D1191194

Sources Of
American Spirituality

Phoebe Palmer
SELECTED WRITINGS

Edited by Thomas C. Oden

PAULIST PRESS
New York ◇ Mahwah

Library of Congress Cataloging-in-Publication Data

Palmer, Phoebe, 1807–1874.
  [Selections. 1988]
  Phoebe Palmer : selected writings / edited by Thomas C. Oden.
    p.   cm. — (Sources of American spirituality)
  Bibliography: p.
  Includes indexes.
  ISBN 0-8091-0405-9
  1. Spiritual life—Methodist authors. I. Oden, Thomas C.
II. Title. III. Title: Selected writings. IV. Series.
BV4501.P259 1988
287'.6–dc19   88-6624
                                                                                               CIP

Published by Paulist Press
997 Macarthur Boulevard
Mahwah, N.J. 07430

Printed and bound in the United States of America

CONTENTS

To
Sallie Eliza Walker Oden
(1868–1953)
and
Centennial Germany Seeger Clark
(1876–1970)

GENERAL INTRODUCTION

Few have spent more effort studying the mystical element of religion than Baron Friedrich von Hügel. In his massive study of the life of St. Catherine of Genoa, he determined that the mystical element could not be seen apart from its relation to other aspects of the religious experience: the institutional and the intellectual elements. In certain individuals and in certain movements one of these elements is more pronounced than the others. For the mystic, it is the element that stresses a direct experience of God through contemplation and ultimately through union that is central.

Although the experience of Phoebe Palmer, a nineteenth-century American woman, is the product of a thoroughly different age than the sixteenth-century Liguorian world of Catherine of Genoa, there was in her life also a modified though discernible emphasis on what von Hügel would call the mystical element. For Phoebe Palmer, though, "mystical" was a dirty word. She was weaned on Wesleyan piety—a piety that was weary of what its creator John Wesley called "the trap of the mystics." It reacted with distrust to talk of pure love, of ultimate stillness, of the quiet of the heart and chose instead to speak of good works done in evangelistic fervor, of social reform, of revival, of the fire of the Lord, and the enthusiasm of the heart strangely warmed.

If one looks further at the structure of the two women's experiences, one sees more similarities. There was the emphasis on total commitment of life which for Catherine meant consecration to pure love and to Palmer meant holiness. In either case the results were similar. Good works, whether ministering to the dying in a Genovese hospital or to the urban poor at Five Points in Manhattan, flowed from the beliefs about God and humanity that so engaged the intellects and affections of these women. There was also the common experience of the ineffable, which not only formed the basis for their work but enticed their imaginations and proved to be the inspiration for much of their writing. Both also experienced the mystical element within the larger context that von Hügel was so insistent upon seeing. Their mystical raptures, their experiences of what Palmer called the "tongue of fire upon the daughters of the Lord," took place within the framework of institutional religion. In many ways both women were on the margins of the dominant religious institutions of their times. Catherine, a woman and a wife, was known during her lifetime for her good works. Only after her death did her writings, filtered as they were through the hands of her male confessors and editors, attain popularity. Palmer, the product of a brave new world and an age of reform that gave new opportunities to women, was a crusader for women's ministry in a church that still reflected a male hegemony among the clergy. She found success and even public acclaim through creating her own structures for ministry, such as the famous Tuesday Meetings for the Promotion of Holiness. In both lives the institutional element acted as a foil against which the unique and immediate experiences of those women were played out.

This discussion of two figures, so diverse and dissimilar in many ways, takes its motivation from the fact that many of Mrs. Palmer's friends and disciples found the Genovese saint an apt illustration of the rightness of their own Palmer-inspired views of holiness. It was Thomas C. Upham, a professor of philosophy at Maine's Bowdoin College, converted at one of the Tuesday Meetings for the Promotion of Holiness, who set the pace with his 1845 work *The Life of Catherine Adorna* (he insisted on using her surname, rather than referring to her as "St. Catherine"). Others like Methodist editor George Peck, and Oberlin professor John Morgan followed.[1]

The comparison of these two women also suggests more than this historical oddity, however. It aids us in seeing that Palmer's quest for what she called "holiness" was part of a larger, more ancient tradition. Although she was strapped with the language of frontier Methodism with its unsophisticated philosophy, its biblical literalism, and its anti-intellectualism, she searched for ways to express the profound experiences of God that she had had. Though an activist more than a contemplative, she could not help returning to that ineffable something that churned inside of her, that pulled her on and compelled her to seek a more perfect love. Relentlessly she strove to respond to that nameless grace more fully, and to possess its beatitudes.

The fact that she is part of that great mystical stream that runs like a golden river down through the ages is important, and is alone justification

---

[1]John Farina, "Nineteenth Century Interest in Saint Catherine of Genoa," *The Catholic Historical Review* 70 (April 1984): 250–62.

for including her in a series of books on spirituality in America. But she is also worth remembering for her innovations.

She, like many of her fellow American religionists, experimented with new forms. She pushed out the borders of the sacred to include the heartfelt, but often troublesome, experience of grace that was so much a part of Revivalism and gave it, as it were, an air of Northeast sophistication and gentility. She changed the venue for the moment of ecstasy from the rugged camp meetings of places like Cane Ridge, Kentucky to the almost-refined parlors of her New York City home. There, in the middle-class equivalent of a sophisticated Continental salon of a *spirituel* like Madame Guyon, Mrs. Palmer brought Pentecostal fire.

She spread that fire with the new technology that the circuit riders of the 1830s did not have: cheap books and magazines. With the invention of the Hoe Rotary Press and the introduction of inexpensive wood-pulp paper during the 1840s, the era of mass publishing had begun, and no one on the American religious scene used it better than she, as her long lists of books with their impressive sales figures attest. Whether it was through the enormously popular book *The Way of Holiness*, or through articles in Timothy Merrit's magazine *The Guide To Holiness*, Mrs. Palmer spread her message across denominations. She was quick to see the advantages of rail and steamboat transportation that enabled her to extend her campaigns throughout the U.S., and even to Canada and the British Isles.

Hers, then, is truly a remarkable and, up until recently, neglected story that I am happy to present.

John Farina

INTRODUCTION

Suppose one came into possession of information showing that a relatively unrecognized individual was influential in American history and a worldwide religious movement, far surpassing any general acknowledgement of these facts. Suppose that person was seldom mentioned or only slightly treated in standard historical accounts.

Suppose one discovers upon investigation that this person had helped launch one of the earliest inner city missions to the poor in America; that she had been the principal founder of her church's mission to China; that she had been a direct progenitor of a dozen different Protestant denominations that have survived a century later.

Suppose one then discovers that major universities and colleges (such as the University of Michigan, Northwestern University, Syracuse University, Wesleyan University, Boston University, University of Georgia, American University, Drew University, and many others) had founders, early presidents or major leaders who were influenced directly by this person, though she seldom appeared in their official histories.

Suppose, too, that long before the popular feminism of the turn of the century, this woman had established patterns of public speaking and mass communication that influenced feminist advocates decades later.[1] Suppose one finds that this person was a prolific author who for years edited one of the most widely read religious journals of her time during the height of its influence. Suppose that dozens of subsequent authors would directly pattern their work and language after hers. Would not one expect such a woman would be widely studied and noted?

Suppose one also discovers that this individual served as a vital spiritual mentor to many, that dozens of major American religious leaders of different denominations credited this person with decisively shaping their

1

own personal religious development;[2] and that she had significantly influenced the embryonic development of major international religious groups or movements as diverse as Methodist bodies, the Salvation Army, the Wesleyan Church, the Free Methodist Church, The National Camp Meeting Association for the Promotion of Holiness (out of which several denominations emerged), the Evangelical Association and the Keswick Movement in England, the Church of the Nazarene,[3] the Assemblies of God, the worldwide Pentecostal movement, and numerous modern charismatic movements.[4]

Would one not be amazed that such a figure would remain virtually unmentioned in standard church history textbooks? Leading histories of religion in America that contain no reference whatever to this individual include those by Edwin S. Gaustad, *A Religious History of America,* H. Sheldon Smith, Robert T. Handy, and Lefferts Loetscher, *American Christianity,* J. Gordon Melton, *Encyclopedia of American Religion,* William McLoughlin, Jr., *Modern Revivalism,* and *Eerdman's Handbook of Christianity in America.*[5]

Suppose that this person had developed a theology that had distinctly and directly influenced key theologians, clergy, and lay leaders in major Protestant groups of her day—Congregational, Presbyterian, Baptist, Quaker, Methodist.[6] Yet she did not even think of herself as a theologian, eschewing any such pretentious description of herself (yet she decisively shaped widely recognized definitions of such concepts as conversion and sanctification).

Suppose, as well, that this individual had been responsible for the practical fashioning and development of some of the earliest forms of modern ecumenism in European and American religious life,[7] while remaining loyal and influential within her own denomination.

Suppose that the summer camp meeting tradition was deeply shaped by this individual, with whom the names Chautauqua, Martha's Vineyard,[8] Vineland, and Ocean Grove[9] would be inseparably connected.[10]

Suppose finally that one had been studying church history and teaching theology for years, and felt that one knew reasonably well the theological works of one's own tradition, yet had read very little of this person during almost three decades of teaching. The entire hypothesis is highly improbable. Thus, imagine the amazement that I felt when I began to discover all these stunning facts about Phoebe Worrall Palmer a few years ago. I could not understand why it had taken me so long to meet her. As Søren Kierkegaard remained virtually unknown for almost fifty years after his death, so Phoebe Palmer, after having been one of the most widely known women of her time in England and America,[11] has remained virtually unknown during the past hundred years, except by a handful of religious historians who have known their own roots exceptionally well (among them Timothy L. Smith, John L. Peters, Kenneth Rowe, Charles Edwin Jones, Melvin E. Dieter, Paul Bassett, Vincent Synan, Donald W. Dayton, Charles E. White, and a few others).[12]

Who is Phoebe Worrall Palmer? This book seeks to answer that question. It may seem that such extravagant claims made about a single person easily might be shown to be exaggerated. It seems unlikely that such diverse assertions could be made of the same person. The purpose of this volume is to bring this person to life for the reader and to show through her own writings how she understood herself and her mission as she worked through the intriguing problems that confronted her. The reader will be left to judge whether these claims about her are accurate.

A PIVOTAL FIGURE NEGLECTED

John Wesley had been dead only sixteen years when Phoebe Worrall was born. Her father, Henry Worrall, had been powerfully moved by John Wesley's preaching at Bradford, England.[13] He moved to New York in 1792 and became a specialist in transport engineering.

Phoebe was the fourth of fifteen children, eight of whom attained maturity. Her life spanned roughly the first three quarters of the nineteenth century (Dec. 18, 1807–Nov. 2, 1874). During her thirty-seven years of public ministry, 1837–1874, she became one of the most influential women of her era.[14]

She was among the first women of the nineteenth century to become a celebrated public figure, a widely-travelled, much sought public speaker, and a highly visible religious leader and author.[15] Her work has deeply affected the roots of American social activism,[16] the Wesleyan tradition of spirituality to which she belonged, and numerous other holiness, camp meeting, and revival movements that grew out of her unpretentious "Tuesday Meetings for the Promotion of Holiness," held in her home in New York City beginning in February, 1836. Charles E. White probably does not exaggerate in describing her as "the most influential woman in the American Methodist Church in her century."[17]

Here is one example among many that reveals a century of scholarly neglect of a pivotal figure in American religion: the relation of Phoebe Palmer and higher education. It is gradually becoming more clear that Mrs. Palmer's life and work profoundly touched the founding and early development of many institutions of American higher education. The list of founders and presidents of major American universities and colleges who were confidants and associates of Phoebe Worrall Palmer is stunning. Here is a preliminary inventory of major American universities and colleges whose early presidents or key leaders (and in many cases founders) were significantly influenced, according to their own testimony, by her work: University of Michigan (President Erastus O. Haven, 1863–69), Northwestern University (Matthew Simpson, 1863–65, Prof. Daniel Kidder, President Randolph Sinks Foster, 1856–60, President Erastus Otis Haven, 1869–72), Evanston College for Ladies, Founding President (Frances E. Willard, 1871), Boston University (Founding President of antecedent General Biblical Institute, Elijah Hedding, 1847–66, early trustees Gilbert Haven and Daniel Steele), Syracuse University (President Erastus O. Haven, 1874–81, President, Board of Trustees, J. T. Peck), Wesleyan University (President Wilbur Fisk, 1831–39, President Nathan Bangs, 1841–42, President Stephen Olin, 1842–51, President Cyrus D. Foss, 1875), University of Georgia (Prof. Stephen Olin, 1826–34), Oberlin College (Founding President, Charles Grandison Finney), Dickinson College (President J. T. Peck, 1848–52, Agent Edmund Storer Janes), University of the Pacific (President of Board of Trustees, J. T. Peck), American University (Founding President John Fletcher Hurst, 1891–1902), McKendree College, Illinois (President Robert Allyn, 1863–1874), Randolph-Macon College (President Stephen Olin, 1834–36), DePauw University (President Matthew Simpson, 1839–48), Adrian College (Founding President Asa Mahan, 1859–1864, 1867–1871), Simpson College (named after Matthew Simpson), and Hamline College (named after Leonidas Hamline). All of these persons had long-term, well-established association with Mrs. Palmer, either as personal friends, serious correspondents, Tuesday Meeting participators, or direct contributors to her movement and its journal, the *Guide to Holiness*. Hence it can be argued that through these associations and influences, she may have affected American higher education as much as any other woman of her period.

A separate monograph should be written on the ways in which Mrs. Palmer influenced higher education in America. Drew University, however, can serve as one of many examples of a university founded by persons who either directly or tangentially belonged to the Palmer circle, some of whom attended the Tuesday Meetings, contributed to the *Guide to Holiness,* or wrote on Christian perfection in Palmerian terms. Among them were the first three presidents of Drew—John McClintock (contributor to the *Guide to Holiness*), Randolph Sinks Foster (former pastor of Washington Square Methodist Church in New York City, author of *Christian Purity*), and John Fletcher Hurst,[18] as well as trustees such as the Palmers' long-time friends, Bishops Edmund Janes and Matthew Simpson, and early teachers at Drew such as Daniel Kidder, Samuel Upham, and Henry Anson Buttz.[19] In addition the Palmers knew Daniel Drew himself, their fellow

Methodist and near neighbor living at Broadway and 17th St. (After living for years at 51 Rivington Ave., the Palmers lived at 23 St. Mark's Place from 1865–1870, and at 316 East Fifteenth St., across from Stuyvesant Park, after 1870.)

WHY THE SPIRITUAL WRITINGS OF PHOEBE PALMER ARE DUE RESTUDY

There is an abundance of good reasons why Phoebe Palmer is belatedly receiving serious attention today in the rediscovery of the sources of American spirituality. Among them are the following:

She developed an effective strategy with distinctive methods for the holiness revival which ultimately influenced millions of lives. She is arguably the best representative figure, male or female, of the beginnings of the holiness tradition of spirituality in America, which subsequently has continued to have such astonishing influence around the world. She developed a holiness theology that has deeply affected four worldwide religious traditions: Wesleyan, Holiness, Pentecostal, and Charismatic.[20]

She is in the central stem of the direct root of many worldwide Protestant denominations that have been spawned by her own Methodist tradition (in addition to those named above, groups like the Pentecostal Holiness Church, Primitive Methodists, Pilgrim Holiness, Four-Square Gospel Church, Apostolic Faith Movement, and several member groups of The Christian Holiness Association),[21] and far-flung radio and television ministries that have emerged out of related holiness traditions.[22] Nancy Hardesty described Phoebe Palmer as "the 'Mother of the Holiness Movement,' which eventually gave birth to such denominations as the Church of the Nazarene, the Church of God (Anderson, Indiana), the Salvation Army, and also Pentecostal groups like the Assemblies of God, the Pentecostal-Holiness Church, and the Church of God (Cleveland, Tennessee)."[23]

Although she did not advocate a secularized egalitarian feminism or even "women preaching, technically so called,"[24] she became a plausible and decisive model for numerous later advocates of women's ordination, women's political rights, the women's temperance movement, and for women becoming actively engaged in social change in urban life among the poor.[25] On the subject of the ministry of women, she authored the most important treatise written by male or female in the Christian tradition from the first to the nineteenth century.[26] She countered conservative apologists by showing that Paul's admonition was not specifically against women speaking in public, but against the usurpation of legitimate authority. "Her defense of women's ministry was only the first of many in the holiness-

Pentecostal tradition which led such churches to ordain women more than fifty years before more 'mainline' denominations began to do so.''[27]

She was the most influential woman in the largest, fastest growing religious group in mid-nineteenth century America—Methodism.[28] From within her sphere of influence in Methodism, numerous leaders emerged, catechetics developed, church legislation was fashioned, social reformation sought. Mrs. Palmer's movement for the promotion of holiness impacted heavily upon the election of Methodist Episcopal Church bishops from 1844 until the end of the century. Among bishops that clearly stood out as advocates of the way of holiness were: Leonidas Lent Hamline, Edmund Storer Janes, Matthew Simpson, Randolph Sinks Foster, Stephen Mason Merrill, Gilbert Haven, Jesse Truesdell Peck, Cyrus David Foss, John Fletcher Hurst, Erastus Otis Haven, Willard Francis Mallalieu, and William Taylor. All of the above (and perhaps several others) personally knew and were by their own testimony deeply influenced by Mrs. Palmer. A separate article or monograph on the relation of Mrs. Palmer to nineteenth century Methodist episcopal leadership is greatly needed to clarify the intricacy and detail of these associations.

In 1839 Phoebe Palmer and her sister, Sarah Lankford, encouraged the establishment of the Journal, *Guide to Christian Perfection,* later *Guide to Holiness (GTH),* and promised its founding editor, Timothy Merritt, that she would contribute to it.[29] Subsequently, until the turn of the century, it remained the primary organ of literary productivity, information, and general clearing house for the ecumenically-oriented evangelical holiness revival movement. It was read avidly by revival participants, fueled by summer camp meetings. Dr. and Mrs. Palmer took over its editorship in 1864. By 1870 it had one of the largest circulation lists among religious journals in America (37,000 subscribers).

Beyond the circle of holiness revivalism, she enjoyed wide acquaintance with a great many of the leading writers, benefactors, and leaders of American Protestantism of her time. She was vitally linked with many of the most influential leaders in book and periodical publishing: general publishers such as the Harper brothers (James, John, Joseph Wesley, and Fletcher Harper, New York Methodists, founders of J. & J. Harper, 1817, and Harper and Brothers, 1833), and other editorial leaders of American Protestantism (especially Methodists) of the time—virtually all of the book stewards and key publishing agents of the Methodist Episcopal Church of her time (Thomas Mason, Nathan Bangs, John Emory, Beverly Waugh, George Lane, P. P. Sanford, John M. Phillips, Sandford Hunt); most of the editors of the *Christian Advocate (Christian Advocate and Journal,* New York—among them, N. Bangs, George Peck, Abel Stevens), of the *Western Christian Advocate* (Matthew Simpson, Stephen M. Merrill), of the

Methodist Review (N. Bangs, George Peck, John McClintock), of Church School Publications (Daniel P. Kidder, Daniel Wise), and Timothy Merritt, George Hughes, H. V. Degen, D. S. King, John A. Roche, William McDonald, and of course Walter C. Palmer, Walter C. Palmer, Jr., and her son-in-law, Elon Foster. These names were to dominate Wesleyan and holiness religious publishing in nineteenth century America.

Thirty years before Jane Addams' Hull House in Chicago, Mrs. Palmer was one of the founding directors of America's first inner city mission—New York's Five Points Mission on the Bowery. Since the day of her father's funeral in 1847, Mrs. Palmer was committed to persuading the Ladies Home Missionary Society to establish a mission to the poor in the most dismal neighborhood of lower Manhattan. Overcoming considerable resistance, the mission was organized and operational by 1849.[30] Serving with Mrs. Palmer in this early effort on the Board of the Old Brewery Mission were Daniel Drew, J. B. Cornell (principal benefactors of Drew and Cornell Universities), as well as L. Kirby, W. B. Skidmore, and A. Worrall.[31]

Mrs. Palmer figured prominently in the formation of other early efforts seeking social betterment amid the misery of the urban poor. These included food relief, rent-free housing, the care of orphans, care of the poor, alcoholism rehabilitation, and ministry to immigrants.

She contributed decisively to the influence of lay persons in American religious history, especially in the history of revivalism. Her encouragement of lay leadership was singularly influential in the democratization of the Methodist tradition, and the enabling and extension of its mission. Her 1857 series of essays on ''A Laity for the Times'' became a significant component in inaugurating one of the most intensive periods of lay-influenced revival activity in America and Canada, 1857–59.[32] She remains one of Christianity's most important lay theologians—male or female.

She is rightly counted among the earliest advocates of the ecumenical (or proto-ecumenical) movement in both Europe and America. Among the societies that anteceded the modern ecumenical movement were Evangelical Associations on both sides of the Atlantic that were closely attuned to the multi-denominational revival movement in which she was a key figure.[33]

By Mrs. Palmer's nurture and initiative, far-flung missions were undertaken, camp meetings instituted, a revival hymnody composed, and many thousands attested the completely transforming power of divine grace.

She is acknowledged as one of the founding mothers of world missions in the American Methodist tradition, having seriously considered going to the Orient herself (with her physician husband), and then having decided that her role was better cast as one who would support and equip missionaries in Asia, Africa, and elsewhere. In 1846 she and Dr. Palmer directly raised the funds necessary to send the first Methodist missionaries, Moses C. White, Robert S. Maclay, and Henry Hickok, to China in 1847. The China mission was undertaken when the Palmers "offered to subscribe $1000, payable in ten annual installments, and to procure if possible twenty-nine other like subscriptions," May 18, 1846.[34] She earnestly (but unsuccessfully) sought, against opposition, to initiate a mission to Palestine. Meanwhile at home, she personally initiated what may be the first Christian ministry to Jews in the New York area.

A VITAL TRADITION OF SPIRITUALITY

Any one of the above points might justifiably qualify her for reexamination as a significant and ignored figure in American religious history. But please note that the deeper concern of this series is not historical importance or influence. Rather it is the quality of spirituality that has developed in the American tradition.

The central thesis of this volume is that Phoebe Palmer's spirituality, as shown especially through her autobiographical writings and her spiritual-counsel essays, is deeply grounded in classical Christianity, not on the fanatic, idiosyncratic fringe of centerless enthusiasm. She deserves to be counted among the most penetrating spiritual writers of the American tradition.

It is hoped that this volume will serve as a useful primary sourcebook for the renewed serious study of the spiritual writings of Phoebe Palmer. It is likely that her works will be increasingly attended not only by devotional readers, but also by students of American religious history, women's spirituality, and the history of social work and social activism. She was and is a formidable figure in any of these arenas.

Some students of American religious history have heard vignettes and scraps about Phoebe Palmer, but too few have rigorously studied anything by her, or have encountered her literary power directly through her own plain, forceful sentences. Some have met her only in caricature form—for example in the notion that the "shorter way" simply meant an easier way. Rather, in her view, the way of entire devotion was a radical, demanding way thoroughly enabled by grace.

After numerous press runs in the nineteenth century, most of her books and virtually all of her tracts and journal articles have remained unpublished for over a century. Some may have prematurely concluded that women were not influencing the Christian tradition in the mid-nineteenth century. Her work constitutes striking evidence to the contrary.[35] She is a key exemplar of the thesis that evangelical religion contributed to the movement for the expansion of women's rights.[36]

She was not an academic theologian, and constantly disavowed that she had anything original to contribute to theology. She considered herself simply a "Bible Christian" who took scripture with experiential seriousness. Nonetheless, she has contributed much to the precise definition and terminology of the Christian teaching of sanctification, both in terms of her wide public influence and the precision of her definitions.[37] Central to this contribution were her definitions of the altar covenant, the way of holiness, entire devotion, the baptism of the Holy Spirit, and sanctification.[38]

A concise summary of major characteristics of her contribution, as viewed in Great Britain in 1857, accompanied the announcement of the six-volume British edition of her works:

> The chief characteristics of Mrs. Palmer's works may be summed up thus: First, A lofty and pure ideal of Christianity and the Christian life. Second, She is deeply in earnest to exemplify this ideal,—not by fitful endeavors, but by a steady and persistent strife,—in her there is no tinge of quietism. Third, Her writings are well adapted to set everybody in motion, with whom they come in contact,—we know of no human book that will stir a person's soul to its lowest depths, as her 'Faith and Effects,'[39]—her books make working Christians. Fourth, They exhibit a rare insight into the Scriptures, a clear view of the temptations of the enemy, and the method provided for our escape; while, at the same time, they open up so clearly the great doctrine of holiness, that no one in earnest to find it need stumble. Fifth, As a crowning excellence, they indicate a present salvation.[40]

In his excellent recent biographical study, Charles E. White cogently summarized six ways in which Phoebe Palmer developed John Wesley's teaching of entire sanctification:

> First, she followed John Fletcher in his identification of entire sanctification with the baptism of the Holy Spirit. Second, she developed Adam Clarke's suggestion and linked holiness with power. Third, like Clarke, she stressed the instantaneous elements of sanctification to the exclusion of the gradual. Fourth, again following Clarke, she taught that entire sanctification is not

really the goal of the Christian life, but rather its beginning. Fifth, through her 'altar theology' she reduced the attainment of sanctification to a simple three-stage process of entire consecration, faith, and testimony; and sixth, she held that one needed no evidence other than the Biblical texts to be assured of entire sanctification.[41]

BIOGRAPHICAL SKETCH OF PHOEBE WORRALL PALMER

Since the selections that follow will serve as a substantial textual presentation of key writings that review her life's work, we will limit our biographical sketch to the most essential, introductory points.[42] Our purpose is to gain an initial sense of Phoebe Palmer's social location, historical context, family, and vocation.

A prolific author and leading evangelist of the holiness movement, Phoebe Worrall Palmer was also a poet, hymn-writer, theologian, humanitarian, early feminist advocate, and editor of the *Guide to Holiness*. A lifelong New Yorker, she was born December 18, 1807, in lower Manhattan, the fourth child of a pious American Methodist mother, Dorothea Wade,[43] and English father, Henry Worrall, who had become a Methodist through Wesley's preaching in Bradford, England. She married Walter C. Palmer, a Rutgers-educated New York physician, on September 28, 1827. Of the Palmers' six children, only three survived infancy.

The Palmers participated actively in lower Manhattan's Allen Street Methodist Church, which experienced a remarkable sanctificationist revival under the leadership of Samuel Merwin,[44] beginning in 1831 and continuing for many months. Phoebe's sister, Sarah Worrall, who married Thomas Lankford, attested the reception of sanctifying grace on May 21, 1835, and began leading prayer meetings for women. On February 9, 1836, the two families, Lankfords and Palmers, moved into the same house at 54 Rivington Street, very near the Allen Street Church, and there Sarah and Phoebe began their influential Tuesday Meetings for the Promotion of Holiness.

The Palmers' first two sons, Alexander (September 28, 1828–July 2, 1829) and Samuel (April 29, 1830–June 19, 1830), died in infancy. Their first daughter, Sarah, was born April 11, 1833. Death soon claimed their third child, however, in a tragic crib fire on July 29, 1836.

Almost exactly a year later, on July 26, 1837, Mrs. Palmer experienced that memorable "Day of Days," in which she herself received sanctifying grace amid the making of an irrevocable "altar covenant" with God in the entire dedication of all her redeemed powers. Her own carefully described account of this experience and its meaning is found in chapter 4. By 1839 she was speaking frequently at camp meetings, and learning to attest her experience. In that year she became the first woman to be appointed Methodist "class leader" in New York.

The Tuesday Meetings, led in their early phase by Sarah, increasingly came under the spell of Phoebe Palmer's powerful intellect and spiritual vision. This informal lay-led experience, characterized by earnest prayer, study of scripture, spontaneous testimony to the fully cleansing activity of the Spirit, radical personal openness, and frank encounter concerning the need for present holiness, was destined to influence deeply the course of the holiness revivals of the nineteenth century. With the visit in December of 1839 of Professor Thomas Cogswell Upham, a leading Congregationalist philosopher of Bowdoin College, men began attending the Tuesday Meetings. These Tuesday Meetings became an international pattern for attesting the way of holiness. They would continue for sixty years or more.[45] By 1886 at least 238 similar meetings were being held regularly in such distant places as India and New Zealand.

To the Palmer home came many of the most influential leaders of American Protestantism to hear attestations of the way of holiness. Among her closest associates and frequent guests in her home were George Hughes, editor and publisher, John Dempster, founder of Boston and Garrett seminaries, university presidents Asa Mahan, Wilbur Fisk, and Jesse Truesdell Peck, and a long list of Methodist bishops and their wives. Among the bishops were Leonidas L. Hamline, who attested full salvation under Mrs. Palmer's guidance in the early 1840's, and Matthew Simpson, who would become a confidant of President Lincoln. Among other notable persons who experienced the reception of sanctifying grace in her meetings were Frances Willard, leading figure of the Women's Christian Temperance Union, Benjamin Titus Roberts, founder of the Free Methodist Church, and John Inskip, who would lead the National Camp Meeting Association for the Promotion of Holiness, out of which numerous holiness organizations and denominations emerged. In England, William and Catherine Booth, founders of the Salvation Army, would be powerfully affected by her ministry.

Her vocation as a writer formed early. After writing numerous early poems and keeping a writer's notebook, this vocation took clearer shape in 1841 with the publication of *Mary, Or the Young Christian*, a Sunday School book providing a model for youthful religion, probably adapted from the diary of her friend, Mary D. James. With the *Way of Holiness*, first published in 1842–43 as a series of articles, and in 1843 as a book, (with printings totalling 24,000 copies in six years), her reputation spread.

Entire Devotion to God was published in 1845, followed by *Faith and Its Effects, Israel's Speedy Restoration* in 1854, and *Incidental Illustrations of the Economy of Salvation* in 1855.

She taught that the promises of scripture were not to be taken tentatively, but rather were within reach of ordinary individuals willing to commit to them, receive the help of grace, and the Spirit's testimony in our hearts to God's acceptance of our act of entire devotion. These promises were not intended to be delayed, but to be received now, and were fully available through faith in Christ.

In her revival meetings she taught both pardon and purity—conversion, grounded in classical Protestant teaching of justification by grace through faith, and sanctification, that the Holy Spirit seeks to reclaim the whole person. The reception of sanctifying grace could be expected with an act of entire devotion. She resisted emotive, subjective pietism, inordinately focused on human experience, and rather focused on the adequacy and clarity of the promises of scripture.

For Phoebe Palmer, the experience of divine grace led directly to an energetic life of active social service. Rather than following an individualistic pattern frequently associated with Protestant pietism, she became a leading innovator of social action and reform in urban American Protestantism. She established one of America's earliest prison ministries, visiting prisoners regularly in New York's notorious prison, The Tombs. She contributed materially to the relief of the urban poor, worked at alcoholic rehabilitation, and cared personally for orphans and the hungry.

She was a Founding Directress of the first Protestant mission to the poor in America, the Five Points Mission in the Bowery area of New York, which provided rent-free housing, bathing facilities, food, clothing, schooling, and spiritual care for the urban poor of lower east side Manhattan. Five Points became the precursor of many settlement houses for the urban poor. Long before the formal founding of Five Points, however, she had engaged in social service work for the poor in and around the Bowery area. From 1847–1857 she served as corresponding secretary of the New York Female Assistance Society for the Relief and Religious Instruction of the Sick Poor. Dr. and Mrs. Palmer's commitment to the poor led them in 1848 to leave the middle class Allen Street Church and help develop a faltering church in a poor neighborhood on Norfolk Street.

During all this activity, Mrs. Palmer remained busy with domestic duties in raising her three surviving children: after Sarah came Phoebe (born 1839), and Walter Clark Palmer, Jr., (born Nov. 20, 1842).

Among her close associates and followers were numerous individuals whose names are legend in the history of Methodist missions: Robert S.

Maclay, William Taylor, Abel Stephens, Matthew Simpson, Amanda Smith, and Daniel Kidder.

She had been active since the mid-1830's in the abolitionist and temperance movements, and her sympathies were strongly with the northern Methodist Episcopal Church when Methodism divided, and with President Lincoln in the conflict between north and south. She thought that the failure of Methodism to unite against slavery was a key link in the chain of events that led to the Civil War.

Mrs. Palmer was not without her critics. In 1851 she came under attack in a lengthy controversy with polemicist Hiram Mattison concerning the attainability of sanctification.[46] Among points charged against Mrs. Palmer (which she and her defender, J. H. Perry, largely denied as misconstrued), were the following: that sanctification was a mere consecration; that it followed the pattern of "the Jewish altar"; that the Holy Spirit was ignored; that feeling was repudiated; that one must publicly profess entire sanctification or backslide; that church members are to be divided into "sanctified" and "unsanctified," leading to censoriousness and fanaticism; and that she believed that the faith by which we are to be sanctified is to believe that we are sanctified.[47] Although her movement elected numerous Methodist bishops, their teaching became increasingly controversial toward the end of the century.

In 1857 the Palmers published a plea for lay witness in Protestantism, "A Laity for the Times." Their Canadian mission, begun in 1853, reached its zenith in 1857 and 1858, strongly shaped by lay witness and Pentecostal themes. These themes were expanded to include a plea for the public testimony of women in the publication in 1859 of the *Promise of the Father,* which was destined to influence virtually all subsequent apologias for women in ministry.

From 1859 to 1863 the Palmers were in England, Scotland, Wales, and Ireland, holding services extensively, with multitudes attesting pardon and heart purity, as reported in *Four Years in the Old World* (published in 1867). Upon their return in 1864 the Palmers purchased the *Guide to Holiness,* and Phoebe became its editor. "Circulation rose immediately from 13,000 to 30,000, and Mrs. Palmer remained as editor until her death."[48]

During her last decade (1864–74), Mrs. Palmer travelled extensively, usually with Dr. Palmer, throughout the Midwest, Canada, down the Mississippi River to New Orleans (in 1867), and to California in 1870. By 1872 Mrs. Palmer was suffering with nephritis. She died Nov. 2, 1874. Her book of poetry, *A Mother's Gift,* was published in 1875. Few women in history have been so fully called and enabled to bear witness to the full extent of divine grace.

IS PHOEBE PALMER THE LEADING
WOMAN PROTESTANT THEOLOGIAN?

Between Teresa of Avila and Georgia Harkness, it is difficult to iden-
tify a woman theological writer of greater intellectual power than Phoebe
Worrall Palmer. If one is asked to specify what other women prior to Mrs.
Palmer might have reasonable claim to being Protestantism's most important woman theological writer, a preliminary list might include Anne
Hutchinson, Susanna Wesley, Mary Bosanquet Fletcher, Sarah Crosby,
Elizabeth Richie Mortimer, Hester Ann Rogers, Isabella Graham, Joanna
Graham Bethune, and others whose work perhaps remains inadequately as-
sessed. But it cannot be easily claimed that any of these produced a body
of theological literature and reflection as broad-ranging, historically
grounded, exegetically detailed, theologically well argued, practically useful, and widely recognized as those of Mrs. Palmer. According to these
criteria, Phoebe Palmer's theological writings excel notably among Protestant women. Hence, if Phoebe Palmer is not the most influential woman
theologian of Protestantism of her time, it becomes extremely difficult to
make a serious case for an alternative.

Yet such claims would amuse Mrs. Palmer, who never thought of herself in the slightest as a theologian. A major aim of this volume of annotated
texts is to show that her powers of theological reasoning were subtle, original, biblically and classically grounded, historically aware, clear, extraordinarily influential, and spiritually vital.

Further, if one asks about women who were born after Mrs. Palmer
who have reasonable claim to being the most significant woman Protestant
theologian following her, the nineteenth century list is strikingly filled with
women directly influenced by her, according to their own attestations: Catherine Mumford Booth, Frances E. Willard, Hannah Whitall Smith, Antoinette Brown Blackwell, Amanda Berry Smith, Maggie Newton Van Cott.
These are the remarkable women—the daughters of Phoebe Palmer—who
took primary early leadership in the temperance, holiness, mission, social
service, and early feminist movements, and also in the beginnings of feminist theology.[49] Others may debate whether any women following Mrs.
Palmer in the nineteenth and early twentieth centuries, such as Catherine
Ward Beecher, Susan B. Anthony, and Mary McLeod Bethune exemplified
her detailed exegetical competence, sound theological depth, and public
communication skills. It would be difficult to identify a more influential and
substantive Protestant woman theological writer of the time than Mrs. Palmer because of the extraordinary range, depth, and international character
of her ministry and authorship.

We are not attempting to include in such an assessment the various

Catholic and Protestant women theologians writing in the last twenty years—Rosemary Radford Ruether, Mary Daly, Letty Russell, Elizabeth Schuessler-Fiorenza. But if one asks further how Phoebe Palmer has influenced contemporary feminist theology, it seems clear that her influence is massive, subtle, and increasing. For Phoebe Worrall Palmer provided one of the first plausible role models and a substantive intellectual structure for the social realism, hermeneutic, and feminist critique of later exegetes like Phillis Tribble, historians such as Nancy Hardesty, and theologians like Mildred Bangs Wynkoop and Rosemary Skinner Keller.

CLASSICAL AFFINITIES OF MRS. PALMER'S SPIRITUALITY

The ancestral line of the Pentecostal Movement is defined by Frederick Dale Bruner as: the anointed ecstatics of the Old Testament (Num. 11; 1 Sam. 10), the Corinthian enthusiasts (1 Cor. 12–14), Gnostics, Montanists, medieval spiritualists, Anabaptists, and Quakers.[50] None of these stand prominently in the background of Phoebe Palmer. Her rationalistic tendency distinguished her from those who emphasize experience predominantly without rigorous reflection on scripture.

Although she decisively influenced the language and self-understanding of Pentecostalism, her theological bearings are far better understood as standing squarely within the tradition of triune orthodoxy, especially as represented by those Eastern patristic writers who focused intently upon the fullness of the holy life lived out of faith. Among those that best express the patristic tradition with which Mrs. Palmer's work had such direct affinity are Macarius, Gregory of Nyssa, John Chrysostom, and Western exponents of the holy life—Ambrose, Augustine, Jerome, and John Cassian—and the ecumenical consensualism of Vincent of Lerins.[51] They are all quiet constituents of her spiritual heritage.

Phoebe Palmer's spirituality came more directly out of her essentially Methodist education than any other source. Her most basic mentors were the founders and early leaders of Methodism: Susanna Wesley, John and Charles Wesley, John Fletcher and Mary Bosanquet Fletcher, and her dear friends and Tuesday Meeting associates, Nathan Bangs and Timothy Merritt. There is evidence that she had some Latin skills and had directly studied the texts of some patristic writers, but most of this tradition was indirectly mediated to her through Wesley, who had been deeply affected by the revival of patristic studies at Oxford immediately preceding his time, and through Wesleyan standard writers (Adam Clarke, Joseph Benson, William Carvosso, Richard Watson, and her own catechist, Nathan Bangs). There are residual evidences in her writings that Mrs. Palmer had read much of

Wesley's Christian Library, whose first volume was deliberately chosen: Macarius's *Homilies,* alongside Clement, Ignatius, and Polycarp. Wesley had taken William Beveridge's edition of patristic texts with him to Georgia. From Eastern Orthodox spirituality he had learned a distinctive pneumatology which became "the font of Wesley's most distinctive ideas about prevenient grace and human freedom and, most crucially, of his peculiar doctrine of perfection as *teleiosis* (perfecting perfection) rather than *perfectus* (perfected perfection). . . . His central theme (divine-human participation) was learned in large part from Macarius, Gregory of Nyssa, and Ephrem Syrus."[52]

The pre-Wesleyan Protestant antecedents of her spirituality may be found chiefly in the works of Thomas Cranmer, John Jewell, William Beveridge, John Pearson, Richard Baxter, John Owen, Johann Arndt, and William Law, again mediated through standard Wesleyan sources.[53] Of medieval writers whose thoughts centered upon complete consecration of life to God, the patterns set by Francis of Assisi, Bonaventure, Catherine of Genoa, and Thomas a Kempis[54] have deep affinities with those Protestant patterns later espoused by Phoebe Palmer, but there is little evidence of her firsthand knowledge of these—only of a profound spiritual affinity which is evidenced in her hunger for undiminished life in Christ, in radical renunciation of idolatrous dependencies, and in the constancy of her life of prayer.[55] Such a varied list of names may give the reader bibliographical vertigo, but they have one central interest in common: They all in varied (Eastern, Western, Roman, Protestant) ways have hungered for what Mrs. Palmer was later to call the way of holiness and entire devotion to God.

For a discussion of the links between the Wesleyan tradition and patristic-matristic sources, the reader is referred to studies by Albert C. Outler, Vivian H. H. Green, Frank Baker, and K. Stephen McCormick.[56] One of Mrs. Palmer's most important early sources for the Wesleyan tradition was Timothy Merritt, *The Christian's Manual: A Treatise on Christian Perfection, with directions for obtaining that state; compiled principally from the works of the Rev. John Wesley.*[57]

PHOEBE PALMER AS THE MISSING LINK
BETWEEN METHODIST AND PENTECOSTAL SPIRITUALITY

Phoebe Palmer is the key figure in the crucial yet inadequately understood link between Wesleyan revivalism and modern Pentecostalism, between eighteenth century perfectionism and twentieth century glossolalia, between Aldersgate and Asuza Street.[58] "Methodism is the most important of the modern traditions for the student of Pentecostal origins to understand, for eighteenth century Methodism is the mother of the nineteenth-century American holiness movement, which, in turn, bore twentieth century Pentecostalism. Pentecostalism is primitive Methodism's extended incarnation."[59]

The journey from Wesley to modern Holiness, Pentecostal, and charismatic movements is ostensibly a stark transition from episcopal leadership to greater lay leadership, from Anglican assumptions about the sacraments to those resembling Quaker and Baptist, from a greater stress upon reasonable religion to emotive intensity, from the Prayer-Book to glossolalia, from a relatively hierarchical patriarchal form of leadership to one in which women take an increasing part, from triune theology to a greater focus upon the Holy Spirit, and from water baptism to Spirit baptism.[60] Yet those who look more closely at these transitions see that the changes were subtle, involving gradual shifts, but with momentous effect.

Ever closer inspection of these transitions shows that almost everywhere along the way one finds the footsteps of Phoebe Palmer. Most of these changes occurred unobtrusively, even hiddenly, and were not clearly understood even at the time of her death in 1874. "Those who look for the differences between original Wesleyanism and the tone and teaching of the American holiness movement will probably discover that there were no radical differences in theology and belief, but rather, they will find subtle differences in emphases that derive from the application of all that was America in the nineteenth century to the promotion and practices of the Wesleyan emphasis."[61] The key pivot in the transition was Phoebe Palmer.

Charles G. Finney is sometimes assigned this pivotal transitional role as viewed, for example, by F. D. Bruner: Finney was "the major historical bridge between primitive Wesleyanism and modern Pentecostalism,"[62] as "the major, and the theologically immediate, predecessor of the late nineteenth-century holiness movement, the immediate source, in turn, of the Pentecostal movement."[63] Our reasons for assigning this role instead to Phoebe Palmer will only gradually become evident as this study develops. White astutely summarized:

> Her popularization of Pentecostal language, her emphasis on immediate sanctification, her understanding of faith, and her insistence on testimony laid a firm foundation for later Pentecostal developments. Even the three steps commonly taught as a means of receiving the baptism of the Holy Spirit in most sections of the movement today are similar to the steps Mrs. Palmer taught. Seekers for the full baptism in Pentecostalism are usually told: (1) be converted, (2) obey God fully, and (3) believe.[64] These three steps were elaborately charted by Phoebe Palmer.

Finney borrowed decisively, yet on an occasional basis, from Wesleyan sources on sanctification and made their ideas plausible to Congregational and pan-Protestant audiences. Mrs. Palmer, on the other hand, under the direct mentoring of Bangs and Merritt, more actively shaped sanctification into a cohesive tradition of revival preaching and lay theology, as well as ecclesiological institution-building, spiritual guidance, and religious practice. There doubtless were many voices in the labored transition from Methodist to Pentecostal spirituality, among them James Caughey, Matthew Simpson, William Arthur, Asa Mahan, William E. Boardman, John S. Inskip, B. W. Gorham, Robert Pearsall Smith, Hannah Whitall Smith, and Dwight Moody.[65] All of these doubtless had important parts to play. Note that all were profoundly influenced by Mrs. Palmer. Their thinking and spirituality emerged in significant dialogue with her.

The selections which follow will help make the subtleties of some of these transitions more clear and plausible. In the work of Mrs. Palmer, "American revivalism gave perfectionist promotion new and effective methods, and Methodist perfectionism provided American revivalism with enlarged vision of the possibilities of normal Christian life."[66]

Wesley had argued that justification and sanctification were experientially received as distinguishable experiences: "We do not know a single instance, in any place, of a person's receiving, in one and the same moment, remission of sins, the abiding witness of the Spirit, and a new, clean heart."[67] "A gradual work of grace constantly precedes the instantaneous work both of justification and sanctification," he had written in 1784, "but the work itself (of sanctification as well as justification) is undoubtedly instantaneous. As after a gradual conviction of the guilt and power of sin you was [sic] justified in a moment, so after a gradually increasing conviction of inbred sin you will be sanctified in a moment."[68] Phoebe Palmer and her associates were seeking experiential embodiment of the promise of full salvation, of sustained and complete cleansing from sin, and of the blessings of a life lived wholly toward God, with no other intent than to implement the Wesleyan vision.[69]

Among holiness revival advocates after the Civil War who constitute the subtle links between Wesley and the Charismatic and Pentecostal Movements, many followed in specific detail Mrs. Palmer's theology, spirituality, methods, and even language to an extraordinary degree. There are a series of key terms that became closely connected with the Palmer revivals, so much so that wherever these terms appear later in recurrent clusters, there is reason to believe that Mrs. Palmer's language (or the language of those closely associated with her movement) has been reappropriated.[70] For example, wherever one sees the phrase, "the promotion of holiness," one is tracking the steps of Mrs. Palmer. The same is true of the phrase "the way of holiness,'' and the motto: ''Holiness to the Lord.'' Furthermore she spawned a whole system of language which has come to be referred to as ''the altar terminology'' (including phrases like ''keeping all upon the altar,'' and ''perpetual covenant''). Wherever one hears of the ''Tuesday Meetings'' or the ''holiness camp meeting,'' these are almost certainly echos of Phoebe Palmer. Much of her language was shared with other holiness revivalists, who spoke of ''entire sanctification,'' being ''cleansed from all sin,'' and ''baptism of the Spirit.'' But other phrases are more distinctively characteristic of Mrs. Palmer: ''preaching pardon and purity,'' ''heart purity,'' ''entire devotion,'' ''entire consecration,'' ''the shorter way,'' ''the witness of holiness,'' ''profession of the blessing,'' ''the baptism of fire,'' ''the effects of faith,'' and the ''tongue of fire on the daughters of the Lord,'' the metaphor of ''Beulah Land,'' and ''claiming the power of faith.'' This list does not imply that all these terms were coined by Mrs. Palmer, but that they recur frequently in her vocabulary. They became key phrases in the movements that would follow her, so as to trace, to some degree, the influence of her language and terminology upon subsequent Christian spirituality.

Among those whose spirituality and theology Mrs. Palmer affected would be leaders of widely varied traditions—a representative short list would have to include Congregationalist Thomas C. Upham, Episcopalians Charles and Lucretia Cullis, Baptist William E. Boardman, Salvation Army Founders William and Catherine Booth, Presbyterian W. H. Williams, Dutch Reformed Isaac M. See, Quaker Hannah Whitall Smith, and numerous Methodists.[71] For readers who wish to review testimonies of the experiences of such persons in the Palmer and similar revivals, a large number of them are collected in the volume *Pioneer Experiences*, and in another volume entitled *Forty Witnesses*, edited by Stephen Olin Garrison. It would be difficult to identify any Protestant denomination of mid-nineteenth century America or Britain that did not feel her influence. Clergy and laity of these denominations would later contribute to the pivotal holiness camp meetings and conferences at Manheim, Pennsylvania, Vineland, New Jersey, Brighton and Keswick, England.[72]

PHOEBE PALMER'S LOCUS WITHIN REVIVALISM

Since the following collection of writings will review step by step the development of Mrs. Palmer's work in initiating and nurturing the holiness revival, we will not here try to anticipate these developments in miniature. It is sufficient to note anticipatively that her participation in the revival movement may be understood in several stages: her preparation leading to her own decisive experience of full salvation (1837), her early revival activity (1837–43), the maturing extension of the revival, especially as seen in her writings (1844–59), her mission to the British Isles (1859–63), and her last decade (1864–74). For introductory purposes, it is useful to place her briefly in her context as she arrived on the scene of American revivalism and became an increasingly public figure during the 1840's.

During the period from 1842 to 1850 the membership of the Methodist Episcopal Church gained almost 200,000 members, making it a formidable force in American religious life. By 1848 Nathan Bangs noted that the subjects of Christian perfection and entire sanctification had ''very considerably revived within six or seven years past; and that a more than usual number have sought and found the blessing of 'perfect love.' ''[73] Among those most responsible for this reawakening, not only in the United States, but also in Canada following 1856, and England following 1859, was Phoebe Palmer.

Several types of revival movements preceding Mrs. Palmer's succeeded to some degree in reawakening seekers to the importance of sanctificationist themes, yet failed in other ways to achieve the proper balance between justification and sanctification, consecration and testimony, faith and works. The chief antecedents of Mrs. Palmer's spirituality were Methodist advocates of revival.[74] Among her primary immediate predecessors were Nathan Bangs, Samuel Merwin, and Timothy Merritt. They in turn stood in the tradition of John Wesley, John Fletcher, Francis Asbury, Adam Clarke, Joseph Benson, William Carvosso, Richard Watson, and Elijah Hedding.[75] These were the primary exegetical, intellectual, moral, and spiritual mentors underlying Mrs. Palmer's revival activity, and she very largely represented their views, although she reshaped, reinterpreted, and practically reappropriated them in a newly emergent historical context. Phoebe Palmer remained a lifelong friend and protegée of Nathan Bangs, who ''supported Phoebe Palmer at almost every point, not least on the highly controversial view that no one could remain sanctified who did not openly testify to his sanctification. His influence partly explains hers.''[76]

Her predecessors were less effective in holiness revivalism than she in three ways: (a) in engendering lay leadership for the holiness revival, (b) in precisely articulating holiness teaching in a way that was eminently consistent with American assumptions and cultural conditions, and (c) in discovering a practical method of promoting the teaching of scriptural holiness within the American setting.

The preaching of Congregationalist Charles G. Finney (1792–1876), President of Oberlin, became the recognizable prototype for a prevailing sort of revivalism concurrent with Mrs. Palmer. Finney incorporated certain Wesleyan sanctificationist teachings into an experiential Calvinism.[77]

There is little evidence that Finney had a strong or direct influence upon Mrs. Palmer. Rather it appears more likely that the same Wesleyan exponents that were influencing Mrs. Palmer were also influencing the early Finney (and his colleague, Asa Mahan, who had a much closer relation with the Palmers).[78] Both Finney and Palmer were advocates of a holiness form of revivalism, but differed subtly in theology and ecclesiology, and these differences largely hinged upon the differences of tilt toward Congregational or Methodist theological assumptions.[79]

Less in the mainstream but intriguing is John Noyes, who led his experimental community at Oneida, New York, into a mystical perfectionism that involved sexual experimentation abhorrent to the Wesleyans, who by 1844 were aware that they could hardly even use the tainted term "perfectionist" because it had been co-opted by "wild fanatics" and "antinomians."[80]

Orange Scott was a perfectionist advocate who separated from the Methodist Episcopal Church in 1843.[81] Benjamin Titus Roberts led an antislavery and "free-pews" movement in 1859[82] that resulted in the formation of the Free Methodist Church.[83] Their views on sanctification were largely shared by Mrs. Palmer, yet she found regrettable the separationist tendency that would prove to be latent in various holiness and para-church movements. She sought mitigation and reconciliation within the Wesleyan family, and remained intensely loyal to the Methodist Episcopal Church.

William Miller had predicted the second coming of Christ in 1843. His "Adventist" movement attracted many Methodist followers in the early 1840's, and his preaching was influenced by sanctificationist themes. Mrs. Palmer waited until after 1843 to call upon him to renounce chiliastic aspects of his preaching (see entry for Oct. 24, 1844 below).[84]

These types of revivalist and sanctificationist movements preceded Mrs. Palmer (or proceeded concurrently), but she is easily distinguished from all of them except the Methodist revivalists. All of these movements excepting Noyes were a part of the mid-nineteenth century camp meeting revival tradition.

ORGANIZATION AND PERIODIZATION OF TEXTS

The organization of the material that follows is chronological except for the first chapter, which is her essay entitled "Tongue of Fire on the Daughters of the Lord" (her own summary of her longer work, *Promise of the Father*), presented as the lead essay of this volume. It introduces the reader to a moving argument that has remained unpublished for over a hundred years—a concise statement of her view of the contribution of

women to the church's ministry of testimony. This essay introduces her at
the point of her greatest influence and reveals her rhetorical power, exegetical skill, and historical attentiveness.

The remainder of the chapters are organized chronologically to cover
these periods of her life and thought:

> The Young Phoebe Palmer (1807–1828)
> Early Married Years: Diary and Poetry (1828–1836)
> Reception of Sanctifying Grace (1837)
> The Beginnings of the Holiness Revival (1837–1843)
> The Way of Holiness (1843)
> Entire Devotion to God (1845)
> The Revival Spreads (1844–1859)
> Four Years in the Old World (1859–1863)
> Last Decade (1864–1874)
> Conclusion: Refining Processes

All titles abbreviated in the notes will be found with full bibliographical information in an abbreviation section at the end of the book.

I am greatly indebted to Drew University Library and the Archives of
the United Methodist Church at Drew University for numerous kindnesses,
and especially to my colleagues Paul Hardin, Thomas W. Ogletree, Kenneth Rowe, Russell Richey, Charles Yrigoyen, and Arthur E. Jones. I owe
a special debt of gratitude to Paul Bassett of Nazarene Theological Seminary
in Kansas City for carefully reviewing the manuscript and helping me avoid
numerous errors. The most significant work yet to be written on Phoebe
Palmer is the recent study by Charles Edward White, *The Beauty of Holiness: Phoebe Palmer as Theologian, Revivalist, Feminist, and Humanitarian* (Grand Rapids: Francis Asbury Press, Zondervan, 1986, hereafter *BT*).
I have greatly benefited not only from this excellent book, which comple-
ments this selection of primary source writings, but also from his perceptive
critique of my manuscript. Regrettably the book by Harold E. Raser,
Phoebe Palmer; Her Life and Thought, (Lewiston: Edwin Mellen Press,
1987) was published only after this manuscript was in the last stages of pro-
duction. To Timothy L. Smith, Donald W. Dayton, and Melvin E. Dieter,
acknowledged experts in the body of literature surrounding Phoebe Palmer,
I express sincere appreciation. I am deeply grateful for much help and astute
insight from my able graduate assistants, David C. Ford and Leicester
Longden.

T.C.O.
The Drew Forest, Pentecost, 1987

Notes

1. Nancy Hardesty, *Women Called to Witness: Evangelical Feminism in the Nineteenth Century* (Nashville: Abingdon, 1984) (*WCW*); Amanda Porterfield, *Feminine Spirituality in America* (Philadelphia: Temple University Press, 1980) (*FSA*).

2. Cf. Stephen Olin Garrison, ed. *Forty Witnesses: Covering the Whole Range of Christian Experience,* Introduction by Cyrus D. Foss (New York: Phillips and Hunt, 1888) (*FW*), dedicated to alumni of Drew Theological Seminary, including testimonies to the pursuit of the way of holiness by Dwight L. Moody, Quakers Hannah Whitall Smith and Dougan Clark (Earlham College), Baptist E. M. Levy, and Methodists Frances E. Willard, James Mudge, Daniel Steele, et al.

3. Current membership approximately one-half million.

4. See Melvin Easterday Dieter, *The Holiness Revival of the Nineteenth Century* Scarecrow Press (Metuchen, NJ, 1980) (*HRNC*), 156ff.; Vinson Synan, *Aspects of Pentecostal-Charismatic Origins* (Plainfield, NJ, Logos International, 1975) (*APCO*).

5. Gaustad (New York: Harper, 1966); Smith, Handy, and Loetscher (New York: Charles Scribner's Sons, 1963); Melton (Wilmington, N.C.: McGrath, 1978); McLoughlin (New York: Ronald Press, 1959) (*MR*); E. Noll, N. Hatch, G. Marsden, D. Wells, J. Woodbridge, eds., *Eerdmans's Handbook of American Christianity* (Grand Rapids: Eerdmans, 1983). Earlier histories of American Protestantism with no mention of Phoebe Palmer include: William Warren Sweet, *The Story of Religion in America* (New York: Harper, 1950); Andrew L. Drummond, *The Story of American Protestantism* (London: Oliver and Boyd, 1951); Ernest Sutherland Bates, *American Faith: Its Religious, Political, and Economic Foundation* (New York: W. W. Norton, 1940), and Jerald C. Brauer, *Protestantism in America: A Narrative History* (Philadelphia: Westminster Press, 1953). Even standard Methodist studies covering her period make no direct reference to Mrs. Palmer (see Robert E. Chiles, *Theological Transition in American Methodism, 1790–1935* [New York: Abingdon, 1965], and William Warren Sweet, *Methodism in American History* [New York: Abingdon, 1933]).

6. Editorial, "Mrs. Palmer—Views Entertained of Her by Other Sects," *GTH* 30(1856):64.

7. John Wesley White, "The Influence of North American Evangelism in Great Britain Between 1830 and 1914 on the Origin and Development of the Ecumenical Movement," Ph.D. dissertation, Oxford University, 1963. Cf. Richard Carwardine, *Trans-Atlantic Revivalism: Popular Evangelicalism in Britain and America, 1790–1865* (Westport, Conn.: Greenwood Press, 1978) (*TAR*), 159ff.; Dieter, *HRNC*, pp. 156–204.

8. H. Vincent, *A History of the Wesleyan Grove, Martha's Vineyard, Camp Meeting, 1835–1858* (Boston: Rand & Avery, 1858), 142–46. Many of Mrs. Palmer's close associates—H. V. Degen, R. W. Allen, B. W. Gorham—were active, long-term participants in Martha's Vineyard services.

9. Morris S. Daniels, *The Story of Ocean Grove, Golden Jubilee, 1869–1919* (New York: Methodist Book Concern, 1919); cf. Dieter, *HRNC*.

10. B. Pomery, *Vision from Modern Mounts: Vineland, Manheim, Round Lake, Hamilton, Oakington, Canton, et al.* (Albany: Van Benthuysen, 1871); cf. Hughes, *DP;* Jones, *PPHAM.*

11. Charles E. White, *BH*, p. 2; cf. Richard Wheatley, *The Life and Letters of Phoebe Palmer,* hereafter designated *Memoirs,* pp. 15ff.; Roche, *LSLP,* p. 17.

12. Timothy L. Smith, "The Holiness Crusade," in E. S. Bucke, ed., *HAM,* vol. 2, pp. 608–27; *Called Unto Holiness* (Kansas City: Nazarene Publ. Co., 1962) (*CUH*); "Righteousness and Hope: Christian Holiness and the Millennial Vision in America, 1800–1900," *American Quarterly* 31/1 (1979):22ff.; John L. Peters, *Christian Perfection and American Methodism* (New York: Abingdon, 1956) (*CPAM*); Kenneth Rowe, ed., *The Place of Wesley in the Christian Tradition* (Metuchen: Scarecrow Press, 1980); Charles Edwin Jones, *Perfectionist Persuasion: The Holiness Movement and American Methodism, 1867–1936* (Metuchen, N.J.: Scarecrow Press, 1974) (*PPHAM*); Melvin E. Dieter, *The Holiness Revival of the Nineteenth Century* (Metuchen: Scarecrow, 1980) (*HRNC*); Paul Bassett, "A Study in the Theology of the Early Holiness Movement," *Methodist History* 13 (1975):61–84; Vincent Synan, *The Holiness-Pentecostal Movement in the United States* (Grand Rapids: Eerdmans, 1971) (*HPM*); Donald W. Dayton, *Discovering an Evangelical Heritage* (San Francisco: Harper, 1983); Charles E. White (*BH*); cf. Thomas Langford, *Practical Divinity: Theology in the Wesleyan Tradition* (Nashville: Abingdon, 1983) (*PD*). See also works by John Kent, *HF*, Richard Carwardine, *TAR*, Albert Outler, Dale Dunlap, and Nancy Hardesty.

13. Wesley preached in Bradford at 5 A.M., July 24, 1784 (also April 23, 1786); cf. White, *BH*, pp. 1, 2; *Journals of the Rev. John Wesley, A.M.*, ed. Nehemiah Curnock, 8 vols. (London: Epworth Press, 1938) (*JJW*), vol. 7, 4; cf. p. 157. *GTH* 66 (1874): 42–43; *Memoirs,* pp. 13–14.

14. John A. Roche, "Mrs. Phoebe Palmer," *LR* (Feb. 1866): 65–70; cf. W. J. McCutcheon, "Phoebe Palmer," in *Notable American Women,* vol. 3, pp. 12ff.

15. Anne C. Loveland, "Domesticity and Religion in the Antebellum Period: The Career of Phoebe Palmer," *The Historian* 39, no. 3 (May, 1977): 455–71 (*DRAP*).

16. Cf. Norma Taylor Mitchell, "From Social to Radical Feminism: A Survey of Emerging Diversity in Methodist Women's Organizations, 1869–1974," *Methodist History* 13/3 (1975): 21–44.

17. Charles Edward White, *The Beauty of Holiness: Phoebe Palmer as Theologian, Revivalist, Feminist, and Humanitarian* (Grand Rapids: Francis Asbury Press, Zondervan, 1986) (*BH*), 2.

18. John McClintock, *Guide to Holiness* 52 (1867): 72, Randolph Sinks Foster, *Christian Purity* (New York: Hunt & Eaton, 1869), and John Fletcher Hurst (cf. Albert Osborn, *John Fletcher Hurst: A Biography* [New York: Eaton & Mains, 1905], 33). See Mrs. Palmer's letter of counsel to Foster, *Northern Christian Advocate,* 10:33 (Nov. 12, 1851) 2.

19. On Daniel Kidder, see *Memoirs*, p. 451; on others, see Joy, *Teachers of Drew*, pp. 53–58.

20. Cf. Smith, *CUH*; Jones, *PPHAM*; W. Hollenweger, *The Pentecostals* (New York: 1972); Synan, *HPM*: Bloch-Hoell, *PM*. For various analyses of the antecedents of the charismatic movement, see Arnold Dallimore, *Forerunners of the Charismatic Movement* (Chicago: Moody, 1983); Leslie Davison, *Pathway to Power: The Charismatic Movement in Historical Perspective*. Watchung, N.J.: Logos, 1972; Richard Quebedeaux, *The New Charismatics*, San Francisco: Harper and Row, 1983.

21. Constant H. Jacquet, Jr., *Yearbook of the American and Canadian Churches, 1985* (New York: Abingdon, 1985).

22. Cf. *Directory of Religious Broadcasting*, 1985, ed. Ben Armstrong (Morristown, NJ: National Religious Broadcasters, 1985).

23. *Great Women of Faith* (Grand Rapids: Baker, 1977), 88, 89 (*GWF*).

24. *The Promise of the Father* (New York: Walter C. Palmer, 1859) (*PF*), 1.

25. Cf. Nancy Hardesty, Lucille Sider Dayton, and Donald W. Dayton, "Women in the Holiness Movement: Feminism in the Evangelical Tradition," *Women of Spirit*, eds. Rosemary Ruether and Eleanor McLoughlin (New York: Simon and Schuster, 1979); Nancy Hardesty, *Women Called to Witness* (Nashville: Abingdon, 1984); Amanda Porterfield, *Feminine Spirituality in America* (Philadelphia: Temple University Press, 1980).

26. *Promise of the Father* (Boston: H. V. Degen, 1859).

27. Nancy Hardesty, *GWF*, p. 90.

28. See C. C. Goss, *Statistical History of the First Century of American Methodism* (New York: Carlton & Porter, 1866), 104ff. For an interpretation by a holiness advocate of why Methodism grew, see Anthony Atwood, *Causes of the Marvelous Success of Methodism in this Country in the Past Century* (Philadelphia: National Publ. Assoc. for Promotion of Holiness, 1884).

29. Hughes, *TM2*, p. 162; *GTH* 66 (1874): 20.

30. *GTH* 68 (1875):125; 66 (1874):42–43; *Memoirs*, pp. 224–25.

31. Mrs. Palmer was a Founding Directress: "The first officers of the Missionary Society were Mrs. Bishop E. L. *sic* Janes . . . Mrs. Dr. Palmer, Third Directress" (*CM*, p. 679). The Old Brewery was torn down and a new mission house erected in 1853. For early histories of Five Points, see "The Old Brewery and the New Mission House at Five Points" in *Ladies of the Five Point Mission* (New York: Stringer and Townsend, 1854); "The Five Points House of Industry," *American Church Monthly* 3 (1858): 209–22; E. R. Wells, "Five Points Mission," *CAJ* 35 (1860): 173. Cf. *Memoirs*, pp. 224, 227.

32. *CAJ* (Feb., Mar. 1857): 25, 29, 33, 41; cf. Smith, *CUH*.

33. Cf. John Wesley White, op. cit.; Ruth Rouse and S. C. Neill, editors, *A History of the Ecumenical Movement* (London: S.P.C.K. 1954); *Record of the Convention for the Promotion of Scriptural Holiness Held at Brighton* (Brighton: W. J. Smith, n.d.) (*Brighton, Record*); J. E. Orr, *SEAA, SEAB*.

34. Barclay, *HMM 3*, p. 367; see 1847 entry below, cf. *Memoirs*, pp. 230–32.

35. In "Domesticity and Religion in the Antebellum Period: The Career of Phoebe Palmer," *The Historian*, 39 (1977):455, Anne C. Loveland astutely showed that Phoebe Palmer's experience "belied the confident statements" of the "cult of true womanhood" described as a normative mid-nineteenth century phenomenon by Barbara Welter, "The Cult of True Womanhood: 1820–1860," *American Quarterly* 18 (1966):153.

36. Keith Melder, "The Beginnings of the Women's Rights Movement, 1800–1840," Ph.D. dissertation, Yale University, 1964, 47ff., 70ff., 92ff; see also Melder, *Beginnings of Sisterhood: The American Women's Rights Movement, 1800–1840* (New York: Schocken, 1977).

37. Dieter, *HRNC;* cf. James Blaine Chapman, *The Terminology of Holiness* (Kansas City: Beacon Hill, 1947).

38. White, *BH*, ch. 5.

39. Referring to *Faith and Its Effects*.

40. *Memoirs*, p. 498; cf. "Mrs. Palmer's Works in England," *GTH* 32 (1857):62.

41. White, *BH*, conclusion, p. 232.

42. For other biographical information, see Jones, *PPHAM*, Dieter, *HMNC*, and articles by John A. Roche, Harold E. Raser, Earnest Wall, W. J. McCutcheon, Donald W. Dayton, Anne C. Loveland, and Nancy Hardesty in the bibliography.

43. Her gravestone reads Doretha.

44. It is likely that their second son, Samuel M., was named after Samuel Merwin.

45. E. Dale Dunlap, "Tuesday Meetings, Camp Meetings, and Cabinet Meetings: A Perspective on the Holiness Movement in the Methodist Church in the Nineteenth Century," *Methodist History*, 13 (1975):85–106.

46. Professor Mattison had a reputation as a fierce polemicist. He quarrelled alternatively with "Annihilationists, Arians, Presbyterians, Roman Catholics, Seventh-day Baptists, Spiritualists, Unitarians, Universalists, and worldly Methodists" (*BH*, p. 53).

47. H. Mattison, "Believe," *CAJ*, Dec. 20, 1855, p. 201. Cf. J. H. Perry, "Prof. Matison and His Eight Propositions," *CAJ* (Jan. 10, 1856): 10. When in 1857 Nathan Bangs, a Tuesday Meeting "regular," warned that "the theory which teaches that we are *to lay all upon the altar or surrender up our hearts to God by faith in Christ and then without having any evidence of the Holy Spirit that it is accepted, or having any change in our disposition, or any emotion of joy and peace, more than we had before,* is not sound, is unscriptural, and anti-Wesleyan," Stevens, *NBLT*, p. 398, he was not attacking Mrs. Palmer's views generally, but the caricature of those views, and the aspect of her views most prone to misinterpretation—faith without evidences of fruit.

48. W. J. McCutcheon, *Notable American Women*, III, p. 13.

49. Catherine Booth, *Female Ministry* (London: Morgan & Chase, 1859); Frances E. Willard, *Glimpses of Fifty Years: The Autobiography of an American Woman* (New York: Hacker, 1970); cf. Garrison, *FW*, pp. 90–100; Hannah Whitall Smith, *Philadelphia Quaker: The Letters* (New York: Harcourt and Brace, 1950);

FW, pp. 144–58; *Amanda Smith, An Autobiography* (Chicago: Meyer and Bros., 1893); Maggie Newton Van Cott, *The Harvest and the Reaper,* intro. by Gilbert Haven (New York: Tibbals, 1876). Mrs. Van Cott was involved in the Five Points Mission during the same period in which Mrs. Palmer was active in it (White, *BH,* p. 300).

50. *THS,* p. 35; cf. Synan, *HPM;* Bloch-Hoell, *PM.*

51. "Macarius the Egyptian" (ca. 300–390), *Fifty Homilies* (London, SPCK, 1921); Ephraem Syrus, ca. 306–73 *(NPNF,* 2, XIII), 330–36; Gregory of Nyssa, (331–94) *Ascetical Works, FC,* 58; *Dogmatic Treatises, NPNF,* 2, V; John Chrysostom (347–407) *(NPNF,* 1, IX–XIV), 50; Ambrose, *Theological* and *Dogmatic Works, FC,* 44; Augustine, *The Christian Combat, FC,* 2; Jerome, *NPNF* 2, VI; John Cassian, *Writings, NPNF,* 2, XI; Vincent of Lerins, *Commonitory, NPNF,* 2, XI.

52. Outler, ed., *WJWB,* vol. I, *Introduction to the Sermons,* 74, 75.

53. Thomas Cranmer, *Works,* ed. J. E. Cox, 2 vols. (Cambridge: University Press, 1844–46); John Jewel, *Works,* ed. J. Ayre, 4 vols. (Cambridge: University Press, 1845–50); John Owen, *Works,* 28 vols., ed. T. Russell (Oxford: J. Parker, 1826); William Beveridge, *Synodikon* (Oxford: Wells and Scott, 1672); John Pearson, *An Exposition of the Creed,* 1659 (Oxford, University Press, 1833); Richard Baxter, *Autobiography* (New York: E. P. Dutton, 1938), 103ff; Wm. Law, *A Serious Call to the Devout and Holy Life* (Grand Rapids: Baker, 1977); cf. Frank Baker, *John Wesley and the Church of England,* op. cit.; Robert C. Monk, *John Wesley: His Puritan Heritage* (Nashville: Abingdon, 1966).

54. *Francis and Clare: The Complete Works* (New York: Paulist Press, 1982) Bonaventure, The Soul's Journey Into God, New York: Paulist Press, 1978 *CWS,* and *Works,* 5 vols. (Chicago: Franciscan Herald Press, 1972); *Catherine of Genoa,: Dialogue* (New York: Paulist Press, 1979); Thomas a Kempis, *The Imitation of Christ* (New York: Doubleday, 1955).

55. For an account of the history of the idea of perfection, see Newton Flew, *IPCT,* and Martin Foss, *The Idea of Perfection in the Western World* (Princeton: Princeton Univ. Press, 1946); cf. N. Flew and Rupert Davies, *The Catholicity of Protestantism* (London: Lutterworth, 1953).

56. Outler, ed., John Wesley, *LPT,* introduction and annotations; cf. Outler, ed., *Sermons, WJWB,* vols. 1–4, introductions and annotations; Vivian H. H. Green, *John Wesley* (London: Thomas Nelson, 1964); Frank Baker, *John Wesley and the Church of England* (Nashville: Abingdon, 1970); cf. K. Stephen McCormick, Drew University Ph.D. dissertation on John Wesley's Use of John Chrysostom on the Christian Life, 1984. Cf. John Wesley, *A Farther Appeal to Men of Reason and Religion,* Part I, *WJWB,* vol. 11, 155–69.

57. (New York: Bangs and Emory, 1825). Cf. Timothy L. Smith, "How John Fletcher Became the Theologian of Wesleyan Perfectionism, 1770–1776," *WTJ* 15/1 (1980): 68–87; David L. Cubie, "Perfectionism in Wesley and Fletcher: Inaugural or Teleological?" *WTJ* 11 (1976): 22–27.

58. For bibliography and preliminary discussion of the problems of the relationship between these movements, see Donald W. Dayton, *The American Holiness*

Movement: A Bibliographic Introduction (Wilmore, KY: Asbury, 1971); Dayton, "The Doctrine of the Baptism of the Holy Spirit: Its Emergence and Significance," *WTJ* 13 (1978):114–26; Dieter, *HMNC;* Smith, *CUH;* Jones, *PPHAM;* White, *BH;* Bruner, *THS;* Bloch-Hoell, *PM.*

    59. Bruner, *THS,* p. 37; cf. Bloch-Hoell, *Pentecostal Movement,* pp. 128ff. (*PM*); B. Warfield, *Perfectionism* 2 vols. (NY: Oxford Univ. Press, 1931), I, 3; cf. Donald W. Dayton, *Theological Roots of Pentecostalism,* Grand Rapids: Francis Asbury Press, 1987 (*TRP*).

    60. Cf. Hollenweger, *The Pentecostals* (Minneapolis: Augsburg Press, 1972).

    61. Dieter, *HR,* p. 20.

    62. *THS,* p. 40.

    63. *THS,* p. 42n: cf. D. Dayton, TRP.

    64. White, *BH,* p. 158.

    65. Donald Dayton, TRP; cf. Synan, *HPM, passim.*

    66. Dieter, *HRNC,* p. 22.

    67. Wesley, *A Plain Account of Christian Perfection* (London: Epworth, 1952), 24.; *WJW* XI, p. 380.

    68. Wesley, *LJW,* ed. Telford, vol. 7, p. 222, June 21, 1784.

    69. Chiles, *TTAM,* 33ff.; cf. L. L. Pickett, *Entire Sanctification from 1799 to 1901* (Louisville, KY: Pickett, 1896); Ivan Howard, "Wesley v. Phoebe Palmer: An Extended Controversy," *WTJ* 6 (1971):31–40; L. H. Scott, "Methodist Theology in America in the Nineteenth Century," Ph.D. dissertation, Yale University, 1960.

    70. For a critique of this language, see Theodore Hovet, "Phoebe Palmer's 'Altar Phraseology' and the Spiritual Dimensions of Woman's Sphere," *Journal of Religion* 63(1983):264–80; cf. John Winebrenner, *Doctrinal and Practical Sermons* (Lebanon, Pa.: Church of God, 1868).

    71. Cf. *PE* and *FW, passim.*

    72. Dieter, *HRNC;* Dieter, "From Vineland and Manheim to Brighton and Berlin," *WTJ* (1974):15–27. Cf. B. Pomery, *Visions from Modern Mounts: Vineland, Manheim, Round Lake, Hamilton, Oakington, Canton, etc.* (Albany: Van Benthuysen, 1871).

    73. *The Present State, Prospects, and Responsibilities of the Methodist Episcopal Church,* New York, Lane and Scott, 1850, 58ff.

    74. William Warren Sweet, *Revivalism in America: Its Origin, Growth, and Decline* (New York: Scribners, 1944); cf. Abel Stevens, *HMUS;* Bucke, *HAM.*

    75. John Fletcher, *Works,* 4 vols. (New York: Carlton & Porter, n.d.); Francis Asbury, *Journals and Letters,* ed. E. T. Clark, 3 vols. (Nashville: Abingdon, 1958); Adam Clarke, *Discourses,* 2 vols. (New York: Waugh & Mason, 1832); Joseph Benson, *The Holy Bible With Notes* (New York: Harper, 1823); William Carvosso, *The Great Efficacy of Simple Faith in the Atonement* (New York: Lane & Tippett, 1847); Richard Watson, *Theological Institutes,* 2 vols. 26th ed. (New York: Carlton & Lanaham, 1850); Nathan Bangs, *The Necessity, Nature, and Fruits of Entire*

Sanctification (New York: Phillips and Hunt, 1888); cf. Lorenzo Dow, *History of Cosmopolite* (Philadelphia: Joseph Rakestraw, 1815).

76. John Kent, *HF*, p. 314.

77. Finney, *Lectures on Revivals of Religion,* New York: Leavitt, Lord & Co., 1835, reprint: *Reflections on Revivals* (Bethany Fellowship, 1979).

78. Lewis A. Drummond, *Charles Grandison Finney and the Birth of Modern Evangelism* (London: Hodder and Stoughton, 1983); cf. Asa Mahan, "Oberlin Perfectionism," *CAJ* 19(1885):169f.; Donald W. Dayton, "Asa Mahan and the Development of American Holiness Theology," *WTJ* 9(1974):60–69.

79. Finney, *Lectures on Systematic Theology,* ed. J. H. Fairchild (South Gate, Calif: Colporter Kemp, 1944), [1878], 382ff.

80. *GTH* VI (Dec. 1844): 131; cf. Whitney R. Cross, *The Burned-Over District* (New York: Harper Brothers, 1950).

81. For the story that led to the founding of the Wesleyan Church, see Lucius C. Matlack, *The History of American Slavery and Methodism, from 1780 to 1849;* and *History of the Wesleylan Methodist Connection of America* (New York: Wesleyan Methodist Book Room, 1849).

82. B. T. Roberts, *Why Another Sect* (Rochester: Earnest Christian Publishing House, 1879); *Holiness Teaching Compiled from the Editorial Writings of the late Benjamin Titus Roberts,* North Chili (New York: Earnest Christian Publishing House, 1893).

83. For clarification of the influence of Mrs. Palmer on B. T. Roberts, see White, *BH;* cf. Leslie R. Marston, *From Age to Age a Living Witness: An Historical Interpretation of Free Methodism's First Century* (Winona Lake, Ind.: Light and Life Press, 1960).

84. *Memoirs,* p. 512.

I

TONGUE OF FIRE ON THE
DAUGHTERS OF THE LORD

All who value the gifts of women in ministry owe a debt to Phoebe Palmer, who wrote the first extensive defense of women testifying publicly in the church. Published in 1859 as a large book, The Promise of the Father, *it was later edited by her into a slender monograph entitled:*
Tongue of Fire on The Daughters of the Lord; or, Questions in Relation to the Duty of the Christian Church in Regard to the Privileges of Her Female Membership *(New York: Walter C. Palmer, Jr., 1869).*

Though ignored by many and attacked by some,[1] these views on women's testimony proved to be a century ahead of their time. The Promise of the Father has been recognized subsequently as the prototype exegetical-historical defense of women in ministry.

This shorter version, Tongue of Fire, is the only monograph to be included in full text in this collection.[2] Having lain unpublished during the last hundred years since its original appearance, copies now are extremely rare. It is featured here as the best way to gain initial acquaintance with Mrs. Palmer's spirituality for three reasons:

(1) *It is her own concise, definitive statement of the crucial importance of the gifts (charismata) of women in the service of the church. It stands among the earliest[3] such statements, and is a spare résumé of her definitive exposition,[4] in a long history of such defenses that would follow and develop her pattern.[5]*

(2) *It reveals her protofeminist, critical method of exegesis, her pungent rhetorical style, and her spirited mode of argument. Her procedure is to retrace the history of exegesis of Joel 2:28–29, Acts 1 and 2, 1 Cor. 6–14, and other biblical references, beginning with Justin Martyr and Irenaeus, through Henry Dodwell and Hugo Grotius to modern inter-*

31

preters, thus displaying a rich and resourceful hermeneutic. She argued that Paul's commands against women testifying in public had to do specifically with the usurpation of authority in Corinth, and could not be transferred to other situations where those conditions did not prevail. Hence she directly challenged the common view that Paul rejected the idea of women prophesying in the church, which he elsewhere clearly affirmed.[6]

(3) Moreover, Tongue of Fire shows clearly how Phoebe Palmer remains a major spiritual forerunner not only of the spirituality of the modern Wesleyan family of churches (United Methodist, A.M.E. Zion, Church of the Nazarene, Wesleyan Church, Free Methodist, Salvation Army, etc.), but also of the modern charismatic movement and the worldwide Pentecostal movement. Watch for major clues of proto-Pentecostal theology in (a) her use of Acts as the central textuary of theology for the ministry of women; (b) her strong emphasis upon baptism of the Holy Spirit, Pentecostal gifts, and the disciples, including women, speaking "as the Spirit gave them utterance"; and (c) her constant witness to sanctifying grace. Ironically, recent Catholic renewal has met and come to understand Protestantism through the charismatic movement as much or more than through mainstream Protestantism. Phoebe Palmer has been a quiet mediator in that relinkage.

Mrs. Palmer anticipated numerous subsequent feminist concerns and modern exegetical procedures:

- She was not willing to let the problems of inclusive language pass unnoticed, e.g., preferring "kins-folk" to "kinsmen" in the translation of Romans 16:7.
- She anticipated "audience criticism" in the interpretation of texts on women, taking into account the special circumstances of the audience to which a text was addressed.
- She set forth textual grounds for arguments that women were ordained by bishops in the New Testament period.
- She astutely showed that alleged general biblical claims that women should not teach were directly connected with and limited to that teaching which seeks to usurp authority.
- Anticipating contemporary analyses of social repression, she interpreted the situation of faithful women silenced in the church as a "crucifying process."
- She regarded this repression as having a demonic source in the "ancient Enemy," and placed the question of injustices toward women in escha-

tological perspective, calling for repentance or expecting divine judgment upon ecclesial sins.

● She was among the first women to investigate key patristic interpreters of scripture on women's issues (Chrysostom, Theophylactus, etc.).

● She deftly penetrated the rationalizations and spurious arguments that buttressed male chauvinism.

● She protested the "entombing of endowments of power" of women in the church and called for the "resurrection of women's gifts." The argument is a tour de force of nineteenth century protofeminism.

TONGUE OF FIRE ON THE DAUGHTERS OF THE LORD (1859)

I. FEMALE PROPHESYING;
OR,
DAUGHTERS OF THE LORD ALMIGHTY

When the founder of our holy Christianity was about leaving his disciples to ascend to his Father, he commanded them to tarry at Jerusalem until endued with power from on high.[7] And of whom was this company of disciples composed? Please turn to the first chapter of the Acts of the Apostles. We see the number assembled in that upper room was about one hundred and twenty.[8] Here were Peter, James, John, Andrew, Philip, Thomas, Bartholomew, Matthew, James the son of Alpheus, and Simon Zelotes, and Judas the brother of James.[9] "These all continued with one accord in prayer and supplication, with the women, and Mary, the mother of Jesus, and with his brethren."[10]

Let us observe that here were both male and female disciples, continuing with one accord in prayer and supplication, in obedience to the command of their risen Lord: they are all here waiting for the promise of the Father.[11]

And did all these waiting disciples, who thus with one accord continued in prayer, receive the grace for which they supplicated? It was the gift of the Holy Ghost that had been promised. And was this promise of the Father as truly made to the daughters of the Lord Almighty as to his sons?— See Joel ii.28,29. "And it shall come to pass afterward, that I will pour out my Spirit upon all flesh; and your sons and your daughters shall prophesy, your old men shall dream dreams, your young men shall see visions. And also upon the servants and upon the handmaids in those days will I pour out my Spirit."[12] When the Spirit was poured out in answer to the united prayers of God's sons and daughters, did the tongue of fire descend alike upon the women as upon the men? How emphatic is the answer to this question.

"And there appeared unto them cloven tongues, like as of fire, and it sat upon *each of them.*"[13] Was the effect similar upon God's daughters as upon his sons? Mark it: "And they were all filled with the Holy Ghost, and began to speak as the Spirit gave utterance."[14] Doubtless it was a well-nigh impelling power which was thus poured out upon these sons and daughters of the Lord Almighty, moving their lips to most earnest, persuasive, convincing utterances. Not alone did Peter proclaim a crucified, risen Saviour, but each one, as the Spirit gave utterance, assisted in spreading the good news; and the result of these united ministrations of the Spirit, through human agency, was that three thousand were in one day pricked to the heart. Unquestionably, the whole of this newly baptized company of one hundred and twenty disciples, male and female, hastened in every direction, under the mighty constrainings of that perfect love that casteth out fear;[15] and great was the company of them that believed.[16]

And now, in the name of the Head of the Church, let us ask, Was it designed that these demonstrations of power should cease with the day of Pentecost? If the Spirit of prophecy fell upon God's daughters alike as upon his sons in that day, and they spake in the midst of that assembled multitude as the Spirit gave utterance, on what authority do the angels of the churches[17] restrain the use of that gift now? Who can tell how wonderful the achievements of the cross might have been, if this gift of prophecy in woman had continued in use as in apostolic days? Who can tell but long since the gospel might have been preached to every creature?[18]

Evidently this was a specialty of the last days, as set forth by the prophecy of Joel. Under the old dispensation,[19] though there was a Miriam,[20] a Deborah,[21] a Huldah,[22] and an Anna,[23] who were prophetesses, the special outpouring of the Spirit upon God's daughters, as upon his sons, seems to have been reserved as a characteristic of the last days. "This," says Peter, as the wondering multitude beheld the extraordinary endowment of the Spirit falling alike on all the disciples,—"this is that which was spoken by the prophet Joel: 'And also upon my servants and upon my handmaidens will I pour out my Spirit.' "[24]

And this gift of prophecy, bestowed upon all, was continued and recognized in all the early ages of Christianity. The ministry of the word was not confined to the apostles. When, by the cruel persecutions of Saul, all the infant church were driven away from Jerusalem, except the apostles, these scattered men and women of the laity "went everywhere preaching the word;[25] "that is, proclaiming a crucified, risen Saviour."[26] And the effect was that the enemies of the cross, by scattering these men and women who had been saved by its virtues, were made subservient to the yet more extensive proclamation of saving grace.

Impelled by the indwelling power within, these Spirit-baptized men and women, driven by the fury of the enemy in cruel haste from place to place, made all their scatterings the occasion of preaching the gospel everywhere;[27] and believers were everywhere multiplied; and daily were there added to the church such as should be saved.[28]

Justin Martyr, who lived till about A.D. 150, says, in his dialogue with Trypho the Jew, "that both *women* and *men* were seen among them, who had the gifts of the Spirit of God,[29] according as Joel the prophet had foretold, by which he endeavored to convince the Jew that the *latter days* were come; for by that expression Mannassah Ben Israel tells us all their wise men understood the times of Messias."[30]

Dodwell,[31] in his dissertations on Irenaeus, says, "that the extraordinary gift of the spirit of prophecy was given to others besides the apostles; and that not only in the *first* and *second,* but in the *third* century, even to the time of Constantine, men of all sorts and ranks had their gifts; yea, and *women* too."[32] Therefore we may certainly conclude that the prophetic saying of the Psalmist, lxviii.11, was verified: "The Lord gave the word, and great was the company of those that published it." In the original Hebrew, it is, "Great was the company of women publishers, or women evangelists." Grotius explains, Ps. lxviii.11, *"Dominus dabat sermonem, id est, materiam loquendi uberem, nempe ut feminarum praedicantium (victorias) multum agmen diceret, scilicet, eaquae sequuntur."*—"The Lord gave the word, that is, plentiful matter of speaking, so that he would call those which follow the great army of preaching women, viz., victories, or female conquerors."[33]

The Hebrew scholar, Rev. J. Benson, in his voluminous and deeply spiritual commentary, says the clause here given, "The Lord gave the word, great was the company of those that published it," literally translated, is, *"Large* was the number of women who published the glad tidings."[34] The eminent linguist, Dr. Adam Clark, quotes the original text, and follows it with the literal reading, *"of the female preachers there was a great host."*[35] And then, as though he anticipated the incredulity with which this literal rendering would be received, and resolved on relieving himself of the responsibility of a non-reception of it, he affirms, "Such is the literal translation of the passage," and leaves it with the reader to make the application, with the exclamation, "The reader may make of it what he pleases."[36]

But though this excellent commentator suggests that the reader make what use of it he please, it certainly ought to be assumed that all sincere

Christians, whether male or female, will in their Scripture searchings, make it their highest pleasure to ascertain the mind of the Spirit, adopting the Bible mode of interpreting the Scriptures by comparing Scripture with Scripture,[37] fearful that he may be compelled to the sustainment of some unpopular theory, is not in a state of mind to warrant the belief that he shall know of this or any other doctrine, whether it be of God.

Schaff's "History of Christ's Church"[38] says, "Woman, among the early Christians, had the fullest freedom in the house of worship; and the consequence was, not only that she added vastly to the success of Christianity in those times, but her own character was wonderfully elevated, and her genius developed, by this equality of right. It is said that Libanius, on seeing the mother of St. Chrysostom, a most noble woman, exclaimed, 'What women these Christians have!' "[39]

Eusebius speaks of Potominia Ammias, a prophetess in Philadelphia, and others, who were equally distinguished by their zeal for the love which they bore to Jesus Christ.[40]

Chrysostom and Theophylact take great notice of Junia, mentioned in the apostle's salutations. In our translation (Rom. xvi. 7), it is, "Salute Andronicus and Junia, my kinsmen and my fellow-prisoners, who are of note among the apostles." By the word *kinsmen,* one would take Junia not to have been a woman, but a man.[41] But Chrysostom and Theophylact were both Greeks; consequently, they knew their mother-tongue better than our translators, and they say it was a woman: it should therefore have been translated, "Salute Andronicus and Junia, my kinsfolk."[42] The apostle salutes other *women* who were of note among them, particularly Tryphena and Tryphosa, who labored in the Lord,[43] and Persis, who labored much in the Lord.[44]

We could refer to many women who in the apostolic age used this gift to the edification of the Church, particularly Phebe,[45] the *servant of the Church,* or deaconess, as the Greek word signifies, of the *church at Cenchroea.*[46] Deaconesses were ordained to the office by the imposition of the hands of the bishop. Theodorus says, "The fame of Phebe was spread throughout the world, and she was known, not only to the Greeks and Romans, but also to the barbarians";[47] which implies that she travelled much, and propagated the gospel in foreign countries.[48] "It is reasonable to suppose, in view of her being a succor of many," says the Rev. Mr. Benson, "that this acknowledged servant of the Church was a person of considerable wealth and influence; or we may suppose the appelation, 'servant of the Church,' was given her on account of the offices she performed as a deaconess."[49] Says another able divine on this subject, "There were deaconesses in the primitive Church; and it is evident that they were ordained to this office by the imposition of the hands of the bishop; and the form of prayer used on the occasion is still extant in the apostolic constitution.['']⁵⁰ And this order was continued for several centuries in the Church, *until the reign of the man of sin* commenced.

The Christian churches of the present day, with but few exceptions, have imposed silence on Christian woman, so that her voice may but seldom be heard in Christian assemblies. And why do the churches impose it? The answer comes from a thousand lips, and from every point, "The Head of the Church forbids it, and the churches only join in the authoritative prohibition, 'Let your women keep silence in the churches.' "⁵¹ And here we come fairly at the question: If the Head of the Church forbids it, this settles the question beyond all controversy.

But under what circumstances was this prohibition given? Was it not by way of reproving some unseemly practices which had been introduced into the Corinthian Church, and which in fact seem to have been peculiar to *that* church? for it is in connection with this and kindred disorders which had been introduced among the Corinthian believers, in connection with the exercise of the gift of prophecy, that Paul says, "We have no such custom, *neither the churches of God*"; that is, the other churches of God over which the Holy Ghost had made him overseer. It is evident that the irregularities here complained of were peculiar to the church of Corinth; and, in fact, not even applicable to other Christian churches of Paul's day, much less Christian churches of the present day, as no such disorders exist. The irregularity complained of was not the prophesying of women; for this the apostle admits, and directs how the women shall appear when engaged in the duty of praying or prophesying. The prohibition was evidently in view of restraining women from taking part in those disorderly debates which were not unusual in the religious worship of those days. In the Jewish synagogue, it was a matter of ordinary occurrence for persons to interrupt the speaker by introducing questionings which frequently resulted in angry altercations.⁵² It was in reference to this reprehensible practice that Paul enjoins silence, and not in reference to the exercise of the gift of prophecy, which, in connection with this subject, he so plainly admits. Otherwise the apostle's teachings were obviously contradictory.

But if Paul's prohibition, "Let your women keep silence in the churches," is to be carried out to the letter in relation to the prophesying of women,—that is, her speaking "to edification, exhortation, and comfort,"⁵³—regardless of explanatory connections and contradictory passages, why should it not be carried out to the letter in other respects? If the apostle intended to enjoin silence in an absolute sense, then our Episcopalian friends trespass against this prohibition at every church service, in calling out the responses of women in company with the men, in the Liturgy, and when they repeat our Lord's Prayer in concert with their brethren.

And thus also do they trespass against this prohibition every time they break silence and unite in holy song in the church of God of any or every denomination. And in fact we doubt not but it were less displeasing to the Head of the Church that his female disciples were forbidden to open their lips in singing, or in church responses, than that they should be forbidden to open their lips when the spirit of prophecy has been poured out upon them, moving them to well-nigh irrepressible utterances.

But Paul also says, "I suffer not a woman to teach, nor usurp authority over the man."[54] It will be found by an examination of this text, with its connections, that the sort of teaching here alluded to stands in connection with usurping authority. As though the apostle had said, "The gospel does not alter the relation of women in view of priority. For Adam was first formed, then Eve. And though the condition of woman is improved, and her privileges enlarged, yet she is not raised to a position of superiority, where she may usurp authority, and teach dictatorially, for the law still remains as at the beginning."

But the sort of teaching to which the apostle here alludes, in connection with usurping authority, cannot be the same to which he refers, 1 Cor. xiv. Here Paul admits the prophesying of women in public assemblies,[55] and, of course, could have had no intention in his Epistle to Timothy to forbid that sort of teaching which stood in connection with the exercise of the gift of prophesy, which arose from the immediate impulses of the Holy Ghost, and which is rendered abundantly plain by another passage in his Epistle to the Corinthians, in which he notices the public prophesying of females, and gives particular directions respecting their conduct and appearance while engaged in that sacred duty. "Every man *praying* or *prophesying,* having his head covered, dishonoreth his head. But every woman that prayeth or prophesieth with her head uncovered, dishonoreth her head."[56]

With respect to the prophesying to which the apostle here alludes, as exercised by both men and women in the churches of the saints, he defines its nature (see 1 Cor. xiv. 3). The reader will see that it was directed to the "edification, exhortation, and comfort of believers"; and the result anticipated was the conviction of unbelievers and unlearned persons. "Such," says the author of an excellent work, "were the public services of women which the apostle allowed; and such was the ministry of females predicted by the prophet Joel, and described as a *leading* feature under the gospel dispensation. Women who speak in assemblies for worship, under the influence of the Holy Spirit, assume thereby no *personal authority* over others. They are instruments through which divine instruction is communicated to the people."[57]

But by whom has the exercise of the gift of prophesy in woman been most seriously resisted? Has not the use of this endowment of power been withstood mainly by those[58] whose lips should keep knowledge? Have not the people who have sought to know the law on this important topic been met with the dissuasive teachings, as though God's ancient promise had not been fulfilled? We cannot resist the conviction that the restraining of the gift of prophecy as given to woman in fulfillment of the promise of the Father involves far greater responsibilities than has been apprehended. The subject of which we treat stands in vital connection with the salvation of thousands; and if so, may we not anticipate that he, whose ceaseless aim is to withstand the work of human salvation in every variety of form, will, as an angel of light, withstand the reception of truth on this subject?

Again we repeat that it is our most solemn conviction that the use of a gift of power delegated to the Church as a specialty of the last days has been neglected,[59]—a gift which, if properly recognized, would have hastened the latter-day glory. We believe that tens of thousands more of the redeemed family would have been won over to the world's Redeemer if it had not been for the tardiness of the Church in acknowledging this gift. We believe it is through the workings of the Man of Sin, whose aim it is to withstand the upbuilding of Christ's kingdom on earth, that this deception has been accomplished. We believe that he who quoted Scripture to our Saviour has in all deceivableness quoted Scripture to pious men,—men who would not wickedly wrest the Scriptures to their own destruction,[60] but who, from a failure in not regarding the Scriptural mode of interpretation, by comparing Scripture with Scripture, have unwittingly followed the traditions of men, and have thereby been guilty of the egregious error of making the inspired teachings appear contradictory, and of withstanding the workings of the Holy Spirit in accordance with those teachings, in the hearts of thousands of the daughters of the Lord Almighty.

We believe that the attitude of the Church in relation to this matter is most grievous in the sight of her Lord, who has purchased the whole human family unto himself, and would fain have every possible agency employed in preaching the gospel to every creature. He whose name is Faithful and True[61] has fulfilled his ancient promise, and poured out his Spirit as truly upon his daughters as upon his sons.

God has, in all ages of the Church, called some of his handmaids to eminent publicity and usefulness; and when the residue of the Spirit is poured out, and the millennium glory ushered in, the prophecy of Joel being fully accomplished in all its glory, then, probably, there will be such a sweet blending into one spirit,—the spirit of faith, of love, and of a sound mind;[62] such a willingness to receive profit by any instrument; such a spirit of humility, in honor preferring one another,[63]—that the wonder will then be, that the exertions of pious females to bring souls to Christ should ever have been opposed or obstructed.

The earnestly pious of all denominations seem now disposed to recognize Wesley as having been greatly instrumental, under God, in the revival of primitive Christianity. To those acquainted with the history of the Church at the time this great reformer was raised up, we need not say that the reception of the full baptism of the Holy Ghost was but faintly, if at all, recognized as the privilege of the believer. But as soon as this primitive flame again revived, just so soon was this gift of power, anciently promised as a specialty of the last days, newly recognized. What a host of "laborers together in the gospel"[64] were quickly raised up! And who that has read the correspondence and journal of Wesley but has marked his special recognition and appreciation of this endowment of power?[65] No more appreciatively did an ancient apostle regard "those women that labored with him in the gospel"[66] than did this modern apostle and his coadjutors.

A recognition of the full baptism of the Holy Ghost as a grace to be experienced and enjoyed in the present life was the distinguishing doctrine of Methodism.[67] And who can doubt but it was this specialty that again brought out a host of Spirit-baptized laborers, as in the apostolic days? And the satisfaction with which this apostolic man recognized and encouraged the use of this endowment of power is everywhere observable throughout his writings.[68] Says one, "Mr. Wesley pressed into the service of religion all the useful gifts he could influence." He well knew that in the ratio in which the devoted female, or any other instrumentalities, were calculated to be useful, to just that degree would the grand adversary raise up opposing agencies to withstand.

To his friend Miss Briggs, he writes, "*undoubtedly* both you and Philothea, and my dear Miss Perronet, are now more particularly called to speak for God. In so doing, you must expect to meet with many things which are not pleasing to flesh and blood; but all is well: so much more will you be conformed to the death of Christ.[69] Go in his name and in the power of his might.[70] Suffer and conquer all things.[71] Over a century has rolled away, and still we may thankfully record that this ancient flame, though not cherished as it might have been, has not died out."[72]

Mr. Wesley, in his journal, thus introduces the name of one of his female helpers, Miss Sarah Mallett, afterwards Mrs. Boyce: "I was strongly importuned by our friends at Long Stratton to give them a sermon. I had heard of a young woman there who had uncommon fits, and of one that lately preached; but I did not know that it was one and the same person. I found her in the house to which I went, and talked with her at large. I was surprised. Of the following relation which she gave me, there are numberless witnesses.

"Some years since it was strongly impressed upon her mind that she ought to call sinners to repentance. This impression she vehemently resisted, believing herself quite unqualified, both by her sin and ignorance, till it was suggested, 'If you do it not willingly, you shall do it, whether you will or no.' She fell into a fit, and, while utterly senseless, thought she was in the preaching-house of Lowestoft, where she prayed and preached for nearly an hour to a numerous congregation. She then cried out, 'Lord, I will obey thee; I will call sinners to repentance!' She has done so occasionally from that time, and her fits returned no more.[73]

["][74]Perhaps this was intended to satisfy her own mind that God had called her to publish salvation, in the name of Jesus, to perishing sinners, and to incline her to take up that cross which appears to have been more painful to her than death itself; and also to convince others that *even now* God hath poured out his Spirit upon his handmaids and upon his daughters,[75] that they may prophesy or preach in his name the unsearchable riches of Christ.

The author of "The Heroines of Methodism," says, "Probably the experience of this young woman, and the wonderful dealings of the Lord with her, greatly helped to enlarge the views of John Wesley upon the subject of female preaching. It is very evident, from his letters and conduct towards her, that he believed her, as a preacher, to be doing what the Lord required at her hands."[76]

Says Miss Mallett, "At thirteen, I became member of the Methodist Society, and the Lord made known to me what he would have me do. But oh, how unfit did I see myself to be! From that time, the word of God was an unsealed book: it was my companion day and night. My love to God and souls increased. I have been often led to cry out, in the bitterness of my soul, 'O Lord! I am but a child, I cannot preach thy word';[77] but the more deeply was it impressed on my mind, 'Woe is me if I preach not the gospel,'[78] till my distress of soul destroyed my body.

"In my twentieth year, the Lord answered my prayer in a great affliction and made known to others, as well as to myself, the work he would have me do; and fitted me in the furnace for his use. From that time, I began my public work. Mr. Wesley was to me a father, and a faithful friend. I have not, nor do I seek, either ease or wealth or honor, but the glory of God and the good of souls; and, thank God, I have not run in vain,[79] nor labored in vain.[80] There are some witnesses in heaven, and some on earth. When I first began to travel, I followed Mr. Wesley's counsel, which was to let the voice of the people be to me the voice of God, and where I was sent for to go.[81] To this counsel I have attended to this day. But the voice of the people was not the voice of some of the preachers. Mr. Wesley, however, soon made this easy, by sending me a note from the conference held at Manchester, 1787, by Mr. Joseph Harper, who was that year appointed for Norwich. The note was as follows: 'We give the right hand of fellowship to Sarah Mallett, and have no objection to her being a preacher in our connection, so long as she preaches the Methodist doctrine, and attends to our discipline.' ''[82]

We believe that hundreds of conscientious, sensitive Christian women have actually suffered more under the slowly crucifying process to which they have been subjected by men who bear the Christian name than many a martyr has endured in passing through the flames. We are aware that we are using strong language; but we do not use it in bitterness, but with feelings of deep humiliation before God that the cause of truth demands the utterance of such sentiments. We conscientiously believe, and therefore must speak.

Thousands are in this day enduring this crucifying process, perhaps as never before. God has given the word; and in this wonderful season of the outpouring of the Spirit, great might be the company who would publish it.[83] This, in a most emphatic sense, is the day of which the prophet spake,—when God would pour out his Spirit on his sons and daughters.[84] Though many men have in these last days received the baptism of fire, still greater, as in all revivals, has been the number of females.[85] These constitute a great company, who would fain, as witnesses for Christ, publish the glad tidings of their own heart-experiences of his saving power, at least in the social assembly.[86]

And when the reception of the gift of prophecy is thus recognized in all the disciples of the Saviour, whether male or female, the last act in the drama of man's redemption will have opened.[87] Says the distinguished Dr. Wayland, ''private believers will feel their obligation to carry the gospel to the destitute as strongly as ministers.''[88] Oh! if the word of the Lord, unrestrained by human hinderances, might only have free course, how great would be the company who, with burning hearts and flaming lips, would publish it![89]

A large proportion of the most intelligent, courageous, and self-sacrificing disciples of Christ are females. ''Many women followed the Saviour''[90] when on earth; and, compared with the fewness of male disciples, many women follow him still. Were the women who followed the incarnate Saviour earnest, intelligently pious, and intrepid, willing to sacrifice that which cost them something in ministering to him of their substance?[91] In like manner, there are many women in the present day, earnest, intelligent, intrepid, and self-sacrificing, who, were they permitted or encouraged to open their lips in the assemblies of the pious in prayer, or speaking as the Spirit gives utterance,[92] might be instrumental in winning many an erring one to Christ. We say, were they permitted and encouraged; yes, encouragement may now be needful. So long has this endowment of power been withheld from use by the dissuasive sentiments of the pulpit, press, and church officials, that it will now need the combined aid of these to give the public mind a proper direction, and undo a wrong introduced by the "man of sin"[93] centuries ago.

But more especially do we look to the ministry for the correction of this wrong.[94] Few, perhaps, have really intended to do wrong; but little do they know the embarrassment to which they have subjected a large portion of the Church of Christ by their unscriptural position in relation to this matter. The Lord our God is one Lord.[95] The same indwelling spirit of might which fell upon Mary and the other women on the glorious day that ushered in the present dispensation[96] still falls upon God's daughters. Not a few of the daughters of the Lord Almighty have, in obedience to the command of the Saviour, tarried at Jerusalem; and, the endowment from on high having fallen upon them, the same impelling power which constrained Mary and the other women to speak as the Spirit gave utterance impels them to testify of Christ.

"The testimony of Jesus is the spirit of prophecy."[97] And how do these divinely-baptized disciples stand ready to obey these impelling influences? Answer, ye thousands of heaven-touched lips, whose testimonies have so long been repressed in the assemblies of the pious! Yes, answer, ye thousands of female disciples of every Christian land, whose pent-up voices have so long, under the pressure of these man-made restraints, been uttered in groanings before God![98]

But let us conceive what would have been the effect, had either of the male disciples interfered with the utterances of the Spirit through Mary, or any of those many women who received the baptism of fire on the day of Pentecost. Suppose Peter, James, or John had questioned their right to speak as the Spirit gave utterance before the assembly, asserting that it were unseemly, and out of the sphere of woman, to proclaim a risen Jesus, in view of the fact that there were men commingling in that multitude.[99] How do you think that He who gave woman her commission on the morning of the resurrection, saying "Go, tell my brethren," would have been pleased with an interference of this sort?

But are not doings singularly similar to these being transacted now? We know that it is even so. However unseemly on the part of brethren, and revolting to our finer sensibilities, such occurrences may appear, we have occasion to know that they are not at all unusual in religious circles. We will refer to a Christian lady of more than ordinary intellectual endowments, of refined sensibilities, and whose literary culture and tastes were calculated to constitute her a star in the galaxy of this world.[100]

2. A LIFE-PICTURE

I have seen a lovely female turn her eye away from the things of time, and fix it on the world to come. Jesus the altogether lovely, had revealed himself to her; and the vision of her mind was absorbingly entranced with his infinite loveliness, and she longed to reveal him to others. She went to the assembly of the pious. Out of the abundance of her heart, she would fain have spoken,[101] so greatly did her heart desire to win others over to love the object of her adoration. Had she been in a worldly assembly, and wished to attract others with an object of admiration, she would not have hesitated to have brought out the theme in conversation; and attracted listeners would have taken her more closely to their hearts, and been won with the object of her love.

But she is now in the assembly of the pious. It is true many of them are her brothers and sisters, but cruel custom sealed her lips. Again and again she goes to the assembly for social prayer and the conference meeting, feeling the presence and power of an indwelling Saviour enthroned uppermost in her heart, and assured that he would have her testify of him. At last, she ventures to obey God rather than man.[102] And what is the result? A committee is appointed to wait on her, and assure her that she must do so no more. Whisperings are heard in every direction, that she has lost her senses; and, instead of sympathizing looks of love, she meets averted glances and heart repulses.[103] This is not a fancy sketch; no, it is a life-picture. Ye who have aided in bringing about this state of things, how does this life-picture strike you?

3. WHO WAS REJECTED?

Think of the feelings of the Christian lady, who has thrown herself in the bosom of your church community in order that she may enjoy the sympathies of Christian love and fellowship. Has grace divested her of refined sensibilities? No: grace has only turned those refined sensibilities into a sanctified channel, and given her a yet more refined perception of every thing pure and lovely and of good report.[104] What must be the sufferings of that richly-endowed, gentle, loving heart? But was it not her loving, gentle, indwelling Saviour, that fain would had her testify for him? and in rejecting her testimony for Jesus, did not Jesus, the Head of the Church, take it as done unto himself?

Just as we were about closing the preceding paragraph, the activities of our pen were interrupted by the call of a valued minister of the gospel, whose early religious training was in the bosom of a sect where the testimony of Jesus from the lips of women was not permitted in the church. We will introduce him to our readers. He tells us of an experience, in connection with the theme of our work, with which some husbands may sympathize. But we will let him speak for himself.[105]

4. THE SEAL BROKEN[106]

Never shall I forget the conflicting emotions of my poor heart, when, for the first time, the voice of my wife was heard in a religious meeting. She had been trained from childhood in the Congregational Church, her father having been a deacon in the same for fifty years. I had been born and raised, and educated for the ministry, in the Episcopal Church. All know the oppressive silence imposed on woman's lips, by both these denominations, in their social meetings for prayer and Christian conference. But the voice of my wife, now for the first time, breaks upon my ear. We had only joined the Methodist Church the evening previous. I had anticipated some things in the new church not altogether in harmony with my views and tastes. But never had it entered my heart that my wife should so far forget custom of silence among females in the house of God.

My mortification for a few moments was indescribably keen. I would have dissolved our union with the church instantly, and retraced our steps, had it been possible. Such license, such disobedience to custom, I felt for the moment to be intolerable. My mortification arose, not from a conviction that God was dishonored, Christ displeased, or the Holy Ghost grieved, but that the community, our former friends in the church we had just left, would be grieved, and some point the finger of scorn. It was not a care for God's pleasure so much as a dread of violating long-established customs, wounding the hearts of old friends, that troubled me.

It was suggested to my mind that I had not religion enough to allow my wife to do what she deemed to be a duty to her Saviour; that my prejudices must be her standard of activity. I at once saw the injustice, both to my wife and to my Saviour, of thus thrusting my feelings and preferences between her and the cross.[107] I was deeply humbled; and, lifting up my heart to God in prayer, forgiveness was at once bestowed. I was made happy, and blessed to enjoy woman's voice, in spite of former prejudices, in prayer and prophesying.

"I would have consulted you, my dear husband, had I imagined, before going to church, such a duty would have been impressed upon me," said my wife.

"It is well you did not, for my consent could not have been obtained. It is done now. It nearly killed me for the moment; but I have the victory, and your testimony both rebuked and encouraged me. Henceforth, please Christ, and not your husband.''

I have often thought, since then, how cruel to woman it is to compel her to stifle her convictions, to grieve the Holy Spirit,[108] to deny the Saviour the service of her noble gifts, because the pleasure of the Church (not surely the world, for it favors woman's liberty) must be regarded above that of God.

The Church a Potter's Field,[109] where the gifts of women are buried! And how serious will be the responsibilities of that church which does not hasten to roll away the stone,[110] and bring out these long-buried gifts! Every church community needs aid that this endowment of power would speedily bring. And what might we not anticipate as the result of this speedy resurrection of buried power! Not, perhaps, that our churches would be suddenly filled with women who might aspire to occupy the sacred desk.[111] But what a change would soon be witnessed in the social meetings of all church communities! God has eminently endowed woman with gifts for the social circle. He has given her the power of persuasion, and the ability to captivate. Who may *win* souls to Christ, if she may not?[112]

And how well-nigh endless her capabilities for usefulness, if there might only be a persevering effort on the part of the ministry to bring out her neglected gifts, added to a resolve, on the part of woman, to be answerable through grace to the requisition. Our friend speaks too truly of the Church as the only place where woman's gifts are unrecognized;[113] that is, the church estranges herself from woman's gifts. To doubt whether woman brings her gifts into the Church would be a libel on the Christian religion.

Let us contemplate that lovely, fascinating lady, whose cultivated tastes, richly-endowed mind, and unrivalled conversational powers, made her the soul and star of every worldly circle in which she moved.[114] Did she move in the festive-hall, or the refined social circle, charmed worldlings, irrespective of sex, gathered around her, and, as they greeted her gifts by unrestrained manifestations of approval, acknowledged themselves won by her endowment of power over mind.

Surely there has been no tardiness of the children of this world in acquainting themselves with her gifts. But the Holy Spirit comes to the heart of this interesting worldling, bringing to her remembrance that she is not her own, but bought with the price of her Redeemer's blood.[115] She now apprehends, through the enlightening influences of the Holy Spirit, that all her various gifts have been purchased at an infinite price, and must all be brought into the Lord's storehouse,[116] in order that they may be used for his glory.

Sin has its short-lived pleasures, and she has enjoyed the pleasure of securing the smiles of an appreciative world. But the Holy Spirit assures her that she must come out from the world, and be separate;[117] and she sees that she must renounce the world and sin, and through Christ give herself up to God and his church, if she would become a member of the household of faith,[118] and secure life everlasting. How crucifying to flesh[119] is the struggle! but she has resolved rather to endure the death of nature than to perish everlastingly. The struggle is severe. Nature, unreproved by God, will often suffer intensely in passing through the struggle which ensues in emerging from the death of sin to a life of holiness. God will not reprove, because he knows that nature clings to earth. But the struggle past, the emancipated soul, with all its redeemed powers, is at once taken to the heart of infinite love. This point gained, it is the divine order that all the issues of future life should flow out upon a redeemed world in unison with the Head of the Church. The church militant is Christ's visible body.

And now these gifts, so often in requisition, and so prized in the social assembly of the children of this world, have been brought into the Church. We said it were a libel on the religion of Jesus to assert that natural gifts of a high order, bestowed by the God of Nature, are recalled or buried when the possessor becomes a recipient of grace, and a child of the kingdom. The God of Nature is also the God of all grace:[120] and whatsoever was lovely becomes now more lovely; and that which was of good report becomes of far better report[121] through the refinings of grace, and far more effectual for good.

And now that these natural endowments of power, which were so captivating and commanding, and so appreciatively recognized in worldly assemblies, are laid as a sacrifice on the altar of the service of the Church, what becomes of them? Does the church acquaint herself with these gifts? No! she is both a stranger to them, and estranges herself from them.[122] In most church organizations, she authorizes no church assemblies, where she brings her sons and daughters together to call out these gifts for mutual edification and comfort. What means of grace does she acknowledge where her female members, in common with her male members, may use the gift of utterance with which God has endowed her?[123] And, if the Church authorizes no means by which she may acquaint herself with the gift which God has bestowed on women, what becomes of them? Why, of course they are buried. And where are the sepulchres in which they are entombed?[124] Why, the Church.

And when the Head of the Church comes to receive his own with usury,[125] and demands that these buried gifts be brought forth, who will be required to meet the demand? Church communities are made up of individuals. Will it be some one individual member of that church session? or will it be that minister who has failed to acquaint himself and his church session, and other members of his flock, of their responsibility before God in thus entombing an endowment of power which might have been instrumental in the spiritual life of thousands? What wonder, then, that our devoted friend said, that the Church is as a Potter's Field to bury strangers in; for the Church estranges herself from woman's gifts, and buries them within her pale.[126]

But the spirit of inspiration within us and around us, from every point, seems to say, that the time is coming, and now is,[127] when woman's gifts, so long entombed in the Church, shall be resurrected.[128] The command, "Come forth!"[129] is already penetrating the sepulchre where these gifts have been buried. Faith sees the stone being rolled away.[130] And what a resurrection of power shall we witness in the Church, when, in a sense answerable to the original design to God, women shall come forth, a very great army,[131] engaging in all holy activities; when, in the true scriptural sense, and answerable to the design of the God of the Bible, woman shall have become the "helpmeet"[132] to man's spiritual nature! The idea that woman, with all her noble gifts and qualities, was formed mainly to minister to the sensuous nature of man, is wholly unworthy [of] a place in the heart of a Christian.[133]

And here, in the presence of the God of the Bible, we are free to declare that a consistent Christian man—we mean one who has been baptized into the spirit of his divine Master—will not cherish such an idea. Nominal or meagre Christianity may tolerate it; and we think we see reasons most palpable, and such as should alarm all professing Christians, why the ancient Tempter, in his enmity towards woman, should have thrust this repulsive particle of old leaven[134] into the Church, and have taken so much pains to keep it there. We sincerely believe, before God, that it is this repulsive doctrine that has so much to do towards keeping Christianity meagre; ay, so repulsively meagre, that men of the world, who believe in the doctrines of Christianity, fail to see in many so-called Churches any thing answerable to a social want of man's spiritual nature,—a want which the God of Nature hath himself implanted in the human heart, and which would be abundantly met in the precious bosom of the Church, if it were not for this ingredient of wrong which has been thrown in by the Arch-Enemy. We speak with confidence and with carefulness, in the presence of Christ, the glorious Head of the Church, who would have her stand forth before the world in symmetrical proportions of unrivalled beauty, and in inviting attitude.

In the name of the Lord Jesus, who hath purchased the Church with his blood,[135] and hath made abundant provision, not only for her purification, but for her beauty and strength, we implore those who minister at the altar of Christian churches to look at this subject. Christ would not have the Church unseemly in the eyes of his enemies. How grievous in his sight that repelling influences should emanate from her whom he would call his beloved,[136] and whom he would fain have stand forth without spot, wrinkle, or any such thing;[137] so attractive in beauty and strength as to draw all men to her holy shrine!

Surely the Church should present a model of all the blessed proprieties of grace. He by whose forming hand she should be modelled would have her inward construction and exterior surroundings all so truly in the *beauty of holiness*[138] as to invite investigation and admiration. Why should she not be an embodiment of every thing pure, lovely, and of good report?[139] And such she must, in fact, be through Christ, or her Lord can never receive her approvingly, and say to her, "Thou art all fair, my love: there is no spot in thee."[140] Yet such she cannot be, while she entombs in her midst the gift of prophecy intrusted to her daughters.[141]

Oh the endless weight of responsibility with which the Church is pressing herself earthward through the depressing influences of this error! How can she rise while the gifts of three-fourths of her membership are sepulchred in her midst? Would that we might speedily see her clothed in strength, and coming up out of "the wilderness leaning on her Beloved,[142] fair as the moon, clear as the sun, and terrible as an army with banners"![143]

"Daughter of Zion, from the dust
   Exalt thy fallen head;
Again in thy Redeemer trust:
   He calls thee from the dead."[144]

Notes

1. Cf. Catherine Booth's response to attacks on Mrs. Palmer, *Female Teaching: Or the Rev. A. A. Rees Versus Mrs. Palmer* (London: J. G. Stevenson 1861; reprint, New York: Salvation Army, 1975).

2. For an earlier expression of the title metaphor, see William Arthur, *The Tongue of Fire: or the True Power of Christianity* (New York: Harper & Bros., 1856).

3. See Zechariah Taft, *Thoughts on Female Preaching, With Extracts from the Writings of Locke, Henry, Martin, etc.* (Dover: G. Ledger, 1803); Among antecedents, less detailed and explicitly developed, that could have affected her views, see Hugh Bourne, *Remarks on the Ministry of Women* (Bemersley, England: Office of the Primitive Methodist Connection, 1808); and Antoinette L. Brown, "Exegesis of 1 Corinthians, xiv:34,35 and 1 Timothy ii:11, 12," *Oberlin Quarterly Review* 3 (1849):358–73.

4. *The Promise of the Father.*

5. See Catherine Booth, op. cit.; Frances Willard, *Women in the Pulpit* (Chicago: Women's Temperance Publ. Assoc., 1889); Amanda Smith, *An Autobiog-*

raphy (Chicago: Meyer and Bros., 1893); *Hannah Whitall Smith, Philadelphia Quaker,* ed. L. P. Smith (New York: Harcourt and Brace, 1950).

6. For an assessment of related works of the period, see Nancy A. Hardesty, *Women Called to Witness: Evangelical Feminism in the Nineteenth Century* (Nashville: Abingdon, 1984).

7. Cf. Luke 24:49.

8. Acts 1:15.

9. Acts 1:13.

10. Acts 1:14.

11. Acts 1:4.

12. For an analysis of Phoebe Palmer's understanding of the prophetic role of women, see Nancy Hardesty, "Minister as Prophet? Or as Mother?" in *Women in New Worlds,* ed. Hilah F. Thomas and Rosemary Skinner Keller, vol. 1 (Nashville: Abingdon, 1981), 88–101.

13. Acts 2:3.

14. Acts 2:4, her emphasis.

15. Cf. 1 John 4:18.

16. Cf. Acts 11:21.

17. Cf. Rev. 2:1, 8, 12, etc.; Mrs. Palmer refers elsewhere to church pastors as "angels of the churches," i.e., "ministering spirits" within the church.

18. Cf. Mark 16:15.

19. I.e., the Old Testament, the dispensation of law prior to grace, wherein women received the Spirit's gifts.

20. Exod. 15:20.

21. Judg. 4:4.

22. 2 Kings 22:14.

23. Luke 2:36.

24. Acts 2:16–17.

25. Cf. Acts 8:1 and 4, her emphasis.

26. Quotation marks inaccurately placed in text. Cf. Acts 2:23, 36, 4:10.

27. Cf. Mark 16:20.

28. Acts 2:47, her emphasis.

29. *Dialogue with Trypho,* ch. 88, *ANF,* I, 243.

30. The last of this quotation, beginning with "according as Joel," is a paraphrase.

31. It may seem remarkable that she was apparently reading in Latin the works of Henry Dodwell (1641–1711), prolific, nonjuring Anglican theologian of Oxford. For neither Dodwell nor the following quotation from Grotius were available to her in English translation. It should not be surprising, however, that a young woman well brought up in a pious New York environment should read some Latin.

32. Dodwell, *Dissertationes in Irenaeum* (Oxford: Sheldon Theatre, 1689).

33. Hugo Grotius, *Annotationes in Vetus and Novum Testamentum* (London: Jos. Smith, 1727), vol. 1, 214.

34. Joseph Benson, *The Holy Bible with Notes* (New York: Harper, 1823), vol. 2, 795.

35. Adam Clarke, *The Holy Bible with A Commentary and Critical Notes* (New York: J. Emory and B. Waugh, 1829), vol. 3, 218.

36. Ibid., p. 218.

37. Cf. Adam Clarke, *Christian Theology* (Salem, Ohio: Schmul, 1967), 47–63.

38. Philip Schaff, *History of the Christian Church.*

39. Ibid., 1886 edition, revised from 1867, vol. 3, p. 934.

40. Eusebius, *Church History*, v. 17, *NPNF*, 2, I, p. 234.

41. Modern advocates of gender equity in language may be amazed that such a point was being made in the middle of the nineteenth century. The implication is that the word kinsman is tilted in the direction of reference to males. Phoebe Palmer wished to see such language shift toward greater equity and accuracy, hence, kinsfolk. The point is not a petty one. For she is trying to demonstrate that women were named by Paul as ''among the apostles.'' She was willing to use ancient Greek authorities to make her linguistic point.

42. John Chrysostom, *Homilies on Romans*, XXXI, *NPNF*, 1st series, XI, pp. 554, 555. Cf. Theophylact or Theophylactus of Bulgaria, Archbishop of Okhrid, fl. 1078, *Commentarius in Epistolam ad Romanos*, J. P. Migne, *Patrologia Graeca*, Paris: Migne, 1857–66, vol. 124 (1864), 551 (it is not likely that an English translation of Theophylact was available to Mrs. Palmer, though private translations could have been available).

43. Cf. Rom. 16:12.

44. Cf. Rom. 16:12.

45. Sic: Phoebe.

46. Cf. Rom. 16:1–2.

47. Should be Theodoret, *Interpretatio Epistolae ad Romanos*, in *Patrologiae Cursus Completus* (Series Graeca), ed. J. Migne (Paris: 1859), vols. 82, 218, 219.

48. Cf. Eric Berne, *What Do you Say After You Say Hello?* (New York: Grove, 1972), argues that person's names are crucial factors in ''scripting.'' Could Phoebe's name have affected her sense of calling to diaconal service? She too ''travelled much'' and ''propagated the gospel in foreign countries.''

49. Joseph Benson, *HBN*, V., p. 359 (somewhat paraphrased by Mrs. Palmer). Cf. Benson, V, pp. 120–21: ''We may suppose the name was given her on account of the office she performed to many as a deaconess.''

50. The quote is from Adam Clarke, *The New Testament With a Commentary and Critical Notes*, (HBC) (New York: Carlton and Porter, 1851), vol. 6, 161, but it ends with ''apostolic constitution'' (quote not closed in text; cf. *Apostolic Constitutions* VIII.19–20, *ANF*, VII, p. 492). Clarke goes on to say that the office of deaconess continued in the Latin church until the 10th or 11th century, and to the end of the 12th century in the Greek church. The following sentence, apparently, is Mrs. Palmer's own. It remains puzzling as to whether some historical figure such as Constantine was implied in her reference to the ''man of sin,'' or whether simply the Devil. It would not be unusual for a Protestant reference of this period to refer in this way to Constantine or more generally of the period of papal hegemony, but that could not have been consistently asserted if Mrs. Palmer had fully accredited

what followed in Clarke's commentary. Paul Bassett suggests that the "man of sin" might have reference to Gregory VII (Hildebrand, c. 1023–85).

51. 1 Cor. 14:34.

52. Paul's argument reconstructed: In urging women to "remain silent in the churches," (1 Cor. 1:34), Paul is reproving a particular unseemly practice found at Corinth: that of interrupting the speaker, and of disorderly debates. Mrs. Palmer argues that this practice was peculiar to the Church of Corinth, and not found elsewhere, hence inapplicable elsewhere, unless that abuse should appear. It is in relation to the usurpation of authority that Paul enjoins silence, not generally of women who are not usurping authority. It could not apply to the prophesying of women, which he elsewhere commends.

53. Cf. 1 Cor. 14:3.

54. 1 Tim. 2:12.

55. The distinction between exercising the gift of prophecy and usurpation of authority is the crucial one for Paul, as viewed by Mrs. Palmer. The former he approves, the latter he rejects.

56. 1 Cor. 11:4–5.

57. Cf. Clarke, *NT Commentary*, vol. VI, p. 250, on 1 Cor. 11:5.

58. Clergy.

59. Recapitulating this crucial turn of argument: The gift of prophecy is commended by scripture to both males and females. This gift, when given to women, has been resisted by male clergy, whom one would expect most to welcome it. This is evidence of the power of sin. Those who, by quoting scripture, resist the prophesying of women are deceived by demonic reasoning. But in these last days amid a renewal of the reception of Pentecostal gifts, Mrs. Palmer thought, this gift too is being recovered.

60. Cf. 2 Pet. 3:16.

61. Rev. 19:11.

62. Cf. 2 Tim. 1:7.

63. Cf. Rom. 12:10.

64. 1 Cor. 3:9 with 2 Thess. 3:2.

65. There is indeed a significant body of literature on the special place of women in the Wesleyan tradition. For bibliography, see Kenneth E. Rowe, *Methodist Women: A Guide to the Literature* (Lake Junaluska, N.C.: United Methodist Commission on Archives and History, 1980); see Taft, *HW;* George Coles, *Heroines of Methodism* (New York: Carlton & Porter, 1857); Jesse T. Peck, *True Woman* (New York: Carlton & Porter, 1857); Abel Stevens, *The Women of Methodism* (New York: Carlton and Porter, 1866); Gabriel P. Disosway, *Our Excellent Women of the Methodist Church in England and America* (New York: James Miller, 1873); Warren C. Black, *Christian Womanhood* (Nashville: Methodist Publishing House, 1888); Alice Cook, *Women of the Warm Heart* (London: Epworth, 1952); Earl Kent Brown, "Standing in the Shadow: Women in Early Methodism," *Nexus* 17/2 (1974):22–31, and "Women of Mr. Wesley's Methodism," *Studies in Women and Religion*, vol. 11 (New York: New York University, 1956); cf. biographies in *CBTEL, EWM, CM.*

66. Cf. Phil. 4:3.

67. By "full baptism of the Holy Ghost," she means sanctification as preached by the Wesleys. It would be inappropriate to read into this phrase post-Palmerian nuances, such as glossolalia, which she did not associate with it.

68. It should be remembered that Wesley never made wide use of the phrase "baptism of the Holy Ghost," (nor did he identify that phrase with entire sanctification), or of the "endowment of power," and he never publically claimed to have attained what he called "entire sanctification" (preface to "A Collection of Forms of Prayer for Every Day of the Week" 1775, *WJW*, XIV, p. 272). Yet there is testimony in his works to his interest in those who had attained it, especially where he speaks of examining others who claimed to have received it. His preaching, a model for Mrs. Palmer's, strongly commended the gifts of the Spirit, to be received now, and by all.

69. Cf. Phil. 3:10.

70. Cf. Eph. 6:10.

71. The quotation ending "conquer all things" is in a letter to Elizabeth Briggs, from Athlone, April 14, 1771 (*Letters,* vol. V, p. 237, Telford edition). The rest of the quotation does not appear in Telford. Endquotes misplaced.

72. Endquotes misplaced (see above note).

73. *Journal,* Mon., Dec. 4, 1786, ed. N. Curnock (London: Epworth Press, vol. VII, pp. 226–27). The quotation ends here.

74. This paragraph was erroneously included within quotation marks. It is written by Mrs. Palmer, not Wesley.

75. Cf. Joel 2:28.

76. George Coles, *Heroines of Methodism* (New York: Carlton and Porter, 1857), 291.

77. Cf. Jer. 1:6.

78. 1 Cor. 9:16.

79. Cf. Gal. 2:2.

80. Cf. 1 Thess. 3:5.

81. Mrs. Palmer frequently followed this advice herself.

82. More about Sarah Mallett is in Zachariah Taft's *Holy Women* (London: Kershaw, 1825), vol. 1, 79–90. Cf. Sarah Crosby, "The Grace of God Manifested in the Account of Mrs. Crosby of Leeds," ed. Elizabeth Richie Mortimre, *Arminian Magazine* 19 (1806): 418–73, 516–21, 563–68, 610–71; Hester Ann Rogers, *An Account of the Experience of Hester Ann Rogers* (New York: Bangs and Emory, 1828); John Lancaster, *The Life of Darcy, Lady Maxwell, of Pollock* (New York: Mason and Lane, 1837); Mary Bosanquet Fletcher, *Jesus Altogether Lovely: Or, a Letter to Some of the Single Women in the Methodist Society* (Bristol: n.p., 1766); Mary Barritt Taft, *Memoirs* (Ripon, England: John Stevens, 1827).

83. Cf. Ps. 68:11.

84. Cf. Joel 2:28–29.

85. A monograph is needed on the relative number of women attending and influencing the holiness revivals of the mid-nineteenth century.

86. Social assembly, as distinguished from " 'Women's Preaching,' technically so called," *PF*, p. 1, i.e., in the service of public worship.

87. That the last days begin with the full reception of the gifts of prophecy is a theme that would increasingly influence holiness revivalism.

88. Francis Wayland, *Sermons to the Churches* (New York: Sheldon, Blakeman, 1858), 21ff. Dr. Wayland was president of Brown University, Providence, R.I.

89. Cf. Lucille Sider Dayton and Donald W. Dayton, "Your Daughters Shall Prophesy: Feminism in the Holiness Movement," *Methodist History* 14 (1976): 67–92; "Women as Preachers: Evangelical Precedents," *Christianity Today,* 23 May, 1975, 4–7.

90. Cf. Luke 23:49 with Matt. 27:55.

91. Luke 8:3.

92. Cf. Acts 2:4.

93. Cf. 2 Thess. 2:3.

94. Mrs. Palmer invested great energy in a ministry to ministers, and felt that their role was crucial in this instance—tragically so.

95. Deut. 6:4.

96. The reference is to the resurrection appearances of Jesus to women, which initiated the Christian dispensation.

97. Rev. 19:10.

98. The fundamental idea of repression receives clear expression here. These energies are destined to break through, however long pent up.

99. The humor is wry and biting: The risen Lord gives commands to women; the disciples question and prevent their fulfillment.

100. It is likely that this lady was among Mrs. Palmer's circle of friends, but insufficient clues are given for positive identification.

101. Cf. Matt. 12:34.

102. Cf. Acts 5:29.

103. The dynamics of polite rejection, so familiar to those bereft of power who have sought reformation in religious traditions, are deftly described here by Mrs. Palmer with a subtlety that is hardly exceeded among nineteenth century writers. These dynamics are circumspectly described and courageously confronted.

104. Cf. Phil 4:8.

105. Here begins the testimony of a formerly Episcopalian, later Methodist, clergy husband of a woman who bore testimony in religious meetings.

106. At least the following five paragraphs are a quotation, source unidentified.

107. A nineteenth century example of "consciousness-raising"?

108. Cf. Eph. 4:30.

109. Cf. Matt. 27:7; a powerful image of lost gifts, buried competencies in the church—the burial metaphor requires resurrection.

110. Mark 16:3.

111. I.e., pulpit.

112. Mrs. Palmer thought that women were naturally more gifted for some acts of ministry than men—in persuasive gifts, where grace transmutes nature.

113. Mrs. Palmer apparently viewed the Church as more repressive than the society in this instance.

114. Here begins a rich description of the redeemed powers of a natively gifted woman.

115. 1 Cor. 6:19–20.

116. Cf. Mal. 3:10.

117. Cf. 2 Cor. 6:17.

118. Gal. 6:10.

119. Cf. Gal. 5:24.

120. The nature-grace relation is intuitively grounded in the Thomistic tradition, probably received through Anglican sources, see Thomas Aquinas, *ST*, I–IIae, Q109.

121. Cf. Phil. 4:8.

122. The dialectic of estrangement is intuited by Mrs. Palmer as both self-chosen and in a sense objective. This is a powerful indictment of the failure of the Church as an institution to recognize, develop, and utilize the gifts of women.

123. The Pentecostal traditions of preaching would later form powerfully around particular interpretations of this phrase not yet envisioned by Mrs. Palmer.

124. Cf. Matt. 23:27–29; Luke 11:47, 48.

125. Luke 19:23; Matt. 25:27. The tomb image of the religious institution used by Jesus is employed powerfully to speak of the deadly entombment of women's gifts.

126. This damning critique of the lost possibilities of the Churches runs counter to those who tend to associate holiness revivalism with ecclesiastical conservatism.

127. Cf. John 4:23.

128. Cf. John 5:25.

129. Cf. John 11:43.

130. Cf. Mark 16:4; Luke 24:2.

131. Joel 2:25.

132. Cf. Gen. 2:18.

133. The modern feminist critique that woman is demeaned by being viewed only or primarily in relation to man's sensual needs is clearly anticipated here by Mrs. Palmer.

134. The "repulsive particle of old leaven" (cf. 1 Cor. 5:6–8) is the assumption that woman exists only to serve man's physical needs—a device of the enemy, and a morally unworthy assumption to be made by both males and females in the Christian community. Mrs. Palmer was convinced that it was the work of nothing less than supernatural demonic power (eventuating in social sin) that so rigorously kept women bound to submissive roles in the church.

135. Acts 20:28.

136. Rom. 1:7.

137. Cf. Eph. 5:27.

138. Cf. Ps. 29:2.

139. Phil. 4:8.

140. Song 4:7.

141. Cf. Donna Alberta Behnke, "Created in God's Image: Religious Issues in the Women's Rights Movement of the Nineteenth Century," Ph.D. dissertation, Northwestern University, 1975.

142. Song 8:5.

143. Song 6:10.

144. James Montgomery, *HUMEC*, 1850, #229, v. 1, entitled "Daughter of Zion, from the Dust"; C. S. Nutter, Hymn Studies, NY: Hunt & Eaton, n.d.

II

THE YOUNG PHOEBE PALMER:
EARLY DIARY, LETTERS, POEMS
AND RECOLLECTIONS (1807–1828)

I. CHILDHOOD AND EARLY YOUTH (1807–1820)

The "pious parental solicitude" of Phoebe's parents, Mr. and Mrs. Henry Worrall,[1] combined with Phoebe's early developed moral sensitivities to elicit a disposition of "well-intentioned scrupulousness." As she later looked back upon her childhood in lower Manhattan,[2] she could recognize the tracings of providence in her parental guidance, early instruction in experiential religion, and even her anguish over guilt (Faith and its Effects, p. 62):

I will proceed to present the more prominent portions of my experience in the things of God[3] from my infancy; for from that early period I trace his hand leading me to himself.[4]

My parents, prior to my being intrusted to them, were rather devotedly pious. I was therefore early instructed[5] in experimental[6] religion. Of the necessity of its affecting my life, and even in minute things inducing a change of conduct, I was in the morning of my existence aware. I shall never forget the intense anguish I suffered in consequence of telling an untruth, when but about three and a half years old.

This extreme sensitiveness, as to moral and religious obligation, grew up with me; so much so, that I was sometimes smiled at for my well-intentioned scrupulousness, and at other times almost censured for carrying it to a troublesome excess. I then regarded refuge in God as the safe sanctuary for the recital of the little grievances incident to childhood. Thanks be to

God that the maturer knowledge of later years has never erased the principles thus early cherished by the operation of the Holy Spirit, and pious
parental solicitude.

*At eleven years the precocious young Phoebe was writing poetry. Her
first known poem was written, dated, in the fly leaf of a New Testament
given her by the British Consul, George Buchanan, a friend of her father's.*[7]
*What is remarkable about this poetry is not only the aesthetic balance and
mature use of language by an eleven year old, but also its spiritual subtlety
(Memoirs, p. 18; by* Memoirs, *we refer to Richard Wheatley,* The Life and
Letters of Mrs. Phoebe Palmer *(New York: W. C. Palmer, Jr., 1876),
which includes both her correspondence and diary entries):*

Diary, 1818:

This Revelation—holy, just, and true—
Though oft I read, it seems forever new;
While light from heaven upon its pages rest,
I feel its power, and with it I am blest.

Within its leaves, it grace divine displays,
Makes known the Almighty's will, in various ways;
Justice, it speaks to those who heaven defy,
And with ungracious lips its truths deny.

'Tis here the wearied one, in sin's rough road,
May find the path mark'd out that leads to God,
And when oppressed by earth, *all* here may find
Sweet promises of peace to cheer the mind.

To this blest treasure, O my soul, attend,
Here find a firm and everlasting friend—
A friend in all life's varied changes sure,
Which shall to all eternity endure.

Henceforth, I take thee as my future guide,
Let naught from thee my youthful heart divide
And then, if late or early death be mine,
All will be well, since I, O Lord, am thine![8]

A brief account of her childhood and youth appeared in The Way of
Holiness, *revised from her diary (pp. 72–76):*

At the dawn of life she had been intrusted to parents to whom the Father of spirits[9] had said, "Take this child and bring it up for me."[10] They felt the solemn responsibility, and endeavored to train her up for God.

God did not forget to encourage their efforts. He watered the seed sown with the dews of grace[11] from her earliest recollections. When not four years old,[12] powerful conviction for sin gave assurance that the Holy Spirit was true to the performance of its promised aid.

Though for many happy years she was enabled to testify, with perfect assurance, that she had passed from death unto life, yet the precise time when that change took place she could not ever state.[13] Not to have an experience like most others born into the kingdom of Christ, who are so fully able, from the overwhelming circumstances of the occasion, to state the precise moment, was a fruitful source of temptation, resulting in years of painful solicitude.

From a child it was her error to treasure up, in careful remembrance, those outward exhibitions, which are given by many sincere disciplines, of the inward workings of the Spirit. Hence she was too often led to pronounce upon the magnitude of the work wrought in the heart by the outward manifestations of feeling.

Not unfrequently she felt like weeping because she could not weep, imagining if she could plunge herself into those overwhelming sorrows, and despairing views of relationship to God, spoken of by some, she could then come and throw herself upon his mercy with greater probability of success.[14]

Over and again, after having had a long season in wrestling with God,[15] she would, as a last resource, say, "If thou wilt but direct me by thy word, and permit me to open to some passage suited to my case, I will, through thy grace assisting me, abide by its decisions." And at several never-to-be-forgotten periods did the Lord condescend to give the most direct answers of peace in this manner. For a time she would rejoice in the assurances received, and glory in the assurances of the blessed word as in verity the voice of God to her soul; but as soon as the freshness of these visitations passed over, she would again give way to dissatisfaction with her experience.

This dissatisfaction did not generally arise from the consideration that her experience was unscriptural, but from the fact that it was so unlike what she conceived to be the manner of the Spirit's operation on the hearts of others, who, as she conjectured, had received the assurance of acceptance in some such luminous manner, independent, in part, from Scriptural demonstration, that they had been constrained *irresistibly* to believe.

Uncertainty and spiritual depression were the consequences resulting from these repeated turnings away from the word of the Lord to the feeble testimony of men.[16] And it is not surprising while this course, which was so dishonoring to God, was, in any degree, persisted in, that she should be left to comparative desertion. Yet this was for years her course.[17]

Sometimes, during this period, the adversary tried to urge upon her mind that the ways of the Lord were unequal; intimating that he bestowed a much larger share of spiritual illumination on some than on others, when the true state of the case was, that she was possessed of the spirit of a Naaman,[18] or of the unbelieving Jews[19] resolved that, unless she should see *signs and wonders,*[20] she would not believe.

On reviewing this portion of her experience, she afterward saw that the ways of God could not have been justified, in imparting any other state of experience than that of uncertainty and spiritual depression, inasmuch as he hath said, "If ye will not believe, surely ye shall not be established. . . ."[21]

Yet, notwithstanding all this waywardness she greatly desired God as the portion of her soul,[22] and often felt as if she could say, that his favor was more desirable than life. With deep groaning of spirit,[23] her heart gave utterance to its emotions in saying,—

"Let me no more, in deep complaint,
　'My leanness! O, my leanness!'[24] cry;
Alone consumed with pining want,
　Of all my Father's children I."[25]

"Believe—only believe," was the oft-repeated admonition of the friends of Jesus; and her heart would as frequently silently ejaculate, "But *what* and *how* am I to believe?" till she became nearly wearied with what seemed to her an almost unmeaning admonition, unaccompanied, as it most generally was, with the necessary explanations.

2. YOUTHFUL EXPERIENCE OF RELIGION (1820–1827)

At age thirteen she became "a seeker of salvation, and united herself with the people of God." This experience of religion is to be distinguished from a later conversion experience at seventeen. She worried that she did not have a dateable experience of rebirth, to which so many of that period attested.

The following passages show that (1) dream analysis was a consistent resource for her self-examination; (2) she recognized in herself a strongly rationalist bent even in her early years; (3) she developed early the steady practice of intercession for others; (4) her youthful search for sanctifying

*grace did not permit any neglect of social or temporal responsibilities; (5)
by intentionally ordering her priorities as a young woman, she discovered
on her own (anticipating later feminism) that many things that young
women were conventionally expected to do could be omitted without harm;
(6) from an early period she had developed the habit of thinking concretely
out of her own experience, anticipating existentialist thinkers like Kierkegaard (1813–55) and pragmatist thinkers like William James (1842–1910);
(7) like Kierkegaard's Johannes de Silentio, her inward, silent, hidden
struggle was seldom grasped or recognized by others; (8) she resolved as a
youth to seek to make daily advances in the way of holiness. She wrote
thoughtfully and self-critically of her childhood (The Way of Holiness, pp.
76–101):*

When about thirteen[26] she acknowledged herself, before the world, as
a seeker of salvation, and united herself with the people of God. One night,
about this time, after having wrestled with the Lord till about midnight, she
sought the repose of her pillow with feelings expressed by the poet—

"I'll weary thee with my complaint,
  Here, at thy feet, for ever lie,
With longing sick, with groaning faint—
  O! give me love, or else I die."[27]

She believed herself to have fallen asleep when, with a power that
aroused body and mind by its heavenly sweetness, these words were spoken
to her inmost soul,—

"See Israel's gentle Shepherd stands,
  With all-engaging charms;
See how he calls the tender lambs,
  And folds them in his arms."[28]

The place seemed to shine with the glory of God;[29] and she felt that
the blessed Saviour indeed took her to the bosom of his love, and bade her
"be of good cheer."[30] All was light, joy, and peace.

She had no recollection of ever having heard those sweet lines before,
and regarded them as spoken directly from the lips of the good Shepherd to
her heart; but on observing them some years afterward in a sabbath-school
hymn book, she conjectured that the words might have been seed sown in
her infant heart at a very early age, when cherished in one of these nurseries
of the Lord.[31]

The consolation at this time derived was of several days' duration, but she again yielded to her former unwise course, and began to measure herself by the standard of experience established by others, instead of going to the law and the testimony,[32] as enjoined by the word, and it would, as before observed, have been inconsistent with the declarations of that word for her to enjoy an established state of experience, while indulging in such a course. Had she taken "the sword of the Spirit, it would have guarded the way of life. . . . "[33]

At another time, about a year subsequent to the period just alluded to,[34] the Lord again greatly comforted her soul during the night season. She had again, as on the former occasion, been for a long time wresting earnestly with God, till nature had become wearied, when on falling asleep, she dreamed she was standing without.[35] The canopy of a beautiful midnight sky was spread out above her; the firmament was cloudless, and the full moon was silently walking the heavens. A stillness, that seemed hallowed to something unusual, reigned, but her eye was intently fixed, and her mind all absorbed by the attraction of a bright star. Presently it began to enlarge its circle, wider and yet wider,[36] when (as she continued to keep her eye fixed on the point where it first began to rest) the form of the infant Saviour was presented, and these words were proclaimed, "For unto us a child is born, unto us a son is given. . . . And his name shall be called WONDERFUL, COUNSELOR, THE MIGHTY GOD, THE EVERLASTING FATHER, THE PRINCE OF PEACE."[37]

In the mean time, while these words were being proclaimed, the circle rapidly widened, until the whole heavens had become encircled in one glow of glory.

The happy experience of succeeding years, when, by keeping her eye steadily fixed upon the Day-star from on high,[38] her spiritual horizon had become enlightened, and, as she had continued to gaze, had rapidly taken in yet wider and still wider circles of glory, until the whole firmament of her soul had become radiant with its blissful beams, assured her that this communication was intended to convey a greater infinitude of meaning than her feeble capacities comprehended at the time. . . . [39]

Being naturally much given to reasoning, seldom disposed to credit an assertion without an ostensible wherefore, she sometimes almost yielded to the suggestion, that her constitutional temperament was so greatly to her disadvantage, she need scarcely expect to be strong in faith—imagining that persons naturally credulous had in spiritual matters greatly the advantage of those who required a specified reason for every item of belief, and who most cautiously examined step by step the validity of the ground, ere the venture was made to tread firmly.

Yet this very trait of character, which she had habituated herself to regard as so unpropitious, when brought into obedience to Christ, was made subservient to her spiritual advantage. . . . [40]

But she lost beyond all calculation by thus lingering for years in this comparatively undecided course. Some estimation of the irreparable loss sustained may be conceived by an allusion to one who in a given time is required to build an edifice. He lays the foundation, and begins to advance with the superstructure, but, fearful of some mistake, he overthrows it, and then again commences, and after having made, perchance, still higher advances, again demolishes it from the fear that something may yet be wrong. And this was precisely her unwise course. . . . [41]

And here it might be well to state in reference to the members of her household, she proved that it was not an unmeaning service to follow in the footsteps of God's ancient servant Job,[42] who arose early and bore the individual members of his family before the mercy-seat, by presenting the offerings, ordained by God, in their behalf, in order, through this medium, to crave the acceptance of their persons. Even thus she found it to be a very satisfactory exercise, to present, through the merits of the sin-atoning Sacrifice, not only her own soul, but also the case of each individual member, imploring for them individually that they might be permitted, through the merits of Christ, to abide as in the presence of God, under the direct rays of the Sun of righteousness, during the day. . . . [43]

When she first made up her mind that every earthly consideration should be in the highest degree subservient to the prominent object of attaining the witness of entire consecration, she had no other expectation than that of entering heart and soul into her earthly cares again, for the Lord had written this lesson upon her heart[:][44] "He that careth not for his own household is worse than an infidel";[45] and she did not, at this interesting point of her experience, intend to neglect them, but only resolved that they should cease to be *absorbing* until this assurance was gained; and it was at this precise point in her pilgrimage that Almighty grace gained a signal victory over a naturally over-anxious spirit . . . [46]

But by a careful attention to the instructions of the blessed word, she found that much which had formerly augmented her cares was easily to be dispensed with, without any infringement either on the happiness of others or her own; and in many respects these omissions *increased* the happiness of all.[47] Take, for instance, the admonition contained in the prophetic sentiment, "In that day shall there be upon the bells of the horses, HOLINESS UNTO THE LORD, and the pots of the Lord's house shall be like the bowls before the altar; yea, every pot in Jerusalem and in Judea shall be HOLINESS TO THE LORD OF HOSTS."[48]

By this she observed that there was nothing with which she had a right to do that was either *too high* or *too low* to be inscribed with ''HOLINESS UNTO THE LORD''; and she resolved not to be absorbed with any pursuit that would not unequivocally bear this inscription. . . . [49]

That which is learned by *experience* is much more deeply written upon the heart than what is learned by mere precept.[50] By this painful process, the lessons of grace remain written in *living* characters upon the mind, and we are better able to tell to travelers coming after us, just how and where we met with this and the other difficulty, how we overcame, and the peculiar lessons learned by passing through this and that trial, and thus be not only advantaged in our own experience, but helpful to our fellow-pilgrims.

Yes, she was called to endure trials. To the observation of those unacquainted with the Christian warfare such a statement could hardly be understood or accredited. Consequently, the number of those who knew *just how* to sympathize was not great. Probably for this reason, in part, she seemed seldom called to dwell upon the particulars of those deep mental conflicts which she was permitted to endure, when she was called to wrestle, ''not against flesh and blood, but against principalities and powers, &c. . . . ''[51]

These mighty conflicts were repeated yet again and again, and through each succeeding year of her pilgrimage; with each conflict it seemed, while engaged in the contest, as though it had reached the summit of human endurance, yet the succeeding one was found to be proportionate in magnitude to the increase of strength that had been gained by the former trial, and the intermediate interval for growth, and knowledge, and spiritual stature.[52]

These trials, though they sometimes arose from outward causes, were generally inward and the struggle they caused is indescribable; in the midst of which she was often called to lean so entirely, ''with *naked* faith, upon a *naked* promise,''[53] that nature was sometimes tempted in its shrinkings to say, ''My God, why hast thou forsaken me?''[54], but still holding with an unyielding grasp upon that promise, ''I will never leave nor forsake thee. . . . ''[55]

''Ye have to pass a way that ye have not passed heretofore,''[56] said the courageous Joshua to the unbelieving Jews, who had been forty years accomplishing in zig-zag, and almost aimless wanderings, a journey that might have been performed in fewer days than they had taken years.

It was thus, she conceived that many professed followers of Jesus, in consequence of unbelief, necessarily ending in disobedience, are years in accomplishing that which might have been performed in fewer days.

She could find no Scriptural reason, why each successive day might not witness the heavenly traveler at a higher point of elevation in his homeward course than the day previous and she felt confident that there should not be a perfect rest of spirit, without this assurance. In the early part of her

career in the way of holiness, she resolved not to be satisfied without knowing that she was thus making *daily* advances in the knowledge and love of
God—"the way of holiness."[57]

*By the time she was eighteen, Phoebe appears to be a regular attendant
at Duane Street Methodist Church (Memoirs, pp. 20, 21):*

May 18, 1825[58]

To be deprived in any measure of retirement, and time alloted to secret
prayer, is ever a spiritual loss. My heart, prone to wander, needs every
available inspiration to urge it heavenward. Heard Rev. D. DeVinne
preach, this morning. Text, "If any man will come after me, let him deny
himself, take up his cross daily, and follow me."[59] It was his first sermon
to our people of the Duane St. Church, and was good. Its precepts, followed, would surely make me a more useful and happy disciple. Rev. T.
Mason preached a farewell sermon this afternoon, from the words, "I have
not shunned to declare unto you the whole counsel of God."[60] Well, indeed, will it be for any minister, who can, with the faithful Paul, truthfully
say thus. Rev. Nathan Bangs discoursed this evening, from the words, "Be
not conformed to this world."[61]

Jan. 1, 1826

I have abundant cause of gratitude and praise for the goodness and
mercy that has followed me[62] through the past year. Health of body has been
awarded, and endeared friends have gathered around me. O, that I may
manifest my grateful love to the Lord, my Redeemer, by entire devotedness
to his service. I am endeavoring to lean on Jesus, and to be more conformed
to his image.

3. VOCATION AND MARRIAGE (1827):
A SPIRITUAL SELF-EXAMINATION

*Two entries in her diary indicate how earnestly Phoebe Worrall reflected on the spiritual meaning of her marriage to a young doctor, Walter
Clark Palmer.[63] The wedding was on September 28, 1827. She was nineteen years old, he was twenty-four (Memoirs, pp. 22–23):*

Diary, August 12, 1827

The most eventful period of my life is approaching. During the past
eleven months, friendship has been ripening into a mature affection between myself and a kindred spirit, who, I have reason to believe, is in every

respect, worthy of my love. I have not approached this crisis without careful circumspection and prayer. I have ever felt that it was a step too momentous to be hastily taken, fixing as it does, life's destiny. It has, therefore, been a subject of prayerful solicitude with me, that the avenue to my heart's sanctuary might be guarded. I have dared to present a definite request, which I trust has long stood answered, that the Lord would not permit my affections to flow out in a way bordering on marriage toward any one, other than as ordered by Divine Providence. I have regarded it as cruel—in fact, wicked, on the part of a lady, to encourage a manifestation of affection, that she did not intend to reciprocate, and since my earliest approaches to womanhood, I have been very guarded on this point.[64] The Bible is alike true on this point as on all others, "With what measure ye mete, it shall be measured to you again."[65] Repeated approaches have been made on the part of three or four different individuals, whom I might not have thought unworthy of my love; but as I did not see my parents' approving smile, I have carefully avoided their society, resolved not to favor attentions that I could not return. No credit is due to me in relation to these matters. But in view of the great change I now contemplate, in removing ere long from my father's house, it is proper to say, that I owe much to the grace of God, that I have been so carefully fostered under the parental eye. Obedience from infancy has been the rule of the household. Severity has not been necessary. Doubtless, the kindness of my dear parents would have induced them to use the "rod of correction,"[66] had I refused obedience, as enjoined in the Bible, but having been taught from my cradle, that my parents' wishes were the governing law of the household domain, the rod of correction has not been necessary. I do not remember ever to have been wilfully disobedient to any parental command.[67] If I have loved and honored my parents,[68] and if their expressed wishes with me have been equal to their known commands, is it not because *God* has in these regards written his law on my heart?[69] And here, at this eventful period of my life, I pause, and raise an Ebenezer of Praise, for, hitherto, the Lord hath helped me![70]

And now, having been wary in the bestowal of my affections, I find them permanently and strongly fixed on one, who I believe is, in the order of infinite Love, designed to be a helpmeet.[71] In religious, moral, and intellectual endowments, he stands approved.[72] The best of all is, that he is a servant of the Lord. On his thirteenth birthday he was powerfully converted, and now, in his twenty-fourth year, he is still holding on his way. I cannot but believe that heaven approves, and as my dear friend has consulted my parents, and they have given their consent, I indulge in pleasant anticipations that all will be well. Glory be to the Father, Son, and Holy Spirit, for all the goodness and mercy which have followed me all my days.[73]

*Two months after the wedding she amusingly noted her surprise that
she had not continued to keep her spiritual diary during that period. She was
keenly aware that even though she had older siblings, she was the first of
the Worrall children to "break the family circle" (Memoirs, pp. 23–24):*

Diary, Nov. 24, 1827

Strange, indeed, that such an eventful period of my life should have
passed, and no scrap of entry in my note-book. But O, how indelibly has
memory inscribed on its tablet thought that will ever be cherished. September 28th, 1827, I was united in marriage to Dr. Walter C. Palmer. The ceremony took place at my father's house, in the presence of a number of
relatives and friends. Rev. Nicholas White, pastor of the Duane St. M. E.
C.,[74] officiated. Among the guests was my loved one's old preceptor, Dr.
David Hosack. After a little jaunt abroad,[75] and an incessant round of visiting new and old relatives, we are now settled down in our new home. I
have shed some tears in thinking of the loved ones at home. I was the first
one to break the family circle. My dear father always looked with almost a
jealous eye, on any gentleman who, he imagined, might covet one of his
daughters. The next morning after my marriage, I left for my wedding trip,
at an early hour. I was affected to hear from one of the dear ones present,
at the next gathering around the family altar, how keenly my precious father
felt the loss of the absent member. Said one, "It seemed almost like a funeral occasion. Thus it is, our family circle has commenced to break. One
has gone, and perhaps ere long another will go, till we shall all be separated." It is well for us, that such feelings do not always last. I do not doubt
but my father feels that I have married one every way worthy of my love.
And as for myself, I have no tears of sorrow to shed, though I have felt the
pang of separation from the dear household circle. I know that all is right.

The experience of every day confirms me in the persuasion that our
union is of the Lord. The family altar has been established, and we are aiming mutually to acknowledge the Lord in all our ways.[76] I feel that I am
surrounded by mercies. But, O, what a lack in my religious experience! I
am so often fearful and unbelieving. I shrink from crosses, and often bring
condemnation upon my soul. I approve of the things that are excellent, but
am wanting in courage, faith and fervour.[77]

*We are including in this collection a number of poems from her early
period, partly because they are significant biographically, but more so because they are effective literary efforts of a young, sensitive, cultured
woman. Her poetry from the early period of the marriage, and from subsequent celebrations of the marriage, reveals an extraordinary gift of imagination. "Love's Vicissitudes" is intricately constructed, each verse*

beginning with a question, the answer to which builds upon a sequence of metaphors: the flame (the emergence of first love); the blush (the recognition of love); the speech of the heart (impatient love); binding (covenant love); the twin flowers (connubial love); the storm (inconstant love); and the eternal bloom (heavenly love)—(From A Mother's Gift, *pp. 96–97):*

Love's Vicissitudes

What was that burning flame?
How kindled, when and where?
'Twas smothered, then a fresh blaze came,
And vented in a tear;
The tear then spoke felicity,
And but inflamed its fervency;
'Twas love's first dawn.

What is that crimson blush,
Which fain would be conceal'd;
The more 'twas chid,[78] the more 'twas hushed,
The more it was revealed;
A something that she could but feel,
And yet 'twas inexpressible?
'Twas maiden's love.

What was that in the heart
That spoke exquisite bliss;
That said I cannot from thee part;
That happy restlessness;
That pleasing strife, that joyful tear,
That longing for its object near?
'Twas love impatient.

What is it binds those hearts
In such endearing ties,
That says we'll never, never part
While time and mem'ry lives;
But vow eternal constancy,
And live in blissful unity?
'Tis love cemented.

What are those fair twin flowers,
That rear their lovely hours,

Alike in calm and sunny hours,
 Alike amidst the storm;
  That fairest blooms where all is drear,
  And spreads its sweetest perfume there?
   'Tis love connubial.

What are those scentless flowers
 That bloom in sunshine weather,
But when the storm of fortune low'rs,
 They fade and die together;
  And leave no fragrance o'er the tomb,
  Nor never knew a sweet perfume?
   'Tis love inconstant.

What is that beauteous flower
 No earthly blast can sever,
That blooms till life itself is o'er,
 And then shall bloom forever;
  Imparting sweetest fragrancy,
  In time and in eternity?
   'Tis love celestial.

Later Phoebe Palmer would often take the occasion of various wedding anniversaries to write poetic expressions of the vitality of her love for her husband. Many of these, as the example below, express the vibrant religious depth of their covenant. The premise of what follows is that she is looking at and reflecting upon their certificate of matrimony (Memoirs, pp. 98–99):

To My Husband
On the Thirteenth Anniversary of our Marriage[79]

Dear Love! my tearful eye doth rest
 Upon a little scroll
Which tells the day when we were blest,
 'Tis here I see enrolled
Your name with mine: my maiden name;
 I bade it then adieu,
And from that joyous hour became
 One heart and soul with you.
'Twas then the lover's name was changed

To husband! mine to wife,
'Twas not that love should be estranged,
    Sweet husband of my life;
'Twas but that those by God made one,
    By nature one in heart,
Together through life's course should run,
    Some say, "Till death doth part."[80]
But not such our ambitious thought,
    He who hath made us one,
For us eternal life hath bought;
    Then when time's course is run,
Eternal friendship, far o'er this
    Our earth-cemented love,
Shall reunite in worlds of bliss;
    And in those realms above,
Dear husband, I will tell thee all
    My full heart now would say,
For memory sure will there recall
    Our happy marriage-day.

Walter's birthdays were also celebrated with pungent, witty verse (A Mother's Gift, pp. 103–104):

A Birthday Gift
To My Husband
(undated)

A birth-day present for thee, love,
    Though small yet may it be,
A speaking talisman to prove,
    That I remember thee.

Remember thee! Ah, shall I say,
    Since first I called thee mine,
More deep with each successive day,
    My heart doth thee enshrine.

Then take this small memento,[81] love,
    And may it ever be,
A kind remembrancer to prove,
    The love I bear to thee.

And oh! may He whose power alone,
    Preserves the life He gave,
Who bought and claims thee as His own,
    His feeble servant save.

And 'till life's changing scenes are o'er,
    May bliss thy steps attend,
And Heaven grant many a birthday more,
    Ere time with thee shall end.

Notes

1. Henry Worrall was born Nov. 15, 1771 in Bradford, near Sheffield, York-shire, England, died April 27, 1849. He received a membership ticket to the Methodist Society in Bradford from Wesley himself, see *WJW*, 7, p. 4, 157 (July 23, 24, 1784 and April 23, 1786); cf. *GTH* 66 (1874): 42ff; *Memoirs*, pp. 13f. At about twenty-five years of age (1796) he came to America, (Roche, *LSLP*, p. 17) and married Dorothea (or Doretha Wade, born Feb. 13, 1786, died Sept. 13, 1856), settling in New York City. He is described as an engineer who built and serviced the steamboat and other industries of the early period of industrialization. See John A. Roche, "Mrs. Phoebe Palmer," *LR* 26 (1866): 65. The Worralls had fifteen children, only eight of whom reached maturity: Henry C. (married Sarah Shields), Caroline R. (married Kendric Rehorn), Sarah A. (married Thomas Lankford), Phoebe, Noah M., Mary Jane (married Joseph A. Kellogg), Wade B. (married the daughter of Methodist minister Peter Moriarity), Hannah Angelina (married the brother of Walter C. Palmer, Miles W. Palmer), and Dr. Isaac G. Worrall (married the grandaughter of Rev. Billy Hibbard; *LSLP*, p. 18; *Memoirs*, p. 16; White, *BH*, p. 2). Henry Worrall was described as "a man of mental vigor, of mechanical genius, and by skill and success in business secured ample means for the culture and comfort of his hospitable home" (*LSLP*, p. 18).

2. The Duane Street Area, directly east of the present Civic Center (City Hall) near the Hudson River, between Greenwich Village West and the present World Trade Center. See Lewis Jackson, *Walks About New York* (New York: Mission and Tract Society, 1865).

3. 1 Cor. 2:10.

4. She perceived a special providence at work from the beginning of her life.

5. Abel Stevens, *Life and Times of Nathan Bangs* (New York: Carlton and Porter, 1863), reports that Phoebe Palmer was one of Nathan Bangs's catechetical students at about age nine.

6. I.e., experiential.

7. That Mr. Worrall was a friend of the British Consul supports the hypothesis that the family probably had considerable social status, and sufficient resources to provide Phoebe with a reasonably good education in terms of early nineteenth cen-

tury standards. For background, see Timothy L. Smith, "The Transfer of Wesleyan Religious Culture from England to America," *Historical Bulletin of the World Methodist Historical Society* 14 (1985): 2–16; Frank Baker, *From Wesley to Asbury: Studies in Early American Methodism* (Durham, N.C.: Duke, 1976).

8. Many themes developed later appear here in embryonic form: the decisive authority of scripture, a keen personal awareness of death, an intense inwardness, a desire to be led by God, and excitement in spiritual journey. Her biographer, Richard Wheatley, reports that she "composed the following lines, and wrote them upon the fly leaf of the Testament" (*Memoirs*, p. 18). Since Wheatley had known her for twenty-three years (ibid., introduction p. 4), it is likely that he learned of her authorship directly from her. It is conceivable that she wrote another's poem in her Bible. There is considerable internal evidence, however, in addition to the testimony of Wheatley, that the young Phoebe indeed wrote it, for it reveals the themes of entire devotion, the special anxiety over early death, and friendship transcending the earthly. It employs phrases she would frequently use ("blest treasure," "feel its power," "endure to eternity") and must have been written by a young person ("my youthful heart").

9. Hebr. 12:9.

10. Cf. Exod. 2:9.

11. Hos. 14:5.

12. By 1811. The account in "The Experience of Mrs. P. P.," of disputed authorship, *GTH* 19 (Jan. 1851–July 1851): 134ff. (*EMPP*), refers to scrupulosity, but not assurance, at age three and one half. Paul Bassett has suggested the possibility that this essay may have been written by Persis Wing Peck, wife of Bishop Jesse T. Peck, born Sept. 2, 1807, died Dec. 7, 1897, *Christian Advocate* (NY) 72 (1897):824, PBL.

13. She felt something was amiss in that a precise time could not be specified for her conversion. Later she would be able to point to a specific date, July 26, 1837, not for her conversion but for complete reception of sanctifying grace.

14. The dialectic is intricate. She despaired even over the lack of despair that could lead to redemption. Hence she wept over her lack of weeping. The dialectical subtlety is intuitively similar to, though not dependent upon, that of Quidam in Kierkegaard's *Stages Upon Life's Way*.

15. Gen. 32:24.

16. Lack of trust in scripture was the cause of this "dark night."

17. *WOH*, pp. 72–75.

18. 2 Kings 5.

19. Acts 14:2.

20. John 4:48.

21. Isa. 7:9, *WOH*, p. 75.

22. Cf. Lam. 3:24.

23. Cf. John 11:33, Rom. 8:28.

24. Isa. 24:16.

25. *HUMEC* 1850, #490; *CH*, #392.

26. Early in 1821.

27. *Collection of Hymns* (London, Wesleyan Conference Office 1877), #155 (*CH*).

28. "See Israel's gentle Shepherd stands," *Methodist Hymn Book* (London, Charles H. Kelly 1908), #720, v. 1, *CMC*, p. 245; *LHS*, p. 827.

29. The luminosity theme will reappear frequently.

30. Matt. 14:27.

31. Doubtless the Wesleyan hymnody conveyed to Phoebe Palmer some of the deepest elements of her spirituality.

32. Cf. Is. 8:20.

33. Eph. 6:17; *WOH*, pp. 72–76.

34. At this time, about 1822, Phoebe would have been about fourteen years old.

35. Dream recollection and interpretation was apparently regarded as a means of spiritual insight.

36. The dream is of an ever-widening circle of silent light, out of which the promise of salvation is spoken.

37. Isa. 9:6.

38. Cf. Luke 1:78.

39. *WOH*, pp. 78–80.

40. Again, we see her reasoning subtly and dialectically about the relation of temperament, providence and reasoning: natural gifts without grace may be prone to disadvantage, but with grace to advantage.

41. *WOH*, pp. 82–83. So self-critical was she that she could not be satisfied with any foundations whatever, reminiscent of the mood of ancient Greek skepticism. Later she learned radically to trust the written Word.

42. Job 1:5.

43. *WOH*, p. 87.

44. Colon omitted in text.

45. 1 Tim. 5:8.

46. She viewed her natural temperament as anxiety-prone and excessively rationalistic and scrupulous.

47. She learned early that providence could work precisely through anxiety to elicit a greater happiness than if the conditions of anxiety were disallowed (cf. Augustine, *Enchiridion, LCC*, VII).

48. Zech. 14:20,21. "Holiness to the Lord" was a prevalent ascription in the days of Zechariah, not only on the High Priest's breastplate, but also upon the bells of horses and "every pot." It became one of the leading mottoes of the Holiness Revival.

49. Indeed she would repeat this motto often in her evangelical work.

50. Here is an early, clear recognition of the pragmatic and experiential principle that would constitute one of her major contributions to the history of revivalism. The seeds were in John Wesley, but they reached full bloom only with Phoebe Palmer. Pragmatism as a philosophy would await another half century to emerge articulately.

51. Eph. 6:12.

52. Conflict and suffering were key marks of the Christian pilgrimage. One is reminded of Kierkegaard in this description, of the knight of faith who struggles inwardly, silently, as did Abraham, who quietly prepared to go to Mount Moriah. Cf. *Fear and Trembling*, ch. 1. Yet there seems to be a progression of growth from struggle to struggle that is more evident in Mrs. Palmer than in Kierkegaard.

53. A phrase that is intensely characteristic of Mrs. Palmer, but which she derived from various passages in Wesley, LJW, VII, p. 322, and Fletcher.

54. Ps. 22:1; Matt. 27:46; Mk. 15:34.

55. Hebr. 13:5.

56. Cf. Josh. 3:4.

57. *WOH*, pp. 100, 101; cf. her later suggestions for a "shorter way."

58. At 17 years old.

59. Matt. 16:24.

60. Acts 20:27.

61. Romans 12:2. Note the Methodist luminaries that she was tutored by or who formed models for her early development: Nathan Bangs, Daniel DeVinne, J. B. Stratton, Samuel Merwin, Timothy Merritt, Thomas Mason, and quite likely also Herman Bangs, Daniel Ostrander, and Beverly Waugh. All were active in her lower Manhattan neighborhood at various times.

62. Ps. 23:6.

63. Walter Palmer was a recent graduate of Rutgers Medical College of Physicians and Surgeons in New York. Son of Miles and Deborah Clarke Palmer, born Feb. 9, 1804, he had lived in New York since May of 1804 (see George Hughes, *The Beloved Physician: Walter C. Palmer* (New York: Palmer & Hughes, 1884). His brother Miles married Phoebe's sister Hannah (cf. Roche, *SLP*, p. 18; *GTH* 53 [1868]:5).

64. Her sexual ethic is rigorous: she regarded it as cruel to prompt a manifestation or expression of love that she did not intend to reciprocate on a covenant monogamous basis, with parental approval.

65. Matt. 7:2.

66. Prov. 22:15.

67. A revealing statement of her fidelity to parental care. It seems overweening to modern sensibilities, yet it apparently did not inhibit her creative self-expression.

68. Cf. Exod. 20:12.

69. Jer. 31:33.

70. 1 Sam. 7:12; the verse is associated by many Protestants with the Robert Robinson (1735–1790) hymn, "Come Thou Fount of Every Blessing," *HMEC*, 1879, #726, v. 2.

71. Gen. 2:18. Her reflection upon the vocation to marry places human love in the context of divine love, and assumes radical accountability and fidelity in love.

72. Rom. 14:18; 2 Tim. 2:15.

73. Ps. 23:6.

74. Methodist Episcopal Church.

75. Itinerary uncertain.

76. Cf. Prov. 3:6.
77. Cf. Phil. 1:10.
78. Chided.
79. Sept. 28, 1840.
80. Cf. *Book of Common Prayer* (Philadelphia: Church Pension Fund, 1945), Service of Matrimony, "till death us do part," p. 300.
81. Incorrectly spelled in text.

III

EARLY MARRIED YEARS:
DIARY AND POETRY, 1828–1836

In late September of 1828, exactly a year after their wedding, their first child, Alexander, was born.[1] Much loved, this fragile child died nine months later, July 2, 1829. The young mother, then twenty-one years old, wrote beautifully and tenderly of "Our First-born." Focused on the fragile flower metaphor, among its profound themes are the radical awareness of the potential in created goods to elicit idolatry, the painful struggle with loss, the grief-laden breaking of bonds, resignation, and finally death and resurrection (A Mother's Gift, pp. 91–92):

Our First-born

He was indeed a lovely flower,
   Although of pallid hue,
Whilst love maternal, "magic power,"
Beheld new beauties every hour,
   Unfolding to its view.

The parent stem beheld with joy
   Its first bright bud of bliss,
Their earliest hope, their first-born boy,
Vainly they thought nought would destroy,[2]
   Or blast such loveliness.

But soon a still small voice[3] from Heaven,
   Whispered in accents mild,—
The blessing was in mercy given,[4]
But ah! it draws the heart from Heaven,
   Thou must resign thy child.

And then the flower more pallid grew,
   Oh! then how keen the smart!
Delusive hope perceived its hue,
But still more close and closely drew,
   The idol to the heart.[5]

And when its blighted form had bowed,
   'Neath sorrows with'ring blast,
The whispering voice grew still more loud,—
Resign, resign him to his God,
   The just decree is past.

Oh! then the sad, the rending stroke,
   As in the "midnight" came,[6]
Affection's tender ties were broke,
Which might have loosed when mercy spoke
   And not have given such pain.

The flower transplanted in the skies,
   From sorrow's blast is riven,
The parents' chastened, earthly love,
Their better hopes, transferred above,
   Are centered now in Heaven.

Oh! there our Alexander lives,
   Where beauty's bud ne'er dies!
Though snatched from love's maternal arms,
He's safe from all impending harms,
   And calls us to the skies.[7]

The last two stanzas of "Our First-Born" make clear how the death of Alexander changed the Palmers' understanding of their vocation. Since he had been idolized by them, they gradually came to see that his being taken away could become a significant learning for them on behalf of chastened, purified faith. Through him they learned to fix their faith more upon God than creatures.

Their second son, Samuel M.,[8] *was born April 29th, 1830. They*
would lose him within seven weeks.[9] *With wrenching pathos, she would*
write in her diary on September 28, 1831, the fourth anniversary of her
marriage, and the third anniversary of Alexander's birth (Memoirs, p.
26):

This is the anniversary of my wedding day. Varied have been the vicissitudes through which I have passed since my last record. He who setteth
the solitary in families[10] has entrusted two darling little ones, both of which
he has recalled to his own bosom of love. Alexander H., was born September 27th, 1828. He was a lovely, yet pallid little exotic, and when but nine
months old, was transplanted to a more congenial clime,—beyond the reach
of earthly blight.

In less than three years, another little son[11] was entrusted. The treasure
was lent but seven short weeks and was then recalled; giving us two angel
children in heaven, and leaving us childless on earth. I will not attempt to
describe the pressure of the last crushing trial. Surely I needed it, or it would
not have been given. God takes our treasure to heaven, that our hearts may
be there also.[12] The Lord has declared himself a jealous God; He will have
no other Gods before Him.[13] After my loved ones were snatched away, I
saw that I had concentrated my time and attentions far too exclusively, to
the neglect of the religious activities demanded. Though painfully learned,
yet I trust the lesson has been fully apprehended. From henceforth, Jesus
must and shall have the uppermost seat in my heart.

Now childless, her poetry welled up profoundly from her grief. How
deeply she was wounded by these events is evident in its prevailing themes:
finitude, death, loneliness, grief, resurrection, and eternal life. "The Be-
reaved Parent" reveals her poetic imagination as penetrating, poignant,
sensitive, moving. Although the following poems are undated, they bear
internal evidence that they came from this period. There is no avoidance of
death or denial of grief, but all is seen in the context of eternity (A Mother's
Gift, pp. 23–24):

The Bereaved Parent

Ah! many days have passed so lone and drear,
    Since these deserted arms thy form did clasp,
And all on earth to me most fond and dear,
    Was sternly snatched away by death's cold grasp!

That hour seems ever near, though long gone by,
    When envious angels kissed thy soul from earth,

And thy pure spirit loosed, and soar'd on high,
    And gladsome seemed to hail celestial birth.

Did no regret then steal about those ties
    That bound to earth?—did not this sorrowing heart,
This bosom so bereaved of all it prized,
    Not make thee somewhat loath with life to part?

Perhaps thou didst not hear those wishful sighs,
    Thy spirit so enwrapt in blissful things,
And seraphs softly wooing thee to rise,
    Bore thee away in triumph on their wings.

Sometimes methinks that spirit yet is near,
    And when this heart gives to its sorrows way,
It chides my grief, and whiles away my fear,
    And in love's softest accents seems to say:

"Though I hasted from thy pillowy breast,
From within thy twining arms to rest,
Though so quick and early was removed,
The form of all on earth most loved,
Yet angels are my guardians now,
A wreath of beauty is round my brow,
I gaze on glories unearthly bright,
And hold sweet converse with saints in light,
Through bowers of bliss I lightly roam;
Oh! is not this a far sweeter home?
And yet I so oft am near thee still,
Thy guardian angel from any ill;
To whisper peace to thy weary breast,
And to lull thy earth-born cares to rest,
Till thy spirit released from earth shall rise,
And thy loved one meet thee in the skies."

    It is likely that "Immortality" came from this same period (A Mother's Gift, pp. 10–11):

Immortality

        "Oft bursts my song beyond the bounds of time,
          What then but immortality can please?"

Time! I have dealt with thee, I know thee strong,
    I've seen the blightings left by thy rude touch,
But knew thy flapping wing would cease ere long
        To throw its chill, and looked on thee as such
        Whose withering course should yet be stayed,
        Nor all most lovely droop and fade
        Where'er thy passing shade has been,
        For those bright conquests yet I ween,
Shall light another sphere, when thou hast ceased to be,
Lost in the flowings of eternity.

But who, eternity, hath dealt with thee?
    And from thy landing-place to earth returned?
To tell the vastness of thy boundary,
        Or the profoundness of the mystery learned?
        Ah! none can say; I ask no more,
        Thine is a vast returnless shore;
        And 'tis enough; the lucent ray,
        Sent from on high to guide the way,
Now points where spirits glitter near the throne,
And measure out their bound with God alone.

This inward consciousness, this ceaseless flame,
    Was an enkindling from omnific breath,
It was a spark inbreathed, that lit this flame,
        And animates the whole; and shall stern death
        Extinguish that of heavenly birth?
        Ah, no! when bid to loose from earth,
        'Tis far more glorious in its glow,
        And can no damp'ning conflicts know,
But with new body joined, no more to sever,
It mingles with its source and glows for ever.

*Few memoirs remain from this period. It was largely through poetry that she sought self-understanding and articulated her pilgrimage. Hence we must study her poetry if we are to gain insight into this period of her life. The death of her first two sons became a spiritual ordeal through which she understood that her faith was being tested, and within which she sought and found consolation in God (*A Mother's Gift, *p. 109):*

A Power Stronger Than Death

Oh, Death! we own thee mighty strong,
    Strength, beauty, withers at thy breath,
Remorseless dost thou turn hope's song
    To dreary mournfulness and death.
And helplessness would nature own
Were not a power beyond thee known.

And through that power, hope yet shall break
    The spell of gloom so darkly cast,
Shall yet the tone of gladness wake,
    And sing the darkness overpast.
And faith shall lift her downcast eye,
To pierce beyond earth's gloomy sky.

The recollection of her child remained a luminous source of joy. The sentiments expressed were moving but not maudlin (A Mother's Gift, *pp. 17–18):*

The Hours I've Spent With Thee

Oh no! I never can forget
    The hours I've spent with thee,
My horizon they lighten yet,
    Bright stars in memory.
I thought thee as a bird of spring,
    Sporting in heaven's pure light,
Forever on the joyous wind,
    Of innocent delight.

And oh! when thou didst rest thy plume,
    Careless o'er sorrow's brink,
I grieved that one in thy young bloom
    Should'st its dark waters drink.
That thou, unskilled in guile or art,
    Unknown to drooping care,
The loved, the cherished of my heart,
    So long should'st linger there.

Again I see thee raise thine eye,
    For lo! a form of light,
Hath bid thee mount again on high,
    In a more joyous flight.
Fair one, from henceforth speed thy way,
    Nor let earth's tempting flow
Allure thy heaven bound wing to stay,
    To seek for bliss below.

Is it better that such children not be born than die so soon? Can philosophy speak to the heart amid such grief? Does faith in divine grace transcend our natural suffering? Does grace require the bereaved to forget the loss? These questions of theodicy pervaded her searching poetry, probably of this period (A Mother's Gift, *pp. 20–21):*

Consolation in Bereavement

The blossom's gone: the beauteous one
    In which thy soul delighted,
To bloom 'neath heaven's more genial sun,
    E'er damps of earth had blighted.

Dost thou yet weep, and fondly say,
    Would that it ne'er were planted,
A treasure so soon borne away,
    Were better far not granted.

Ah! that was nature's voice alone,
    Grace prompted not this chiding,
And she, a misty veil hath thrown,
    The joyous future hiding.

Philosophy, perhaps, might say,
    Oh! still thy vain regretting,
Ah! if thou canst her call obey
    Thy lovely one forgetting.

But such is cold philosophy,
    And hard, alas! her teaching;
Grace makes not such demands of thee,
    So far beyond thy reaching.

She asks but that her voice be heard,
    Above fond nature's groanings,
For solace is in every word,
    To soothe those heartfelt moanings.

It[14] gently bids faith's downcast eye,
    Look up to fields all vernal,
That smile beyond earth's gloom-wrapt sky,
    Where blooming is eternal.

Ah! there that bud blooms beauteously,
    In never ending splendor,
The gift thy Father asked of thee,
    Joy, thou hadst it to render!

2. EARLY SOCIAL REFORM, TEMPERANCE,
AND ABOLITIONIST ACTIVITIES
(POETRY AND MEMOIRS, 1831–1835)

Mrs. Palmer's interest in social transformation developed earlier than her religious thought. As early as age twenty-three, she was actively involved in sanctificationist social reform movements, as evidenced especially in her early poetry. Surprisingly, she took the American national independence holiday as an occasion to write on "African Emancipation" (A Mother's Gift, pp. 208–209). The ode reveals her compassionate empathy with the wretched condition of slaves. It is an unequivocal call for immediate emancipation of slaves. It was written in 1831, some years before the broader popularization of the abolitionist cause:[15]

Ode for the Fourth of July
(Written in reference to African Emancipation)

PEACE spreads her wings, and shadows thee,
    From despot's sway that pressed thee long:
And Liberty bends pliantly,
    When thou dost will, O people strong;
Then raise thy notes, land of the free,
The Lord hath done most valiantly.

His power hath wrought thy liberty,
  His own right arm avenged thy wrong:
And now He asks returns of thee,[16]
  For those whose groanings have been long.
His ear hath heard, O people free,
Of those long bondaged held by thee.

'Tis Ethiopia's vented sigh,[17]
  Heard in that grief-imploring moan;
Hear, Christians, hear her anguished cry,
  "Restore, restore to us our own;
Oh! land with sons and daughters free,[18]
Make our long captive ones like thee."

Offended Justice, sword in hand,
  Tells of her claims and bids you give,
As stern atonements quick demand,
  The price that says lorn[19] Afric live!
Live unoppressed, live, joyous, free,
And cease to mourn our wrongs to thee.

Ah! can the parent heart forget
  Its torn-away returnless ones?[20]
Nor can a tearful Afric yet
  Cease sighing for her long lost sons;
'Till clasped again, from slavery free,
Loosed by the voice of charity.

Doth liberty stand mountain-strong,
  And view such claims unsatisfied,
When she hath cried so loud, so long,
  And *Freemen* have her call denied?
Wake! PATRIOTS, wake, cry, *now* be free!
Rise Afric, hail thy liberty.
1831

Her 1832 New Year's poem, probably designed for declamation by young people in a Sunday School setting, reveals her youthful idealism as a woman in her early twenties, expressing a subtle dialectic between religious hope and political realism (A Mother's Gift, pp. 234–36, 157–58). Note especially her political references to the tragedy of Poland's defeat, and the oppression of the Irish:

New Year, 1832

WELCOME young smiling childhood of the year,
   Season when heart meets heart in friendly cheer,
   When kindred gratulations freely flow,
And memory reflects affection's glow.
Yes, mortals hail with joy thy happy birth,
They call thee happy; children of earth
Are ever looking forward; hope's perspective gaze
Is keen and sanguine, until the rays
Of future beams upon them; then, we will not say,
It ill-becomes the gladness of the day,
To trace in fancy's darkening imagery,
A seeming standard for futurity;
Such were inglorious toil, it is enough,
That though the pathway should be smooth or rough,
All will be well at last, if faith's intent
Is in the road of duty firmly bent.
Since then it is not meet to question one
So young and joyous, and when just begun,
His destined course of journeying to the past;
We'll ask his elder brother, who, alas!
Is now no more with us; whose deep-drawn shade
Has left behind him vividly portrayed,
On memory's scroll, things not to be effaced,
Things that have man ennobled, man disgraced.

First, trace the Christian's triumph; see the dawn
Of an eternal day comes hastening on,
See pure religion, offspring of the skies,
Child of Omnipotence, how swift she flies;
O'er all our world she darts her seraph eye,
And 'neath its glance the clouds of error fly.
Her herald angels pass o'er hill and dale,
O'er towering mountains, o'er the humble vale,
And fearless leave their heavenly embassy,
Disclosing life and immortality.
Many that were in heathen darkness bound
Have heard the Gospel trumpet's thrilling sound;
'Twas ransom from the prison shades of night,
A beaming ray of pure millennial light.[21]
The glory of a brighter day beams forth;

The tidings come from east, west, south, and north;
The sun of promise never, never shone,
With lustre so peculiarly its own.
In our own favored land, triumphs of grace,
Like bounding echoes, pass from place to place;
Thousands with joy have gathered to the fold,
And with Immanuel's bands their name enrolled.
All o'er earth's wide domain wonders and signs
Speak the unfolding of some vast designs,
Wars, rumored wars, and kingdoms on the wane,
Seem to presage our great Messiah's reign.

Then mark the fiend of power's destroying tread
Fast congregate his thousands with the dead;
    His unrelenting devastation's sway
The mightiest of the earth has swept away.
    POLAND, lamented Poland, patriot band!
We mourn for thee as for a sister land;
Thy sons were brave, too brave to wear the yoke
Of Russian tyranny, which erst were broke
If victory had rested with the brave;
A freeman's rights were bought e'en with a freeman's
    grave.
Thy foe in numbers their proud conquest told,
Courage alone to thee was thy stronghold;
Alas! thy beacon-star is set in gloom,
And hopes of liberty no more illume
Thy midnight sky; the lowering clouds of fate
Have gathered round thee; pity comes too late!

Oh! EMERALD ISLE, thy harp is hung on high,
And adverse winds in moanings o'er it sigh;
Ah! stern oppression, its bleak chillings throw,
And wakes that deep, deep thrill of heartfelt woe,
'Tis heard in vented groans of wild despair,
From all thy lowly sons of toil and care.
Commotion waves her wand with proud success,
All EUROPE'S wide domain is restlessness.
To vent her inward groanings, great indeed
Have been her throes; and with volcanic speed
She hastes to vent, unless some powerful sway
Her smother'd vengeance hastily allay.

A still more fearful foe than wars or broils
Is gathering in the EAST its many spoils,
So sure its aim, so deathly in its power,
It gathers in its scores with every hour.

Spirit of desolation! could it not satiate thee,
Life's flowing crimson pour'd forth plenteously?
But must its fountains stagnate to thy taste?
Then pass in triumph! to thy banquet haste!
Lessen the sum of human misery,
By making short thy meal till satiety
Has told thy numbers—then the mind at peace
From fear's distracting gnawings soon shall cease.

AMERICA! what shall we say of thee?
Sure an Almighty power has gloriously
Been thy defence; peace dwells within thy land,
And showers her blessings with diffusive hand;
Beneath her shadowy wings sits *liberty,*
With her twin sisters, *truth,* and *equity,*
And with a potent arm outstretched o'er all,
Impartially her wondrous blessings fall.

Earth, with a contemplative mother's care,
Has fed her children with the richest fare,
And to the diligent, both high and low,
A portion of her bounties kindly flow;
Here no oppressive hand dares to secure
Her generous gifts from the deserving poor.

Science, in rising strength, as some fair tree,
Towers in height and spreads majestic'ly
And shelters 'neath it those of every age,
E'en from the lisping infant to the sage;
The infant school the infant mind has taught
To soar into the lofty realms of thought,
To grasp such treasures comprehensively,
As once seemed but for ripe maturity;
And Sabbath schools, known as a nursery,
For rearing plants for immortality,
Have flourished greatly 'neath heaven's fostering care,
And largely in the dews of mercy share.

Our institutions of more classic name
Rank still more prominent in well-earned fame;
Our country's wealth, in scientific lore,
Now proudly vies with boastful BRITAIN'S store.

*Several temperance poems came out of the period of the early 1830's.
Among the best of them is the following (A Mother's Gift, pp. 212–13) that
one can almost see being delivered as a declamation to a religious society
to an approving round of applause.*[22] *Those who imagine that sanctificationist social reformism lacks humor might read aloud:*

The Man that Drank the Adder Up

In size I know I'm not a man,
    And I suppose you've smiled
And said "Do you think this cause can
    Be helped by such a *child?*"
I'll tell you what my mother says,
    "Weight is not *all* in SIZE,
But he shall have it who oft prays
    To God to make him wise;
'Tis *truth weighs* HEAVY, such as taught
    in inspiration's page;
The *child* from such a lesson brought
    May say words like a sage!"
"*Truth* brought in *words!*" can you ask more?
    And now, though not a man,
The question that you asked before
    I'll answer if I can.

The Bible has pronounced a woe
    On him who loves strong drink,
And though I'm young, too well I know
    That MAN is on the brink
Who puts the poison to his lips;
    Who tarries long at wine,
And takes the cup and si-p-s and si-p-s,
    Ah! soon he'll *prove* divine
This WEIGHTY *truth*, an ADDER lurks[23]
    Within the poisoned cup!

Up to the brim it w-o-r-k-s and w-o-r-k-s,
    Ah, soon he'll drink it up!
And oh, it makes my young heart shrink!
    A venomed adder's sting
To gnaw the vitals! only think!
    These WEIGHTY TRUTHS I bring
Right from the Eternal Word of God!
    And heaven and earth shall fail,
And tottering fall beneath his nod,
    Before *His Truth* shall fail.[24]

Now turn from *this* and daily read
    From observation's page,
And say if farther proof you need
    of this rank poisoner's rage?
Look o'er the long black list of crime,
    The murderous midnight scene!
Turn back! still b-a-c-k, the leaves of time,
    Say what does all this mean?
What was it helped that murderous heart
    To stir up scenes of strife?
What did *nerve* to that hand impart
    Which took a fellow's life?
It was that ADDER he drank up!
    It was that poisonous sting
He swallowed from *that* whiskey-cup!
    That *living* venomed thing
Still gathers strength from every sip,
    Frenzies his fevered frame!
Oft as he puts it to his lip
    He feeds anew the flame!
And soon the awful fires of hell
    Will seize upon his SOUL!
And heaven's eternal records tell
    The *whole,* the *fearful* WHOLE!

*   *   *

Worm of the still, thy horrid form,
    When thy true colors shine,
        Personifies the undying worm,
    Brought to the shores of time.

*Once again she chose Independence Day, 1832, to denounce the
wicked oppression of alcoholism. The unabashed analogy is between
America's freedom from bondage to England, and freedom from alcohol
addiction. The anti-colonialist sentiment had remained ebullient twenty
years after the War of 1812 (A Mother's Gift, pp. 215–16):*

*Temperance, or Independence Ode
Composed for the 4th of July, 1832*

HAIL to the day on which were loosed
    The chains that bound 'neath despot's sway
When a proud nation thus refused
    Lordlings and tyrants to obey—
        Day when the voice of Freedom cried,
        Freeman, thy chains are cast aside!

Are cast aside, no longer thou
    Need bend thy neck to foreign power;
No more to the oppressor bow,
    But claim as thine, from this glad hour,
        Thy Birthright; freedom from thy foes
        This freely heaven on thee bestows;

Bestows on *thee*, the strong, the brave;
    Strong through the power that saw thy wrongs,
And brave through Him that's nigh to save;
        'Twas He that turned thy sighs to songs—
        'Tis He that wills you should be free,
        True, valiant sons of Liberty.

A liberty from every foe,
    Other than dynasties impose,
Which our forefathers nobly broke,
    For which our grateful songs arose;
        But, ah! a greater foe[25] we see
        Marking its course with victory.

Disease and death are in its train,
    Thousands have proved its deathly skill,
Aye, tens of thousands have been slain,
    And yet it is insatiate still.

Rouse, sons of Liberty, awake!
For thou canst its enchantment break.

Yes, break his spell, assert thy right,
    Nor let the tyrant longer reign;
"Union is strength," and in its might
    Ye shall the victor's triumph gain,
    And rescued thousands yet may know
    Their INDEPENDENCE of this foe.

3. HER MID-TWENTIES:
FORMATIVE YOUNG ADULT YEARS

Mrs. Palmer's later revival activities are best understood within a longer history of revivalism dating back to the patterns of John Wesley, George Whitefield, Francis Asbury, Lorenzo Dow,[26] *Charles G. Finney, and others.*[27] *An early example of a "holiness revival" that sought to enable both the experiences of pardon and purity was New York's Allen St. (Methodist) Church Revival of 1832, in which Walter and Phoebe Palmer actively participated, as reported in her diary (Memoirs,p. 25):*

April 28th, 1832—A remarkable revival is now going on in the Allen St. Church. It began with a four days' meeting. The beloved pastor, Rev. Samuel Merwin, as he announced on the Sabbath that a four days' meeting would commence on Monday morning at 10$\frac{1}{2}$ o'clock, said that he hoped it might be a forty-days' meeting, and such it has proved to be. My dear Dr. P. and self were both present at the first meeting when the services commenced, in April, last.[28] When those who desired a deeper work of grace were invited forward, feeling that no one could need it more than myself, I was among the first to kneel at the altar,—my husband leading the way. I was quickened in the divine life, and trust that I have since been living nearer to the Lord. My beloved was greatly blest, and has been used in an extraordinary manner in the promotion of this wonderful revival. He seems to be filled with the Spirit, and labors so excessively, that I sometimes fear he will kill himself. I chide myself for the feeling I have, in regard to this matter, and keep my fears to myself, as I would not dare to hinder him from adding stars to the crown of his rejoicing. I do not doubt but scores have been brought to the Lord through his agency.[29] Hundreds have been saved through this great visitation of the Spirit, and still the work goes on in unabated power. I am getting on feebly in the divine life:—not so much lacking in good purposes, as in carrying out my ever earnest resolve. I ought to be more openly active. I lack faith and courage.

*Mrs. Palmer commented upon false and true eloquence in these undated lines that reflect upon communication styles within the revivalism of this period (*A Mother's Gift, *pp. 45–46):*

Eloquence

The mighty spell, the all-empowering trance
    Of every faculty owns its control,
So like as if some magic wand should chance
    To sway its sceptre o'er the ravished soul.
'Tis not bombastic style, or affectation's mien
For ignorance, the vile and palmy screen
To make a show of depth, where shadows glide,
And thus beneath its shadow strive to hide
What is most prominent a want of care,
To tell what such most anxious are to spare,
That 'tis a station they can never fill,
And but a substitute for competence and skill.
Not so true eloquence, most powerful charm,
That error's strongest habiliments disarms,
The truth arrays in knightly armor bold,
And draws the assent, though strongly we withhold,
'Tis nature's gift alone, none else need claim it,
Others may make attempts but she'll disdain it.

*One of her most stunning poems apparently was written upon the suicide of the husband of someone she knew (*A Mother's Gift, *pp. 64–66):*

The Suicide

A DEAFENING sound breaks o'er the gloom of night!
That loud report told of a soul dislodged
In haste from earth! And she, who fondly
Dreamed she slept beside her bosom's lord,
Wakes in amazement wild, as in a lightning glare!
A momentary flash! 'tis gone, and all is dark,
And hushed in silence awful!

She hardly reck'd that in that flash, that glare
The spirit of the one she cherished, and whose
Love was more than life, had passed to worlds unknown!
For frantic consternation, shook from reason's throne,
Its burden; far too oppressive to be borne.

But so it was!
The once so comely form, that spoke a dignity
Of mien, so pleasant to the view, was now
Revolting to the astonished gaze; bereft
Of movement, save a faint fluttering,
Thrilling motion of the unconscious heart,
Deserted by the vig'rous soul, that flew
Unbidden to the land of spirits disembodied;
Where it erst had made its boast, to sleep
In night oblivious! But those ill-omened shades
Of long forgetfulness, may not fall o'er
That awe-awakened soul; oblivion's curtains
Cover nought that wisdom infinite
Hath form'd through power omnipotent!
The beams emitted from the light of truth,
"That lighteth every soul,"[30] had once shone brightly
     there;
But error wilful, darkly sought to obscure
Its rays, by carnal wisdom's reasoning false;
And now, self-condemnation bids despair
Prey on its victim! It trembling stands
Repulsed by Him, who hath said,
No self-destroyer hath eternal life.

But where is she! the young, the beautiful
And now the lonely widow'd one; the truth
Hath broke upon her soul, convulsed
With torture most extreme!
O reason! 'twere almost now unkind in thee
So soon to reassume thy wonted residence;
When truths so fearful, so momentous,
Wait but thy recall, to put on hues
So awful! so appalling!

But what, or who hath done it?
O infidelity! 'twas thy deceptive form,

In league with vile ambition; thou didst
Insinuate illusions false and vain;
And then despoiled the aspirant of his hopes,
And oft in thy known cruelty, doth lull
Thy victim to a seeming rest; all but to show
Thy power so venomous, and then, as in a
Moment, dash them in the sea of justly
Kindled wrath.

                    Thou hast destroyed
Thy thousands,[31] and the one, whom now
We groan, hath felt thy lash but too severely,
And sunk beneath thy powerful arm.

That her early poetry had the capacity to express profound themes of despair, dread, and guilt, is evident from "Soliloquy" (A Mother's Gift, *p. 67):*

Soliloquy

(Occasioned by an alarming dream of being "weighed in the balances and found wanting.")[32]

            O! WHENCE this dread decision!
That tombs in horror's night my future destiny.
Where now is hope? that swift-winged dove of promise,
That erst this dreadful hour, was wont to 'min'ster
Consolation sweet in times so drear and troublous.
O haste! O speed thee quick! ere this convulsive agony
Disable quite my powers to cling to thee!
Why dost thou tarry yet? O why! so long my call resist?
Frantic, I sink to desperation if thou yet delay.
And yet thou dost not come! in vain I look,
And call for thee! I see nor hear thee not!
And hast thou fled? Is this the sealed doom-hour?
O misery extreme! my state is fixed for ever,
And I am left to utter hopelessness.
And is it so? O! can it be, that I, who long had
            cherished hopes
Of blissful immortality and heaven when loosed from earth,
Oft called with seeming ardor on the name omnific,
Trod oft the sacred sanctuary of the Lord most holy,

And swelled high, elate with hope the chorus with the
    saints,
Am thus bereft, undone, and lost for ever?[33]

*One of the most admired leaders of Methodism was biblical scholar,
Adam Clarke,[34] who wrote Old and New Testament commentaries read
by Methodists everywhere, and whom Mrs. Palmer so much admired and
studied so avidly. She wrote two poems on the occasion of his death in
1832, one a eulogy, and the following hymn* (A Mother's Gift, *pp. 76–
77*):

Hymn
Composed for, and sung
at the funeral discourse of Dr. Adam Clark[e].[35]

WE thought to waken melody,
    To sing thy welcome to our land,
But angel choirs have welcomed thee,
    To thine own seat, at God's right hand.

Thy earth-won laurels are laid by,
    Thou dost thine own loved anthem hymn,
And holy, holy, holy, cry,
    To vie with highest seraphim.[36]

Brother, we know our loss thy gain,
    But when we think to man thy worth,
We cannot sorrow's thoughts restrain,
    And sigh that thou art gone from earth.

The Church of God—the little band
    Who knew from infancy thy care,
She saw, and blest thy fostering hand,
    And ever shall thy memory bear.

Nor she alone, where is the heart,
    The name, the age, the clime, the race,
That say we bear in him no part,
    Nor never knew his faith's embrace.

Grasped in his comprehensive soul
    The whole wide world was treasured deep,

And oft in mighty prayer, the whole,
  Presented at the mercy-seat.

Then earth may mourn a friend well proved,
  Science her long most favorite son,
The Church of God a saint removed,
  And seraphs shout a partner won.

Mrs. Palmer went through several periods of intermittent illness—at times dreadfully serious—in the early years of her marriage. One grave illness at age twenty-seven, after the birth of two more children (following the death of her first two children), is recorded in her diary, eliciting an intensification of her sense of religious calling, and of the feeling that she needed to grow further in grace (Memoirs, pp. 27–28):

August, 1835.—What shall I render unto the Lord for all His benefits? I have been raised almost as from the dead, having recently passed through a very critical illness, when, for days in succession it seemed as though any hour might have been my last. The Lord has now blest us with two darling little ones. The eldest is over two years old, and the youngest was given to our arms, but a few weeks since. Both the mother and the youngest born were so near the confines of eternity, that it seems a miracle of mercy, that we did not o'erstep the boundaries of time. I say mercy, because my precious ones were so unwilling to let me go, and also for my own sake, and the blessed cause of my Lord and Saviour. Not that His work might not go on equally well without me, by another being raised up to take my place, but I do not want another to take my crown. I have long felt that the Lord has a work for me to do, but I need an inspiration of power beyond what I now possess.

While flickering between the two worlds, during my late extreme illness, I had views of responsibility, and feelings unlike any I have heard described. I know that I had not been insincere in my feeble attempts to live for God,—I felt that I was trusting alone in the merits of Jesus, for salvation. Knowing that I had come to the Saviour, I was not troubled with harassing fears, that He would cast me out. But O, such a sense of shortcoming and unworthiness! How shall I describe it? A consciousness of having done so little, for Him who had done so much for me . . .

My desire was to get well. Not merely to enjoy life, though my surroundings were happy, and conspired to make life desirable, but that I might live to engage in "instant in-season and out-of-season" activities,[37] in the service of the Lord my Redeemer. Hearing a child passing my window, calling out, "Blackberries for sale!" I thought, How gladly would I live, if it were only to walk the street crying out "Blackberries!" if I might only say to each passer-by, "Do you love my Saviour?"[38] And now that the Lord has, in infinite mercy, raised me up, how shall I worthily magnify his name?[39] May I never forget the solemn teachings of those hours of pain and weakness.

One thing more especially demands a thankful record. I have, since my childhood been in the habit of composing verses, occasionally. I have never dared to give anything to the public, other than I had cause to believe would be for the glory of God. My views of responsibility led me to reason thus. If I have a talent for writing, God has given it.[40] To use that talent in any other way than to promote his glory, would be sacrilegious. And who can tell where the influence of a fragment of thought may end, after having been given to the press? A wrong sentiment may live and speak, when the hand that wrote it is mouldering in the grave. . . . [41]

I have just been spending three or four days at Sing-Sing camp-meeting. The Lord manifested himself most graciously to His people. My own soul was refreshed. The Lord has given me a longing desire for purity. I am sure I would not knowingly keep back anything from God. But alas! there must be some hindrance, or I should consciously enjoy the witness, that Jesus reigns the Supreme Object of my affections.

One cause of oft solicitude has for some time past been settled beyond controversy. Whenever my soul has reached out most ardently for the witness of holiness, the adversary has suggested most persistently the question of my justification. When I let the subject of entire sanctification alone, and do not reach out after higher attainments, then I seem to have rest in the assurance of my adoption.[42]

Reviewing this matter, I became satisfied that it was a stratagem of the tempter, to keep me from rising to higher attainments in the divine life. I then resolved that the vexed question should be forever settled, and reasoned thus: "I *am* either a child or God, or I am *not*. In the eye of God the matter is settled. And now, if I have such an evidence of a new creature as God has given in His Word, in the strength of Omnipotence, never will I doubt again. Whatever my feelings may be, I will believe God's immutable Word unwaveringly, irrespective of emotion." Two test passages were presented by the Holy Spirit to my mind. 1st. "As many as are led by the Spirit of God, they are the sons of God."[43] . . . 2d. "Love is of God, and whoso loveth is begotten of God."[44] "What evidences have I, of love to God?" I asked. "Why is the first thought of the morning,[45] and the controlling idea of the day a desire to please God? Should I desire to please Him if I did not love Him?" "But," said the adversary, "how do you know?"[46] "How do I know I love my parents," I asked. "Would I not do everything out of their presence to please them, just the same as in their presence? I *know* I love them, and on the same principle *I know that I love God,* and therefore I know *that I am a Child of God.*" I then heartily believed, simply because God *said so.* I had the evidence of his WORD, and therefore with confidence said, "I know that I have the evidences of adoption, *I am a Child of God.*" The moment I believed, the witness was given indubitably clear. Yes! the Spirit testified with my spirit.[47] *"He that believeth,* hath the witness in himself".[48] And thus it has been all along through the experience of childhood and riper years; to just the degree I have *believed God's* Word, I have felt happy and assured. But I now see that the error of my religious life has been a desire for signs and wonders. Like Naaman, I have wanted some great thing,[49] unwilling to rely unwaveringly on the still small voice of the Spirit,[50] speaking through the naked Word. It was thus that the question of my adoption was settled, and the witness given with the clearness of noonday.

By August 1835, Phoebe and her sister Sarah Lankford (wife of Thomas Lankford) and their families had decided to live together in a home at 54 Rivington in New York, very near the Allen Street Church. They dedicated their home to the holy life, and pledged to begin a weekly conversation on the "promotion of holiness." This group first met on February 9, 1836. It was to become one of the most significant contributions of the Worrall sisters to the development of American Protestantism.

4. THE THIRD DEATH:

HER DAUGHTER, ELIZA (1836)

The death of her eleven month old daughter Eliza (born Aug. 28, 1835, died in a tragic crib fire, July 29, 1836) again brought anguish to the young mother. The gauze curtain on the cradle caught fire while a nurse charged with attending the sleeping child was refilling an alcohol lamp. The mother's account is filled with shock and pathos. It became the occasion for a profound and fundamental reinterpretation of her vocation, which exactly one year from this date would become unambiguously clear (Memoirs, pp. 30–32):

July 29, 1836.—Never have I passed through a trial so severe, as since the last date. If it were not that the Heavenly Physician had applied the healing balm, I should shrink utterly from a review of the scene. But a life of christian progress presents stepping-stones. Nature may shrink painfully from taking the leap from one stepping-stone to another, and the chasm below look craggy and fearful, but if helped forward by a divine hand, all will be well. I dare not doubt but I am being led forth by a right way, to a city of habitation. Through a distressing casualty, our darling youngest born has suddenly been translated from earth to heaven.

Just before the great trial came upon me, I had attended a camp-meeting, where the Lord was most graciously present, and my own soul shared in the general refreshing from on high. Soon after my return home, I observed that my lovely little daughter Eliza, about eleven months old, though not really ill, appeared to be dropping in health. I don't know why it was but a feeling came over me that she might not be with me long.[51] My motherly fondness might have drawn the picture too strongly, but I thought her an angel-like child, both in disposition and beauty of form. She was robed in virgin white, and her every look seemed so angelic, that I clasped her yet more closely to my breast, and with inexpressible love, exclaimed, "O you little angel!" I sat clasping her in my arms, till she fell into a soft beautiful slumber. A gentleman called, asking to see me. I laid the lovely sleeper in her cradle bed in the nursery, telling the nurse, that after the caller had left, I should retire to my room, and she must bring the infant to me. In less than an hour, an appalling shriek from the direction of the nursery startled me. I flew to the spot, and what a scene met my gaze! The gauze curtain that surrounded the cradle of the sleeping infant, through the carelessness of the nurse, had caught fire. I grasped my darling from the flames. She darted one inexpressible look of amazement and pity, on her agonized mother, and then closed her eyes forever on the scenes of earth. After a few hours the sweet spirit of my darling passed away, leaving me, from the suddenness of the shock, in an inexpressible bewilderment of grief. Turning away from human comforters, I coveted to be alone with God.

After the angel spirit winged its way to Paradise, I retired alone, not willing that an one should behold my sorrow. While pacing the room, crying to God, amid the tumult of grief, my mind was arrested by a gentle whisper, saying, "Your Heavenly Father loves you. He would not permit such a great trial, without intending that some great good proportionate in magnitude and weight should result.[52] He means to teach you some great lesson that might not otherwise be learned. He doth not willingly grieve or afflict the children of men.[53] If not *willingly,* then he has some specific design,[54] in this, the greatest of all the trials you have been called to endure."

In the agony of my soul I had exclaimed, "O, what shall I do!" And the answer now came,—"Be still, and know that I am God."[55] I took up the precious WORD, and cried, "O teach me the lesson of this trial," and the first lines to catch my eye on opening the Bible, were these, "O, the depth of the riches, both of the wisdom and knowledge of God! how unsearchable are his judgments and his ways past finding out!"[56]

It is the Holy Spirit alone that can take of the things of God, and reveal them to the waiting soul.[57] The tumult of feeling was hushed, and with the words came a divine conviction, that it was a loving Father's hand, that had inflicted the stroke. "What thou knowest not now, thou shalt know hereafter,"[58] was assuringly whispered. Wholly subdued before the Lord, my chastened spirit nestled in quietness under the wing of the Holy Comforter.

From that moment the very distressing keenness of the trial passed away, and my loved little one, who during her brief stay on earth, had seemed so akin to heaven's inhabitants, appeared scarcely separated from me. The vail[59] separating the two worlds was so slight, that things unseen became a living reality. Never before have I felt such a deadness to the world, and my affections so fixed on things above.[60] God takes our treasures to heaven, that our hearts may be there also.[61] My darling is in heaven doing an angel service. And now I have resolved, that the service, or in other words, the time I would have devoted to her, shall be spent in work for Jesus.[62] And if diligent and self-sacrificing in carrying out my resolve, the death of this child may result in the spiritual life of many.[63]

Ever since I gave this great trial with all its painful peculiarities up to God, resolved not to look at second causes,[64] a conviction has rested on my mind, that the Lord will make her translation to heaven, the occasion of many being translated out of the kingdom of darkness, into the kingdom of His dear Son.[65] And now my whole being says, with a strength of purpose beyond anything before attained, "My heart is fixed, O, God, my heart is fixed!"[66]

Once again the vital awareness of eternal life transcended her tragic sense of affliction and became expressed in its most native form through her poetry (A Mother's Gift, pp. 73–74):

After a Scene of Affliction

I would not that my lyre should cease,
    Nor sorrow touch its chords alone;
No, come sweet hope, thou breathest peace,
    And thou shalt too command its tone.

I would essay to touch the strain,
    Where mingled grief and bliss doth dwell;
And try, though tremblingly, again
    To raise the tones I've loved so well.

My harp—discourse of yon blue sky,
   Hope thence brought bliss in former days;
But why thus chant in sadness—why?
   Do sighs still interrupt thy lays?

Yet 'tis but right a mournful touch
   Should vibrate for the fate of those
Who pass from earth away, for such
   Whose term of life so soon doth close.

But cease, for lo! faith sees her now
   Pass gently through the gate of Heaven,
Whilst angels crown her beauteous brow,
   And now let highest strains be given.

'Tis meet, for now before the throne,
   She doth full notes of rapture raise,
With harps that know no varying tone,
   She mingles her triumphant lays.

Then what though earth entombs the form,
   Through which the soul of beauty shone,
'Tis not those charms that feed the worm,
   No—look again before yon throne!

*Some years after Eliza's death, Mrs. Palmer expressed poetically that
no subsequent human relationship had been so wonderful for her as her deceased infant daughter. It seems likely that this was written on an annual
recollection of her birth or death (A* Mother's Gift, *pp. 89–90).*

My Ideal

I loved her, yes! from earliest infancy,
When thought just chooses models, then did she
   Within my heart her image shine,
   And had I then sought to define
All I thought good, and kind, and amiable,
I'd think of her, for all seemed there to dwell.

But years have passed since then, and my free thought
Hath taken wing, and many a vision wrought
    Of beauty, excellence, and good;
    Yet none, the test of time hath stood,
Like that dear image infancy enshrined,
Or goodness like to that I then defined.

I loved that meek, that winning gentleness
That beamed on all, as though it all would bless;
    Ah! its diffusiveness was felt;
    That it on my young spirit dwelt
Undying in its strength:—I wonder not,
For it were sacrilege were it forgot.[67]

    But oh! in after life, when her meek eye
Looked forth from creature-love, and the Most High,
    Himself did set His signature
    Of all most lovely good and pure,
Upon her heart:—O! if I loved before
My love and reverence now were ten-fold more.[68]

But she has fled! yet whither is her flight?
Ah, faith hath seen far o'er yon worlds of light
    Her wearied soul at rest with God,
    For she the heavenward pathway trod
While we beheld her; now beyond our love,
In the embrace of God, she rests above.[69]

    On this tragic note, the early phases of Phoebe Palmer's story come to
an end. Her preparatory period ended in the crib fire, the death of her third
child. This became the pivotal crisis that would culminate and decisively
redirect her future self-understanding and activity.
    Keep in mind these dates: Eliza died on July 29, 1836. Mrs. Palmer's
experience of entire dedication to God was to occur almost exactly one year
later on July 26, 1837.

Notes

    1. *Memoirs*, p. 26, says Alexander was born on Sept. 27, 1828, yet the tomb-
stone inscription reads Sept. 28.
    2. The vitality of a prized earthly life elicits the illusion that it will continue.
    3. 1 Kings 19:12.

4. The conclusion that this too, however, painful was an expression of divine mercy, was based on the premise of the good providence of God, but that did not make the temporal separation any less profound.

5. The potential for idolatry is intensified with the excellence and proximity of created goods; cf. Oden, *Structure of Awareness* (Nashville: Abingdon, 1968), ch. 2.

6. Job 34:20; cf. Mark 13:35.

7. *MG,* four more verses in the original, pp. 91–92.

8. Probably named after their former pastor, Samuel Merwin.

9. June 19, 1830.

10. Ps. 68:6.

11. Samuel.

12. Matt. 6:21; Luke 12:34.

13. Exod. 20:4.

14. The solace of grace.

15. For an astute discussion of the religious roots of social activism and the women's movement, see Keith E. Melder, *Beginnings of Sisterhood: The American Women's Rights Movement in the United States, 1800–1840, Studies in the Life of Women* (New York: Schocken, 1977).

16. The theme that those who have benefited from free societies must fight for the freedom of others oppressed recurs subsequently in the work of W.E.B. DuBois and Martin Luther King, Jr.

17. A metaphor of slavery.

18. For further critical discussion of the views of Wilbur Fisk, whom Mrs. Palmer admired, see Douglas J. Williamson, "Wilbur Fisk and African Coloniza- tion," *Methodist History* 23/2 (1985):79–85.

19. Forlorn.

20. The image of returnlessness suggests that she is not proposing the return to Africa as an adequate reparation.

21. Here is some evidence of her early, optimistic post-millennialism.

22. For a picture of the Temperance Movement at about this time, see, "Sta- tus of the Temperance Movement", *CAJ* 16 (1842): 124; for a more wide-ranging discussion of religion and society in this period, see Charles C. Coles, Jr., *The So- cial Ideas of the Northern Evangelists, 1826–1860* (New York: Octagon Books, 1966) (*SINE*).

23. Prov. 23:31–32.

24. Cf. Matt. 5:18.

25. To this point we have simply a patriotic poem. At this point, we notice a drastic reversal of images, so that Satan's triumph through alcoholism becomes viewed by analogy as the new oppressor to be vanquished. What strikes modern ears as a humorous interplay of incongruous images (oppressive colonialism and oppressive alcoholism) apparently had plausibility and cohesion for sanctification activists of the 1830's.

26. Cf. John Kent, *HF,* pp. 48ff.

27. J.E. Orr, *SEAA:* John Kent, *HF:* Timothy Smith, *RSR.*

28. Perhaps "April last" was erroneously transcribed; it might make more chronological sense if it reads "April 1st." It could mean that the revival began in April of 1831. In any event, there are indications that the revival at Allen Street went on intermittently for several years, probably between about 1831 and 1835.

29. Walter's attestation of sanctifying grace preceded Phoebe's by more than five years. During these years Phoebe sought to deepen her spiritual life, but felt she lacked "faith and courage."

30. Cf. John 1:9.

31. Cf. 1 Sam. 18:7.

32. Dan. 5:27. Note the crucial role that dreams apparently played in her self-examination.

33. In the period prior to 1837, she, like Luther, had feared that she might be predestinated among the damned. Subsequently she attested that this despair had been completely overcome.

34. Adam Clarke, (c. 1762–1832), born at Moyberg, County Londonderry, Ireland, studied at Kingswood School, appointed by Wesley to Bradford, Wiltshire in 1782, presided over the British Conference three times. Missionary to the Shetland Islands, orientalist, and leading exponent of sanctification theology, his major contribution was his commentary. See *HBC*, and *Christian Theology* (New York: Lane and Scott, 1851).

35. Clarke's name was variously spelled in America.

36. Cf. Isa. 6:3.

37. Cf. 2 Tim. 4:2.

38. Earlier when near death, she had expressed full readiness to die; now having come through grave illness, she is ready and determined to live to fulfill her mission. If all she did was sell blackberries and witness to grace, that would be sufficient.

39. Cf. Ps. 34:3.

40. In 1835 at age 28 with two surviving children, two having died, she is now more than ever aware of her special vocation as a writer. It was not common in this era for a woman with children to express or even feel a determined sense of vocation in addition to her domestic tasks. But that sense was attested in Phoebe Palmer's notes as a young mother.

41. This suggests a very serious ethic of consequences in communication—that the writer is responsible to some large degree for potential misinterpretations that may emerge even much later out of the writing (note the analogy to her rigorous sexual ethic in the entry of Sept. 28, 1828). This attention to an ethic of consequences later would become an important question in the interpretation of the tradition following Mrs. Palmer—is she to be held accountable for those who "followed after her" yet did so in a distorted way? She appears here to be holding herself to a high ethic of accountability.

42. This is a complex dialectic: She sought the witness of holiness, but felt no enjoyment of it. Each time she would reach out for the fullness of the Christian life, she experienced the demonic temptation that asked her: Are you yet even jus-

tified? Hence she backed away from sanctification, in order to rest assured of her justification. This was the "hindrance."

43. Rom. 8:14.

44. 1 John 4:7.

45. Cf. Ps. 5:3.

46. Whenever she experienced thoughts during self-examination which threw doubt upon the clarity of determination to love God, she perceived therein a demonic detour.

47. Cf. Rom. 8:16.

48. 1 John 5:10.

49. Cf. 2 Kings 5:13.

50. 1 Kings 19:12.

51. Did she by now constantly dread losing those she loved most? Or was this a premonition or precognitive awareness, a kind of anticipatory clairvoyance?

52. Cf. Augustine, *Enchiridion:* God permits evil that a greater good may come from it which otherwise might not have been possible, *NPNF*, 1, III, p. 269. This type of theodicy was reappropriated by Wesley. It is likely, however, that Mrs. Palmer derived this insight largely from the scriptures she cited.

53. Lam. 3:33

54. Her understanding of her vocation is being decisively shaped by her experience of the loss of her children.

55. Ps. 46:10

56. Rom 11:33

57. Here is a dramatic, practical instance of her understanding of the work of the Holy Spirit—a doctrine indeed, but one that is known and tested experientially.

58. John 13:7.

59. Vale, i.e., valley.

60. Cf. Col. 3:2. Eliza's death brought her closely and immediately in touch with the communion of saints, the divine presence, and the heavenly hosts.

61. Cf. Mt. 6:21

62. Here it becomes evident that the power and extraordinary energy of her subsequent ministry was understood in relation to the commitment that she would have had to Eliza had she lived.

63. Far from being meaningless or absurd to Mrs. Palmer, Eliza's death in fact was made meaningful by inspiring the kind of sacrificial faith active in love that resulted in the spiritual life and growth of many.

64. To focus upon secondary causes—the question of who was negligent in the fire, etc.,—in the midst of innocent suffering was in Mrs. Palmer's view a wrong turn. Secondary causality would include all human and natural agencies. The prime cause enabling all secondary causes is God, whom she found trustable even amid these difficult circumstances.

65. Cf. Col 1:13

66. Ps. 57:7

67. It is a razor's edge upon which faith walks in grief: not to fall into idolatry yet to rightly remember the beloved. Forgetting is sacrilege; inordinate valuing is idolatrous.

68. Love had not diminished but increased tenfold through the intervening years.

69. Without the eschatological vision such talk seems hopelessly sentimental. With it, the language is infused with profound meaning: the child rests in God's embrace. She is gone, but in God's hands. The memory of her is still clear, bright, and beautiful.

IV

THE ALTAR COVENANT (1837)

I. THE CRUCIBLE OF VOCATIONAL REASSESSMENT
(MEMOIRS, NOTES, AND POETRY,
JANUARY–JUNE, 1837)

1837 would prove to be a momentous year for Phoebe Palmer. It began in an auspicious way (Memoirs, pp. 33–34):

Diary, January 3, 1837

Yesterday was one of the best days of my life. The enemy persistently suggested to me that I could not pass through the ordeal of seeing so much company without danger of breaking the covenant into which I had solemnly entered on New Year's Eve. Ever since my child-hood I have been in the habit of going to the house of God to attend watch-night service,[1] and to spend the last hours of the year, in reviewing the past, and in renewing my covenant to serve the Lord more faithfully during the coming year.

Sabbath being the first day of the year, and expecting many calls on Monday, I saw reasons that seemed plausible, why I should remain at home, intending to spend the last hour wholly with God, and in solemnly renewing my covenant engagements to be only and forever His. But when the hour came, O, how the enemy withstood. He can quote Scripture, when by taking detached portions, it suits his subtle purpose. "It is better not to vow, than to vow and not perform,"[2] said the adversary. And then such a fear came over me, that I might not be able to keep my vow. "Do not covenant anew till after the festivities of New Year's Day are over," urged the tempter. But I had knelt before the Lord, with the Bible in hand, with a sincere desire to do right. I cried to the Strong for help, when in authoritative tones the Holy Spirit said, "Vow unto the Lord and pay thy vows."[3]

107

With an indescribable weight of responsibility resting on my mind, I said, "O, Lord, if Thou wilt give me something from Thy word to strengthen me, I will take it as my motto during the whole year." I then opened the precious Book of books, and the first words my eye rested on, were these, "I CAN DO ALL THINGS THROUGH CHRIST WHICH STRENGTHEN-ETH ME."[4] How shall I speak of the wondrous manner in which the Holy Spirit made these words spirit and life to my soul. I saw that the strength of Omnipotence was pledged for my sustainment. With a conscious power of purpose, beyond anything ever before realized, I then entered into covenant with God, laying hold upon divine power. Ever since, I seem to have increasing strength to meet the demands of the moment.

Sabbath, January 1st, a divine, soul-hallowing conviction rested upon me, assuring my inmost soul that the Lord my Redeemer is with me and will guide me with strength for all life's emergencies and conflicts.

Yesterday, January 2d, many friends, perhaps not less than a hundred, called.[5] I had resolved in the strength of the Lord that I would not only avoid all mere frivolity of manner and speech, but would endeavor, if possible, to say something that would attract the attention of my visitors, to the One altogether lovely.[6] I was really amazed at the condescensions of grace in helping me. I do not think I ever felt, or manifested, more cheerfulness, or was more successful in promoting the happiness of others, and yet I think no one left the house without thinking more of Jesus, and the interests of eternity.[7] Today I have a realization of having passed the Rubicon.[8] I presume some will say, in thinking of me, "Is Saul also among the prophets?"[9] Yet! and through grace they shall see that Saul will *stay* among the prophets. I seem to feel that it is the voice of Divinity within me, that says, "I will strengthen thee, yea, I will help thee; yea, I will uphold thee with the right hand of my righteoussness, for I, the Lord thy God will hold thy right hand, saying unto thee, fear not."[10]

In February of 1837, a year after the Tuesday Meetings for the Promotion of Holiness had begun, Mrs. Palmer committed herself more deliberately and dutifully to keep a regular record of her spiritual progress in experiential religion,[11] which she called her "Notes," later to be published in The Way of Holiness, *as "Notes By the Way" (*The Way of Holiness, *pp. 117–26). These passages record the crucial stages that led to the experience of sanctifying grace:*

Aware of the proneness of the heart to forget the admonition divinely enjoined, "Thou shalt remember all the way which the Lord thy God hath led thee . . . in the wilderness, to humble thee and prove thee,"[12] she re-

solved from that time to be more diligent in noting down, for future remembrance, the Spirit's gracious leadings, some of which stand briefly
recorded as follows:—

Feb. 23, 18—.[13] For some days past my soul has been longing after
God, I have been waiting at Jerusalem for the promise of the Father;[14]
blessed be God the Father, the Son, and the Holy Ghost, that my waiting
has not been in vain; my faith has been as the dawning of the morning,
clearer and yet clearer; and now the calm sunshine of God's presence il-
luminates my soul.

The precious words, "whereby are given unto us exceeding great and
precious promises, that by these ye might be partakers of the divine nature,"[15] were applied to my soul with much power this evening. Yes, I saw
such comprehensiveness and depth of meaning in them, as I had never before apprehended. What! am I to be made a partaker of the divine nature?
Shout, O heavens! be glad, O earth! . . .[16]

Feb. 24. I have often felt as though God had called me peculiarly to a
life of holiness. I have also felt that in order to be led in this way, the path
of self-denial must be mine.[17] Well, thanks be to God that he has given me
in a gracious degree, a disposition to walk in the way of his appointment.
From the depth of my heart I can say, through grace, that I have deliberately
chosen to walk in the more excellent way, even though the highway to it
may be by passing through trials most contrary to nature. I know that my
heavenly Father loves me. He will not require me to do anything but what
will be eventually for my good and the glory of his great name. . . .[18]

Feb. 27. Glory be to God that I have this day been enabled to resolve
to follow the faith of Abraham, who, against hope, believed in hope.[19] I
now repose in the promises of the unchangeable Jehovah, believing that
what he has promised he is fully able to perform.[20] His promises are all yea
and amen in Christ Jesus.[21] O may I never rest till I have the witness of the
Spirit,[22] that my heart is the temple of an indwelling God,[23] and have the
full confidence that Christ reigns supreme on the throne of my affections,
bringing every thought into obedience to himself.[24]

This is the blessing which I fully believe God has in reserve for me;
"for this my cry shall never cease."[25] For several days past the eye of my
faith has been so intensely fixed on this point, that almost every breath has
been a breathing after it. O Lord, make me holy! establish fully with me
the new covenant. Thou hast said, "I will sprinkle you with clean water,
and ye shall be clean; from all your filthiness and from all your idols will I
cleanse you."[26]

I feel that I have been greatly deficient, and have lost inconceivably,
by not exercising that faith which takes God at his word; that faith which is

apprehended in the simple illustration, "God hath said it, and I believe it."
When looked at in this light, O, how exceedingly sinful does unbelief appear![27]

About this time Abel Stevens was sending out the call for "pious phy-
sicians" to go to China as missionaries.[28] *Ten years later in her 1847 diary*[29]
she was reporting her visit with Rev. and Mrs. Henry Hickok, and Rev.
Robert S. Maclay, three of the first five Methodist missionaries to China,
before their departure. She recalled the vocational crisis that Stevens' call
*had elicited in her and Dr. Palmer (*Memoirs, *p. 231):*

Diary, 1847.—This afternoon, the Rev. Mr. Hickok and lady, and
Rev. Mr. Maclay, missionaries to China, visited us.[30] They are interesting,
and I doubt not truly devoted in spirit to the work to which they have been
called by the Great Head of the Church.

The mission to China has long been a matter of much interest with Dr.
P. and myself.[31] When Abell's [sic] very important call for pious physicians
was put into my hands, nearly ten years since, my mind was strongly impressed that it might be our duty to go.

Shortly after our marriage,[32] my husband expressed a persuasion that
it might be his duty to go on a foreign mission, as physician. I indulged a
secret hope that he might be mistaken, but dared not say anything
dissuasive, from an idea that if it were the will of God, and I should stand
in his way, the Lord would remove me, yet though I did not dissuade, I did
not encourage,[33] and there the matter rested. Now,[34] I seemed to be required
to count the cost.

"Leaving home and friends, and all
The dear delights of ripe society."[35]

I did count the cost, and I believe the Spirit helped me to do it thoroughly.[36] After this, the question was proposed, "Would you be willing to
devote yourself just as fully to the cause of Christ here as though you were
already amid China's dense population?"[37] If you will do so, the Spirit of
Holiness is the spirit which will tell upon missions, and the Lord will make
you instrumental in working upon minds which tell on missions, and you
may, for the present, do more service in aiding missionary work here, than
if you were in China.[38]

I thought of the absorption I should feel, in the work of saving souls,
if thus wholly given up, and I resolved to make the work of the Lord as
absorbing here, as though I were on missionary ground,[39] and my career[40]
has ever since been influenced by these resolves.

Through this humble instrumentality, the Lord has condescended to act directly on my mind, which is now operating[41] the salvation of China.

Mrs. Palmer's special admiration of Ann Wilkins illustrates her early personal interest in the world mission of the church. In September of 1836 Ann Wilkins had been converted at a camp meeting at Sing Sing, New York.[42] *Shortly thereafter she offered herself for service in Africa. Mrs. Palmer was moved to write this poem on the occasion of her departure, June 15, 1837 (from* A Mother's Gift, *pp. 158–60):*

Call of the Missionary

"Get thee out from thy father's house, unto a land that I will show thee." Gen. xx.1.

Written on the Occasion of the Departure of Miss—,[43] the First Female Missionary to Liberia.

Sister, thy home is far away—
    A trackless path between us lies,
Proud ocean's queen hath thus far sway;
    Her mountain billows now defy,
The *hand* that would to thine be prest,
    The *lip* that would love's impress seal,
The *eye* where answering smiles would rest,
    The voice that would the *heart* reveal!

Thus far doth she her sway extend,
    And here her triumphs cease with thee;[44]
For though afar, thou hast a Friend,
    That trod the billows fearlessly;
'Twas He that gave the high command,
    That bade thee rise and haste to go
To sojourn in a stranger land,[45]
    Unto a place which He would show.

And Abram-like faith loosed the ties
    Of kindred, love of friends and home.
Thou conquering faith we saw thee rise,
    And heard thee say, "O Lord! I come."[46]
And now that thou art far away,
    Shall thought dwell on thy loneliness?

No! love's soft smiles still light thy way,
    And seraph-guards around thee press.

The strength of God was all thy boast,
    By this alone thou wast borne hence,
And now the *legions* of His hosts
    Are round thee 'camped for thy defence.
Do thoughts of home or other days
    Thy peaceful bosom ere invade?
They gently chide, and turn thy gaze
    On Him on whom thy help is laid.

Oh! what are earthly loves or ease,
    Or health, or life, compared with this,
That there is One we love and please,
    Whose smile is most consummate bliss;
To know *His* eye doth condescend
    To beam with pleasure, light and power,[47]
On her I love, my chosen friend,
    It is enough, I ask no more.

A dreary clime, a sable[48] race,
    With brightness beams where this doth rest
And where all beauty was effaced,
    This reproduces loveliness.
Courage, my sister; soon this light,
    Which now so sweetly clears thy way,
Shall dissipate dark error's night,
    And usher in eternal day.

*She spent much of June 1837 in secret prayer, seeking the blessing of full salvation. Her resolve to order her daily patterns in the light of eternity was consistent with John Wesley's[49] emphasis upon "redeeming the time" (*Way of Holiness, *pp. 122–26):*

June 17. . . . I have placed the standard of Christian excellence high, and have asked strength of Omnipotence to be enabled to reach the summit of my desires. "My heart is fixed! O, God, my heart is fixed!"[50] and, though the opposition of a perverse will, the infirmities of nature, or crosses indescribably great may oppose, my progress, I trust, will yet, through grace, be onward and upward. I long to be made a monument of what the grace of God can effect on a once rebellious child of Adam. O! this, I am sure, is a holy ambition, and authorized by Scripture. I have been enabled to spend much time in secret prayer this week, and I feel that I have received a new degree of strength for the holy effort; but O, how little to what I might have received, had my faith been more active and persevering! Lord, increase my faith,[51] and enable me ever to go on from strength to strength.[52]

June 18. Of late I have increasingly felt the importance of time. In view of an eternal state of existence, and the short space allotted for its vast concernments, I do indeed feel the force of the admonition, "What thy hand findeth to do, do it with thy might."[53]

"Short is our longest day of life,
  And soon its prospect ends,
Yet on this day's uncertain date
  Eternity depends. . . . [54]

I have thought that some rules for the regulation of my time and the distribution of my duties, might be helpful. I will endeavor to rise at four,[55] spend from four to six in reading the Scriptures, and other devotional exercises; half an hour for closet duties at midday. I will resolve, at this season to bear in special remembrance those who have said, "Pray for me," not forgetting the exhortation, 1 Tim. ii, 1.[56] If practicable I will get an hour to spend with God at the close of the day.

In order to keep a continuous and comprehensive arrangement of Bible truth before my mind, I will resolve to pursue a systematic course of reading. I purpose to read, in proper connection, in the Old Testament in the morning, in the Gospels at noon, and in the Epistles in the evening. This I will endeavor to do, with the most careful circumspection, inasmuch as God hath said, "*Search* the Scriptures,"[57] "*Study* to show thyself approved."[58]

If I meet with portions which I cannot readily comprehend, I will, through grace, seek diligently and go confidently unto Him who hath said, "I will instruct thee,"[59] believing it is his *will* that I should learn some special lesson of grace from *every* portion of his word, whether historical or from those parts deemed more practical. . . . [60]

June 24. In consequence of ill health I have not been able to observe *all* the resolutions in my last, an alteration in domestic arrangements has also, in a measure, frustrated my purposes; I regret that I do not, with greater equanimity of feeling, bear the thwarting of my purposes. O, how much I need establishing grace![61] I know—O! yes, I *feel* that it is, in all its richest plenitude, for me; and yet I live without it.[62] O! when shall my heart be circumcised[63] to love the Lord my God with all my heart?

2. THE DAY OF DAYS, JULY 26, 1837

July 26, 1837, was the critical day of her decisive experience of sanctifying grace and the irrevocable commitment of all her powers, which would thenceforth energize the remainder of her life. The issue concerned Walter—whether she was willing to sacrifice or yield to divine grace the "one dear object" of her affection, her life partner. She wrote in her Notes of the morning of that day (Faith and Its Effects, pp. 68–71):

July 26. On the morning of this day, while with most grateful emotions remembering the way by which my heavenly Father had led me, my thought rested more especially upon the beloved one whom God had given to be the partner of my life. How truly a gift from God, and how essentially connected with my spiritual, as also my temporal happiness, is this one dear object! I exclaimed.

Scarcely had these suggestions passed, when with keenness these inquiries were suggested: "Have you not professedly given up all for Christ? If he who now so truly absorbs your affections were required, would you not shrink from the demand?" I need not say that this one dear object, though often in name surrendered, was not in reality given up. My precious little ones, whom God had taken to himself, were then brought to my recollection, as if to admonish me relative to making the sacrifice. I thought how fondly I had idolized them. He who had said, "I the Lord your God am a jealous God," saw the idolatry of my heart, and took them to himself.[64] The remembrance of how decidedly I had, by these repeated bereavements, been assured that He whose right it is to reign, would be the sole sovereign of my heart, assisted me in the resolve, that neither should this, the yet dearer object, be withheld. . . .

I began to particularize.[65] The thoughts and exercises of the morning occurred again with yet greater power. Can God be about to take from me this one dear object, for which life is principally desirable? thought I. Looking into the future, I said, "What a blank!" Never before had I realized, that the very fibres of my existence were so closely interwoven with his. My impression was, that the Lord was about to take my precious husband from me. The inquiry with me was, whether it were possible that my heavenly Father could require me to make the surrender, when he had authorized my love, by making it my duty to be of one heart and soul with him. But grace interposed; and from more mature consideration, I was led to regard it as extraordinary condescension in God thus to apprise me of his designs, by way of preparing my heart for the surrender.

With Abraham I said, "I have lifted my hand to the Lord."[66] In word, I had again and again made the sacrifice before, and said, "My husband

and child I surrender to thee.'' I had not been insincere, but I now saw that I had not in fact done that which, in word, had often been named. Far, indeed, had I been from realizing the depth of obligation which, in word, I had taken upon myself.

Truth in the inward part[67] I now in verity apprehended as God's requirement. Grace triumphed. In full view of the nature of the sacrifice, I said,

"Take life or friends away."[68]

I could just as readily have said, "Take *life,*" as I could have said, "Take friends"; for that which was just as dear, if not dearer, than life, had been required. And when I said, "Take him who is the supreme object of my earthly affections,'' I, from that moment felt that I was fully set apart for God, and began to say, "Every tie that has bound me to earth is severed.'' I could now as easily have doubted of my existence as to have doubted that God was the supreme object of my affections.

The report of her unconditional reception of sanctifying grace was attested in three accounts: The Way of Holiness *(pp. 125ff.),* Memoirs *(pp. 36ff.), and* Faith and Its Effects *(pp. 65ff., 262ff.).[69] The most concise description is found in her Notes of July 27, 1837, referring to the previous day, to which she would later refer as her "day of days"* (Way of Holiness, *pp. 125–26):*

July 27. The Lord reigns unrivaled in my heart; he has my supreme affections; for some days past I have experienced such a heartfelt want of the assurance of being cleansed from all unrighteousness, to know that the motives influencing every thought, word, and action, originate from a pure fountain, that I last evening resolved I could no longer do without it. Between the hours of eight and nine[70]—while pleading at the throne of grace for a present fulfillment of the exceeding great and precious promises;[71] pleading also the fulness and freeness of the atonement, its unbounded efficacy, and making an entire surrender of body, soul, and spirit; time, talents, and influence; and also of the dearest ties of nature, my beloved husband and child; in a word, my earthly *all—I received the assurance that God the Father, through the atoning Lamb, accepted the sacrifice;* my heart was emptied of self, and cleansed of all idols, from all filthiness of the flesh and spirit,[72] and I realized that I dwelt in God, and felt that he had become the portion of my soul,[73] my *ALL IN ALL.*

A more detailed, probing account was written in her diary of July 27, 1837. It focuses upon the subtleties of her struggle against eight distin-

*guishable ploys or assaults of the adversary to prevent the full consecration
of her powers to God (Memoirs, pp. 36–44):*

I never made much progress in the career of faith, until I most solemnly
resolved,[74] in the strength of the Lord Jehovah, that I would do every duty,
though I might die in the effort. From that hour my course was onward and
upward. I also covenanted with God that I would be a BIBLE CHRISTIAN,[75]
and most carefully seek to know the mind of the spirit, as recorded in the
WRITTEN WORD, though it might lead to an experience unlike all the world
beside. I had often prayed for holiness of heart,[76] before, but do not remember now that holiness, as a blessing in name, was on my mind; my
highest and all-engrossing desire was to be a BIBLE CHRISTIAN.

The day of the Lord is near in the Valley of *Decision.*[77] This was an
important step, and took me much nearer to God, the source of Light and
Love. In a manner that exceeded all former perceptions, the living Word
said to my heart, *"Ye are not your own, ye are bought with a price, therefore glorify God in your body and spirit, which are God's."*[78]

From this I saw that I could not be a BIBLE Christian, without being
wholly consecrated. I rose early, and began every new day with a renewed
solemn consecration. In the name and strength of the Triune Deity, I presented myself to the Lord. And every day, and hour, my soul seemed to be
pressing hard after God. From the depths of my being,[79] I said,

"My heart-strings groan with deep complaint,
    My flesh lies panting,[80] Lord, for thee,
And every nerve and every joint,
    Stretches for perfect purity."[81]

While in this state of longing expectancy, my pastor[82] came in one
morning, and spoke of a lady who, the evening previous, had presented
herself at the altar of prayer, as a seeker, and professed to find the Saviour.
He said that the lady appeared to be an entire stranger, and asked, "Will
you not go and see her?"

I might have hesitated about going to a stranger thus, but the Holy
Spirit whispered, "Did you not consecrate yourself to the Lord this morning; and if so, it is not left optional with yourself whether you will go; the
one and only question is, Would the Lord have you go?"[83]

Looking at the question in that light, the duty was clear. I went; found
the lady a new creature in Christ Jesus. An unconverted, gay[84] sister, was
sitting by, who manifested great displeasure. I asked if she did not feel the

need of the same grace that her sister had received? In a manner exceedingly repulsive, she answered, *No!*

Affectionately, I entreated her to be careful of her utterances before God, as she was in danger of sinning as Ananias and Sapphira[85] did—that is, lying against the Holy Ghost. And here I was withstood. "How much of *self* in this performance," suggested the tempter.[86] Though consciously not insincere, yet the accusation was for the moment almost paralyzing, and from the depths of my soul I cried out, "What shall I do?" The still, small voice whispered, "Stand still, and see the salvation of God!"[87]

"Stand still, and do nothing?" No. "Be steadfast and immovable, always abounding in the work of the Lord, forasmuch as ye know that your labor is not in vain in the Lord."[88] It was thus that the blessed Holy Spirit, through the living Word, deigned to talk with me, making the written word spirit and life.[89]

At this point I perceived the privilege of *knowing that my labors were in the Lord.*[90] Paul must have known it, or he would not have written thus. And to *know* this, I must be conscious that the spring of every motive is pure. It was thus I apprehended heart purity as an absolute *necessity* if I would be *useful.*[91]

On the evening of the third day after the conversation with the young lady, she was powerfully converted, the Spirit having used my lips in convincing her of sin. Between the hours of eight and nine o'clock the same evening,[92] I was led by the Spirit to the determination that I would never rest, day or night, until I *knew* that the spring of every motive was pure, and that the consecration I made of myself was wholly accepted.

The adversary said,[93] "Don't be rash. You may have to wrestle all night, and perhaps all day to-morrow, and the next day too. If you do this, it will be your death." I replied, "God demands present holiness. I cannot glorify Him without holiness; and if I cannot live to glorify God, let me die and glorify Him."

I was then withstood with the suggestion, "How do you know that this is God's *time?*"[94] Again the Spirit, through the written Word, speaking to my inmost soul, said, "Now! is the accepted time, and behold, NOW is the day of salvation."[95]

Had any one asked me, weeks previous to this, "Are you wholly consecrated?" my answer might have been, as far as I know myself, "I am."[96] Otherwise, I could not understandingly have retained a state of *justification,* for, *how* can one on *scriptural* principles retain a state of justification, while *knowingly* keeping back anything from God.[97] "To him that knoweth to do good, and doeth it not, to him it is *sin.*"[98]

But I was not following hard after God,[99] and to the degree my mind was enlightened, was making daily advances Godward. Said Jesus, "I have many things to say unto you, but ye cannot bear them now."[100] He had been saying thus to me as His disciple, and following on lovingly after Him, true to the light revealed, I was walking in *justification* before Him.[101]

In coming to the decision, I WILL be holy NOW, I took a step beyond any I had ever before taken. God is *light.* As I drew nearer to Him than ever before, He drew nearer to me.[102] I had often entered into covenant with God before. Now, by the light of the Holy Spirit, I saw that the High and Holy One would have me enter into a covenant with Him, the duration of which would be lasting as eternity, *absolute,* and *unconditional.*[103]

I felt that the Spirit was leading into a solemn, most sacred, and inviolable compact between God and the soul that came forth from Him, by which, in the sight of God, angels and men, I was to be united in eternal oneness with the Lord my Redeemer,[104] requiring unquestioning allegiance on my part, and infinite love and everlasting salvation, guidance and protection, on the part of Him who had loved and redeemed me, so that from henceforth He might say to me, "I will betroth thee unto Me forever."[105]

That the covenant might be well ordered and sure, I thought "let me *particularize,* taking every step, so that not one may ever have to be retraced." The first object presented to be given up, was one with which every fibre of my being seemed interwoven; with amazement, I asked, can it be that the Lord requires that this one beloved object, dearer to me than life itself, be bound to the altar?[106] What shall I have to live for if I give up this object? The Holy Spirit suggested, "Have you not often said to the Lord, your Redeemer, 'I take Thee as my only portion!'[107] Now, God is taking you at your word."[108]

"What a sacrifice," said the tempter.[109] "Did you ever hear of such a sacrifice being required at the hand of any one?"

Here the tender, loving Spirit interposed. "Did Abraham know *why* he was called to give up Isaac at the *time* he gave him up?[110] But he knows *now.* And are you willing to wait till you get to heaven in order to know why the Lord demands this sacrifice at your hand?" My soul replied, "Yes! Lord, I will wait till knowledge is made perfect.[111] Take this object[112] if Thou dost require. Take life or friends away. I am wholly Thine! There is not a tie that binds me to earth. Every tie has been severed."

"Perhaps there is something that you do not know of, not yet given up," whispered the tempter.[113]

"What will not a man give for his life? and I have given up that which is dearer to me than life. I make no provision[114] for future emergencies, resolved hereafter, as God shall reveal His will, to say, 'Behold Thy willing servant!' "

Arriving at this point, the enemy had no further ground for questioning, relative to the *consecration,* whether it was *entire, absolute, and un-conditional.* From the depths of my being I felt that the consecration was absolute and universal, and in view of all coming time.[115] But at this point I was for a moment perplexed with the question,—

"How do you know that God will receive you?" And here I paused, and pondered, *"How* may I know that the Lord *does* receive me?"[116] To this, in gentle whispers, the Spirit replied, "It is *written,* I WILL RECEIVE YOU."[117] "Must I believe it, because it simply stands written, without any other *evidence* than the *Word of God?"* I exclaimed.[118]

In answer to these questionings, the ever-blessed Spirit (given to guide us into all truth)[119] suggested, "Suppose you should hear a voice, speaking in tones of thunder, from heaven, saying, *'I will receive you,'* would you not believe it then?" I could not help believing it then, because I should have the "evidence of my *senses,"* was my reply.

In a moment I saw the inconsistency of my position, remembering that I was taught by the Scripture most plainly, and had always known, that the blessing of entire sanctification was received by *faith,*[120] inasmuch as it stands written, "Sanctify them through Thy truth, Thy WORD IS TRUTH."[121]

"But," said the adversary, "suppose, after you have believed you don't *feel* any different, what will you do?"[122] Here the blessed Word again met me, intensifying the truth, "The just SHALL live by *faith."*[123] I now saw what *faith* was in all its *simplicity.* Such perceptions of the *Divinity* of the Word I never before had. So true it is that, "if any man WILL do His will, he shall know of the doctrine."[124]

I had thought of the doctrine of faith as difficult. Now I saw that it was only to believe *heartily,* what in fact I had always professed to believe, that is, that the Bible is the WORD OF GOD just as truly as though I could hear Him speaking in tones of thunder from Sinai's Mount, and *faith is to believe it!*

Still the enemy withstood me, with the suggestion, "Suppose you should be called to live a long life, till you are three score or a hundred years old, and never have any of those manifestations that others enjoy—never have anything but the naked Word of God upon which to rely; and should die, and come up before your Judge, without ever having had anything but the naked Word to assure your faith?"[125]

My reply was, "I would come up before my Judge, and in the face of an assembled universe, say, 'The foundation of my faith was Thy immutable Word.' " The moment I came to this point, the Holy Spirit most assuringly whispered, "This is just the way in which Abraham, the father of the faithful, walked." "By *faith* he journeyed, not knowing whither he went."[126]

There is joy in faith. "Can it be that the Lord of the Way is going to honor me thus, as to permit me all along through life, to tread in the footprints of the father of the faithful?''—was the language of my heart.

It was at this point that the Covenant was consummated between God and my soul, that I would live a *life of faith.* That, however diversified life's current might roll, though I might be called to endure more complicated and long-continued trials of my faith, than were ever before conceived of, or even brought to a climax, where, as with the father of the faithful, commands and promises might *seem* to conflict, that I would still believe, though I might *die in the effort,* I would hold on in the death struggle.

In the strength of Omnipotence I laid hold on the Word, ''I WILL RE-CEIVE YOU!''[127]

Faith apprehended the written Word, not as a DEAD letter, but as a living voice of the living God.[128] ''Holy men of God spake as they were moved by the Holy Ghost.''[129] The holy Scriptures were intensified to my mind as the *lively,* or living *oracles*—the voice of God to me, as truly as though I could every moment hear Him speaking in the tones of thunder from Sinai. And now, that through the inworkings of the Holy Spirit, I had presented all my redeemed powers to God, through Christ, how could I doubt His immutable word, ''I will receive you?''

O! with what light, clearness and power, were the words invested, *''Sanctify them through Thy truth, Thy Word is truth!*[130]

Yet, though I *knew* that it could not be otherwise than that God did receive me, my faith was at once put to the test. I had expected that some wonderful manifestation would at once follow as the reward of my faith. But I was shut up to faith—*naked faith in a naked promise.*[131]

Said the adversary, tauntingly, ''Where now is the great joy that you anticipated? Why do you not, from constraining influences, praise the Lord, as many others do who receive the blessing of a clean heart?''[132]

So subtle is Satan, when transformed as an angel of light,[133] that though kept from yielding, I did not perceive that it was the tempter, and, in answer to his subtle suggestion, replied, ''I do not feel so much like praising the Lord from impelling influences now, as on some other occasions.''

True it is that the kingdom of heaven cometh not by observation.[134] But O, the proneness of the human heart to say, Lo! here, and Lo! there![135] And how few seem to remember that the ever-blessed, tender, gentle Holy Spirit, is quiet in its influences. He would fain lead the soul into green pastures, and beside still waters[136]—casting down all high imaginations,[137] and whisper soothingly, ''In quietness and assurance thy *rest* shall be.''[138] And now that Satan would have come in as a flood, the Spirit lifted a standard[139] thus—

''Through what power were you enabled to enter into the bonds of an everlasting covenant with God, yielding up that which was dearer to you than life?''[140] It was through the power of Omnipotence. I could no more have done it of myself than I could have created a world. Every step toward the attainment of this grace has been through the direct inspirations of the Holy Spirit.''

"And upon whose Word do you now rely?" "It is on the Word of the immutable Jehovah. He has given me that Word." Wonderful, indeed, that the Holy Spirit does thus condescend to reason with the human heart;[141] but through these reasonings I saw with the clearness of a sunbeam, that it was all from the first to last the work of the Spirit—"God working in me to will and to do."[142] With the poet, I experimentally apprehended,

"Thou all our works in us hast wrought.
　Our good is all divine,
The praise of every virtuous thought
　And righteous act is *thine*."[143]

Now, that I so clearly apprehended that the power to will and to do, was all so manifestly of the Lord, I began to reason with myself thus: "Do I wait to thank a friend who does me a great favor, till I feel an *impelling* influence to do it? Do I not do it because it is a duty?[144] And now, if the Lord has enabled me to make an unconditional and absolute surrender of all my redeemed powers and faculties, and has given His Word, assuring me that He *does* receive me, shall I refuse to give Him the glory due to His name, till I feel constraining influences?" Ashamed of the thought, I took yet another step in the Divine order, without which, a most important and imperative requirement would have been omitted.

There are distinctive steps[145] in the attainment of the great salvation! In that of ENTIRE CONSECRATION, I had so carefully pondered the path of my feet, that the way back again to self, or the world in any degree, was returnless.[146] The next step, FAITH, in regard to Divine acceptance of all, had also been distinctly taken. And now, as I plainly saw the third step clearly defined in the Word, I took the advance ground—CONFESSION.[147]

Giving God the glory due to His name, I exclaimed, "Through Thy grace alone I have been enabled to give myself wholly and forever to Thee. Thou hast given Thy Word, assuring me that Thou dost receive. I believe that Word! Alleluia! the Lord God Omnipotent reigneth unrivalled in my heart.[148] Glory be to the Father! Glory be to the Son! Glory be to the Holy Spirit forever![149] O! into what a region of light, glory and purity, was my soul at this moment ushered! I felt that I was but as a drop in the ocean of infinite Love, and Christ was All in All.[150]

If any one had asked me, previous to this, "Are any of the graces of the Spirit *perfected* in you?" I might have said, "I am, indeed greatly deficient in all the gifts and graces of the Holy Spirit, but if one grace is nearer perfected than another, it is the grace of *humility.*" But never before did I know the meaning of the word *humility.*[151] How the realization was intensified to my mind, "Not by works of righteousness that we have done!"[152] I saw that I was not sufficient of myself to think a good thought, much less to perform a righteous action. I felt that I could not save myself, even for one moment, and from the depths, my soul cried out,

> "Every moment, Lord, I need
> The merit of Thy death."[153]

But amid these realizations of utter nothingness, I had such views of the unbounded efficacy of the atonement, that if the guilt of the universe had been concentrated and laid upon my head,

> "The stream of Jesus' precious blood
> Would wash away that dreadful load."[154]

Notes

1. Wesley prepared a Watch-Night Service and commended it to his American followers. Those who view Finney as the primary advocate of covenantal language in the holiness tradition do well to recall frequent references to covenant in the pre-Palmer Wesleyan tradition.
2. Eccl. 5:5.
3. Cf. Ps. 76:11.
4. Phil. 4:13.
5. An indication of the strongly gregarious temperament of Mrs. Palmer. Indeed she desired withdrawal at critical times of her spiritual development, but when she did, it was from a great number of steady friendships and associations of deep mutual accountability.
6. Note the important function of "resolve" in the holiness tradition—in this case directed toward a particular day: Let everyone I meet this day recognize something of the "One altogether lovely."
7. She conceived this as an illuminating example of grace ennobling nature, of a woman's natural gifts of cordiality and amenability being strengthened and intensified by divine grace.
8. By Jan. 3, 1837, she was confident that she could sustain her earnest seeking of full salvation. She could envision her vocation in terms of the prophetic pattern, and she knew by then that by grace she could sustain that vocation, so as to "*stay* among the prophets."
9. The reference, 1 Sam. 19:24, is ironic, for it was uttered by those who feared that Saul had grown addled when he stripped off his robes and prophesied in Samuel's presence.

10. Isa. 41:10, 13.

11. This renewal of resolve stands in the tradition of William Law, *Christian Perfection*, reprint edition (Carol Stream: Creation House, 1975); and John Wesley, *WJW*, III, p. 313; VI, p. 297.

12. Deut. 8:2.

13. From the context it is clear that she is speaking of 1837.

14. Cf. Acts 1:4; this text was to provide the title of her book on women prophesying: *The Promise of the Father*. This is a Pentecost-oriented theme that Donald Dayton argues is largely absent from Mrs. Palmer's work prior to 1857, *WTJ* 13 (1978): 118, yet it appears prominently here, even prior to her experience of the summer of 1837.

15. 2 Pet. 1:4; cf. Athanasius, *Incarnation of the Word*, *NPNF*, 2, IV.

16. Cf. Ps. 96:11.

17. Cf. Mark 8:34.

18. Cf. Rom. 8:28. She felt called and enabled by being given a disposition to seek the life of holiness. This calling and enablement drew her will toward full commitment (cf. Augustine, *On Grace and Free Will*).

19. Rom. 4:16–18. Although at this stage she could easily appeal to Abraham as a model, she later learned that her major obstacle to the reception of sanctifying grace was that she had not been willing, as Abraham toward Isaac, to give up her creaturely loves that had been made idols.

20. Rom. 4:21.

21. 2 Cor. 1:20.

22. Rom. 8:16.

23. Cf. 1 Cor. 6:19.

24. Cf. 2 Cor. 10:5.

25. Cf. 1 Sam. 7:8.

26. Ps. 51:7.

27. For background on the theological context out of which this sort of struggle is to be understood, see Robert Chiles, *Theological Transition in American Methodism, 1790–1935* (New York: Abingdon, 1965), pp. 21–49; cf. Tho. Langford, *PD*, ch. 1–4.

28. Stevens, a member of the New England Conference, had in 1837 made a trip to Europe, and upon his return he became a leading advocate of world missions among Methodists. President Wilbur Fisk of Wesleyan University had proposed a China Mission to the Missionary Society Board in May 1835.

29. The precise date of this call is uncertain, but since her diary of 1847 (no month listed) indicates that it came ten years previously, it is reasonable to assume that it came about 1837.

30. The Hickoks (Genesee Conference), and Robert S. Maclay (Baltimore Conference), were not appointed missionaries to China until that year, 1847. So apparently they visited the Palmers just before leaving as the second company of Methodist missionaries, arriving in Foochow in 1848 (*CM*, p. 556). From 1847–72 Maclay was superintendent of the mission at Foochow. After returning to the United States, he was appointed to head the mission to Japan. Later he astutely supervised

Henry G. Appenzeller's mission to Korea (see Daniel Davies' Drew University dissertation on Appenzeller, 1986).

31. Wheatley observed: "The mission to China was established through her efforts. She had spoken with Bishop Janes, and other bishops, and with some of the Board of Managers of the General Missionary Society, on the subject. But they replied that it would take so long before any fruit would appear, that the Board would not undertake it. One morning, while riding out with Dr. Palmer, she said, 'Pa! Would you be willing to give so much yearly, for ten years, if twenty others would give the same amount, for the establishment of a mission to China?' Dr. P. answered in the affirmative, and said, 'I would double the amount named, each year.' The next question was, 'Will you say so at the anniversary of the Missionary Society, this evening?' That evening, in the Green Street church, he did say so. The proposition was no sooner made than Bishop Janes said he would be one of the number. Mr. W.H. Woodbury was the next to volunteer, and the twenty pledges were very quickly made" (*Memoirs*, pp. 230–31).

32. Sept. 28, 1827.

33. It appears to have been a weighty matter of conscience that she did not seek either to dissuade or persuade, knowing that Dr. Palmer had felt the call, and doubtless looked circumspectly to her for confirmation.

34. "Now" apparently refers to the 1837 occasion of Stevens' call for a medical mission to China.

35. Cf. *HMEC*, 1879, #787.

36. This suggests that the China medical missionary vocation was taken with great seriousness, not casually or theoretically.

37. Could it be that Phoebe Palmer was given the courage to pursue her energetic ministry in the holiness revivals by this kind of reasoning: *If* she should not go to China—if her "secret hope" that the China call would be not for her and her husband—*then* she would devote herself fully to Christ's cause *as if in China?*

38. The result of her decision confirms her original intuition. From her parlour on 54 Rivington in New York many dozens of missionaries went around the world and returned periodically to visit the Tuesday Meeting.

39. She viewed herself thereafter as a missionary.

40. It was not common for a woman in this period to speak of "my career." It was this urgent and definite sense of special vocation (distinct from domestic concerns, which she accepted and took for granted) that set Phoebe Palmer apart from many otherwise similar women of the 1840's. It will interest students of feminism that at such an early date we have a clear instance of a woman thinking deliberately about her public vocation or career and the "resolves" that gave it energy and direction.

41. I.e., working for (*opera*, works).

42. Since Phoebe Palmer attended the Sing Sing camp meeting about this time, although the exact date is not known, it is quite possible (even probable in the light of this poem) that she had met and knew Ann Wilkins.

43. Ann Wilkins sailed from Philadelphia on June 15, 1837, with Rev. J.J. Matthias of Newark, who became governor of Bassa Cove, Liberia (*CM*, p. 948).

This is the same Matthias who later would write the preface to Phoebe Palmer's first book, *Mary, Or the Young Christian* (preface written 1840). Phoebe had doubtless known Matthias in the period of her marriage when he was appointed to the Methodist circuit of churches in lower Manhattan.

44. Till now the sea had blocked proclamation in Africa. The hands that could have touched, the lips that could have kissed, the eyes that could recognize friendship, and voices that could reveal the heart—all these communications had been blocked by the defiant sea. Now they are being overcome by Ann Wilkins's courageous answer to the divine call.

45. Cf. Acts. 7:6.

46. Cf. Isa. 6:8.

47. Cf. Ps. 33:18.

48. Black.

49. *WJW*, VII, pp. 67ff.

50. Cf. Ps. 57:7.

51. Cf. Luke 17:5.

52. Cf. Ps. 84:7).

53. Eccl. 9:10.

54. Much of the energy of the revival that was soon to develop under Mrs. Palmer's leadership hinged on this point: This day could be one's last. What occurs today could destine one's eternity. Not in *DH, HUMEC,* Codville or Baketel; for similar themes, cf. *HMEC,* 1879, #950, 956, 964.

55. Following Wesley's pattern.

56. "I urge, then, first of all, that requests, prayers, intercession and thanksgiving be made for everyone" (NIV).

57. John 5:39.

58. 2 Tim. 2:15.

59. Ps. 32:8.

60. This implies a plenary view of the divine inspiration of scripture, i.e., all scripture is inspired, coupled with the view that various parts of scripture must be read differently, with the different intentions of various authors in mind.

61. This refers not merely to grace for repentance or grace to accept divine love, but to become established in it, i.e., sanctifying grace, (cf. Thomas Aquinas, *ST*, I-II, Q. 109–112, vol. II, pp. 1123ff.). She had been reading Robert Philip's *Devotional Guides,* Introduction by Albert Barnes, 2 vols. (New York: Appleton, 1837), which provided an instruction in the seeking of assurance of faith, *WOH,* p. 112.

62. Even after all the seeking of her past, the numerous resolves, the steady disciplines nurtured, and having participated for over a year in the Tuesday Meetings for the Promotion of Holiness, Mrs. Palmer still did not feel that she had received sanctifying grace in late June of 1837. But that was soon to change.

63. Cf. Wesley's sermon on "The Circumcision of the Heart," *WJW,* V, pp. 203ff., XI, p. 368ff.

64. Here the encumbrance to her further progress becomes evident to her:

idolatry—her tendency to idolatrize her husband and children. Once that is recognized and brought into the perspective of faith, the flood of the Spirit begins to rise.

65. By particularize (see also the entry of July 27, 1837) she appears to mean the act of dealing with each particular idolatry or creaturely temptation as a special, intentional act of penitence and consecration.

66. Gen. 14:22.

67. Cf. Ps. 51:6.

68. Charles Wesley, "And Let This Feeble Body Fail," *HMEC*, 1879, #1032, v. 4.

69. Cf. also *GTH* 1 (1839–40) 125ff.

70. This appears to be the precise identification of time (between 8:00 and 9:00 P.M., July 26, 1837) of her altar covenant. A long tradition of Wesleyan literature expecting instantaneous sanctification lies behind this precise concern for witness to a specific date and time. This must be strictly distinguished from conversion, which had occurred in Phoebe Palmer's case as a youth.

71. 2 Pet. 1:4.

72. 2 Cor. 7:1.

73. Cf. Lam. 3:24.

74. Following the advice of William Law, *A Serious Call to the Devout and Holy Life,* and Wesley. This narrative begins several days before July 26, 1837.

75. Being a "Bible Christian" meant that she would simply seek to receive the promises indicated in scripture, cf. *WJWB,* vol. 1, "The Almost Christian," pp. 137–42.

76. Wesley used the phrase, "holiness of heart and life," letter to George Downing, April 6, 1761, *LJW,* (Telford edition), IV., p. 146, and letter to "Various Clergymen," April 19, 1764, *LJW,* IV, p. 237; cf. Outler, *Theology in the Wesleyan Spirit* (Nashville: Tidings, 1975), pp. 65ff.

77. Joel 3:14.

78. 1 Cor. 6:19, 20.

79. Ps. 130:1.

80. Cf. Pss. 38:10, 42:1, 63:1.

81. Hymn source uncertain, not referenced in *DH, HMEC,* Codville or Baketel; however the theme of panting or yearning for heart purity is familiar in many Methodist hymns, among them, *HMEC,* 1879, #491, 501.

82. Probably John Stratten, who was appointed to the Allen Street Church in June 1837.

83. This question would again and again form the basis of her understanding of her specific calling to a given area of service. This visit probably took place on July 23, 1837, three days before her experience of sanctifying grace.

84. Showily dressed, sportively adorned.

85. Acts 5:1.

86. Here begins a series of temptations that will recur throughout the passage. This is the first ploy of the tempter: Are you not merely expressing egocentric interest in your testimony to grace?

87. 2 Chron. 20:17.

88. 1 Cor. 15:58.

89. This passage shows that her understanding of the Spirit's address to her is not without the written word, for it is the Spirit speaking through the word. This is what distinguishes her from much of the tradition of mysticism.

90. Rom. 16:12.

91. To know one's labor is "in the Lord" is to experience the Spirit's witness with our spirit that one's act is accepted, approved.

92. July 26, 1837.

93. This is the second assault. The account of her experience of full salvation is essentially told as a three way dialogue between her, the Spirit, and the adversary. At times a fourth party, a human conversant, appears in the dialogue, but this is largely a report of a three-voiced inward conversation. The psychological description of this dialogue is exceedingly subtle, and the reader is alerted to watch for its subtlety.

94. The third assault.

95. 2 Cor. 6:2.

96. Note that even before July 26, 1837, she had thought herself at times as wholly consecrated. Later she felt that she had on several occasions received, but lost, the blessing of sanctifying grace, as did Fletcher reportedly (cf. *PF*, pp. 159–61). White, *BH*, p. 261, is probably correct in arguing that Mrs. Palmer may have gained her impression of Fletcher's loss of sanctification from the diary of Hester Ann Rogers, August 24, 1781, "An Account," p. 201; cf. *GTH* 1 (1839):147f.

97. Later a lengthy debate would emerge out of this and other writings on sanctification, questioning whether there is any fundamental difference in justification and sanctification. Critics like J.M. Boland would argue that sanctification is indistinct from regeneration, and that holiness is accomplished in regeneration, cf. *The Problem of Methodism: Being a Review of the Residue Theory of Regeneration and the Second Change Theory of Sanctification and the Philosophy of Christian Perfection* (Nashville: Methodist Publishing House, 1888).

98. James 4:7. Many in the Protestant tradition would regard this as an exceptionally rigoristic doctrine of justification.

99. Cf. Ps. 63:8.

100. John 16:12.

101. I.e., lacking sanctifying or perfecting grace.

102. Cf. Ps. 73:28.

103. This covenant was distinguished from previous efforts at entire devotion by its absolute character of unconditionality and irrevocability.

104. Being united with God (Col. 1:15–23), being grafted into Christ's body (Rom. 11:17–36), partaking of God (2 Pet. 1:4; Hebr. 12:8ff.)—all these are themes familiar to ancient Christian piety and askesis, particularly in the Eastern Church tradition (Athanasius, *On the Incarnation of the Word, NPNF*, 2, IV).

105. The covenant to the holy life has the same unconditional and irrevocable character as betrothal; cf. Hosea 2:19.

106. The crucial aspect of particularization: All idols must be bound to the altar. Every created good that has the potential character of an idolatry must be given

up. Hence the placing of her relationship with that one most beloved—her husband, Walter—was preconditional to her readiness to receive sanctifying grace. Cf. James Blaine Chapman, *The Terminology of Holiness* (Kansas City, Mo.: Beacon Hill Press, 1947).

107. Cf. Ps. 73:26; Lam. 3:24.

108. She had often promised that God only was her Lord. If her husband had the potentiality of becoming a pretended substitute for God, then she must show willingness to render that relationship also unconditionally to God.

109. The fourth ploy of the Tempter in this inward drama, following previous ploys ("How much of self in this performance." "Don't be rash." "How do you know this is God's time?"): Isn't the sacrifice too great?

110. She viewed her decision by analogy with the prototype of faith, Abraham (Hebr. 11:8ff.), who trusted God's command to sacrifice his son, Isaac, even though Isaac's death would have jeopardized God's promise to bless many nations through the seed of Abraham. The purpose of the command was not fully understood while it was being obeyed—only later.

111. Cf. 1 John 4:16–18; 1 Cor. 13:8–12. Her unconditional obedience to God must be understood in eschatological context, the divine purpose not being fully knowable within current history, but only at the end of history. She had already given up her three children without knowing why, except that she trusted that in God's own time even that would be made plain. Now she was being required, as with Abraham's sacrifice, to be willing to give up her relation with that one most loved.

112. Walter.

113. The fifth ploy of the enemy appealed to her lack of complete self-knowledge: The whole consecration could be invalidated if *unconsciously* she harbored idolatries that were inconsistent with this one consecration.

114. Cf. Rom. 13:14.

115. That is, irrevocable in future time and universally including all worldly values and goods.

116. Though not dealt with in detail here, the answering of this question would become one of her major contributions, hinging on the altar analogy, and resulting in "the altar theology" for which she became noted. It is noteworthy here that she perceived this as a significant question from the very day of her consecration, and intuited its importance.

117. 1 Cor. 6:17.

118. Note that the guidance comes from the written word, and that the emotive life is not placed on a plane above the written word.

119. John 16:13.

120. It becomes a crucial point to her that sanctification is not attained on the basis of the evidence of the senses, but rather given by faith on the basis of the evidence of the Spirit speaking through Scripture. Cf. Wesley, *Plain Account of Christian Perfection, WJW,* XI, pp. 393–403; 446. Paul Bassett, in personal correspondence (June 2, 1986), writes concerning this pivotal distinction: "This point marks the Great Divide, as it were, between the Holiness Movement and most Pen-

tecostals, as well. I.e., even if there be authentically Christian 'glossolalia' (most Holiness people believe there is no such thing), it, in them, can neither be a way of attaining nor a means of confirming the grace of entire sanctification." It is this sort of guardedness on Mrs. Palmer's part that makes it difficult for some to see any connection between her work and that of later Pentecostalism, or to see her as a source of Pentecostalism.

121. John 17:17.

122. The sixth ploy, later to become the subject of several extended discussions.

123. Rom. 1:17; Gal. 3:11; Hebr. 10:38; cf. Hab. 2:4.

124. John 7:17.

125. The seventh ploy of the enemy: the fantasizing that there would never be any other evidence than the written Word for proceeding on this risky, life-shaping decision—i.e., there would be only Scripture without other immediate, experiential validations, and furthermore that such constricted means of validation could last an entire lifetime. Her answer to this provides the best evidence that Mrs. Palmer is not a pietist in the stereotyped image (see Albrecht Ritschl, *Justification and Sanctification,* Ernst Troeltsch, *Social Teachings of the Christian Churches,* II, and B. B. Warfield, *Lectures on Perfectionism*) of one who focuses upon private experience as opposed to scripture or objective criteria.

126. Cf. Hebr. 8:11.

127. 2 Cor. 6:17.

128. Cf. 2 Cor. 3:6.

129. 2 Pet. 1:21.

130. John 17:7.

131. The notion of "naked" (vulnerable, unprotected, undisguised) faith in the naked Word (i.e., with nothing added to it), is a crucial feature of this account. At this point in her experience, she says, all she had outwardly was the scriptural promise, "I will receive you," and her faith in the sufficiency of that Word. The same notion is found in John Wesley, "Letter to Mrs. Bowman," March 4, 1786, *LJW,* (Telford edition), VII, p. 322; cf. Joseph Benson, *Life of Rev. John W. de la Flechere,* p. 85; Charles White, *BH,* pp. 18ff., 261.

132. The adversary's eighth ploy.

133. Cf. 2 Cor. 1:14.

134. Luke 17:20.

135. Matt. 24:23.

136. Ps. 23:2.

137. Cf. 2 Cor. 10:5.

138. Cf. Isa. 30:15.

139. Cf. Isa. 59:19.

140. Cf. Gen. 17:7ff.; Isa. 61:8.

141. Cf. Isa. 1:18.

142. Cf. Phil. 2:13.

143. Charles Wesley, "Father, to Thee My Soul I Lift," *HUMEC,* 1850, #99, v. 5; last line should read "righteous word is thine."

144. Cf. Kant, *Fundamental Principles of the Metaphysics of Morals,* LLA, for whom moral response was never left to inclination, but at every step hinged on duty. It is unlikely, however, that Mrs. Palmer was in any direct way influenced by Kant, and more likely that she found these moral injunctions directly in scripture.

145. Here in her diary of a single day's experience is a concise outline of Palmer's way of holiness: There are three steps—entire consecration, faith, and witness or confession. These would be later refined and developed.

146. "Returnless" indicates the irrevocable unconditionality that distinguishes this act of consecration from all others. If revocable, it is not entire.

147. By confession she means public testimony, requiring daily attestation, to sanctifying grace.

148. Cf. Rev. 19:6.

149. The Cappadocian Fathers would have taken pleasure in the remarkable fact that often amid *ecstasis* her language becomes unselfconsciously and without apology trinitarian; cf. Gregory Nazianzen, *Theological Orations, NPNF* 2, VII; Gregory of Nyssa, *Dogmatic Treatises, NPNF* 2, V.

150. Despite her strictures against individualistic mysticism (lacking grounding in the written Word), her language in moments of ecstatic joy is often pervaded with the images of luminosity and the oceanic feeling so recurrent in the history of mysticism.

151. Here it appears that humility is learned by stages (an idea familiar to the ascetic tradition), in which the earlier stages do not grasp the formations to come in the later (cf. *Sayings of the Desert Fathers,* trans. B. Ward [London: Mowbray, 1975]). Subsequently, one of the most difficult criticisms her followers would face would be that the attestation of full salvation denied the virtue of humility. On the contrary, in her view, humility was intensified to its greatest degree in the awareness of the power of the Spirit to claim all.

152. Titus 3:5.

153. Cf. Methodist Hymn-book, 1908, #468, v. 4.

154. Verse begins: "If all the sins which men have done," but source uncertain—not in *DH, PWJCW, HMEC, HUMEC,* Codville or Baketel.

V

NURTURING THE HOLINESS
REVIVAL (1837–1843)

Immediately after her experience of July 27, 1837, Mrs. Palmer learned that she could not retain this blessing without testifying to its source. In Faith and Its Effects *(pp. 262–65), she recounted an incident at a camp meeting in August of 1837 in which she felt unavoidably challenged to become a reliable, special witness to this grace:*

A few days after I first received the witness of holiness,[1] I was at a meeting where there was a number of persons deeply agonized in spirit for the salvation of God. Some were groaning for justifying grace, and others for full redemption. O, thought I, if there were only some one here to talk about the simple way of salvation by faith![2] "Why do you not do it?" was suggested. O, thought I, it would require a *special* commission to undertake a duty so formidable;[3] for among the suppliants for full salvation were one or more ministers, and other persons of influence.[4] I was at a camp meeting, and I hastened to a retired place, that I might, without interruption, inquire of God. But I had scarcely knelt before I received the gentle chidings of the Spirit thus: "Did you not, in supplicating guidance for the day, ask that you might be filled with the knowledge of the will of God, and with all wisdom and spiritual understanding?" &c.[5] When you asked, did you not believe that you received the thing you desired?[6] Why then did you not let your conduct correspond with your faith, by acting promptly? . . .[7]

A short time after this I was at a love-feast. My heart was rejoicing in the blessedness of full salvation; and the privilege of sounding it abroad to the ends of the earth would, indeed, have been blissful. It was presented,[8]

You have mentioned it before in this church; and, perhaps, the most here have heard your experience on this point; and here are others who profess to enjoy this blessing, yet they do not speak so *definitely* nor so *often* on that subject, and it will appear more humble to be more reserved. I concluded I would not speak *definitely* of enjoying the blessing, but would leave it to be inferred. I rose to testify, but felt no liberty. I was startled, said but little, and sat down. I thought, Can it be that it was not my duty to speak? No, that duty was clear. If the Lord required the testimony, why did he not help me, was the next question? I inquired the cause. My Saviour was most graciously near and precious, and truly did I feel that he did not condemn me; but in love he assured me, that I had chosen my *own* way to speak, therefore I had not right to expect the special help of the Holy Spirit. . . .

I would urge the importance of looking well to the things which we have gained. A lesson once learned should ever be retained. We as parents would feel ourselves grieved and dishonored by a child who is ever learning, and never coming to the knowledge[9] which we desire to impart. Our heavenly Father is intent on teaching us the lessons of his grace, and if we will not learn otherwise than by *painful* experience, his love may move him to treat us accordingly.

Mrs. Palmer's Diary (scattered throughout the Memoirs, *which include also the letters) contains numerous kernels of insight that later became elaborated in longer writings. In the September 11, 1837, entry, for example, two crucial themes appear that have extraordinary subsequent influence: (1) the subordination of subjective emotion in favor of the address of the written Word of scripture, a strong Reformation theme in her thinking; and (2) the recognition of the importance of that crucial moment in her covenant to the life of holiness—the willingness to give up her most beloved object of affection, her husband—so as to put their relationship also in the hands of God. This was in her mind the "last barrier" to her sanctification. The testing of Abraham in the command to sacrifice his only son would henceforth become for her a principal metaphor of her own experience (*Memoirs, pp. 46–48):

September 11th.—The more I observe the motions of the Spirit on the hearts of others, the more I see that it is according to their faith it is done unto them.[10] Obstinate unbelief receives its punishment by a consequent delay. We must not reject the counsel of God against ourselves. It is our solemn DUTY, if by examining the Word, we can ascertain that we are of those to whom the promises in question are applicable, then it is our solemn *duty* to rely on them, whether our feelings warrant it or *not*. There is no test as a standard for our *feelings*, in Scripture, previous to believing, and if God has not placed one, where shall we fix it? Let us note the testimony of Scripture. If by trying ourselves by the word of God, we find we have but one evidence of Divine relationship, let us glory in this. It is by strong faith, not *feeling*, that we glorify God.[11] By the whole tenor of Scripture we are assured that the trial of our faith is permitted only for its more glorious establishment. I have felt that the Lord has led me peculiarly in this way. Glory be to His name!

Wisdom has marked all His footsteps.[12] He has led me in a way I knew not.[13] The counsels of His grace have been sweetly unfolded in their design and tendency, as I have been led onward. It seems to me now, that when an intimation is given, that in any way bears the impress of His spirit, by which I can recognize it as from Him, I could never again question or hesitate. The Lord grant that I may never disobey the voice of His spirit, or reject the counsels of His grace concerning me.

"Though fearful nature shrinking stand,
I'll follow on at His command."[14]

One circumstance that has a bearing on the above, I can but mention. It is this: the last object that was presented as a barrier to the entire sanctification of all my powers was my precious companion.[15] How natural would it have been for the unbelief of my heart to have exclaimed, "What! am I not permitted to retain this gift of God, connected with which is all my earthly happiness?" Blessed be His name, that the whispers of grace were heard, the voice of duty obeyed, and the absolute consecration of every power was made. Yes, grace conquered. The seal of the Spirit,[16] that I was then set apart, sanctified wholly to the service of the Most High, was given.[17] Why this last sacrifice was required, I then knew not, nor was it for me to question, but it has since been fully and satisfactorily explained. Before, there were always dregs in the cup of my enjoyment, if he was a partaker. My love, as I have since discovered, was far too exclusive. If I went even to the house of God, and experienced the visits of His grace, they were hardly prized to the same degree, unless he also was a sharer. But now, how different. Though my *genuine* affection has increased, I can see him go with a contented heart about his Father's business[18] in his own sphere, and I can go with a light heart to that assigned me. He is perhaps more useful, knowing that I am satisfied with his absence, and I *know* that I am far more useful now. Had I listened to the reasonings of nature so *seemingly* plausible, what would have been the result? The darkness of unbelief and the chidings of an unsanctified nature, unquestionably.[19]

By October of 1837, two months after her "day of days," she was still experiencing the daily sustaining power of grace (Way of Holiness, *p. 150):*

October 6. Still living in the enjoyment of a *present* salvation; my time has been so fully occupied of late, that I have not taken time to record the various loving kindnesses of the Lord as frequently as formerly; I have almost regretted this, for I ever prove it a blessing to be thus engaged, and then I find the review so inspiring for subsequent consideration.

I have been almost inclined to regard remissness in this, unless unavoidable, as remissness in *duty.*[20] But the record is written upon my heart, and I trust, by the help of the Spirit, that the record of my daily walk and my conversation may be a living epistle, read and known of all men,[21] during my life; and in the world above tell for ever on the records of eternity, to the praise and glory of God.

Acknowledging scripture, not her own subjective emotions, as her guide, she sought to develop a daily pattern of utter and unceasing divine praise (Memoirs, *p. 72):*

November 20th, 1837. I have felt, for some time past, most intense desires after conformity to God.[22] These breathings have not been unavailing. I would thankfully acknowledge that an increase of spiritual life has been the result, but I feel conscious that I do not indulge sufficiently in the spirit of praise. I would obey the divine injunction given by the apostle to his Hebrew brethren, when, after expatiating so conclusively on the all-sufficiency of the atonement of our great High Priest, now entered into the heavens for us, he says, ''By Him therefore, let us offer the sacrifice of praise to God continually, that is, the fruit of our lips, giving thanks to His name.''[23] How reasonable that this should be the ceaseless sacrifice of every heart, that feels momentarily the cleansing efficacy of His blood.

The ecstatic awareness of the Spirit's purifying presence was a recurrent theme of her 1837 diary (Way of Holiness, *p. 157; cf.* Memoirs, *Dec. 13, 1837):*

Diary, December 13th, 1837.—To-day I feel all the ardent aspirations of my soul sweetly centering in God. I do not feel that I have one desire apart from that which may promote his glory. He is my all in all. I at present enjoy ''the silent heaven of love.'' The beauty of holiness[24] more and more captivates my enraptured soul, and its requirements appear still more and more reasonable as I daily drink in its spirit. Spirit of Holiness! Continue to breathe upon me thy purifying, soul-transforming influences. My experience has uniformly corroborated the truth, that after every intense season of longing for more co[n]formity[25] to the Divine image, though the soul may not at that moment or hour, realize the attainment of the blessing, or feel a present answer, yet it is invariably given.

Mrs. Palmer struggled against her strong natural reticence toward speaking in public. She would have considered herself badly misunderstood if others derived the impression that she had some native talent for public communication (Memoirs, *p. 176):*

Diary, July 2nd, 1838.—Last evening, in the experience meeting,[26] grace triumphed gloriously over nature. In the early part of the meeting, I felt an unusual shrinking, when the duty of speaking was presented. I felt desirous to avail myself of the opportunity, if assured of its being duty; but the enemy, by repeated suggestions, endeavored to darken my mind.[27] I asked for the light of the Spirit, relative to the requirement, and then abandoned myself, soul and body, into the hands of the Lord. "I am thine," said my confident soul, and I felt conscious assistance from on high, while speaking of the riches of grace manifested toward me in the experience of the past week. I sat down feeling that Jesus was the strength of my soul. As the meeting progressed, rather an unusual backwardness was exhibited. I was impressed to tell them of the way in which I had been led into this wealthy place. Aware of the impropriety of always following impressions, without examining prayerfully the principles leading to action, I looked confidently to my Heavenly Father for guidance, and determined, if another pause ensued, to improve it. I did so, and found it peculiarly blessed, to be obedient to the motions of the Spirit.[28] A plain path seems marked out before me—the path of obedience.

She gained two hours from her busy day as a mother and a witness to God by rising early (4:00 A.M.), "redeeming the time" for intercession and scripture study. The experiment was so surprisingly fruitful that she determined to continue it (Memoirs, *p. 153):*

Diary, 1838.—Punctuality in my engagements with God, is necessary to my advancement. Shall the children of this generation, who have been declared wiser than the children of light,[29] rise up early, and sit up late, and eat the bread of carefulness,[30] to lay up corruptible treasures,[31] while the children of a King consume the early hours of the morning in sleep? He who redeemed me from the service of self and sin, rose while it was yet night, to pray.[32]

I well remember the shrinking of body and mind, when I first began to devise a plan for having uninterrupted time for devotion. I saw that the most eligible opportunity, and the only one that would positively warrant a precise hour of freedom from company, must be taken from the season usually devoted to sleep.[33] The spirit was willing, but the flesh was weak,[34] and for some time after I commenced this practice, by which I gained nearly two hours from my accustomed repose, I was inclined to question its expediency. I found, however, the strength of my spirit so increased, and my heavenward advancement so much accelerated by it, that I could not conscientiously discontinue the experiment. I felt that body as well as soul belonged to Jesus; that both were precious in His sight, and that He knew the sincerity of my motives.

I long more to be a proficient in the science of holy living,[35] and skilled in the art of heavenly warfare, than for any earthly attainment. Time spent in any engagement, not in some way conducive to this end, seems lost. Pleasure or pain, sickness or health were welcome, if assured that this absorbing object was gained.[36] Soon my health began rapidly to improve.[37] Soul and body were invigorated and refreshed, by the smile of Heavenly approbation. I rejoiced in the knowledge that God was pleased with the persevering spirit of sacrifice, in which I was enabled through His grace to persist in.[38]

2. TUESDAY MEETINGS FOR THE PROMOTION OF HOLINESS (1839–1840)

In 1839,[39] Phoebe Palmer and Sarah Lankford encouraged Timothy Merritt to launch the journal, The Guide to Holiness, *with promise of their support and written contributions.[40] This journal was in time to become the primary organ of communication of the holiness revivals over a long period of time (1839–1901),[41] and Phoebe Palmer would herself become its editor in 1864. Mrs. Palmer engaged in a constant ministry of conversation. She retained, however, a capacity to comment humorously on her own unsparing intensity in her diary of September 2, 1839 (*Memoirs, *p. 165):*

To-day has been very much taken up in seeing company, but I have reason to be very thankful that I do not have many trifling visitors. My friends seem to have learned what to expect from me, and if afraid of serious conversation, do not make long visits—unless they become interested in the subject which, in all companies, I feel it a duty to bring forward as most prominent.

In December of 1839 she was pastorally appointed by the Rev. J. L. Gilder to take sole charge of one of the class meetings,[42] "an innovation

on the usages of New York Methodism, '"⁴³ *according to Wheatley (p. 178).*
She set forth and maintained rigorous rules for these classes (Memoirs, pp.
178–179):

Diary, December 5th, 1839:
On Friday evening, I am to take the entire charge of a class. It is to be
formed principally of young converts. I thought it would be well to lay
down some rules by which I should be governed. First, I will ascertain
whether they are furnished with the discipline,—containing our rules, doctrines and usages,—and will labor to enforce the necessity of being thorough Methodists. Second. In order to more fully explain my meaning, I will
furnish each one with Wesley's tract, containing the "Character of a Methodist." Third. I will urge the subject of holiness as a fundamental doctrine.
The Wesleys having been thrust out to raise up a holy people, it consequently becomes their duty to rise up to that standard of experience. Fourth.
In order to keep the subject prominently before them, I will ask them to
covenant before God with each other, to pray at least three times a day for
the attainment of the witness in themselves. Fifth. I will cultivate by every
possible means, a sympathy of feeling among the members, by getting them
to bear one another's burdens.⁴⁴ This will serve to unite them together in
Christian love, and cause them to long for a return of the evening class-
meeting. Sixth. I will impress upon them the importance of praying for her
who has charge over them. May the Lord enable me to be faithful in this
department of labor; and may not the blood of one soul thus committed to
my care, be found upon me, in the day of eternity.⁴⁵

A self-examination after Christmas Day was written to Professor
Thomas C. Upham of Bowdoin College, a leading Congregational theo-
logian, after his auspicious visit to the Tuesday Meeting for the Promotion
of Holiness in December 1839. Professor Upham had come to New York
to supervise the re-publication of his widely respected Treatise on the
Will.⁴⁶ *He was brought, through the influence of Mrs. Upham, to visit the*
Tuesday Meeting. Upham was the first male participant in the Tuesday
Meetings, and the first of many ordained ministers and religious leaders that
would come for her mentoring. Mrs. Palmer entered into an extended dia-
logue with him that developed into a lifelong association.⁴⁷ Here, as early
as 1839, she is already realizing her vocation as a tough-minded counselor
to theologians, willing to admonish, and rigorous in her logic. This letter,
one of Mrs. Palmer's most thoughtful and subtle theological reflections,
was published in Faith and Its Effects, *pp. 339–52 (its last chapter; see also*
Guide to Christian Perfection, *1840, 2:86ff.; and* Tracts on Holiness, *No.*
16.)

No. LV.—To Rev. Mr. U.—.

Christmas day[48] was rendered memorable by my receiving more definite and confirmed views of the precise act of faith, which brings present salvation from all sin.

These views were preceded by an uncommon humiliation of spirit. During the day a temptation to hastiness was continually pressing upon me, and as the tempter had an object to act upon, the suggestion was, that I had, more or less, yielded to its influence. On examination, I could not bring the conviction that I had offended, and consequently did not feel condemnation; yet I was most deeply humbled, under a sense of my unworthiness. While confessing my want of higher degrees of holiness, and lamenting this before the Lord, I was led to question how it was, that I had been enabled to hold fast the beginning of my confidence,[49] and continually witness that the blood of Jesus cleanseth.[50]

I felt that I had not deceived myself, and could appeal to the Searcher of hearts[51] that it was not merely a blessing in *name* that had been gloried in, but an actual realization of his saving and cleansing power. Yes, thought I, in verity I do know, that the blood of Jesus cleanseth—*cleanseth now!* With feelings which even the recollections of that hour reproduce, causing tears of grateful joy, I could say with Paul, "To me, who am less than the least of all saints, is this grace given."[52] Yet, for reasons almost undefinable, but which perhaps cannot be more fully expressed than by saying, the appearance (in the eyes of some) of assuming, by professing this blessing, a higher state of experience than many others whose piety I so much venerate,[53] and especially some of Christ's beloved ambassadors, whom in love I highly esteem for their work's sake, I felt a shrinking tenderness of spirit,[54] relative to the testimony I had given before the world on this point. And yet I realized that the vows of God were upon me, and woe is me if I do not profess this blessing, and urge its attainableness on others. And must I continue to urge its reasonableness, even though it may assume the appearance of taking higher ground in the Christian walk?[55] I felt that I could weep, and even now do weep at the thought. But the plain, direct path, cast up for the ransomed of the Lord to talk in, still presented its track, lit up by the rays of divine truth, as luminously as ever. The way was not to be mistaken. I saw what would be the result of a willful turning, either to the right hand or to the left. It was a blessed thought that I had now given my influence into the hands of the Lord, and could unhesitatingly leave it there, and know that *duty* was mine, and *events* the Lord's.[56] I also most deeply felt that it was not because I was more worthy than others, that I had been enabled, for years past, to bear testimony to the possibility of living in the enjoyment of the *witness* that the blood of Jesus cleanseth from all unrighteousness.[57]

But I would not assume the ground, that I have not trespassed in thought word, or deed, since that time.[58] No. But in this, through grace, I will glory,—I have not, since the memorable hour that witness the entire consecration of all my powers, taken myself from off the altar, but have ceaselessly endeavored to present a living sacrifice of body, soul, and spirit.[59] Since that period, I have not felt as if any of these redeemed powers were for one moment at my disposal. When duty has been presented, however much nature may have shrunk from the requisition, I have been enabled to act upon the principle, that I have given myself irrevocably to God.[60] Though life might be the forfeiture, I have estimated the favor of my God better than life.[61] Neither have I, since that period, knowingly transgressed.[62]

Yet, I do not take this as the precise ground of my confidence; but this state of soul, in conjunction with an act of faith, which as a key opens the door, and brings the soul into the actual possession of full and complete redemption, is that which I have been enabled to render continually available, and by this I have been permitted to enter into that state of light and liberty which is spoken of [in] 1 John 1:7.

But what is this act of faith which brings the soul into the enjoyment of full salvation? By the help of the Lord I will state it, as also the way by which I continue its exercise. I saw that God had erected an altar, whereunto I was commanded to come with faith, nothing doubting.[63] And still further, that he did not require that I should believe, without a thorough foundation for my faith.[64] Perhaps I cannot better explain, than by adverting to what my expectations would be, if a will, which I knew to be in every possible way legally executed, were placed in my hands, and I authorized, from undoubted authority, in believing myself the rightful heir of an inheritance.[65] Would I hesitate in availing myself of its provisions, and think it mysterious that I was to come into possession by merely believing the validity of the document? And yet the knowledge of the fact, without the act of taking possession, would leave it just as unavailable for my present necessities, as though there were no such inheritance for me.[66]

Thus I saw that God had declared it his will, even my sanctification,[67] and that he had also rendered that will very explicit by the command, "Come out from among them, and be ye separate, touch not the unclean thing," conjoined with the declaration, "I will receive you."[68] In view of this declaration of my heavenly Father, had I any reason to doubt that it was his will, even my sanctification? What then remained for me, but, through the strength of grace, to "come out and be *separate?*" With this requisition I was enabled to comply. Would it not have been strangely inconsistent, after having come to this point, not to have believed that God would accept? And did it require any extraordinary effort of faith to believe that I was indeed one of his covenant people? It was thus, therefore, in the simplicity of my heart, I was ready to exclaim, Why, it is hardly of faith, but rather of knowledge; it is so easy.[69] It is all here. I have given myself wholly to God. He has accepted the offering, and sealed me irrevocably his. And would it not be strange, and in effect doing great dishonor to the faithful Jehovah, by an intimation of inconsistency, if, when he had required the entire surrender, and enabled me to comply, I were not to believe he would be true to his own part of the engagement?

But to get at the more definite answer that presented itself in reply to the inquiry, how I, so unworthy, was permitted to be clear in the enjoyment of this blessing, when there were so many whose piety I held in such high esteem who were not? The only explanation I could give was this: I have faith in God, and believe fully in the validity and feasibility of the plan devised by infinite wisdom, by which the polluted may be cleansed. . . . [70]

It is this implicit trusting in God, with a resolute determination not to proportion *faith* to *feeling;*[71] believing, if he permit your faith to be tried, by a seeming delay, it is only that you may be accounted worthy of being a more victorious example of its power;[72] which will produce a fixedness of purpose, and an established state of experience, beyond expression glorious. Look well to the terms. Holiness and sanctification most expressively signify the state intended. You cannot consistently expect it, until you make up your mind to live in the *continuous act of unreserved consecration*. Consequently, you *cannot* believe that there is an entire acceptance on the part of God, until you come to this point, even though you were as desirous, and should shed as many tears, by way of imploring the acceptance of your sacrifice, as did the ancient Jews, who covered the Lord's altar with tears, until he became weary, and regarded not the offering any more. (See Malachi ii, 13.) It is *unreasonable* not to live in the entire and continuous surrender of soul, body, and spirit, to God. All are *already* his, by the right of redemption. If you withhold aught, you keep back part of the price. It is, therefore, *unreasonable* not to be holy.[73] O then enter at once into the bonds of a covenant never to be broken, to be wholly the Lord's! Count the cost fully, and then lay the offering upon the altar. *While you present it, the blood of Jesus cleanseth.*[74] In the strength of Omnipotence venture now, and you will find, what you had thought to be the mystery of faith, simplified.

Yours, in the bonds of perfect love.

The story of Professor and Mrs. Upham's visit to the Tuesday Meeting was recounted in the diary (Memoirs, pp. 239–40):

January 3rd, 1840—On Tuesday, Mrs. Upham, wife of Professor Upham, of Bowdoin College, Maine, came to meeting. Though a member of the Congregational church, she has for several months, stood as a witness of the present attainableness of holiness, firm and unbending, among many who regarded her peculiar views as not only novel but unpopular. Difficulties arose in the way of her professing what God had done for her. The views of the denomination, discountenancing female speaking, was a great trial.[75] She was told that it must be a snare of the enemy; but grace sustained her, and enabled her to bear a noble testimony for God.

The simple testimony of a Methodist sister, led her to think there was something more for her, experimentally, to know. She resolved on searching the scriptures diligently,[76] to see whether the present enjoyment of holiness was a blessing, the witness of which might be expected in this life. She gave herself up wholly to the pursuit. Some of the Epistles she read and re-read, and the more she studied, the more confirmed was she, in the belief that it was not only her privilege, but her solemn duty to be entirely sanctified. She sought the blessing with all her heart, and entered into its enjoyment.

From that time, her husband, who for twenty-five years had been teaching others the way of life, became an object of intense interest. For several months, he was skeptical as to his privilege in reference to this blessing, but lately he has also been assured of the glory of his inheritance, and is now a witness of this grace.[77] His establishment in grace seemed peculiarly marked by the finger of God. He was called to the city to attend to the publication of a theological work—on the ''Will''—and Mrs. Upham was led to the Tuesday meeting. The spirit of freedom,[78] which invited inquiry and discussion, together with the clear witnesses of this grace, inclined her to ask the privilege of bringing her husband[79] the Tuesday following.

On Thursday, I had an interview with him, and it was rendered a mutual blessing. His views became clearer, and his desire for the present attainment of the blessing, more ardent. And here let me ascribe to the glory of God, the Divine influence, I realized, while answering the questions which he proposed. I felt that they were asked with a sincere desire to elicit truth. We parted, having spent the evening at my sister Lankford's, in a truly Christian manner.

On my return home, the burden of his soul was laid upon me with so much weight, that I continued for a long time, wrestling with the angel[80] of the covenant, in his behalf. I saw that the Redeemer's kingdom needed an advocate in the denomination of Christians to which he belonged,[81] in defence of this doctrine. Standing, as he did, with an important college, it was greatly desirable, that he should be a witness of its attainment.[82] I laid myself down for repose, but the spirit of supplication still continued, and my sleep was broken by the breathings of intense interest for this subject of solicitude. When I awoke in the morning, it was still pressing upon me. I arose early, and instead of what is usually my first exercise, praise and thanksgiving, I began immediately to unburden my soul with increased earnestness. My faith began to rise, and to lay claim to a present answer. "Is it not according to Thy will, that he should be *blessed now?*" I asked. I felt that it must be so. The manner in which his case had been laid upon my mind, assisted to the increase of my faith. The suggestion was made, that he would probably, at that hour, be asleep. But I remembered, what had been my exercise during the night. I felt confident that his must have been similarly exercised. I was reminded that I had asked, with a measure of faith, that he might not rest without the blessing. With these reflections, I urged my plea, and said, "Whether asleep, or otherwise, Thou canst bless; and O! grant him, even *now*, a manifestation of Thyself, and clear views of the simplicity of faith." I felt that my prayer was heard. I had asked that which was according to the will of God, and had received the thing I desired of Him, and prayer was mostly lost in praise.

The next evening, he came to the house, and I found that just about that time,[83] he had received a very powerful manifestation of the Spirit. Such a view of the simplicity of faith burst upon him, as seemed to bring a new creation with it; and now his cry is, *"O, the power of Faith!"*

I never felt more like devoting all my powers to God. While pleading for Professor Upham, I promised the Lord, if he would impart the blessing, I would, through grace, make it an especial subject of praise, not only through time, but also through all eternity, and that, if the entire devotion of my life to his service were in any way possible, it should, as a ceaseless thank-offering, be rendered.[84] I feel it a duty to make memoranda of such instances of His condescension, that they may enduringly stand as memorials of his loving kindness, for the confirmation of my faith.

The following letter to Mrs. Palmer's dear friend, Mrs. Mary D. James,[85] illustrates the way in which dream interpretation had apparently become a standard aspect of self-examination in the "promotion of holiness." The mystical experience of the holy Trinity is a recurrent theme of her religious history (Memoirs, pp. 96–98).

New York, November 17th, 1840
BELOVED SISTER:

I am reminded of a dream I had, I think the next morning after I parted with you. I seemed to be in social interview with two or three of the Redeemer's chosen ones.[86] When prayer was proposed, I thought: "O, I wish such a one would pray," for he was signalized in my mind as one strong in faith, and I wanted someone to pray, who would take me right up in the arms of faith, to Jesus. Immediately, a gentle chiding filled me with holy shame before the Lord, and the Spirit said, in language which I trust will ever rest as living truth on my heart, ''The Blessed Jesus will Himself take you up in His arms.'' I received the precious lesson with joy, saw I had been over solicitous about outside agencies,[87] and took courage. After this, I was permitted to enjoy a very blessed state of experience. Condescending love seemed to invite me to take the place of the beloved disciple.[88] I was conscious of the possession of that grace whereby I was enabled to feel the experimental blessedness of breathing out of my whole existence to God,[89] and in the language of my own heart; and the frequently expressed sentiment of my lips, was—

> ''While on His breast I lean my hand,
> And breathe my life out sweetly there.''[90]

My soul was wrapped in unutterable visions of glory. I hesitate in attempting to describe the inconceivable glory that passed before me.[91] I am at a loss for language, and I have been asking the Lord to empower me, so that I may be able to give some faint idea of it. The holiness of God was presented to my ravished soul, yet it did not seem inapproachable, like the burning bush.[92] No voice issued forth, but love,—infinite love. Such a joyous consciousness of *oneness* of spirit, such a consciousness of identity in this atmosphere of glory, in which I seemed to be bathing, when these words came with such power;

> ''A drop of that unbounded sea
> Is ours, a drop derived from Thee.''[93]

While beholding the unutterable glory, though no form of words was used, the *Everlasting Father* revealed immediately afterward, *Christ, the Gift of God,* and then I realized that the *Holy Spirit* was taking of the things of God, and showing them unto me. I never felt before in such blessed unity, the unity of the God-head.[94] While the vision lasted, the spirit of the words quoted above, ''a drop of that unbounded sea,'' was continually present with me, and soon afterward, these words were proclaimed, as in perfect unison of sentiment, ''Beloved, *now* are we the sons of God.''[95] O, the inexpressible glory!—my body shrank, unable to participate with the spirit in such excessive raptures, while the spirit struggled in its extreme joyousness, as if to disengage itself from the shackles of mortality. The effect of this manifestation has been hallowing. Pray, dear sister, that it may be permanently so. O, the beauty of holiness! My soul is increasingly captivated.[96]

3. FIRST BOOK:
MARY, OR THE YOUNG CHRISTIAN (1841)

Mrs. Palmer's first book, published without author identification, was Mary, Or the Young Christian. It serves as a splendid example of early Protestant Sunday School literature for young people, and also sheds light upon Mrs. Palmer's literary activities in her formative period as a writer around 1840. Professor Paul Bassett has correctly identified "Mary" as Mary Dagworthy Yard James (Mary D. James, previously referred to), born Aug. 7, 1810, the birth date of the "Mary" of this account.[97] *It seems fitting to include sections of this charming little book as an example of Mrs. Palmer's interest in the way in which pious youth of the early nineteenth century were brought up and experienced religion.*

That this is not merely a fictional account is seen in the full title: "Mary, the Young Christian—An Authentic Narrative By One Who Was Intimately Acquainted with Her from Her Infancy." It is unlikely that Mrs. Palmer would have chosen such a definite subtitle for an account purely fictional. It was published by Carlton and Porter, Sunday School Union, 200 Mulberry St., New York (Preface, 1840, copyright, 1841), a lower Manhattan address not far from where the Palmers lived, and a location frequented by them. The copy held by the United Methodist Archives at Drew University appears to be Mrs. Palmer's own copy,[98] *annotated by Mrs. Palmer herself, probably in preparation for a proposed revision that never occurred. In this edition, published in 1841, perhaps scheduled to be republished by the Sunday School Union, several manuscripts are attached (apparently in Mrs. Palmer's handwriting) that indicate that Mary, A Young Christian, is "A True Story, or Protrayings from real life of the model child of the finished home, by the author of the Way of Holiness, Faith and Its Effects, Incidental Illustrations, Entire Devotion, Useful Disciple, Sweet Mary, Promise of the Father, etc." If this was written by Mrs. Palmer, as it appears to be, and as the other attached manuscripts appear to be (one is signed by her in similar handwriting, an attached bill), then several probable indications are suggested: (1) Mrs. Palmer was quite likely considering republishing Mary, A Young Christian, first published in 1841, at some later date. (2) Phoebe Palmer and Mary Yard were childhood friends ("intimately acquainted with her from her infancy"). (3) Mary was not viewed by Mrs. Palmer as a fiction made from whole cloth, but a "portraying from real life," probably reconstructed from letters and diaries as well as personal conversations. (4) The purpose of the biography was the teaching of young people about entire devotion to God.*

It is clear from its September 1840 preface by John J. Matthias of West Bloomfield, New Jersey, that Mary was a real individual, known by Mat-

thias since 1831 until "the present time" (1840); Mary's health was frail; she displayed, like Phoebe, a "close application to literary pursuits"; and the motive of the writer was "to benefit the young Christian"—for Matthias expected that "pious youth will read this book." Until this work was discovered in the Drew Archives and distinguished from a later book by Mrs. Palmer entitled Sweet Mary *(London: Simpkin and Marshall, 1862), it was generally thought that her first book was* The Way of Holiness. *Only now has it become clear that her first book was this Sunday School curriculum story published more than a year before* The Way of Holiness *which was to make her reputation as a writer (*Mary,[99] *or the* Young Christian, *pp. 7–9):*

The subject of this narrative was born August 7th, 1810. From the earliest period of her recollection, her mind was seriously impressed on the subject of religion, and frequently most deeply concerned for the salvation of her soul. She enjoyed the unspeakable blessing of a pious mother, who from the first moment of her little daughter's existence, had fervently prayed, that she might be a child of God and an heir of heaven. To signify her solicitude that her little one might choose the good part, and ever sit at the feet of Jesus, she called her Mary.[100]

As soon as little Mary began to discern good from evil, her mother was continually endeavoring to lead her youthful mind to heavenly objects, and instill into it the principles of the blessed gospel; and she had the happiness to discover that her beloved child drank in the salutary instructions with an avidity which only equalled the ardent desires of her fond parent that she might be "made wise unto salvation."[101] Her inquiring mind was ever seeking to know "the things that belonged to her peace."[102] She asked many questions concerning her accountability to God, the state of the glorified in heaven, and the lost in hell, which her superiors in years and in wisdom could not satisfactorily answer. Thus left in the dark upon subjects which she deemed of vital importance, she would retire to her chamber, and strive by her own efforts to solve the mysteries which perplexed her, and implore the Source of all wisdom to enlighten her mind on the great truths of the holy gospel, whereby she might discern the good and the right way of the Lord.

When, through the volatility of her disposition, and the example of her young companions, she was led into trifling or rude behaviour, she felt great remorse of conscience, and wept and prayed for hours together, fearing she had offended God; and frequently did she resolve to engage no more with her associates in their plays and amusements, and rejected their invitations to join them in their little parties, lest she should bring condemnation on her soul, by incurring the divine displeasure . . . . When Mary had arrived at about the age of ten years, she gave her heart to God and became a decided Christian.[103]

At age ten, Mary experienced the assurance of her conversion. She had heard her grandmother say to her mother concerning her conversion, "I am the more astonished that you encouraged her in it,—for I am sure there can be nothing real or lasting in it."[104] *When Mary ran upstairs to pray (Mary, pp. 13–14):*

She had scarcely knelt down, before such a flood of divine light, and love, and joy as poured into her heart, that she was quite overwhelmed, and for some time scarcely conscious that she was on earth!

"The Omnipotent himself drew nigh,
And seal'd the gift himself had given!"[105]

He spoke to her heart the joyful words, "It is I, be not afraid![106] Thou art indeed my child; and now be strong! fear not; though earth and hell thy way oppose, I am with thee, to defend and preserve thee: cleave to me, and thou shalt be secure."[107] Now indeed her joy was full, for she felt that she was owned and blessed of God. She could now no more doubt the genuineness of her conversion, than she could doubt her natural existence.[108]

Mary attended a camp meeting at age eleven (September 1821). The account provides an intriguing glimpse of the sort of dialogue that must have occurred there among pious youth seeking religion. She reports her sense of penitence over having neglected scripture and prayer while visiting her friends in the country. Note the strong emphasis in the revivalism of the time upon sustaining the state of grace (Mary, pp. 17–18):

I[109] felt more than ever distressed on account of my unfaithfulness while in the country: I saw I had grieved the Spirit of God, and now my heart was all broken in pieces. I wept, and prayed, and asked others to pray for me; and while a servant of the Lord was praying for me, I fell to the ground by reason of the power of God;[110] for the tent seemed filled with his presence and glory. My heart too was soon filled with peace and joy, and I was restored to the blessed state which I had lost by that sad visit. For two weeks there was no interruption in my happiness; but after that Satan came in like a flood, and I was constrained to fight against the powers of darkness, which lessened my rapturous joys; but still my heart was fixed to do the will of God.

Mary's diary entries of the following winter (January–February 1823, Mary, pp. 20–25) reveal the inward struggle of a deeply pious youth seeking full salvation:

I cannot rest till I am wholly sanctified. Satan tells me I must not expect to get the blessing yet,—that I must fast and pray more, and struggle longer. But Jesus tells me now,—now is the time that I must look to him, and to him only, not so much to the *means,* that it is through *his merits alone* that I am to receive the blessing.

Jan. 10th.—Now I can go to rest in peace, and sleep in quietness, having the love of Christ in my soul. O, where shall I begin to praise him for his goodness to me! He has brought me to enjoy so much of his love, even while in my childhood! O, may I grow up to be a pattern of piety, and a pillar of the church of God; and when I leave this vale of tears, may I go to the realms above, where I shall have nothing to do but to love and serve my God for ever! It is now nearly two years[111] since I enlisted under the banner of Jesus, and he has kept me by his power until that time. I have had many temptations and trials; and sometimes I have not lived as near to God as I ought to have done.[112] But blessed be his name, he has upheld me by his gracious hand; and I am this moment a witness, that his precious blood cleanseth from all sin.[113] O, blessed be the Lord for what I feel in my soul! I would not exchange it for ten thousand such worlds as this.

Feb. 2nd.—This day my soul has truly been fed with heavenly food. While partaking of the Lord's supper, my heart was melted to tenderness, and mine eyes to tears. I feel stronger in the faith than I ever did before. The path of holiness grows brighter and brighter. My peace is like a river. . . . [114]

Feb. 15th.—To-day I have been conversing with the people of the world a great deal, and have had many temptations. But they have not prevented me from enjoying communion with my God. Satan often tried to make me believe that I have been deceived concerning the great blessing of perfect love,—that I did not receive it, when I supposed I did; but I feel that Jesus reigns in my heart *without* a rival, and he fills my soul with his love from day to day. I am sure, if I were in a delusion, I should not be so happy. Sometimes I am lost as in an *ocean of love* and seem to forget that I am still an inhabitant of earth. . . .

Feb. 27th.—This evening I went to a love feast. It was indeed a feast of love to my soul. I thought I would not speak, as I had spoken so often; but "the love of Christ constrained me"[115] to declare the goodness and mercy of the Lord to me. These words were spoken to my heart, "Open thy mouth wide, and I will fill it."[116] *I obeyed,* and the *promise was verified to me.* O! blessed be the Lord for ever, for what I enjoy of his love![117]

The pastor was looked to for spiritual guidance by young people
(Mary, pp. 35–39):

Rev. J.L.[118] was a friend to Mary, whom she will ever remember with
the warmest gratitude. He succeeded Rev. S.S. in the pastoral charge of the
church of which Mary was a member. As soon as he arrived in the place of
her residence, he inquired, "Where is little Mary?" On her being introduced to him, he took her hand, and then affectionately said, "This is the
little girl that father S. told me to *nurse,* is it? Well my dear, I will try to
take care of the lambs of my flock; and I am happy to find that you are one
of them."

He did indeed fulfill his promise. During the two years in which he
was her pastor, Mary was an object of his special care. . . . [119]

A poignant account follows of the intense struggle of Mary's mother
with feelings of damnation, and how Mary became significantly responsible
for bringing her parents into fellowship with seekers of holiness (Mary, pp.
36–44):

Mary's mother was a truly pious woman although at the time that her
daughter made a profession of religion she was not a member of any church.
Yet for a number of years she had enjoyed the comforts of divine grace.
Soon after Mary joined the Methodist Episcopal Church, she was induced
to do so likewise, from a conviction of duty as well as the urgent solicitation
of her daughter. It may not be improper here to relate the circumstances of
her conversion, as it may tend to show the moving power of gospel truth,
and magnify the grace of God.

After she had been married for some years and spent all the early part
of her life in gaity and folly, though not without frequent admonitions of
conscience, she was one day standing before a looking-glass, adjusting her
hair, and arranging her dress, when she was suddenly arrested by the Holy
Spirit, and saw herself in the gospel mirror as "poor and miserable, and
blind, and naked,"[120] a guilty sinner, exposed to the indignation of a just
and holy God. . . . She accordingly commenced the great work of seeking
her soul's salvation in earnest; but while thus engaged she was visited by a
minister of the gospel, who endeavoured to persuade her that the work was
already wrought, and that it was now her *duty* to be *baptized;* and that she
must come forward and do her duty, and then she would be happy. He did
not cease to urge her till she finally yielded, though with some reluctance.
Hoping that her mind would be comforted by the performance of what she
was taught to believe was required of her, she was induced to comply, and
went forward. But alas! she was disappointed. She found that being im-

mersed in the water had not the efficacy to wash away her sins. Her distress of mind increased after her baptism; and fearing that she had sealed her damnation by taking upon herself the profession of religion when she was yet in an unregenerated state, she sunk into despondency, and for two years afterward was incapable of attending to her family concerns. Her agony of mind was almost insupportable, believing as she did that she was a reprobate, and must inevitably be lost. One sabbath morning she was solicited to go to Methodist meeting, but manifested much reluctance, saying, "It will do me no good,—there is no comfort for me,—my doom is fixed,—I am lost for ever!"

Her prejudices had been strong against the Methodists. From her infancy she had been taught to look upon them as ignorant fanatics. And she had little hope of being benefited at one of their meetings. She concluded, however, to go; for she thought it could not increase her wretchedness, and she would hear what they could say. Against one of the preachers she entertained a particular antipathy, and *him* she thought she *would not hear.* But it so happened that soon after her arrival at church, this very preacher arose in the pulpit to commence his discourse. She was about to leave the house, when the thought occurred to her, "How unbecoming it will appear for me to go out just after having seated myself; I will try to endure it, and stay till meeting is over."

He announced his text. It was 2 Cor.13.5, "Examine yourselves whether ye be in the faith; prove your own selves; know ye not your own selves, how that Christ is in you, except ye be reprobate?" She thought, "Well, I was unspeakably wretched before, but now, my agony is to be increased by hearing my awful doom. I am indeed a reprobate, and soon I shall realize all the horrors of my dreadful destiny." As the minister proceeded in his discourse, light shone upon her darkened soul, and she thought, "Why, every word is for me!—surely some one has told him all about me,—and even of such as sinner as *me* he says *there is mercy. . . .*"

Most gladly would this newly released captive have immediately united herself with the votaries of the blessed doctrine through which she had been set free, but she was prevented by the opposition of her husband. She, however, regularly attended the ministry which had been rendered so great a blessing to her; and the people whom she had before despised were now greatly to be loved by her, and no privilege was so sweet to her as to mingle with these devoted servants of the Most High in their devotions.

Years had passed away since the happy period of her conversion, when she saw her little daughter go forward to unite her with these people of God; and she would fain have accompanied her, but was restrained by the same reason which had at first hindered her. . . .

It must be asked with reference to Mary's joining the Church, How did she obtain her father's consent, while it was denied to her mother? Mary at first also anticipated opposition, and presenting her cause before the Lord, and fervently praying that he would change her father's heart to accede to her wishes, she felt a strong confidence to believe that her desires would be accomplished. One day, when he was alone, she approached him and throwing her arms around his neck, with tears in her eyes she asked him, if he would not grant her the privilege of joining the Methodist Church? He at first hesitated, but seeing his daughter so extremely anxious, he looked affectionately at her and said, "My dear, why do you desire to become a Methodist?" She replied, "I want to *get to heaven*, father, and I think it will be a great help to me in the way to heaven, to join the Methodist meeting." He said, "Well, if you think it will do you any good, you may do so, but I cannot consent for you to attend the *night meetings.*"

Young converts who had received the blessing of salvation were expected to witness to it (Mary, pp. 82–83):

When Mary attended school, she was in the habit of conversing with her schoolmates on the subject of their eternal interests. On one occasion, when her teacher was absent, and she was left as monitor, she introduced her favourite topic, and with much earnestness urged them to seek *then* that heavenly treasure, which was the joy of her heart.

Mrs. Palmer's account of Mary's youthful religious journey concludes with this counsel to vigilance (Mary, pp. 87–88):

An extract of a letter written by Mary to one of her associates will perhaps be to the point here:—

"While in this world we are in a state of warfare. We have a mighty *triple* foe to contend with, and *three weapons* are necessary in order to vanquish our enemy: vigilance, prayer, and diligence in duty. *These,* if kept in vigorous exercise, will effectually subdue the powers of earth and hell, which ever and anon our way oppose. All-conquering, indeed, they are— for if you are ever *watching* you cannot be *ignorant* of the approach of the enemy—consequently, he cannot take you by surprise. If ever praying, you will continually be receiving supplies from above, which will form an invulnerable *coat of mail,*[121] as it were, around you that will repel the darts[122] as soon as they are thrown, and they will fall powerless at your feet.

And if diligently running in the way of the Lord's commandments, the adversary cannot possible reach you. Always keep in mind this one blessed truth, that Satan cannot harm you while you *keep in the path of holiness.*"

4. INCREASING INFLUENCE OF THE
HOLINESS REVIVAL WITHIN METHODISM
(1841–1843)

Beginning about 1840, Mrs. Palmer increasingly became influential among leading figures in Methodism. She had attended her first Methodist Episcopal Church General Conference of May 1840 in Baltimore,[123] the home of her husband's parents. Upon hearing acrimonious debates at the Conference, she confessed her dissatisfaction with church policy decision-making devoid of spirituality (Memoirs, p. 259):

I know I may be thought by some, to be too contracted in my views, but it is an established truth in my mind, that should the spirit of holiness preside, these conflicting opinions would be much more easily tranquilized. "Charity hopeth all things, believeth all things, is not easily provoked."[124]

Her growing commitment to a ministry to ministers is seen in her Diary reporting the New York Conference of 1841, where the Mary and Martha metaphor was poignantly employed (Memoirs, pp. 163–164):

On May 10th, 1841, the New York Conference[125] commenced its sessions in the Allen Street Church. Being in the immediate neighborhood we were favored with much of the company of the Lord's annointed ones. In part, I took Martha's place; although I believe I had Mary's heart,[126] I enjoyed sweet fellowship of spirit with some of these beloved ambassadors of the Lord,[127] but I am fearful that the first few days were not quite so profitably spent as they might have been. Conference business was absorbing during the hours they were in. I thought possibly I might not be called upon to urge so prominently the subject so important to me.[128] As there did not appear much of an opening as usual, I feared an abatement of zeal, and I began to inquire resolutely the cause. My mind reverted to the fact, that I had been less definite in urging the necessity of a present witness of holiness. Though I could not refer to any opportunity neglected, I did not feel perfectly satisfied with the course pursued. In the afternoon a brother came in. I darted prayer to heaven, that if I had been in any measure laboring under temptation, that it might be dissipated by the effort I was about to make. I spoke more pointedly than usual, and was powerfully tempted to think that the brother would consider me officious. But I felt my own courage rising immediately after the effort, and a joy in the thought that I had tried to do my duty. This dear minister in a few days sent me word, that he had been greatly blessed through that afternoon's conversation.

Memorandum.—I solemnly covenanted with God on Friday, the 12th of June, that if He would condescend to bless that effort, I would endeavor thereafter, under similar temptations "that perhaps it is not *duty* to be so explicit in urging the subject,—especially to ministers,"[129] to regard it as the voice of any enemy; and to be more truly "instant in season and out of season,"[130] than I have heretofore been. The Lord helps me to keep my covenant.

By 1841 she was travelling more and more, declaring her dual witness of pardon and purity both to laity and clergy. From Mount Holly, New Jersey, she wrote her husband a sympathetic letter that nonetheless explained how difficult it had been to get time to write, and "that I do not know what to say about coming home" (Memoirs, pp. 260–61):

Mount Holly, N.J.,
November 22d, 1841

My Precious Husband:

Will not wonder that the interests of the kingdom of God, still keeps me from him, when I tell him that I know that He has permitted me to be in a measure helpful in bringing about the establishment of this blessed kingdom, in the hearts of others, during my absence. I know that your heart will exult; I was about to say, I know you will not repine at the thought of my absence,[131] but I shrank from the very mention of the word repine, when the interests of the Master are served by our being parted in the flesh. "We part in body, not in mind."

"Our minds continue one;
While each in sweet communion joined,
We hand in hand go on."[132]

O, how sweet I find it, to present to my God, you, my beloved, and those precious little ones. Kiss them for me; tell them that Ma sends one hundred kisses each.[133]

I find it a sweet privilege to present all the members of my household, through Jesus, before the throne of God, morning and evening.

She requested the special prayers of her friend, Mary D. James,[134] when, under fire for her views on holiness, she felt that she needed wisdom to respond rightly. This letter reveals her developing thinking about her special vocation as a woman called to public witness to pardon and purity (Memoirs, pp. 264–65):

New York, December, 1841

To Mrs. James:
Since my return, my hands have been full. A variety of pursuits seem to engage every moment. I can say with truth,

"With me, no melancholy void,
No moment lingers unemployed,
Or unimproved below."[135]

I have been attending meetings in Jersey City, of much the same character as those at Burlington; I cannot describe to you the weight of responsibility I at times, feel to be resting upon me, in view of these various calls, as they seem to be accumulating.[136] By the manner in which I am sustained, I have no reason to think otherwise than that the invitations I receive, and the providential openings which seem to say, "Go forward," should be regarded as the voice of God.

Those extraordinary outpourings of the Spirit which I am often led to anticipate,[137] as a proof to others that I am called to this peculiar work,[138] as Moses and Gideon,[139] seem to be delayed. The Lord gives me liberty of speech, favor in the eyes of His servants, and the affections of those to whom I endeavor to be useful. Notwithstanding all this, I am tempted with the suggestion, that an extraordinary work, should, to prove its validity to others, be accompanied with more extraordinary effects.[140]

I often think of the words of the beloved Fletcher, "We will not ask signs, Polly."[141] It was the sin of Israel that they asked signs. And my heart says, "Lord, I will not, as Gideon, ask signs."[142] It is enough that I hear Thy voice. Thou hast said, "Ye have need of patience!"[143] And Thou art proving me; Shall I repine? The Lord blesses my labors, and the blessed portion of the word, "For as much as ye know that your labor is not in vain in the Lord!"[144] causes me to triumph. O, bless his name!

I am at present placed in very responsible circumstances. Can you not meet me daily at the throne of grace, at two P.M.?[145] Pray especially, that I may have *wisdom* to direct in every step. It is in reference to the articles I have written on holiness. I fully believe the hand of God is in the whole affair, for good.

The ecumenical character of her work was enriched and intensified in the summer of 1842, when she was invited by the Presbyterian minister of Newburgh, New York, to make her witness there. The outcome reveals how difficult it was for Presbyterian ministers to become associated with her effort, and the costly nature of ecumenical risk. Her ministry of hospitality—

especially directed to ministers—subsequently became extended to ministers and laity of many denominations, notably Presbyterian, Anglican, Baptist, Congregational, and Quaker (Memoirs, pp. 197–99):

Diary, August, 1842.—Have been permitted to enjoy an interesting interview with the Rev. Mr. Hill of Newburg, Pastor of the Presbyterian church, of that place. A month since, I was solicited to attend a meeting where a number of friends of the Presbyterian, and other denominations, were convened, to talk and pray on the subject of Holiness. The meeting was social in its character, and not only brothers, but sisters also,[146] were invited to give in testimony in reference to the subject. When brother Hill was introduced to the meeting, and expressed his hearty belief of the doctrine, theoretically, and his intense desire to know experimentally, of its blessedness, a deep sympathy of soul seized me, and a burden which found its only relief in bearing his case to a throne of grace.[147] His deep humility and ardent expressions, reminded me strongly of what I had pictured to my mind of a Fletcher. I asked the Lord for a message that might touch his heart. I felt that my request was granted, but the time was so short, I did not deem it expedient to say all that was in my heart. In the afternoon, I anticipated an opportunity to say what still remained on my heart as a burden, but the same cause as in the morning, influenced me. For two or three days succeeding, I continued to feel so assured that my testimony to that brother was unfinished, that I at last yielded to what appeared to be the solicitations of duty, and consented to write, what I would have communicated to him at the meeting . . . .

Brother Hill did not come with the intention of staying that night, but during the evening, became so deeply absorbed in wrestling prayer, in which we alternately engaged, that it was midnight, before he seemed to be aware of it, and he staid with us, not only all night, but until near noon of the next day.[148]

During the deep exercises of the evening, he felt that he was enabled to lay all upon the altar, but did not become quite so clear, in the witness of its acceptance, as he desired.

On the day of his arrival, I had set apart a room, that had lately become unoccupied, for the more especial use of God's servants; or, as I said before the Lord, while dedicating it to his service, a "prophet's chamber."[149] How little did I then imagine, that its acceptance was to be so signally given, and so soon. But it was sweetly hallowed by this servant of Christ. The last sound, as I fell into the repose of sleep, was praise and prayer, and the first that reached my ear in the morning, was the same blissful sound. "Bless the Lord, O, my soul, and forget not all his benefits."[150]

On Wednesday, we went in company with him, and several other

Christian friends, to Newark, to attend a meeting similar to the one in New-burg. My dear husband accompanied us. O, what a blessed day is ushering in upon us! Christians of different denominations meeting on one common ground, "Holiness to the Lord. . . . "¹⁵¹ But a short time since, and the most of them would have condemned as fanatical, and perhaps as almost heretical, a female, that would dare give in a testimony for God, before the Church. Now, they invite and urge such testimonies.

Only a few days later she would write (Memoirs, p. 267):

RAMAPO VALLEY
Monday, August 22d. [1842]

Here we again met with our Presbyterian brethren, spoken of before. Brother Hill's noble testimony had led two into the belief of full salvation, while their united testimony led many to the Saviour. They were as flaming torches, filled with the Spirit. In a couple of weeks, they will be called to answer before the Presbytery, for what is termed by that body, "heresy." But if the Lord is as eminently present with them, as at this time, they have nothing to fear.

Will it be believed a score of years hence, that men were arraigned before an ecclesiastical tribunal of this description, for no other reason, than that of declaring as their belief, that man may be cleansed from all unrighteousness in this life,¹⁵² and be enabled to fulfill the great command, "Thou shalt love the Lord, thy God, with all thy heart, soul, mind, and strength"?¹⁵³

For this peculiarity of belief, these brethren will probably be condemned, as guilty of heresy.

By June 7th, 1843, The Way of Holiness had been published. In presenting several copies to Rev. Leonidas Hamline, editor of the Ladies' Repository, who became her lifelong friend, and who was soon to be elected a Methodist bishop, she wrote (Memoirs, p. 481):

On giving the numbers into the hands of the printer, it was thought they would make a fair volume,¹⁵⁴ but the sequel proved that the printer, as well as ourselves, was mistaken, and so it was insisted by my dear husband, that I should furnish other matter. I could conceive of nothing more proper than "Notes by the Way," the taking of which from childhood had been rather a favorite pursuit with me. I have therefore condensed the "Notes," taken during the two or three first years of my journeying in the way of holiness, with the hope that they may be, in some degree, helpful toward illustrating the nature and privileges of the way.

Notes

1. Another incident somewhat similar to this is reported in *F&E,* p. 84 (cf. *GTH* 1 [1839–40: 210]), in which she felt called upon, for the first time, to first testify to her experience of the reception of sanctifying grace at the Tuesday Meeting, August 1, 1837, "that I might have clear, enlightened views of the *precise* ground upon which I obtained, and might retain, this blessing."

2. This question became the motivating energy of her subsequent vocation. It also shows that she thought of her activity in classical Protestant language as being a simple expression of salvation by faith.

3. She assumed or felt, at this early stage, that she needed a special commission in order to witness. Whether she was referring obliquely to ordination or something analogous to it is unclear. In any event, it seemed out of reach. This would soon change, and by 1859 she would write *The Promise of the Father* in forthright defense of women bearing public testimony.

4. Her vocation to witness to sanctifying grace was made doubly difficult by the fact that she thought it to be the duty of ordained ministers, and she could not think of aspiring to be ordained herself; yet it was evident that this witness was not being adequately accomplished by the ministers she knew.

5. Cf. Eph. 1:17.

6. Cf. Mark 11:24.

7. This reveals a key principle of her understanding of the relation of faith and action: faith not acted upon or attested. Genuine prayer risks taking itself seriously.

8. The demonic temptation urged her not to speak explicitly of the fullness of grace.

9. Cf. 2 Tim. 3:7.

10. Matt. 9:29

11. Mrs. Palmer is due credit here for battling against one of the commonest criticisms of revivalism: excessive and unrestrained emotivity.

12. Cf. 1 Cor. 1:24.

13. Cf. Lam. 3:2.

14. Cf. Mark 2:14; hymn source uncertain—not referenced in *HUMEC, HMEC,* Codville, Baketel, *PWJCW,* or *WJWB* 7; for a similar metaphor, see *HMEC,* 1879, #431.

15. Walter; see July 26, 1837, above.

16. Cf. Eph. 1:13.

17. This passage makes clear the connection in her mind between giving up her most resilient idolatry (her husband), and the readiness of the Spirit to cleanse her from all sin and sustain her growth in grace.

18. Cf. Luke 2:49.

19. This is an intensely complex and subtle psychological analysis of the relation of Walter and Phoebe prior to July 1837. There were dregs in her enjoyment of God because she so desperately wanted to share with Walter all experiences of the visitation of grace. After July 1837, she was willing to let both him and herself go about their Father's business, granting greater distance, and perhaps to some de-

gree relieved of the compulsive need to reveal all to one's partner. Able to be "satisfied with his absence" (one wonders if she might have suffered separation anxieties prior to this time), she now experienced greater lightness of heart and enjoyment of her marriage relationship, once the compulsive quality had been reduced. This was based upon her decision no longer to idolatrize Walter, the basic turning point in her sanctification (cf. Oden, *SA,* part II, pp. 147–155 on the idolatrous intensification of anxiety).

20. Her motives for keeping a spiritual diary (it having been recently neglected due to her intense involvements) were primarily for her own edification and review of progress as an act of daily praise.

21. Cf. 2 Cor. 3:2

22. Cf. Rom. 8:27, 12:1ff., i.e., the desire to be conformed to the divine image revealed in Christ (Phil. 3:10).

23. Heb. 13:15

24. Ps. 29:2.

25. Misprint in original text: comformity; cf. Rom. 8:29.

26. It was called an "experience meeting" because it sought to enable the experience of the holy life, full salvation.

27. A year after her experience of July 1837, she was still struggling inwardly over the third point of her entire consecration: public testimony or confession.

28. A functional distinction seems to have been presupposed here between "following impressions" (i.e., following one's emotive flow, "without examining prayerfully the principles leading to action"), as distinguishable from obedience to the Spirit speaking through the written Word. These are not synonymous.

29. Cf. Luke 16:8.

30. Ps. 127:2.

31. Cf. Matt. 6:19. The rhetorical question suggests: Are those who are diligent in worldly enterprise, who on the basis of self-interest have sufficient determination to get up early, wiser than the sleepy faithful?

32. Cf. Luke 6:12, referring to Jesus.

33. The difficulty of this commitment must have been increased by the fact that she was at this time the mother of small children.

34. Mark 4:18.

35. She regarded holy living primarily as an experiential practice as well as an art, but also as an object of study, an intriguing puzzle about which much more could be known through appropriate inquiry.

36. She appears to be not disturbed by illness except when it should seem meaningless in her experiment in the science of holy living.

37. A debate has continued as to whether Mrs. Palmer's holiness revival placed an emphasis upon healing. In passages such as these, it becomes clear that she herself had moved from sickness to health during this period of radical dedication. She had suffered much illness during the previous early years of her marriage. It was precisely in connection with this rigorous spiritual discipline that she understood her own physical strength to return. Nonetheless, by saying, "pleasure or pain, sickness or health, were welcome . . . ." she showed a remarkable de-

tachment (*apatheia*) from physical circumstances, understanding clearly that spiritual health and growth were more a primary concern than physical health. Such beliefs would never fuel a physical healing revival for which is required an absolute conviction that all sickness is unequivocally evil and must be eliminated through the power of faith.

38. Double preposition in text.

39. The same year that Asa Mahan wrote the *Scripture Doctrine of Christian Perfection* (Boston: D.S. King, 1839). King would later become editor of *GTH*.

40. Her first article: "Letter From a Lady to Her Friend," *GTH* 1 (1839).

41. For an overview of the literature of the holiness revivals, see Donald W. Dayton, *The American Holiness Movement*, (Wilmore, Ky: Asbury Theological Seminary, 1971); Dieter, *HRNC;* Jones, *PPHAM;* cf. John E. Ayars, *Holiness Revival of the Past Century* (Philadelphia: John E. Ayars, n.d).

42. For a discussion of the nature and functions of the class meeting, see John Miley, *Treatise on Class Meetings* (Cincinnati: Poe and Hitchcock, 1866). Later, as professor of systematic theology at Drew Theological School, Miley would become an advocate of that view of sanctification that sees it as distinct from regeneration, but allowing for a gradual process of continuing growth (Miley, Systematic Theology, 2 vols. [New York: Hunt & Eaton, 1984]; cf. Peters, *CPAM,* pp. 159ff., 175ff.).

43. Due to her gender.

44. Cf. Gal. 6:2.

45. Her shepherding responsibility is viewed in the radically serious light of Ezek. 34.

46. Thomas Cogswell Upham, (1799–1872), *A Philosophical and Practical Treatise on the Will* (New York: Harper & Bros., 1853), later designated as "one of the first original and comprehensive American contributions to psychology" by Frank Hugh Foster, *A Genetic History of the New England Theology* (Chicago: University of Chicago Press, 1907), p. 249. Subsequently Upham would contribute to sanctification theology by writing *The Principles of the Interior or Hidden Life, Designed Particularly for the Consideration of Those Who Are Seeking Assurance of Faith and Perfect Love* (Boston: D.S. King, 1843). His book on *A Treatise on Divine Union* would be published by the Palmers, (New York: Walter C. Palmer, Jr., 1870), and many of his articles would appear in *GTH*. He also wrote *The Life of Faith*, (Boston: Waite, Pierce, 1845); and *The Life and Religious Opinions and Experience of Madame de La Mothe Guyon*, London: Allenson, 1908.

47. See *Hughes, Fragment Memories of the Tuesday Meeting and the Guide to Holiness and their Fifty Years Work for Jesus* (New York: Palmer & Hughes, 1886), *TM1,* pp. 27, 28; *F&E,* p. 170; *Memoirs,* pp. 238ff.

48. Probably drafted originally just after Christmas 1839, since it appeared in the *Guide to Christian Perfection, GTH* 2 (1840): 26. It is by inference, and not direct identification, that this letter appears to have been addressed to Upham. The internal evidence strongly suggests that Upham is its recipient. It reveals her intellectual strengths and capacity for self-critical dialogue, willing to match wits with a splendid theological mind.

49. Cf. Hebr. 3:14.

50. Cf. 1 John 1:7.

51. Cf. Ps. 139:23; Rom. 8:27.

52. Eph. 3:8.

53. She was keenly aware of the temptation to deception which would imagine a higher state had been entered into.

54. Cf. Wesley, *WJW*, VII, pp. 191ff., on a "tender conscience." She was not unaware, as an attestor of holiness, of her own continuing fallibility, human frailty, finitude, temptability, and weakness. She continued to evidence a healthy capacity for self-criticism. This realism appears to have conflicted at times with her strong sense of duty to witness to the way of holiness. She felt a strong moral claim, based on scripture, to profess that she had received sanctifying grace. In the light of this, however, there was disinclination to seem to be morally superior, especially in relation to elders who would be expected to be far more experienced in the Christian life. In times of such a "shrinking tenderness of spirit" as she was now reporting, she candidly expressed this tension. Wesley was spared such wrestlings, since he did not publicly claim to have attained entire sanctification in a sustained way, ("not as though I had attained," Phil. 3:12, *WJW*, VI, pp. 1ff., 506ff.), yet still powerfully preached the possibility of a life unreservedly claimed by grace.

55. The apparent dilemma: if the blessing is prematurely or conspicuously professed, it tempts to pride, and tends easily to self-deception, and seems to lock one into not freely admitting continuing sin; yet if not professed, she was convinced that faithful following in the way would not be sustained. This is what made her position so poignant, when taken with utter moral seriousness.

56. A powerful image suggesting the release of control, and willingness to following in obedience to the Spirit.

57. 1 John 1:7. For years, at least since 1831, she had been living in the midst of a community in which this witness to sanctifying grace was being attested.

58. Those who look for some acknowledgement in Mrs. Palmer that she had fallen short of the mark after the reception of sanctifying grace can find her response here.

59. Cf. Rom. 12:1. The decisive point is not that she had not faced temptation or trespassed since July 1837, but that she had not taken herself from the altar.

60. Note that irrevocability is the one quality that distinguished this covenant from lesser covenants. If it ever should be regarded as revocable, it would cease being entire consecration.

61. Cf. Ps. 63:3.

62. The operative word is "knowingly," yet even with this qualifier, the statement strains credibility. She is relying upon Wesley's definition of sin as the "wilful transgression of known law" (*WJW*, V, pp. 154ff.).

63. Cf. Acts 10:22; 11:12.

64. Accordingly, irrational faith without understanding (or a sacrifice of intellect) is not required by scripture. Faith, as Pascal said of the heart, has reasons that reason does not know. Cf. Thomas Aquinas, *ST*, I, 1, Q11ff.

65. Cf. Gal. 3:29ff.; Rom. 4:13ff.

66. To fail to take possession of a will is to nullify its effect.

67. 1 Thes. 4:3.

68. 2 Cor. 6:17. The "come-outers" would later use this text as an argument for separation. Cf. C.E. Jones, *PPHAM*, pp. 47ff.

69. Faith is not thereby reduced to knowledge. She was aware that justification by faith through grace alone is intimately conjoined with sanctification. It became a short step for some of those who followed in her train to tend to make faith either a work or a new *gnosis*.

70. She had taken the most direct route (at long last!)—faith, as declared in scripture. Others might have great piety and not yet be willing to risk this direct faith through entire consecration.

71. If one seeks faith in that proportion that corresponds to one's current feeling, the scripture is not being attentively followed. She is warning against a pious stress on feeling (so familiar to the central stream of pietism), appealing to faith in God according to scripture which may run directly counter to fleeting feelings. This is why she is not easily or simply described as a pietist.

72. I.e., even if Providence permits the delay of the experience of full salvation, there is purpose in the "seeming delay," that it may elicit a more "victorious example of its power."

73. Cf. Rom. 12:1, RSV.

74. Cf. 1 John 1:7.

75. Mrs. Palmer clearly recognized by 1840 that strictures against public testimony by women caused a devastating injustice to women and an irrecoverable loss for the church. Two decades later, in 1859, she would publish the first full-length, definitive, exegetical-historical apologia for women testifying in public.

76. Cf. John 5:39; Acts 17:11.

77. Prof. Upham wrote Mrs. Palmer on September, 1840: "Our visit to New York, the last winter, was greatly blessed to us. To me, personally, it was in religion, the 'beginning of days,' and although you will think me right in ascribing everything in its ultimate source to the goodness and mercy of God, yet I am compelled to say, I have ever felt the most sincere and grateful obligation to the respected and beloved sister, who, for the sake of one so unworthy as myself, was willing to assume the responsibility of a perpetual vow" (*Memoirs*, p. 241). For a full discussion of Upham, see Darius Salter, *Spirit and Intellect: Thomas Upham's Holiness Theology*. (Metuchen, N.J., Scarecrow Press, 1986.)

78. Cf. John 8:32ff.

79. The first of many subsequent male attendants of the Tuesday meetings.

80. Cf. Gen. 32:24–30.

81. Congregational.

82. It is no small tribute to Mrs. Palmer's education, about which we know almost nothing, and probably it was largely self-education, that she was able to confront and instruct one of the principal theological minds of her time, and lead him into what he was to regard as the pivotal religious experience of his life.

83. Apparently while she was praying for him, at some particular point in the night, he attested to receiving the Spirit, mutually confirmed the next day. This ex-

perience of simultaneity of intercession and sanctification was to be further attested in the revivals to follow.

84. Such memorials were apparently taken with rigorous seriousness by Mrs. Palmer, especially as seen in the cases of Professor Upham, and Bishops Janes and Hamline and their wives.

85. That this crucial moment of ecstatic vision was reported by letter to Mary D. James indicates or suggests that Mrs. James may have been an important spiritual mentor or at least soul friend to Mrs. Palmer as a young woman (32 years old). See selection from *Mary, Or the Young Christian,* which is an account of Mrs. James's youthful experience of religion.

86. Perhaps a reference to persons at the Tuesday Meeting.

87. She learned through this dream that an inordinate dependence upon "outside agencies"—i.e., secondary causes that themselves depend upon prior divine permission—could stand as an obstacle to direct dependence upon and communion with the triune God.

88. John 20:2; 21:7,20. The allusion suggests that she was permitted in this dream to be as close to the Redeemer as John, the beloved disciple, had been.

89. Note how often the image of breathing recurs in her descriptions of mystical experience.

90. Isaac Watts, "Why Should We Start, to Fear to Die," *HMEC,* 1879, #976; cf. John 13:25, 21:20.

91. Here follows an ecstatic experience of the vision of God made known in a dream.

92. Exod. 3:1–6.

93. *PWJCW,* V, 419, v. 3; also in *A Collection of Hymns,* London: Wesleyan Conference Office 1877, #513.

94. This vision of God is thoroughly trinitarian, with all the key elements of triune teaching intact: unity, distinguishability, and tri-unity of the God-head. The ecstatic experience of unity is as intense as she had experienced, and once again contains the allusion of the unbounded sea.

95. 1 John 3:2.

96. Her writings that would follow in 1841 are: "Closet Reflections on the Subject of Gospel Holiness," *GTH* (1841); and several essays that later were included in *The Way of Holiness*—"What is Gospel Holiness or Sanctification?" and "How May We Enter into the Enjoyment of Sanctification," *GTH* (1841).

97. Hence about two and one half years younger than Phoebe Palmer, PBL. For the testimony of Mary D. James, see Stephen Olin Garrison, *Forty Witnesses* (New York: Phillips and Hunt, 1888), p. 245. Mrs. James was also a hymnwriter; see Metcalf, *American Writers and Compilers of Sacred Music* (New York: Abingdon, 1925).

98. It may be the only one in existence. The book is not listed either in the Union Catalogue or the Library of Congress.

99. The primary biblical allusion appears to be less to the mother of Jesus than to the sister of Martha. That this Mary was a favorite figure of Mrs. Palmer's is clear from her frequent references to Mary and Martha of the

Gospels, and from the fact that she wrote two different books with Mary in the title: *Mary, the Young Christian,* 1841, and *Sweet Mary, A Bride Made Ready for Her Lord,* 1862. Later, in notices announcing the latter, she urged persons who knew someone named Mary to give *Sweet Mary* as a gift book to them.

100. Luke 10:42, in reference to the sister of Martha.

101. 2 Tim. 3:15.

102. Luke 19:42.

103. An account here follows of Mary's conversion, which she dated Tuesday evening, Feb. 18, 1821.

104. *Mary, or the Young Christian (MYC),* p. 12.

105. Cf. John 3:33; Rom. 4:11; hymn source unidentified.

106. Matt. 14:32; Mark 6:50.

107. Cf. Job 11:8; Pss. 59:1, 64:1.

108. This phrase Phoebe would later use often about herself.

109. Here the narrative shifts from third person (apparently reconstructed from notes and conversations by Phoebe Palmer) to first person singular, apparently the record of a diary written by Mary D. James (similar in form to the "Notes" Mrs. Palmer wrote).

110. Apparently a common occurrence in the camp meetings of the period, as if struck by the Spirit.

111. Feb. 21, 1821 to Jan. 10, 1823.

112. Cf. Isa. 41:10; *BCP,* Prayer of General Confession.

113. 1 John 1:9.

114. Cf. Isa. 48:18, 66:12.

115. 2 Cor. 5:14.

116. Ps. 81:10.

117. *MYC,* pp. 7–24.

118. Joseph Lybrand, S. O. Garrison, *FW,* p. 245.

119. *MYC,* p. 35.

120. Rev. 3:17.

121. 1 Sam. 17:5.

122. Cf. Eph. 6:16.

123. Incorrectly reported by Wheatley as 1841 (*Memoirs,* p. 259).

124. 1 Cor. 13:8.

125. An Annual Conference (of New York) as distinguished from a quadrennial General Conference, as at Baltimore, mentioned in the previous entry.

126. Cf. Luke 10:38–42, John 12:2–3.

127. She considered many leaders of the New York Conference saintly exponents of sanctification: Timothy Merritt, Nathan Bangs, Samuel Merwin, and others.

128. She was more sharply defining her vocation in relation to Methodism—to call it to its original purpose, and directly to confront ministers concerning their understanding of the witness to the way of holiness.

129. After her covenant of June 12, 1841, she increasingly viewed it as her

solemn duty to witness to full salvation in a persistent and distinct way to ministers of the gospel, whose influence potentially was so vast.

130. 2 Tim. 4:2.

131. Although she is keenly aware of her absence from her husband, she seems assured of his commitment to her efforts.

132. Charles Wesley, "God of All Consolation, Take," *HUMEC*, 1850, #10, v. 3; second line reads: "And each to each in Jesus joined."

133. This passage suggests that the parenting was seriously being shared between Phoebe and Walter. Doubtless they had domestic help during these periods of her absence, but Walter Palmer was an active parent.

134. Phoebe's friend, Mrs. Mary D. James (the subject of *Mary, Or the Young Christian*, wife of Henry B. James), a resident of Mount Holly, New Jersey, is distinguished from Mrs. Janes, wife of (soon to be Bishop) Edmund Janes.

135. Charles Wesley, "How Happy, Gracious Lord! Are We," *HUMEC*, 1850, #911, v. 2; first line reads: "With us no melancholy void."

136. It appears that by this time Mrs. Palmer was increasingly being asked to take major responsibilities in public meetings witnessing to pardon and purity.

137. This suggests that she understood herself to experience some precognitive awareness of these outcomes.

138. She came to regard the astonishing changes in persons that accompanied these meetings as evidence that she was "called to this peculiar work." Later she would write *The Promise of the Father*, defending varied forms of the ministry of women. At this point it is useful to note how gradually this sense of special calling had developed through her revival activities, of which this letter is evidence.

139. Cf. Exod. 4:1–5; Judg. 6:18–23.

140. The examination of the extraordinary effects of faith is developed extensively in her later work, *Faith and its Effects*.

141. In John Wesley's "A Short Account of the Life and Death of the Rev. John Fletcher," in *WJW*, XI, p. 359.

142. Judges 6:17.

143. Heb. 10:36.

144. 1 Cor. 15:58.

145. This suggests that she felt the special efficacy of the prayers of one whose faith and prudence she trusted. She had several covenants to mutual intercession (Mary D. James, Thomas Upham, Sarah Lankford, her husband and family, and later, Bishop and Mrs. Janes and Hamline).

146. A milestone for many Presbyterians, to allow women to offer testimony in the church.

147. She may have had some anticipatory awareness of the risk and trouble he would soon face as a result of this profession.

148. This illustrates how the Palmer-Lankford home functioned not only as a meeting place for the promotion of holiness, but also as a hostel for seekers of holiness, especially ministers—attentive to all their needs.

149. An overnight accommodation for ministers seeking the way of holiness.

150. Ps. 103:2.

151. The proto-ecumenical implications of her work were just beginning to dawn upon her. They were later to make a decisive contribution, especially in England, to the history of ecumenism. Among the earliest beginnings of holiness ecumenism were the events described in this summer of 1842 in Newburgh, New York, in connection with Reverend Hill.

152. Cf. 1 John 1:7.

153. Mark 12:30.

154. The first nine sections of *The Way of Holiness* had originally appeared in the *New York Christian Advocate and Journal,* and in *GTH* (1843). The "other matter" was "Notes by the Way," revised from her diary of 1837–39, published in *The Way of Holiness* (1843), and *GTH* (1844).

VI

THE WAY OF HOLINESS (1843)

In 1843 Mrs. Palmer published a small book, The Way of Holiness, *gathered largely from "Notes" on her own religious experience, which was destined to catapult her into the public eye. Although she had published articles and an anonymous book for Christian education curriculum, it was through the wide circulation of this book that her international reputation grew. Thereafter, her good name preceded her whether she went to Canada or California, Chicago, London or Glasgow. Its publication, the first part in the* Christian Advocate and Journal *of 1842,[1] and then in the* Guide to Christian Perfection *in 1843, and first published as a book in 1843,[2] marked a milestone in her public life. After its publication she was frequently on the road, responding to a flood of invitations to provide testimony to the way of holiness.[3] Henceforth she was destined to be a "public figure," in fact one of the few women of the mid-nineteenth century who could be found constantly speaking in public on religious issues.*

The full title she gave the book was The Way of Holiness, with Notes by the Way: Being a Narrative of Religious Experience Resulting from a Determination to be a Bible Christian. *By 1867 it had gone through fifty editions.[4] In the preface to the second edition (1844) she wrote (pp. 7–8):*

For the kindness with which the first edition[5] of this little volume has been received, the author acknowledges herself under obligation to the Christian public. She regards it as no small favor that the mantle of charity has been thrown over its imperfections, and its humble aim to guide the sincere seeker into the way of holiness, not wholly unanswered. A desire to present entire consecration as a duty enjoined in the Scriptures, and not merely the peculiarity of a sect, induced the author, before issuing the first edition, to query, whether the volume should be entitled "Bible Christi-

165

anity,'' or "The Way of Holiness.'' The latter was decided upon, from the consideration that the Bible presents but one way to heaven, and that "The *Way* of Holiness.'' But from the encouragements received from gentlemen of different evangelical churches,[6] she, with gratitude to God, acknowledges the fact, that her aim to present "Bible Christianity'' has not been unsuccessful.[7]

The book's initial question, "Is there not a shorter way?", does not seek or imply a cheap shortcut or easy way, but asks whether the way of holiness[8] necessarily requires a long, detailed, circuitous process of religious development or psychological growth. Or—could the road to the holy life be shortened or compacted by a clearly defined, step by step, life-changing decision of total responsiveness to grace? (the following selections are from The Way of Holiness, *pp. 2–70):*

IS THERE NOT A SHORTER WAY?

SECTION I.

"Be always ready to give an answer to every man that asketh you a reason of the hope that is within you, with meekness and fear.''—Peter.[9]

"I have thought,'' said one of the children of Zion to the other,[10] as in love they journeyed onward in the way cast up for the ransomed of the Lord to walk in; "I have thought,'' said he, "whether there is not a *shorter way* of getting into this way of holiness than some of our * * *[11] brethren apprehend?''

"Yes,'' said the sister addressed,[12] who was a member of the denomination alluded to; "Yes, brother, THERE IS A SHORTER WAY![13] O! I am sure this long waiting and struggling with the powers of darkness is not necessary. There is a shorter way.'' And then, with a solemn feeling of responsibility, and with a realizing conviction of the truth uttered, she added, "But, brother, there is but one way.''[14]

Days and even weeks elapsed, and yet the question, with solemn bearing, rested upon the mind of that sister. She thought of the affirmative given in answer to the inquiry of the brother—examined yet more closely the Scriptural foundation upon which the truth of the affirmation rested—and the result of the investigation tended to add still greater confirmation to the belief, that many sincere disciples of Jesus, by various needless perplexities, consume much time in endeavoring to get into this way, which might, more advantageously to themselves and others, be employed in making progress in it, and testifying, from experimental knowledge, of its blessedness.

How many, whom Infinite Love would long since have brought into this state, instead of seeking to be brought into the possession of the blessing at once, are seeking a preparation for the reception of it![15] They feel that their *convictions* are not deep enough to warrant an approach to the throne of grace, with the confident expectation of receiving the blessing now.[16] Just at this point some may have been lingering months and years. Thus did the sister, who so confidently affirmed "there is a shorter way." And here, dear child of Jesus, permit the writer to tell you just how that sister found the "shorter way."

On looking at the requirements of the word of God, she beheld the command, "Be ye holy."[17] She then began to say in her heart, "Whatever my former deficiencies may have been, God requires that I should now be holy. Whether *convicted,* or otherwise, *duty is plain.* God requires *present* holiness." On coming to this point, she at once apprehended a simple truth before unthought of, i.e., *Knowledge is conviction.* She well knew that, for a long time, she had been assured that God required holiness. But she had never deemed this knowledge a sufficient plea to take to God—and because of present need, to ask a present bestowment of the gift. . . .

Deeply conscious of past unfaithfulness, she now determined that the time past should suffice, and with a humility of spirit, induced by a consciousness of not having lived in the performance of such a "reasonable service,"[18] she was enabled, through grace, to resolve, with firmness of purpose, that entire devotion of heart and life to God should be the absorbing subject of the succeeding pilgrimage of life.

SECTION II.

"We by his Spirit prove,
And know the things of God,
The things which freely of his love
He hath on us bestow'd."[19]

After having thus resolved on devoting the entire service of her heart and life to God, the following questions occasioned much serious solicitude:—How shall I know *when* I have consecrated all to God? And how ascertain whether God *accepts* the sacrifice—and how know the manner of its acceptance? Here again the blessed Bible which she had now taken as her counselor, said to her heart, "We have received not the spirit of the world, but the Spirit which is of God, that we might know the things freely given to us of God."[20]

It was thus she became assured that it was her privilege to *know when she* had consecrated all to God, and also to know that the sacrifice was *accepted,* and the resolve was solemnly made that the subject should not cease to be absorbing until this knowledge was obtained.

Feeling it a matter of no small importance to stand thus solemnly pledged to God, conscious that sacred responsibilities were included in these engagements, a *realization* of the fact, that neither body, soul, nor spirit, time, talent, nor influence, were even for one moment, at her own disposal began to assume the tangibility of living truth to her mind, in a manner not before apprehended.

From a sense of responsibility thus imposed, she began to be more abundant in labors, "instant in season and out of season."[21]

While thus engaged in active service, another difficulty presented itself. How much of self in these performances? said the accuser.[22] For a moment, almost bewildered at being thus withstood, her heart began to sink. She felt most keenly that she had no certain standard to raise up against this accusation?

It was here again that the blessed word sweetly communed with her heart, presenting the marks of the way, by a reference to the admonition of Paul: "Therefore, my beloved brethren, be ye steadfast and unmovable, always abounding in the work of the Lord, forasmuch as ye know that your labor is not in vain in the Lord. . . . "[23]

SECTION III.

. . . These exercises, though so deep as to assure the heart, most powerfully and permanently, that "the word of the Lord is quick and powerful, and sharper than any two-edged sword, piercing to the dividing asunder of the soul and spirit, and of the joints and marrow, and is a discerner of the thoughts and intents of the heart,"[24] were not of that distressing character which, according to her preconceived opinions, were necessary, preparatory to entering into a state of holiness.

So far from having those overwhelming perceptions of guilt, on which she afterward saw she had been too much disposed to place reliance, as somewhat meritorious, she was constantly and *consciously* growing in grace daily—yea, even hourly her heavenward progress seemed marked as by the finger of God.[25]

No gloomy fears that she was *not a child of God* dimmed her spiritual horizon, presenting fearful anticipations of impending wrath. There had been a period in her experience, some time previous to that under present consideration, from which she had not *one lingering doubt of her accept-ance with God, as a member of the household of faith.*[26] But, conscious that she had *not the witness of entire consecration to God,* neither the assurance that the great deep of her heart, the fountain from whence action emanates, was pure, which at this time stood before the vision of her mind as two distinct objects, (yet which, as she afterward perceived, most clearly merged in *one*),[27] and impelled onward also by such an intense desire to be *fruitful in every good work,*[28] the emotions of her spirit could not perhaps be more clearly expressed than in the nervous language of the poet—

"My heart strings groan with deep complaint.
    My flesh lies panting, Lord, for thee;[29]
And every limb, and every joint
    Stretches for perfect purity."[30]

And yet, to continue poetic language, it was a "sweet distress," for the *word of the Lord* continually said to her heart, "The Spirit helpeth our in-firmities;"[31] and conscious that she had submitted herself to the dictations of the Spirit, a sacred conviction took possession of her mind that she was being led into all truth.[32]

"Stand still, and see the salvation of God,"[33] was now the listening attitude in which her soul eagerly waited before the Lord,[34] and it was but a few hours after the above encouraging admonition had been spoken to her heart that she set apart a season to wait before the Lord, especially for the bestowment of the object, or rather the two distinct objects previously stated.

On first kneeling, she thought of resolving that she would continue to wait before the Lord until the desire of her heart was granted. But the ad-versary, who had stood ready to withstand every progressive step, sug-gested, "Be careful, God may disappoint your expectations, and suppose you should be left to wrestle all night; ay, and all the morrow too?"[35]

She had ever felt it a matter of momentous import to say, either with the language of the heart or lip, "I have lifted my hand to God";[36] and for a moment she hesitated whether she should really determine to continue in a waiting attitude until the desire of her heart was fulfilled; but afterward concluded to rest the matter thus: One duty can never, in the order of God, interfere with another; and, unless necessarily called away by surrounding circumstances, I will, in the strength of grace, wait till my heart is assured, though it may be all night, and all the morrow too.[37]

And here most emphatically could she say, she was led by a "way she knew not;"[38] so simple, so clearly described, and urged by the word of the

Lord, and yet so often overlooked, for want of that child-like simplicity[39] which, without reasoning, takes God at his word. It was just while engaged in the act of preparing the way, as she deemed, to some great and undefinable exercise, that the Lord, through the medium of faith in his *written word,* led her astonished soul directly into the "way of holiness," where, with unutterable delight, she found the comprehensive desires of her soul blended and satisfied in the fulfillment of the command, *"Be ye holy."*[40]

It was thus, waiting child of Jesus, that this traveler in the King's highway was directed onward, through the teachings of the word of God and induced so confidently to affirm, in reply to the brother, *"There is a shorter way."*

SECTION IV.

. . . It was on this wise that the word of the Lord, the "Book of books," as a "mighty counselor,"[41] urged her onward, and by unerring precept directed every step of the way. And as each progressive step by which she was ushered into the enjoyment of this blessed state of experience was as distinctly marked, by its holy teachings, as those already given, may it not be presumed, that some heretofore wavering one may be induced to rest more confidently in the assurance that "the word of the Lord is tried,"[42] and is the same in its immutable nature as the Faithful and True,[43] by stating, as nearly as will comport with the brevity required, the steps as successively taken by which this disciple of Jesus entered?

Over and again, previous to the time mentioned, had she endeavored to give herself away in covenant to God. But she had never, till this hour, deliberately resolved on counting the cost,[44] with the solemn intention to "reckon herself dead *indeed* unto sin, but alive unto God through Jesus Christ our Lord;"[45] to account herself permanently the Lord's, and in verity no more at *her own* disposal, but *irrevocably the Lord's property,*[46] for time and eternity. Now, in the name of the Lord Jehovah, after having deliberately "counted the cost," she resolved to enter into the bonds of an everlasting covenant, with the fixed purpose to *count all things loss* for the excellency of the knowledge of Jesus,[47] that she might know him and the power of his resurrection, by being made conformable to his death, and raised to an entire newness of life.[48]

Apart from any excitement of feeling, other than the sacred awe inspired by the solemnity of the act, she now, in experimental verity, *did* lay hold upon the terms of the covenant, by which God has condescended to hand himself to his people, being willing, yea, even desirous to bring down the responsibility of a perpetual engagement upon herself, even in the sight of heaven. So intensely was she desirous that earth should usurp a claim no more, she asked that the solemn act might be recorded before the eternal throne, that the "host of the Lord that encamp round about them that fear him"[49] might bear witness, and also the innumerable company of the redeemed, blood-washed spirits, should behold yet another added to their choir in spirit, and also in song; and though still a resident of earth, they should witness the ceaseless return of all her redeemed powers, *through Christ,* ascending as an acceptable sacrifice.[50] The obligation to take the service of God as the absorbing business of life, and to regard heaven as her native home, and the accumulation of treasure in heaven[51] the chief object of ambition, was at this solemn moment entered upon.

On doing this a hallowed sense of consecration took possession of her soul; a divine conviction that the covenant was recognized in heaven, accompanied with the assurance that the seal, proclaiming her wholly the Lord's, was set;[52] while a consciousness, deep and abiding, that she had been but a co-worker with God in this matter, added still a greater confirmation to her conceptions of the extent and permanency of those heaven-inspired exercises, by which a mighty work had been wrought in and for her soul, which she felt assured would tell on her eternal destiny, even after myriads of ages had been spent in the eternal world.

But she did not at the moment regard the state into which she had been brought as the "way of holiness," neither had the word holiness been the most prominent topic during this solemn transaction. *Conformity to the will of God in all things*[53] was the absorbing desire of her heart. Yet after having passed through these exercises she began to give expression to her full soul thus: "I am wholly thine!—Thou dost reign unrivaled in my heart! There is not a tie that binds me to earth; every tie has been severed, and now I am wholly, wholly thine!" While lingering on the last words, the Holy Spirit appealingly repeated the confident expressions to her heart, thus: What! wholly the Lord's? Is not this the holiness that God requires? What have you more to render? Does God require more than all? Hath he issued the command, "Be ye holy," and not given the ability, with the command, for the performance of it?[54] Is he a hard master, unreasonable in his requirements? She now saw, in a convincing light, her error in regarding holiness as an attainment beyond her reach, and stood reproved, though consciously shielded by the atonement from condemnation, and enjoying the blessedness of that soul "to whom the Lord will not impute sin."[55] And now the eyes of her understanding were more fully opened, and founded on eternal faithfulness did she find the words of the Saviour, *"If any man will do his will he shall know of the doctrine."*[56]

SECTION V.

"Let us, to perfect love restored,
Thine image here retrieve,
And in the presence of our Lord
The life of angels live.

"But is it possible that I
Should live and sin no more?
Lord, if on thee I dare rely,
The *faith shall bring the power*.[57]

She now saw that holiness, instead of being an attainment beyond her reach, was a state of grace in which every one of the Lord's redeemed ones should live, that the service was indeed a "reasonable service,"[58] inasmuch as the command, "Be ye holy,"[59] is founded upon the absolute right which God, as our Creator, Preserver, and Redeemer, has upon the *entire* service of his creatures.

Instead of perceiving anything meritorious in what she had been enabled, through grace, to do, that is, in laying all upon the altar, she saw that she had but rendered back to God that which was already his own.[60]

She looked upon family, influence, earthly possessions, &c., and chidingly, in view of former misappropriation, said to her heart, "What hast thou, that thou hast not received? And if received, why didst thou glory in them as of thine own begetting?"[61] And though with Abraham in the sacrifice of his beloved Isaac, she was called seemingly to sacrifice what was of all earthly objects surpassingly dear,[62] yet so truly did she now see that the "Giver of every good gift"[63] but rightfully required his *own* in his *own time*, that she could only say, "The Lord gave, and the Lord hath taken away, blessed be the name of the Lord."[64]

And O, what cause for deep and perpetual abasement before God did she now perceive in that she had so long kept back part of that price which, by the requirement of that blessed word, she now so clearly discerned infinite love had demanded! and when the inquiries were presented, "Is God unreasonable in his requirements? Hath he given the command 'Be ye holy,' and not given the ability, with the command, for the performance of it?"[65] her inmost soul, penetrated with a sense of past unfaithfulness, acknowledged not only the reasonableness of the command, but also the unreasonableness of not having lived in obedience to such a plain Scriptural requirement. . . .

Still her insatiable desires were unsatisfied; and yet she continued to wait with unutterable importunity of desire and longing expectation, looking upward for the coming of the Lord; while the Spirit continued to urge the Scriptural declarations, " *'Now is the accepted time,'*[66] I will receive you.[67] Only believe! Trust all, *now* and *forever,* upon the faithfulness of the IMMUTABLE WORD, and you are *now* and *for ever* the *saved* of the Lord!'' And now an increase of light in reference to the sacredness and immutability of the word of God burst upon her soul![68] An assurance that the Holy Scripture is, in verity the WORD OF THE LORD, and as immutable in its nature as the *throne of the Eternal,* assumed the vividness and vitality of TRUTH, in a manner that she had never before realized.

These views were given in answer to an inquiry that rose in her mind, thus—''Shall I *venture* upon these declarations without *previously* realizing a change sufficient to warrant such conclusions? Venture now, merely because they stand thus recorded in the *written word!*[69] She here perceived that the declarations of Scripture were as truly the WORD OF THE LORD to her soul, as though they were proclaimed from the holy mount in the voice of thunder, or blazoned across the vault of heaven in characters of flame. She now saw into the simplicity of faith in a manner that astonished and humbled her soul; she was astonished she had not before perceived it, and humbled because she had been so slow of heart to believe God. The perceptions of faith and its effect[70] that then took possession of her mind were these: *Faith is taking God at his word,* relying unwaveringly upon his truth. The nature of the truth believed, whether joyous or otherwise, will necessarily produce corresponding feeling. Yet, *faith* and *feeling* are two distinct objects, though so nearly allied.

Here she saw an error, which, during the whole of her former pilgrimage in the heavenly way, had been detrimental to her progress. She now perceived that she had been much more solicitous about *feeling* than *faith*— requiring *feeling,* the *fruit* of faith, previous to having exercised faith.[71]

And now, on discerning the way more clearly, she was enabled by the help of the Spirit to resolve that she *would take God at his word,* whatever her emotions might be. Here she was permitted to linger for a moment, to count the cost of living a life of faith on the Son of God. The question was presented, ''Suppose after you *have* ventured upon the bare declaration of God—resolved to believe that *as you venture upon his word he doth receive you just because* he hath said, 'I will receive you,'[72]—and then should perceive no change, no extraordinary evidence, or emotion, to confirm your faith, would you still believe?'' The answer from the WORD was, *''The just shall live by faith.''*[73]

She now came to the decision that if called to live *peculiarly* the life of faith, and denied all outward or inward manifestations to an extent before unheard of, with the exception of him who ''journeyed'' onward in obedience to the command of ''God, not knowing whither he went,''[74] she would still, through the power of the ALMIGHTY, who has said, *"Walk* before me, and be thou perfect,"[75] journey onward through the pilgrimage of life—*walking by faith*[76]—resolved that the shield of faith[77] should *never be* relinquished, but retained even with the unyielding grasp of death, should the powers of darkness be permitted to assail her thus formidably. Never can the important step that followed be forgotten in time or in eternity.

SECTION VI.

. . . From the preceding views she discerned clearly, that *one* more step must be taken ere she could fully test the faithfulness of God. "Faithful is he who hath called you, who also *will do* it"[78] was now no longer a matter of opinion, but a truth confidently believed, and she saw that she must relinquish the confident expression before indulged in, as promising something in the *future,* "Thou wilt receive me," for the yet more confident expression, implying *present* assurance, "Thou *dost* receive!"[79] It is, perhaps, almost needless to say, that the enemy who had heretofore endeavored to withstand every step of the Spirit's leadings, now confronted her, with much greater energy. The suggestion that it was strangely presumptuous to believe in such a way, was presented to her mind with a plausibility which only Satanic subtilty could invent. But the resolution to believe was fixed; and then the Spirit most inspiringly said to her heart, "The kingdom of heaven suffereth violence, and the violent take it by force."[80]

And now, realizing that she was engaged in a transaction eternal in its consequences, she here, in the strength, and as in the presence of the Father, Son, and Holy Spirit, and those spirits that minister to the heirs of salvation,[81] said, "O, Lord, I call heaven and earth to witness that I *now lay body, soul,* and *spirit,* with *all these redeemed powers, upon thine altar, to be for ever THINE!*[82] *'TIS DONE!* Thou has promised to receive me! Thou canst not be unfaithful! *Thou dost receive me now!* From this time henceforth I *am thine—wholly thine!"*

The enemy suggested, " 'Tis but the work of your own understanding—the effort of your own will." But the Spirit of the Lord raised up a standard[83] which Satan, with his combined forces, could not overthrow. It was by the following presentation of truth that the Spirit helped her infirmities:[84] "Do not your perceptions of right—even your *own understanding—* assure you that it is matter of *thanksgiving to God* that you have been thus enabled to present your all to him?" "Yes," responded her whole heart, "it has all been the work of the Spirit. I will praise him! Glory be to God in the highest! Worthy is the Lamb to receive glory, honor, and blessing! Hallelujah! the Lord God Omnipotent reigneth!"[85] Yes, thou dost reign unrivaled in my heart! Thou hast subdued all things to thyself, and now thou dost reign throughout the empire of my soul, the Lord God of every motion!'' The SPIRIT now bore full testimony to her spirit,[86] of the TRUTH *of* THE WORD! She felt in experimental verity that it was not in vain she had believed; her very existence seemed lost and swallowed up in God; she plunged, as it were, into an immeasurable ocean of love, light, and power, and realized that she was encompassed with the ''favor of the Almighty as with a shield['']:[87] and felt assured while she continued thus, to rest her entire being on the faithfulness of God, she might confidently stand ['']rejoicing in hope,''[88] and exultingly sing with the poet—

''My steadfast soul from falling free
    Shall now no longer rove,
But Christ be all in all to me,
    And *all my soul be* LOVE.''[89]

She now saw infinite propriety, comprehensiveness, and beauty, in those words of DIVINE origin from which she had before shrunk, as implying a state too high and sacred for ordinary attainment or expectation.

HOLINESS, SANCTIFICATION, *perfect love,* were words no longer so incomprehensible, or indefinite in nature or bearing, in relation to the individual experience of the Lord's redeemed ones. She wondered not that it should be said, in reference to the ''WAY OF HOLINESS,'' ''The *ransomed of the Lord shall walk there!*''[90] She perceived that these terms were most significantly expressive of a state of soul in which *every* believer should live, and felt that no words of mere earthly origin could imbody[91] to her own perceptions, or convey to the understanding of others, half the comprehensiveness of meaning contained in them, and which stand forth so prominently in the word of God, thereby assuring men that they are given by the express dictation of the Holy Spirit. . . .

SECTION VII.

. . . So reasonable did it appear, that *all the Lord's ransomed ones,* who had been so fully redeemed, and *chosen out of the world,* should be *sanctified,*[92] set apart for holy service, as chosen vessels unto God, to bear his hallowed name before a gainsaying world, by having the seal legibly enstamped upon the forehead,[93] proclaiming them as ''not of the world,''[94] a ''peculiar people to show forth his praise;''[95] that all the energies of her mind were now absorbed in the desire to communicate the living intensity of her soul on this subject to the heart of every professed disciple. . . .

It was in that same hallowed hour when she was first, through the blood of the everlasting covenant, permitted to enter within the veil,[96] and *prove* the blessedness of the "way of holiness," that the weighty responsibilities, and also inconceivably-glorious destination of the believer, were unfolded to her spiritual vision in a manner inexpressibly surpassing her former perceptions.

She seemed permitted to look down through the vista of the future, to behold herself as having begun a race, in a way luminously lit up by the rays of the Sun of righteousness,[97] with the gaze of myriads of interested spectators—ay, even the gaze of the upper, as also the lower, world—intensely fixed upon her, watching her progress in a course that seemed to admit of no respite, or turning to the right or to the left,[98] and where consequences, inconceivably momentous, and eternal in duration, were pending.[99]

Have you brought yourself into this state of blessedness? Is it through your own exertions that this light has been kindled in your heart? were the inquiries which were now urged upon her attention. She deeply felt, as her heart responded to these interrogatories, that it was *all* the work of the Spirit; and never before did such a piercing sense of her own demerit and helplessness penetrate her mind as at that hour, while her inmost soul replied, 'Tis from the "Father of lights," the "Giver of every good and perfect gift,"[100] that I have received this precious *gift.* Yes, it is a *gift* from God, and to his name be all the glory!

The Spirit then suggested, *If* it is a *gift from God,* God is not exclusive in the impartation of his gifts, and you will be required to declare it; to declare it as his gift, through our Lord Jesus Christ, ready for the acceptance of all, as his free gift; and this, if you would regain the blessing, will not be left to your own choice. You will be called to profess this blessing before thousands![101] Can you do it? And here she was permitted again to count the cost. She had been saying, Rather let me die than lose the blessing, for Satan had suggested that she would ever be vacillating in her experience; one day professing the blessing, and another not; that she was so constitutionally prone to reason, it would require an *extraordinary* miracle to sustain her amid the array of unpropitious circumstances, which, like a mighty phalanx, crowded before the vision of her mind: but the Spirit brought to her remembrance the continuous miracle of the Israelitish nation, fed daily with bread directly from heaven.[102] And though assured that a miracle equal in magnitude would be constantly requisite for her support, yet she gloried in the assurance that the same almighty power stood continuously pledged for its performance. . . .

The matter was decided thus: Some settled principles must be established in the soul, by which it may be known what shall constitute duty in reference to this subject. Duty must be determined by a reference to the requirements of the Word, and being settled thus, the voice of duty is literally the *voice of God to the soul*. She was then enabled to decide the matter of testifying to the work of the Spirit thus: The church is represented as Christ's body. I am one of the members of that body. If I, by testifying of the spirit's operation in my heart, am individually benefited, the whole body is advantaged, by a more healthy action being produced throughout, while if I neglect to testify, and, in consequence, suffer loss, my relation to the body will of necessity cause it to participate in that loss. It is plain, therefore, and beyond all contradiction, my duty to declare the work of God. The health of my own soul and that of the precious body of Christ, of which I am a member, demand its performance.

The inquiry then arose, But am I by my own power of reasoning to determine in matters so momentous? The answer was, If you have power to reason above an idiot, or the beasts that perish, God has given that power; it is a talent intrusted, for which you will be called to render an account of stewardship. *Natural* abilities are as truly *gifts from God* as those termed by men *gracious* abilities. Grace does not render natural endowments in any degree useless, it only turns them into a *sanctified* channel. . . .

It was now that the Scriptural meaning of the words, "The very God of peace sanctify you wholly,"[103] "body, soul, and spirit,"[104] "thy will be done on earth as it is done in heaven,"[105] "ye are not of the world, I have chosen you out of the world,"[106] "redeemed from all iniquity,"[107] "a *peculiar* people,"[108] "strangers,"[109] "pilgrims,"[110] "sojourners,"[111] "fellow-citizens with the saints in light,"[112] &c., poured torrent after torrent of light upon the peculiar nature, responsibilities, and infinite blessedness of the way upon which she had newly entered. And in answer to the inquiry, Can you declare this great salvation to others?[113] her heart responded, Yea, Lord, to an assembled world at once, if it be at thy bidding! . . .

'Tis done! the great transaction's done,
   I am my Lord's, and he is mine;
He drew me, and I follow'd on.
   Charm'd to confess the voice divine.
Now rest, my long-divided heart,
   Fix'd on this blissful centre rest.
Nor ever from thy Lord depart,
   With him of every good possess'd."[114]

THERE IS BUT ONE WAY

SECTION VIII.

. . . She now found that *"there is but one way,"* and this way far better, and *"shorter,"* also, by bringing every diversified state of experience, however specious or complex, to compare with the "law and the testimony."[115] And if not *according* to *these,* she became assured it was because the true light had not been followed. From this period, therefore, it became an immovable axiom with her, never to deem an experience satisfactory that could not be substantiated with an emphatic, *"Thus saith the Lord. . . . "*

SECTION IX.

. . . God, in his infinite love, has provided a way by which lost, guilty men may be redeemed, justified, cleansed, and saved, with the power of an endless life. Provision has thus been made for the restoration of man, by availing himself of which, in the way designated in the Scriptures, he may regain that which was lost in Adam—even the image of God re-enstamped upon the soul.

To bring about this restoration, the Father so loved the world that he gave his only-begotten Son,[116] who from eternity had dwelt in his bosom. At the appointed time, Christ, the anointed of God, was revealed, and, as our example, lived a life of disinterested devotion to the interests of mankind; and, as the Lamb slain from the foundation of the world,[117] laid himself upon the altar; "tasted death for every man,"[118] and "bore the sins of the whole world in his own body."[119] As an assurance of the amplitude of his grace, and that he is no respecter of persons,[120] he hath said, "and I, if I be lifted up, will draw all men unto me."[121] "The Spirit of truth which proceedeth from the Father, he shall testify of me."[122] The Spirit, true to its appointed office, reproves of sin, righteousness, and judgment.[123] And now the entire voice of divine revelation proclaims, *"all* things ready!"[124] The Spirit and the Bride say, Come![125]

The altar, thus provided by the conjoint testimony of the Father, Son, and Holy Spirit, is Christ. His sacrificial death and sufferings are the sinner's plea; the immutable promises of the Lord Jehovah the ground of claim. If true to the Spirit's operations on the heart, men, as workers together with God,[126] confess their sins, the faithfulness and justice of God stand pledged not only to *forgive,* but also to *cleanse from all unrighteousness.*[127]

By the resolve to be a "Bible Christian," this traveler in the "way of holiness" placed herself in the way to receive the direct teachings of the

Spirit, and in the *one* and the only *way* for the attainment of the salvation promised in the gospel of Christ, inasmuch as it is written, "He became the author of eternal salvation to all them that *obey him.*"[128]

And by the determination to consecrate all upon the altar of sacrifice to God, with the resolve to "enter into the bonds of an everlasting covenant to be wholly the Lord's for time and eternity," and then acting in conformity with this decision, *actually laying all upon the altar,* by the most unequivocal Scripture testimony, she laid herself under the most solemn obligation to *believe that the sacrifice became the Lord's property; and by virtue of the altar upon which the offering was laid, became "holy" and "acceptable."*[129]. . . .

And though she apprehended that nothing *but the blood of Jesus* could *sanctify* and *cleanse* from sin, yet she was also scripturally assured that it was needful for the recipient of this grace, as a worker together with God, to place himself believingly *upon* "the altar that sanctifieth the gift,"[130] ere he could prove the efficacy of the all-cleansing blood. Gracious intentions, and strong desires, she was convinced, are not sufficient to bring about these important results; corresponding *action* is also necessary; the offering must be *brought* and believingly *laid upon the altar,* ere the acceptance of it *can* be realized. In this crucifixion of nature, the Spirit helpeth our infirmities,[131] and worketh mightily to *will*—but *man must act.*

As illustrative, in a degree, of her views of responsibility, she would refer to a would-be offerer at the Jewish altar, for months graciously intending to present the sacrifices required by the law, yet deferring, from a variety of causes, seemingly plausible, to *comply* with the requirement by handing over his gift, until the law which he had ever acknowledged "just and good,"[132] cuts him off from the community of his people. And thus she was apprehensive that many who graciously *intend* to be holy, by laying all upon the Christian altar, from various seemingly-plausible causes, are delaying to comply with the requirement, "Be ye holy,"[133] until, at an unlooked-for hour, the law, which they have ever pronounced "just and good,"[134] excludes them from the community of the redeemed, bloodwashed company in heaven.

She also found one act of faith not sufficient to insure a continuance in the "way of holiness," but that a *continuous* act was requisite. "As ye have received Christ Jesus the Lord, so walk ye in him,"[135] was an admonition greatly blessed to her soul. Assured that there was no other way of retaining this state of grace but by the exercise of the same resoluteness of character, presenting *all* and *keeping* all upon the hallowed altar, and also in the exercise of the same faith, she was enabled, through the teachings of the Spirit, "to walk by the same rule, and mind the same thing,"[136] and for years continued an onward walk in the "way of holiness."

Notes

1. "Is There Not a Shorter Way?", *CAJ*, 1842.

2. *Guide to Christian Perfection*, "The Way of Holiness," 4 (1842–43): 200ff.; *The Way of Holiness* (New York: Piercy and Reed, 1843).

3. Others were also writing on these themes. About the same time Mrs. Palmer was completing her writing of *The Way of Holiness*, George Peck published *The Scripture Doctrine of Christian Perfection Stated and Defended: With a Critical and Historical Examination of the Controversy Both Ancient and Modern* (New York: Lane and Sandford, 1842). The Pecks and the Palmers had interlacing interests, and it is probable that Mrs. Palmer read this work shortly after it was published, but it is also probable that most of the articles constituting the *Way of Holiness* had been written before the publication of Peck's book. Peck would shortly thereafter write *Appeal From Tradition to Scripture and Common Sense: An Answer to the Question What Constitutes the Divine Rule of Faith and Practice* (New York: Lane and Sandford, 1844). After the Conference of 1844 which separated the Methodists, North and South, Peck wrote *Slavery and Episcopacy* (New York: Lane and Tippett, 1845). In 1854 he edited an edition of *Wesley's Explanatory Notes on the New Testament*. Cf. Asa Mahan, *The Scripture Doctrine of Perfection*, Boston: D.S. King, 1839.

4. Recently republished in *The Devotional Writings of Phoebe Palmer*, The Higher Christian Life Series, ed. by Donald W. Dayton (New York: Garland Publishing, Inc., 1985); this volume includes *The Way of Holiness*, 50th American edition, and *Faith and Its Effects*, 27th edition.

5. 1843.

6. Her writing ministry was conceived from the outset as reaching out for all evangelical Christians, hence, an ecumenical ministry.

7. The book is prefaced by brief commendatory reviews by Asa Mahan, president of Oberlin College and Congregational minister, and Leonidas Hamline, who in 1843 was editor of the *Ladies' Repository*, soon to be elected Methodist bishop.

8. Isa. 35:8.

9. 1 Pet. 3:15.

10. The question was posed to Mrs. Palmer by Presbyterian Elder, Dr. Bull, "in a convention of earnest Christian friends" in which Mrs. Palmer was a participant, *Memoirs*, p. 480. The question prompted the reflection which resulted in the articles leading to this book.

11. Methodist.

12. Mrs. Palmer is speaking of herself.

13. Shorter did not mean easier for Mrs. Palmer. The term "shorter way" has been pounced upon by critics, and frequently interpreted by her detractors as if she meant simply a quick and uncomplicated way of circumventing difficulties and suffering. The shorter way was in fact a more immediate route to total commitment, a more direct way to giving up one's idolatries and consecrating oneself wholly to God. Modern readers whose consciousness is formed by one hundred years of pragmatism that Mrs. Palmer preceded may draw the wrong conclusion from this language.

14. Cf. John 14:6.

15. This presupposes a Wesleyan distinction between gradual and instantaneous sanctification. Wesley thought both were possible (*WJW*, VI, pp. 53ff., 490ff.; XII, pp. 207, 275, 333ff.). Mrs. Palmer is arguing for an accurate description of a method or way by which ordinary individuals can learn to move directly, here and now, to seek to receive sanctifying grace.

16. This must have been a significant obstacle to the continued growth of the holiness revival for many. Persons felt that their emotive strength was insufficient for the commitment required to seek the blessing of full salvation now, without delay.

17. 1 Pet. 1:16.

18. Rom. 12:1.

19. Charles Wesley, "We By His Spirit Prove," *HUMEC*, 1850, #460.

20. I Cor. 2:12.

21. 2 Tim. 4:2.

22. The rehearsal of ploys of the tempter parallels to some degree the report of her experience of July 26, 1837.

23. 1 Cor. 15:58.

24. Heb. 4:12.

25. She had by this time become aware that she had too long placed excessive emphasis upon the imagined efficacy of guilt-consciousness and the arcane syndromes of pietistic anxiety. The shift of consciousness now is toward continued daily (hourly!) growth—not progress in an immanentistic or automatic sense, but as continuing receipt of the gift of divine grace.

26. Cf. Eph. 2:19.

27. The two distinct objects appear to be total consecration and assurance. Yet it also could be that the two dimensions merging into one, in this complex sentence, are the intense desire of the heart and outward acts (or fruitful good works) of faith.

28. Cf. Col. 1:10.

29. Cf. Ps. 63:1 with Ps. 42:1.

30. Allusions such as these are frequently found in the Methodist hymnody (e.g., *HMEC*, 1879, #446, 496, 503, etc.), but the specific hymn is not specified (no reference in *DH, PWJCW,* Codville, Bakatel).

31. Cf. Rom. 8:26.

32. Cf. John 16:13.

33. Cf. Ex. 14:13.

34. Cf. Pss. 33:20, 62:1, 130:6.

35. The tempter wishes to tempt the believer with the thought that high expectations will be disappointed, and the wrestling continue without meaning or fulfillment.

36. Cf. Ps. 141:2.

37. Cf. Pss. 62:5, 130:5.

38. Cf. Josh. 3:4.

39. Cf. Matt. 18:1–5; Luke 1:17.

40. 1 Pet. 1:16.

41. Cf. Prov. 19:20–21; Isa. 9:6.

42. 2 Sam. 22:31.
43. Rev. 19:11.
44. Cf. Luke 14:28.
45. Cf. Rom. 6:11.
46. Cf. Rom. 14:8.
47. Cf. Phil. 3:8.
48. Cf. Phil. 3:10–11.
49. Cf. Ps. 27:3.
50. Cf. Rom. 12:1f.
51. Cf. Luke 12:32–34.
52. Cf. 2 Cor. 1:22; Eph. 4:30.
53. Cf. Rom. 12:1f.
54. No requirer can reasonably require a commandment if the ability is not even potentially there to perform it. Hence, nothing makes the command of God (to be holy) more absurd than the insistence that it is impossible (cf. J. Arminius, *Works*, 3 vols. [London: Longman, Hurst, 1825–73]).
55. Rom. 4:8.
56. John 7:17. In using this motto, holiness teaching viewed practice of the divine will as prior to the knowledge of doctrine. It is a preliminary anticipation of a secularizing pragmatism that would later make a philosophical program and educational philosophy of "learning by doing," a motto often attributed to John Dewey, but which may have been co-opted by him from some religious source similar to Mrs. Palmer.
57. Charles Wesley, "God of Eternal Truth and Peace," *HMEC*, 1879, #523, v. 4.
58. Cf. Rom. 12:1–2.
59. 1 Pet. 1:16.
60. Pelagianism and works–righteousness were thereby strictly ruled out, contrary to the imagination of some Reformed-tradition critiques of sanctificationist teaching, cf. B.B. Warfield, *Perfectionism*, 2 vols. (New York: Oxford, 1931, 1932).
61. 1 Cor. 4:7; cf. Matt. 10:8; John 1:16.
62. Gen. 22.
63. Cf. James 1:17.
64. Job 1:21.
65. Lev. 11:44–45; 19:2; 20:7; 1 Pet. 1:16. This point is stressed repeatedly. To Immanuel Kant is often ascribed the insight that the sense of moral obligation presupposes (and proves) freedom, and that no commandment could be rightly given without presupposing the ability to respond to it (*Critique of Pure Judgment; Metaphysics of Morals*, LLA). Phoebe Palmer is not here relying upon Kant, but a pre-Kantian Arminian-Anglican tradition that has its roots in Origen, John Chrysostom, John of Damascus, Thomas Aquinas, Erasmus and the Arminian Anglican tradition that was mediated to Mrs. Palmer through Wesley, Fletcher, Clarke, and Bangs.
66. 2 Cor. 6:2.
67. 2 Cor. 6:2.

68. Ps. 119:142–144. That the divine Word is unchanging does not imply that God lacks capacity to respond to changing historical conditions; rather God's Word addresses all contingent conditions precisely because God is eternally communicative.

69. The demonic temptation is to distrust the written word.

70. Later this would become the central theme of the book, *Faith and Its Effects*.

71. To place feeling before faith would have been to return to the condition of her struggle before July 26, 1837. A less precise grasp of the relation of faith and feeling did indeed come to plague the holiness revival that followed Mrs. Palmer, despite her admonitions.

72. Cf. 2 Cor. 6:17.

73. Rom. 1:17.

74. Heb. 11:8.

75. Gen. 17:1.

76. Cf. 2 Cor. 5:7.

77. Eph. 6:16.

78. Cf. 1 Thess. 5:24.

79. 2 Cor. 6:17 says, "and I will receive you."

80. Matt. 11:12.

81. Cf. Heb. 1:14.

82. The essence of entire consecration: laying all one's redeemed powers (body, soul, spirit) continually upon the altar in the light of the divine promise.

83. Cf. Isa. 59:19.

84. Cf. Rom. 8:26.

85. Cf. Rev. 5:12, 9:11, and 19:16.

86. Rom. 8:12–17.

87. Cf. Ps. 5:12.

88. Rom. 12:12. Brackets indicate omitted quotation marks.

89. Charles Wesley, "Jesus Thine All Victorious Love," *HUMEC*, 1850, #536, v. 5. Fourth line reads: "And all my heart is Love."

90. Cf. Isa. 35:8–10.

91. Embody. It is not that all words are thoroughly incapable of carrying or embodying the meaning of the terms holiness, sanctification, and perfect love (for she had just noted that these heretofore incomprehensible terms had taken on new and full meaning for her). Rather, no words of earthly origin could convey it—only scripture.

92. Cf. 1 Cor. 6:11; 2 Tim. 2:21.

93. Cf. Jer. 3:3; Rev. 14:9.

94. Cf. John 17:16.

95. Cf. 1 Pet. 2:9.

96. Cf. Heb. 10:20, 13:20.

97. Mal. 4:2. She seems to have grasped a precognitive vision of the race before her, as if legions of angels were attending.

98. Cf. Prov. 4:27.

99. The attendant angelic powers anticipatively knew that great consequences hinged upon her commitment.

100. Cf. Jas. 1:17.

101. She recognized early, despite her aversion to public testimony, that she would be required to bear wide and frequent public witness.

102. Cf. Exod. 16:4ff. The counterpoint is between the tempter's address ("you will vacillate" in the inconstancy of subjective reasoning), distinguished from the Spirit's daily feeding of Israel in the constancy of grace.

103. Thess. 5:23.

104. Cf. 1 Thess. 5:23, but in reverse order.

105. Cf. Matt. 6:10.

106. John 15:19.

107. Cf. Titus 2:14.

108. Titus 2:14.

109. 1 Pet. 2:11.

110. 1 Pet. 2:11.

111. Lev. 25:23.

112. Cf. Eph. 2:19.

113. Cf. Pss. 40:10, 145:4; Jer. 4:5.

114. Philip Doddridge, "O Happy Day That Fixed My Choice," *HUMEC*, 1850, #451, vv. 3–4.

115. Cf. Isa. 8:20.

116. John 3:16.

117. Rev. 13:8.

118. Cf. Heb. 2:9.

119. Cf. 1 Pet. 2:24.

120. Acts 10:34.

121. John 12:32.

122. John 15:26.

123. John 16:8.

124. Cf. Matt. 22:4.

125. Rev. 22:17.

126. Cf. 2 Cor. 6:1.

127. Cf. 1 John 1:9.

128. Heb. 5:9.

129. Cf. Rom. 12:1.

130. Cf. Matt. 23:19.

131. Rom. 8:26.

132. Cf. Rom. 7:12.

133. 1 Pet. 1:16.

134. Rom. 7:12.

135. Col. 2:6.

136. Phil. 3:16.

VII

ENTIRE DEVOTION TO GOD (1845)

In 1845[1] Mrs. Palmer published a slender volume entitled: Present to My Christian Friend on Entire Devotion to God. *It was to go through twenty American editions in the next ten years, and other editions in Canada and England, and has remained in print during the last century more than any of her books. It addresses the reader in warm, personal terms, and calls for undelayed decision and accountability to the claims of the holy life.[2] It provides a vivid example to modern readers of how her living testimony to sanctifying grace might have sounded had one been able to hear her in person.*

Her theme is the enjoyment of holiness. Carefully she lays the biblical ground for each step commended. Deliberate intentionality is required to enable receptivity to sanctifying grace. This discussion (pp. 6–22; 73–78) sets forth the essentials of her "altar theology":

INTRODUCTION

MY BELOVED CHRISTIAN FRIEND—

Will you accept of this little token of regard from one deeply interested in your welfare? I have received your friendship as a precious gift from God. Yes, "Jesus gives me my friends," and I have resolved on valuing and also cherishing your friendship as a precious gift from Him.[3] You will feel with me that friendships thus bestowed are Divine responsibilities. Then, beloved one, let us be faithful to each other; and may our communings during our short sojourn here be so directed as shall in the highest possible degree tell towards our mutual well-being in eternity.

I would not needlessly sadden your heart, but my thoughts are now

185

dwelling on the certainty of that period when our friendship on earth will close. Perhaps before the expiration of the present year you or I may be called suddenly, "in such an hour as we think not,"[4] to meet the Son of Man. My intense solicitude for you moves me to faithfulness beyond what cold formality might warrant.

Permit me, then, beloved one, to ask, Are you ready? Have you on the white robe?[5] No longer think of holiness as a doctrine peculiar to a *sect,* but rather as a doctrine peculiar to the *Bible,* as the only fitness for admission to the society of the bloodwashed in Heaven.[6]

If you are not a *holy* Christian, you are not a *Bible* Christian. I have been much concerned that till this period you should have remained indefinite in your experience on this point. In endeavouring to show the Standard of Bible fitness for Heaven, and the manner of attaining it, I have taken it in my way to answer three questions, which I am sure you will regard as infinitely important.[7]

I hope you will carry this small token of affectionate regard to your closet,[8] and, in solemn, prayerful waiting, decide there on perfecting holiness in the fear of God.[9] May the Sun of righteousness[10] shine upon your mind, and the Spirit of holiness guide you into all truth,[11] so that, as you read this communication, you may, through the blood of the everlasting covenant,[12] enter into the holiest![13]

P. P.

I

HOLINESS

Dost thou turn away with half-hearted eye, yielding to an impression indefinitely formed, that this, for the present, is a subject that does not demand special attention? Let us for a few moments examine the foundation on which this impression rests, and know whether it is warranted. We will take the word of God for our text-book, and not, "What does my neighbour, or what does my Christian friend, think of the *doctrine* of holiness?" No; for thereby we should be in danger of being influenced by the traditions of men.[14] To the law and to the testimony,[15] and not to the experience or practice of this or that professor, however high in experience or station. What does God say to *me* on this subject? What does He NOW require of me in relation to it? And how should these requirements affect my *present* conduct? And then let us firmly purpose, in the strength of the Lord Jehovah, that every future effort shall be correspondingly directed.

Let us take a declaration from the word of God—a declaration which, at a glance, covers the ground we would occupy, involving requirements weighty and far-reaching as eternity—"Follow peace with all men, and *holiness,* without which no man shall see the Lord."[16] Had attention been called to this article by the words, "To one who intends to seek God, or to make sure work for Heaven," your heart would probably at once, as your eye met the article, have said, "Why, that is something for *me.*" Then you need not be assured that the attainment of the end is utterly impossible without the use of the means. Thus you at once come in possession of the knowledge that it is absolutely necessary that *you* should be *holy,* if you would see God.

But perhaps you may say, "I am convinced that holiness is necessary, and I intend to have it before I am called into the presence of God." Ah! hear His voice saying unto thee, "Watch: for ye know not what hour your Lord doth come."[17] Think of the many, both of the prepared and the unprepared, who have been called without a moment's warning to meet God.

Scores will be in the eternal world before the return of this day next week, who expect it as little as yourself; and the voice still continues to say, "What I say unto you I say unto *all,* 'Watch.' "[18]

Perhaps you are saying, "I would be holy; I would not leave the attainment of it for any future period, not one day; no, not one hour would I delay; but I cannot get my eye distinctly fixed on the object. At times I get a glimpse, but mainly it seems to stand as an attainment quite beyond my reach; and too often do I find myself giving way to the persuasion that it cannot be well apprehended, except by those more deeply experienced in the things of God." Let me assure you, dear friend, that as surely as you need holiness *now,* so surely it is for you *now.* The provisions of the Gospel are all suited to the exigencies of the present time. Are you commanded to be ready for the coming of your Lord *now?* Then holiness is a blessing which it is now your privilege and also your duty to enjoy.

We will now endeavour, as promised, to answer three important questions. First, What is implied in Gospel holiness or sanctification? Second, How may we enter upon the enjoyment of a state[19] of holiness? Third, What will be the advantages to ourselves and others of living in possession of it?

II
WHAT IS GOSPEL HOLINESS, OR SANCTIFICATION?

GOSPEL holiness is that *state* which is attained by the believer when, through *faith* in the infinite merit of the Saviour, body and soul, with every ransomed faculty, are ceaselessly presented, a living sacrifice, to God;[20] the purpose of the soul being steadily bent to know nothing among men, save Christ and Him crucified,[21] and the eye of faith fixed on "the Lamb of God which taketh away the sin of the world.''[22] In obedience to the requirement of God, the sacrifice is presented *through* Christ, and the soul at once proves that "He is able to save them to the *uttermost* that come unto God by Him.''[23]

Holiness implies salvation from sin, a redemption from *all* iniquity.[24] The soul, through faith, being laid upon the *altar* that *sanctifieth* the gift,[25] experiences *constantly* the all-cleansing efficacy of the blood of Jesus.[26] And through this it knows the blessedness of being presented faultless before the throne,[27] and mingles its triumphant ecstasies with the bloodwashed company: "Unto Him that loved us, and washed us from our sins in His own blood, and hath made us kings and priests unto God and His Father, to Him be glory and dominion for ever and ever. Amen.''[28]

Though saved from all sin at present, yet the soul that has been brought into the *experience* of this state well knows that it is not saved to the uttermost. If finds that, in the entire surrender of the world, it has but "laid aside every weight.''[29] And now, with undeviating purpose and unshackled feet, it runs with increasing rapidity and delight in the way of His commandments, gaining new accessions of wisdom, power, and love, with every other grace, daily.

"Holiness," "sanctification," and "perfect love" are terms intimately related in meaning.[30] The terms *holiness* and *sanctification,* being frequently used by Divine inspiration, we may presume to be most significantly expressive of the state to which it is the duty of every believer to attain.

"Sanctification" being a word of much the same prominence as "holiness" in the blessed Word, it may be well to devote a few moments to its investigation, as it will doubtless throw an increase of light on the endeavour to ascertain the *nature* of the blessing.

As we have frequent occasion to observe in Scripture, the term "sanctify," in its most simple definition, means setting apart for any specified purpose.[31] Thus it was that Moses was commanded to sanctify the children of Israel. "And the Lord said unto Moses, Go unto this people, and sanctify them today and tomorrow, and let them wash their clothes, and be ready against the third day: for the third day the Lord will come down in the sight of all the people upon Mount Sinai" (Exod. xix. 10, 11).

The Israelites also were required to sanctify themselves: "Sanctify yourselves therefore and be ye holy: for I am the Lord your God" (Lev. xx. 7). The Saviour sanctified Himself for the redemption of the world: "And for their sakes I sanctify Myself, that they also might be sanctified through the truth" (John xvii. 19). God also is represented as sanctifying His people: "I am the Lord that doth sanctify you" (Exod. xxxi. 13). "And the very God of peace sanctify you wholly" (I Thess. v. 23). "Even as Christ also loved the Church and gave Himself for it, that He might sanctify and cleanse it" (Eph. v. 25, 26). The Saviour prays that His disciples may be sanctified through the truth: "Sanctify them through Thy truth: Thy word is truth" (John xvii. 17). Peter also speaks of the sanctification of the elect, according to the foreknowledge of God, unto obedience and sprinkling of the blood of Jesus (1 Peter i. 2). Paul as above speaks of the sanctification of the Church, cleansed with the washing of water by the Word (Eph. v. 26, 27). The Corinthian brethren are also exhorted to cleanse themselves from all filthiness of the flesh and spirit, by taking hold on the promises (2 Cor. vii. 1). The vessels in the Temple were all, by the special appointment of God, set apart for holy purposes; and though a variety of uses was designated, yet they were sanctified exclusively for the holy service of the sanctuary.

Thus it is that the Christian, redeemed from all iniquity, not with corruptible things, such as silver and gold, but by the precious blood of Jesus,[32] is, by the most explicit *declarations* and *obligations*, required to come out and be separate. "And what agreement hath the temple of God with idols? for ye are the temple of the living God: as God hath said, I will dwell in them, and walk in them; and I will be their God, and they shall be My people. Wherefore come out from among them and be ye separate, saith the Lord, and touch not the unclean thing, and will receive you" (2 Cor. vi. 16, 17). "Go ye out of the midst of her; be ye clean, that bear the vessels of the Lord" (Isaiah lii. 11). "Know ye not that your body is the temple of the Holy Ghost which is in you, which ye have of God, and ye are not your own? For ye are bought with a price: therefore glorify God in your body, and in your spirit, which are God's" (1 Cor. v. 19, 20). "For this is the will of God, even your sanctification" (1 Thess. iv. 3, 4). "If ye were of the world, the world would love his own; but because ye are not of the world, but I have chosen you out of the world, therefore the world hateth you" (John xv. 19). Yet "sanctification," as applied to believers, comprehends inconceivably greater blessedness than a mere nominal setting apart of body and soul, with every power, to God. The sacrifice, or service, however well intended, could not for a moment be acceptable without the washing of regeneration, and the renewing of the Holy Ghost.[33]

And then, in order to be continually washed, cleansed, and renewed after the image of God, the sacrifice must be *ceaselessly* presented. This is implied in the expression, "a *living* sacrifice;"[34] it is thus we are made priests unto God.[35] Through Jesus Christ, the Lamb of God, that taketh away the sins of the world;[36] the Way, the Truth, and the Life,[37] the Door by which we enter in;[38] the Lamb slain from the foundation of the world;[39] the sacrifice ascends unto God a sweet savour of Christ.[40] It is thus that the triumphant believer momentarily realizes the blessed fulfillment of the prayer: "And the very God of peace sanctify you wholly; and I pray God your whole spirit, and soul, and body, be preserved *blameless* unto the coming of our Lord Jesus Christ. Faithful is He that calleth you, who also will do it."[41] Amen. Even so, Lord Jesus.[42]

III

HOW MAY WE ENTER INTO THE ENJOYMENT OF HOLINESS?

Having become convinced that holiness is a state of soul which the Scriptures clearly set forth as an attainment which it is your duty and privilege to be living in the enjoyment of, it is necessary that the *intention* be fully fixed to *live* a holy life.[43]

This will require deep searchings of heart, and will not admit of a secret reserve of this or the other thing, when there is a doubt that the object may be prejudicial to the soul's best interests. The matter must be brought to bear the scrutinizing eye of God; and *must* be decided upon faithfully, though the decision involve a surrender literally painful as that of parting with a right hand or right eye.[44]

Some may be inclined to think this is narrowing the way[45] too much, and with shrinking of heart may solicitously inquire, "Lord, are there few that be saved?"[46] while the Saviour, beholding the many hindrances, replies, "Strive to enter in at the strait gate: for *many*, I say unto you, shall *seek* to enter in, and shall not be able."[47] And why not able? Has the command gone forth, "Be ye holy in all manner of conversation?" (1 Peter i. 15). And has a command with such an infinite weight of consequences (Heb. xii. 14) pending on its non-fulfilment, been issued from the throne where eternal love, power, and wisdom preside, and yet the *ability* for its performance not been given? No! it is the Almighty God, boundless in love, goodness, and power, that says, "Walk before Me, and be thou perfect."[48]

But the words of our Saviour will bring us yet more directly to the point, and will stamp the assertion with the signet of truth,[49] that the *intention* to be holy, resolutely fixed in the mind, is a very *necessary* step toward insuring the object. "If any man will do his will he shall know of the doctrine" (John vii. 17). This, taken in connection with "For the word of the Lord is quick and powerful, and sharper than any two-edged sword, piercing even to the dividing asunder of the thoughts and intents of the heart" (Heb. iv. 12), will yet more fully assure us of the necessity of subjecting ourselves to the deep searchings of the Spirit with the intention decidedly fixed to know nothing among men "save Christ and Him crucified."[50]

We have frequent occasion to observe with the sinner that the last point of extremity, previous to obtaining comfort, is the resolve that though he seek till the hour of his death, and never obtain forgiveness, he will not go back to the world and seek his pleasures there, but will endeavour to serve the Lord, and seek, in the use of all the appointed means,[51] the knowledge of pardon. So with the believer; he must have all his energies concentrated in the one endeavour and *intention* of living a life of entire devotion to God.

If you would raise a superstructure that will endure the searching winds, storms, and rains, which will inevitably beat against it, it is absolutely necessary that you count the cost.[52] Deem not that hand or that heart unfriendly that would assist you in this duty. How needful for the comfort of the soul, as also for the permanency of the work, that a thorough foundation be laid, so that the distressing temptations consequent upon the circumstance of this and the other sacrifice not having been before contemplated, may never successfully obtrude! Many are continually vacillating in their experience, and many more are falling through a failure in this particular. Through this the good way is evil spoken of.[53]

Oh, if you would be holy, and have your name written in *heaven* with those "who have come out of great tribulation,"[54] and on *earth* with those "who adorn the doctrine of God our Saviour in all things";[55] if you would be a living epistle, read and known of all men,[56] count the cost! Say, with the Apostle, "Yea, doubtless, and *I count all things but loss* for the excellency of the knowledge of Christ Jesus my Lord."[57] No less *devotion* of spirit will carry you unpolluted through the world, than carried the martyrs through the flames to Heaven. Though, from the present state of Christianity, its claims in many respects may not be of the same kind, yet the *devotion* of spirit required is precisely the same in *nature* and *extent!* And unless it leads you to an entire renunciation, a *crucifixion to the world,*[58] you have reason to fear that it will not bring you to the same happy Heaven of which they are now in possession.

Be assured that unless you are decided on making the entire sacrifice of all your powers to God, and are willing to be sanctified on the terms specified in the Word, "Come out from among them, and be ye separate, and touch not the unclean thing,"[59] you have no proper foundation for your faith to rest upon, when you endeavour to believe that God will receive the offering at your hand. "And if ye offer the blind for sacrifice, is it not evil? and if ye offer the lame and sick, is it not evil? Offer it now unto thy governor; will he be pleased with thee, or accept thy person? saith the Lord of Hosts" (Mal. i. 8). "And this have ye done again, covering the altar of the Lord with tears, with weeping, and with crying out, insomuch that He regardeth not the offering any more, or receiveth it with goodwill at your hand" (Mal. ii. 13).[60] From these passages you may infer the reason why so many find it so exceedingly difficult to believe. The Faithful and True Witness[61] hath said, as illustrative of the requirements of this way of holiness, and also of its simplicity, "*The unclean shall not pass over it;* the wayfaring men, though *fools, shall not err therein.*''[62] May not, then, the defect in the experience of thousands, who have endeavoured by merely *believing,* without having this *essential preparation* for their *faith,* be accounted for in this way, rather than that the truth of God should be questioned?

The experience of a glorious number of living witnesses who have attested the excellency of the knowledge of this grace, proves that just so soon as they were willing in reality to count *all* things loss, just so soon they found it *perfectly easy to believe.* And as it is by *believing* that we are brought into this blessed state of soul, this is why the writer has spent so much time in what may seem merely preliminary. To prove the point, let me bring two or three out of the many living witnesses that have come under my observation. The first a divine, who has been, for two or three years past, publishing to thousands the blessedness of this way.[63] He stated that he had been nine years interested in the subject of holiness, believing it to be the privilege of all believers to be holy. A considerable part of those nine years was spent in much anxiety and perplexity on the subject. ''Why, brother,'' said I, ''how can you account for the circumstances of your being so long seeking without obtaining the blessing, when you were such a sincere inquirer after truth?'' ''Why,'' he said, ''I think I cannot reply to your question better than by using the words of our Saviour: '*How can ye believe* which receive honour one of another, and seek not the honour that cometh from God only?'[64] For just as soon as I was willing to give up that honour that cometh from the world, willing to have my name literally cast out as evil, and to seek that honour that cometh from God *only, I found it perfectly easy to believe.*''

Another had been more than a year earnestly seeking the blessing, and whenever the question was proposed to her mind, ''Should the Lord give you the blessing, would you be willing to profess it?'' as often as the question recurred, she replied, by her feelings, that she could not; and yet thought that she was willing to give up all for the attainment of the blessing. She at last felt the necessity of it so deeply, that she concluded no sacrifice would be too great. When the Spirit again applied the question, ''Would you be willing to profess the blessing, should you receive it?'' her heart replied, ''Yes, Lord, confess it, or anything; only let me have it!'' The way of faith was at once plain, and her mouth was filled with praises.

Two other cases, coming, as in the instances just mentioned, directly under my own observation, may be instrumental in solving the difficulties in the way of believing with some.[65] Remote from each other resided two individuals, entirely unacquainted with each other's experience; both became deeply interested in the subject of holiness, the Spirit urging them powerfully to the present attainment of the blessing. Yet the way of faith seemed hard to understand,[66] when it was suggested that something must be in the way of believing, as God had declared it easy.[67] Both explained the difficulty by an allusion to such an attachment as is forbidden by the Word (2 Cor. vi. 14). They were told that the would find it utterly *impossible to believe* under such circumstances; that the object must be given up, and they would then find God true to His word.[68] The surrender was made, and they were made the happy possessors of the perfect love of God. These are only transcripts of the experience of scores of living witnesses.

This is a work in which we must most emphatically be workers together with God;[69] for though He saith, "I am the Lord that doth sanctify you" (Exod. xxxi. 13), He also says, "Sanctify *yourselves* therefore, and be ye holy" (Lev. xx. 7). Though the blessing is received through faith, and not by the works of the law,[70] yet it is impossible to exercise that faith which brings the blessing, until we are willing to bring the sacrifice of the body, soul, and spirit, and leave it there.[71] Then shall we find that "God is the Lord, which hath shewed us light: bind the sacrifice with cords, even unto the horns of the altar" (Psalm cxviii. 27).

Then it is that *this* highway, cast up for the ransomed of the Lord to walk in, becomes plain, so plain that the wayfaring man, though a fool, shall not err.[72] In obedience to the requirement, "I beseech you, brethren, by the mercies of God, that ye present your bodies a living sacrifice" (Rom. xii. 1), the offering is presented. And will not that God who hath required it at your hand, accept it, when, in sincerity of heart, it is brought and laid upon the altar? Dare not to charge your faithful, promise-keeping God with such an inconsistency, as for a moment to doubt that He will be true. He cannot deny Himself.

Under the Levitical dispensation, which consisted mainly of outward rites and observances, the comers unto the altar were required to bring such sacrifices as were prescribed by the law, and originally specified by God, such as the firstlings of their flocks, first-fruits, etc. And when, according to the best of their ability, and their knowledge of the nature of the requirement, they brought them, to be presented through their officiating priest to God, have we reason to believe they ever doubted that God, who required, would accept, and not only *would* but *did accept*, at the *time* they were presented? What unwarrantable incredulity, and how dishonouring to God, would it have been, had they said to those around, or even indulged in heart the thought, "According to the ability which God hath given have I brought this oblation, yet I know not whether it will be accepted!" Would not this have been thinking and speaking of God as a hard Master?[73]

Oh, how unlike the conduct induced by the faith of Abraham![74] God was about to make a covenant with him. A sacrifice is required. Abraham brings it. Yet the fire does not at once descend from Heaven and consume it. But does he with impatience remove the sacrifice from off the hallowed altar? No; he judges Him faithful who hath called him to it.[75] With eager, prayerful intensity, he keeps his gaze heavenward, expecting doubtless, *momentarily* that the *token* will be given that will establish him for ever in the knowledge that the covenant is ratified in Heaven. The fowls watch to pollute. This he knows would mar the sacrifice, and render it unworthy the acceptance of his God.[76] He watches their approach, and drives them away. The day passes, and the shades of evening begin to lower, yet still he waits. Imagine, for a moment, that at this juncture Abraham had become disheartened, and had begun to conclude he had mistaken the nature of the requirement in some way; or that the morrow, or some future period, might do as well: would that covenant which secured such important consequences to his posterity have been ratified?

What you want is to enter into—

"The land of rest from inbred sin,
    The land of perfect holiness."[77]

It is your Father's good pleasure to give it you.[78] He will not permit one more pang or struggle in the attainment of it than will be for *your good;* for "He doth not afflict willingly."[79] You will not be called to make *one* sacrifice but what will be for your permanent welfare, and such as you will praise God to all eternity that you were permitted to make. You may be called to some peculiar sacrifice of which you may not know the why and wherefore now, like as Abraham with his beloved Isaac.[80] But the Lord may see some idol in your heart[81] that you have scarcely been appraised of, till thus searched and proved; or He may have a special work in His vineyard,[82] that He intends to fit you with perfect submission to say—

"Mould as Thou wilt Thy passive clay."[83]

Make no provision for future emergencies;[84] give up *all,* whether known or unknown. Resolve that, as duty shall be made plain, you will follow on, in obedience to the command, though death may await you.

If you are thus resolved to "count all things but loss for the excellency of the knowledge of Christ Jesus"[85] your Lord, there is no reason why you may not enter into the enjoyment of this state *this* hour. Jesus, your intercessor, stands at the right hand of the Majesty on high, pleading your cause.[86] He—

"Points to His side, and lifts His hands,
    And shows that you are graven there."[87]

Do you feel a fearful shrinking, which you would fain overcome? Look away *from earth*, from *self*, and fix your eye upon your compassionate JE-SUS. Obey constantly the admonition, "Looking unto Jesus."[88] "And we have *known* and *believed* the love that God hath to us. . . . Herein is our love made perfect."[89] Observe it is not enough to *know*, but we must also *believe* this love. Satan will with all his forces oppose you. Make up your mind to expect this. A door, great and effectual, is opened before you; but there are many adversaries.[90] "The kingdom of Heaven suffereth violence, and the violent take it by *force*."[91] Think of the many evidences your Saviour has given of His infinite willingness and ability to impart this Full Salvation to your soul. When He bowed His head upon the cross, and said, "It is finished,"[92] then a full and complete Salvation, a *redemption from all iniquity*,[93] was made possible for every soul of man. And what shall hinder your now receiving it, if by faith you now lay hold on the *terms* of the covenant, as, in the hallowed presence, and through the Almighty strength, and in the name of the Father, Son, and Holy Spirit, you let *this* be the solemn hour *when you enter into the bonds of an everlasting covenant to be wholly the Lord's for time and for eternity?*

Perhaps you never felt a more piercing sense of your helplessness; but you are now to lay hold on almighty strength. "He giveth power to the faint, and to them that have no might He increaseth strength."[94]

Some desponding, longing one, who may read this communication, may, up to this time have been an unfaithful, cold-hearted professor,[95] so that coming out to profess this state of grace may cause many, whose companionship has before been courted, to say, "Is Saul also among the prophets?"[96] But you are now giving yourself wholly away to Christ, and in His great love He is now saying unto you, "Ye are not of the world, but I have chosen you out of the world,"[97] "and ordained you, that ye should go and bring forth *fruit*; and that your fruit should remain; that whatsoever ye shall ask of the Father in My name, He may give it you."[98] Oh, is not this enough? Mr. Wesley says, "By this *token* you may know whether you seek the blessing by faith or by works. If by works, you want something to be done first before you are made holy. You think, 'I must first be, or do, thus or thus, before I am sanctified.' If you seek it by faith, seek it as *you are;* and if as you *are*, then expect it *now!*"[99]

It is of great importance that you look at this great Salvation as a *present* Salvation, received momentarily from above. The blood of Jesus *cleanseth*;[100] not that it can or will cleanse at some *future* period, but it *cleanseth now*, while you lay your all upon that "altar that sanctifieth the gift."[101] You keep your offering there, even all your redeemed powers—body, soul, and spirit—mind, memory, and will[102]—time, talents, and influence. And as in devotion all these redeemed powers return ceaselessly to God, *through* Christ, it is your *duty to believe*. Do not imagine that you have something indefinite, you know not what, to believe. No; it is the truth just stated you are called implicitly to believe; and if you do not believe, you dishonour God, and grieve the Spirit of love.[103] The inconsistency of your unbelief is here: in obedience to the requirement of God, you, through the assistance of His grace, have been enabled to come out and be separate, resolved to touch not, taste not, handle not the unclean thing.[104] If you had enabled *yourself* to do this, then there might be a shadow of consistency in your unbelief; but now that you have done it through the *power of God,* assured that, apart from his grace, there dwelleth no good thing in you,[105] how unreasonable the thought that He will not fulfil His part of the engagement! *"I will receive you,"*[106] is His own declaration. "I will sprinkle clean water upon you, and ye shall be clean; from all your filthiness and from all your idols will I cleanse you."[107] "Now is the accepted time, and now is the day of Salvation."[108] Then venture upon the truth of His word; you cannot believe God in vain. "The *faith* SHALL bring the *power;"*[109] but do not expect to *feel* the power *before* you have exercised the faith. This would be expecting the fruit before the tree is planted; the power to *live* and *dwell* in God comes *through believing.*

Holiness is a state of soul in which all the powers of the body and mind are consciously given up to God; and the witness of holiness is that testimony which the Holy Spirit bears with our spirit that the offering is accepted through Christ. The work is accomplished the moment we lay our all upon the altar. Under the old covenant dispensation it was ordained by God that whatsoever touched the altar should be holy: "Seven days thou shalt make an atonement for the altar, and sanctify it; and it shall be an altar most holy: whatsoever toucheth the altar shall be holy" (Exod. xxix. 37). And in allusion to this our Saviour says, "The altar that sanctifieth the gift" (Matt. xxiii. 19). As explanatory of this subject, Dr. Clarke says, "This may be understood as implying that *whatsoever was laid on the altar became the Lord's property, and must be wholly devoted to sacred purposes."*[110] Under the new covenant dispensation, the Apostle to the Hebrews says, *"We have an altar whereof they have no right to eat which serve the tabernacle"* (Heb. xiii. 10). Dr. Clarke again says, "The *Christian altar is the Christian sacrifice, which is* CHRIST JESUS, *with all the benefits of His passion and death."*[111] "Hallelujah! Glory be to God in the highest!"[112]

Will you come, dear disciple of Jesus, and venture even *now* to lay your all upon this blessed altar? He will not spurn you away. No; "His side an open fountain is;" "His nature and His name is love."[113] Surely you will now begin to say—

"O Love, thou bottomless abyss!
   My sins are swallowed up in Thee;
Cover'd is my unrighteousness,
   Nor spot of guilt remains on me:
While Jesus' blood through earth and skies,
'Mercy, free, boundless mercy,' cries."[114]

Rest here. Remember, "The just shall live by *faith*,"[115] not *ecstasies.*
HOLINESS is the mark; that state of soul in which all the powers of soul and
body are consciously given up to God. And here you have it. "Cast not
away, therefore, your confidence, which hath great recompense of reward;"[116] "for we are made partakers of Christ, if we hold the beginning
of our confidence steadfast unto the end."[117] Neither former unfaithfulness
nor present unworthiness need hinder your coming *just as you are.*[118] The
blood of Jesus cleanseth from all sin.[119]

"If all the sins which men have done
   In *thought,* in *will,* in *word,* or deed,
Since worlds were made or time begun,
   Were laid on one poor sinner's head,
The stream of Jesus' precious blood
   Could wash away the dreadful load."[120]

Then rest confidently. Resolve that you will not make your *feelings* (as
these may vary by the manner in which God sees most for your good to try
your faith) a standard for your faith. True faith will produce *feeling,* but it
may at first be little other than solid satisfaction, arising from an implicit
reliance on God. As with Abraham, so the most glorious examples, attesting by their lives the excellency of the way of faith, are those whose faith
has been most severely tried. A holy unyielding violence[121] is *necessary* in
order to retain the ground. Let that described by the poet be yours:

"Fix'd on this ground will I remain,
   Though my heart fail, and flesh decay;
This anchor shall my soul sustain,
   When earth's foundations melt away;
Mercy's full power I then shall prove,
Loved with an everlasting love."[122]

Rest now and for ever here, and you *are NOW,* and shall eternally be,
the *SAVED* of the Lord.

XV

A COVENANT[123]

"And because of all this we make a sure covenant, and write it
. . . and seal unto it."—Neh. ix. 38.

"Oh, happy day that seal'd my vows
    To Him who merits all my love!"[124]

In the name and in the presence of the triune Deity, Father, Son, and
Holy Spirit, I do hereby consecrate body, soul, and spirit, time, talents,
influence, family, and estate—all with which I stand connected, near or
remote, to be for ever, and in the most unlimited sense, THE LORD'S.

My body I lay upon Thine altar, O Lord, that it may be a temple for
the Holy Spirit to dwell in.[125] From henceforth I rely upon Thy promise,
that Thou wilt live and walk in me; believing, as I now surrender myself
for all coming time to Thee, that Thou dost condescend to enter this Thy
temple, and dost from this solemn moment hallow it with Thy indwelling
presence. The union is consummated! "Hallelujah to God and the Lamb for
ever!"[126] With comminglings of intense yet solemn joy, and holy fear, I do
at this eventful hour resolve, in the strength of the Lord Jehovah, on minute
circumspection in the sustainment and adornment of my body, to indulge
in only such things as may be enjoyed in the name of the Lord, and bear
the legible inscription, "HOLINESS TO THE LORD."[127]

My present and my future possessions,[128] in family and estate, I here
solemnly yield up in everlasting covenant to Thee. If sent forth as Thy servant Jacob, to commence the pilgrimage of life alone, and under discouraging circumstances; if, like him, homeless, with thought but a stone for
my pillow;[129] yet, with him, I will solemnly vow, "Of all that Thou shalt
give me, surely the tenth will I give unto Thee."[130] If Thou wilt, or hast
already intrusted me with children, I hereby take upon myself the solemn
obligation to train them for Thee. I resolve what my training shall be a view
of fitting them for the self-sacrificing service of God, and laying up treasure
in Heaven,[131] rather than in view of fitting them to make a display in the
world, and lay up treasures on earth.[132] And I resolve, if Thou givest
"power to get wealth," I will still continue to regard this vow, in relation
to my family, as sacredly binding as at the present hour, and will of my
greater abundance "lay by the store" proportionately for charities, and the
evangelization of the world *according* as God hath prospered me.

Believing that the Scriptures are a sufficient rule for my faith and practice, because "*all* Scripture is given for inspiration of God, and is profitable

for doctrine, for reproof, for correction, and for instruction in righteousness;"[133] I resolve that I will search the Scriptures daily[134] on my knees (unless circumstances of health altogether prevent), as in the more immediate presence of God; and that my faith and my duties shall be regulated by the unadulterated WORD OF GOD, rather than by the opinions of men in regard to that Word; and that no impressions in relation to doctrines or duties shall be regarded as coming from God, unless the said doctrine or duty be plainly taught in the Holy Scriptures.

And now, "O Lord, the great and dreadful God, keeping the covenant and mercy to them that love Him and to them that keep His commandments,"[135] confessing that I am utterly unable to keep one of the least of Thy commandments, unless endued with power from on high,[136] I hereby covenant to *trust in Thee* for the needful aid of Thy Spirit. Thou dost now behold my entire being presented to thee a living sacrifice.[137] Already is the offering laid upon Thine altar. I call Heaven and earth,[138] God the Father, Son and Spirit, the spirits of just men made perfect, and the innumerable company of angels now encamped around me,[139] to witness this solemn act of entire, absolute, irrevocable renunciation of sin and self! Yes, my all *is* upon Thine altar. O God, Father of our Lord and Saviour Jesus Christ, behold the offering! By the hallowing fires of burning love, let it now be consumed! Let the purifying, consuming energies of the Holy Spirit now penetrate soul and body, and cause every power of body and mind to ascend in ceaseless flames of love and praise, a living sacrifice. O Christ, Thou dost accept the sacrifice, and through Thy meritorious life and death, the infinite efficacy of the Blood of everlasting covenant, Thou dost accept me as Thine for ever, and dost present me before the throne of the Father without spot:

"No more I stagger at Thy word,
    Or doubt Thy truth which cannot move."[140]

Thou dost condescend to espouse me to Thyself in the bonds of an everlasting covenant in all things well ordered and sure, and from henceforth all my interests in time and eternity are blended in everlasting oneness with the Father and with His Son Jesus Christ, my fellowship is with the triune Deity, my citizenship is in Heaven![141] And now, O Lord, I will hold fast the *profession* of this my faith[142] before Thee, before angels, and before men. The exceeding great and precious promises upon which I have here laid hold, have been *given me*[143] on condition of my complying with the terms thereunto annexed. Through the power of Thy spirit alone I have complied with the conditions laid down in Thy Word upon which thou dost promise to enter into these covenant engagements with me; and now, before angels and men, I will declare my faith in Thee as my covenant-keeping God. And as I solemnly purpose that I would sooner die than break my covenant engagements with Thee, so will I, in obedience to the command of God, hold fast the *profession* of my faith unwaveringly, in face of an accusing enemy and an accusing world. And this I will through Thy grace do, irrespective of my emotions, resolved that my faith in God shall not depend on my uncertain emotions. Now, O God, my covenant engagements are before Thee. Thou hast registered them on the pages of eternity. Already they have been ratified before the throne in the name of the Triune deity, Father, Son, and Spirit. Trusting in Thee to keep me that I may never break from Thee by violating this my solemn covenant, I hereunto set my hand and seal, on this _____ day of _____ , 18_____ .

XVI

SANCTIFICATION RETAINED

HOW ENTIRE SANCTIFICATION IS TO

BE RETAINED

It is only by an entire and continual reliance on Christ, that a state of entire sanctification can be retained. The sacrifices under the old dispensation were sanctified by the altar upon which they were laid.[144] Had the offerer resumed the sacrifice, to the degree he resumed it, to that degree it would have ceased to be sanctified; for it was the *altar* that sanctified the gift. Thus, under the Christian dispensation, the entire sanctification of spirit, soul, and body takes place the moment the entire being is laid believingly *upon* the Christian altar. And when the entire being touches Christ, that moment it is holy. For "whatsoever toucheth the altar shall be holy."[145] As many as touched Jesus, when on earth, were made whole by the virtue that went out of Him.[146]

The only way to *retain* the grace of entire sanctification is by *keeping* all upon the altar. As the soul progresses, increased knowledge and strength involve higher responsibilities. Proportionate to the light are the responsibilities, bringing in to requisition yet more and more of the spirit of sacrifice. In order to retain a state of entire sanctification, these responsibilities must be met. And through Christ, who strengtheneth,[147] they can be met. The *strength of Christ* is imparted to the soul that relies wholly on Him. The soul that thus relies, has only to ask, "Could my Saviour have endured under such a trial? such a cross? or under any circumstances, however varied, in which I may be placed?—then I may endure." "I can do all things through Christ which *strengtheneth* me;"[148] not only who did strengthen, or can strengthen, but who *strengtheneth* just now, and continually, for every emergency as it occurs. It is only by a careful, constant, and entire reliance on Christ, that holiness can be retained.

It is an important consideration, that the entire way to Heaven is narrow.[149] It is the way of the cross. We sometimes hear persons speak of going *around* the cross; but those who speak thus have not carefully acquainted themselves with the chart leading from earth to Heaven. The cross covers all the way to Heaven. He who would be a disciple begins to lift it, in the strength of Christ, the first step he takes in the Heavenward course. Before he entered upon the way, the Spirit presented the *terms* of discipleship, and never could he have become a follower of Christ unless he had resolved on entire compliance with the conditions of discipleship, which, in the Saviour's own words, stand recorded thus: "IF ANY MAN WILL BE MY DISCIPLE, LET HIM DENY HIMSELF, TAKE UP HIS CROSS, AND FOLLOW ME."[150] Yet we would not have it inferred that the soul will have occasion to say, "The burden of the Lord,"[151] while enduring the needful cross, in order to retain a state of entire sanctification; for love knows no burdens. Christ's yoke is easy and His burden light.[152] The *strength of Christ* being imparted to the soul that trusts wholly in Him, how can the burden be otherwise than easy, and even delightsome, when borne in *almighty* strength, and with the soul filled with the constraining love of Christ?

Yet we would have it known that the blessing of entire sanctification cannot be understandingly retained otherwise than by the most careful circumspection in *all things*. The walk of those professing this grace must not be such as rightfully to provoke the inquiry, "What do ye more than others?"[153] The pursuits, the equippage, and the whole exterior, serve as an index to the mind; and to the degree conformity to this world is practiced, is the default in regard to worldly renunciation evident; and to a proportionate degree would a profession of entire sanctification be questionable and uninfluential.

Perhaps some may say, "When I received the blessing of entire sanctification my mind was not convinced that exterior things stand in such close connection with deep internal piety." We would not suspect the sincerity of such but would ask, Have you been faithful to all the convictions you have *since* had in regard to these matters? As you have been going onward in the highway cast up for the ransomed of the Lord to walk in,[154] has not clearer light been given, discovering further responsibilities and sacrifices, as connected with your vows of entire devotion? Did not the Spirit in gentle whispers tell you, that you might be more useful, if more evidently cross-bearing and self-sacrificing in your spirit? Now let me assure you before God, that unless faithful to this increase of light, you cannot retain a state of entire sanctification. Increasing light brings increasing responsibilities.[155] You have already made the sacrifice of your time, talents, reputation—your all—to God. Unless you take your sacrifice from off the hallowed altar, you must conclude to be obedient in these higher duties. You were not insincere when you made the surrender of your whole being to God through Christ; but you may now see that more was involved in that sacrifice than your perceptions at that time apprehended; and surely you will not be guilty of the sacrilegious act of removing an offering from off God's altar; for it was indeed the *Lord's altar* upon which you laid your offering; and it became His property the moment you laid it there. If you shrink from any duty, you will take the offering from off the altar, and then you will *fall* from a state of entire sanctification. If you begin to fall, the Lord only knows how low your fall may be. It will not avail you that you have had a high experience. The greater the height from which an object falls, the greater the *velocity* and the lower the depth to which it sinks! It was because he was so high that he fell so low. Then *keep* all upon the Lord's altar, if you would retain a state of entire sanctification; keep ever in the spirit of sacrifice, and you will ever enjoy the transforming, soul-cheering presence of the Sanctifier. The Father Himself will love you, and come and make his abode with you,[156] and with the sustainings of Christ's blissful, hallowing communings, as your indwelling Saviour, you will prove His infinite ability to keep you from falling, and to present you faultless before the presence of His glory with exceeding joy![157]

Notes

1. Wheatley states that the first edition was published "early in 1845," *Memoirs*, p. 484.
2. For general discussions of sanctificationist teaching of this period, see Peters, *CPAM;* Chiles, *TTAM;* Dieter, *HRNC;* Claude H. Thompson, "The Witness of American Methodism to the Historical Doctrine of Christian Perfection," Drew University dissertation, 1949; Allan Coppedge, "Entire Sanctification in Early American Methodism: *WTJ* 13 (1978): 34–50; S.L.C. Cohard, *Entire Sanctification from 1739 to 1900* (Louisville, KY: Pentecostal Herald Press, 1900); Orville S. Walters, "The Concept of Attainment in John Wesley's Christian Perfection," *Methodist History* 10 (1972): 12–29; cf. John Franklin Knapp, "The Doctrine of Holiness in the Light of Early Theological and Philosophical Conceptions," M.A. thesis, University of Cincinnati, 1924.
3. Cf. John 15:13–15.
4. Cf. Matt. 24:44.
5. Cf. Rev. 7:13; a metaphor of purity of heart, the reception of sanctifying grace.
6. Cf. Rev. 7:14.
7. For attempts to solve some of the problems arising out of the teachings of sanctification and holiness following Mrs. Palmer, see Thomas O. Summers, *Ho-*

liness: A Treatise on Sanctification (Richmond: J. Early, 1850); Randolph Sinks Foster, *Nature and Blessedness of Christian Purity* (New York: Lane and Scott, 1951); John Hunt, *Entire Sanctification: Its Nature, the Way of its Attainment, Motives for its Pursuit* (London: John Mason, 1860); Daniel Whedon, *Entire Sanctification: John Wesley's View* (New York: Hunt and Eaton, n.d.); C.G. Finney, *Lectures on Systematic Theology* (Oberlin: E.J. Goodrich, 1878); Lewis Romaine Dunn, *Relations of the Holy Spirit to the Work of Entire Sanctification* (New York: W.C. Palmer, Jr., 1883); James Mudge, *Growth in Holiness Toward Perfection, Or Progressive Sanctification* (New York: Hunt & Eaton, 1895); John R. Brooks, *Scriptural Sanctification: An Attempted Solution of the Holiness Problem* (Nashville, M.E.C. South, 1899); P.T. Forsyth, *Christian Perfection* (London: Hodder and Stoughton, 1899).

8. Cf. Matt. 6:6.

9. Cf. 2 Cor. 7:1.

10. Mal. 4:2.

11. Cf. John 16:13.

12. Cf. Heb. 13:20.

13. Cf. Heb. 10:19.

14. Cf. Matt. 7:8.

15. Cf. Isa. 8:20.

16. Heb. 12:14.

17. Matt. 24:42.

18. Mark 13:37. The admonition against delay of any sort, a standard aspect of revival preaching, is best viewed in eschatological context.

19. It remains a matter of controversy as to whether the view of holiness elsewhere indicated by Mrs. Palmer is best described as a "process" or "state." "State" suggests a static condition that appears contrary to much that Mrs. Palmer has elsewhere attributed to the life of holiness. The *way* of holiness is a more dynamic term that seems to invite continued growth, intersubjectivity, dialogue, and journey. She does not use the term "state" to imply immobility or quiescence, or lack of ability to respond. The "state" of holiness is precisely a condition of high responsivity, ready attentiveness to grace, and intensified activity.

20. Cf. Rom. 12:1.

21. Cf. 1 Cor. 2:2.

22. John 1:29.

23. Heb. 7:25.

24. Cf. John Wesley, in "A Farther Appeal," part I (*WJWB*, VIII, p. 47): "Now, if by salvation we mean a present salvation from sin, we cannot say, holiness is the condition of it; for it is the thing itself. Salvation, in this sense, and holiness, are synonymous terms. We must therefore say, 'We are saved by faith.' Faith is the sole condition of this salvation."

25. Cf. Matt. 23:19, a pivotal verse in Mrs. Palmer's thought.

26. Cf. 1 John 1:7.

27. Cf. Jude 24.

28. Rev. 1:5–6.

29. Cf. Heb. 12:1.

30. Not precisely synonymous, but deeply intertwined in Wesleyan teaching.

31. From this general definition there follows a series of biblical applications and illustrations of the crucial concept of set-apartness—key building blocks for the doctrine of sanctification.

32. Cf. 1 Pet. 1:18–19.

33. Cf. Titus 3:5.

34. Cf. Rom. 12:1.

35. Cf. Rev. 1:6.

36. Cf. John 1:29.

37. Cf. John 14:6.

38. Cf. John 10:7–9.

39. Cf. Rev. 13:8.

40. Cf. Eph. 5:2; 2 Cor. 2:15.

41. 1 Thess. 5:23–24.

42. Cf. Rev. 22:20: "Even so, come, Lord Jesus."

43. The fixing of attention is a theme found often in the tradition of spiritual formation from John Cassian and John Climacus through Thomas a Kempis and William Law, to Wesley and Fletcher, and of sanctificationist spiritual directors of Mrs. Palmer's period: Carvosso, Philips, Mahan, and Peck, op. cit.

44. Cf. Matt. 5:29–30.

45. Cf. Matt. 7:14.

46. Cf. Luke 13:23.

47. Luke 13:24.

48. Gen. 17:1.

49. Cf. Hag. 2:23; note her later use of this metaphor in the conclusion of this volume.

50. Cf. 1 Cor. 2:2.

51. Cf. John Wesley, "The Means of Grace," *WJW*, V, pp. 185–201; and "The General Rules of the United Societies."

52. Cf. Luke 14:28.

53. Cf. Rom. 14:16.

54. Cf. Rev. 7:14.

55. Cf. Titus 2:10.

56. Cf. 2 Cor. 3:2.

57. Phil. 3:8, a pivotal text in her interpretation of "counting the cost."

58. Cf. Gal. 6:14.

59. 2 Cor. 6:17.

60. I.e., the polluted or blemished sacrifice is not acceptable.

61. Rev. 3:4 with 19:11.

62. Isa. 35:8.

63. Perhaps a reference to J.T. Peck, Asa Mahan, or C.G. Finney.

64. John 5:44.

65. *Faith and Its Effects* contains spiritual direction for those facing just such difficulties.

66. Cf. 2 Pet. 3:16.
67. Cf. Matt. 11:30.
68. For anticipations of the modern psychotherapeutic procedure of paradoxical intentionality (cf. Viktor Frankl, *The Doctor and the Soul*), see Ignatius Loyola, *Spiritual Exercises*, and S. Kierkegaard, *Repetition, Fear and Trembling*. Mrs. Palmer derived her version of this procedure from neither of these, however, but rather from scriptural passages on the combat of idolatry—Jeremiah, Job, Psalms, and Pauline sources—and from Wesleyan commentators, Benson and Clarke, op. cit.
69. Cf. 2 Cor. 6:1. This type of synergism must be careful to assume the priority of grace to human responsiveness, yet without denying or undermining human responsiveness.
70. Cf. Rom. 9:32.
71. Cf. Rom. 12:1; 1 Thess. 5:23.
72. Cf. Isa. 35:8–10.
73. Cf. Matt. 25:24.
74. Cf. Gen. 15:7–17.
75. Cf. 1 Thess. 5:24.
76. Cf. Num. 18:32; Ezek. 7:21, 22.
77. Charles Wesley, *HUMEC*, 1850, #496, v. 2.
78. Cf. Luke 12:32.
79. Lam. 3:33.
80. Cf. Gen. 22:1–14.
81. Ezek. 14:7.
82. Cf. Gen. 9:20; Is. 5:1ff.; Mark 12:1ff.
83. Charles Wesley, "Behold the Servant of the Lord," *HUMEC*, 1850, #830, v. 4; cf. Jer. 18:4–6.
84. Cf. Rom. 13:14.
85. Phil. 3:8.
86. Cf. Rom. 8:34.
87. Charles Wesley, "Jesus the Lamb of God, hath Bled," *HUMEC*, 1850. #444. v. 2. Second line: "And shows that I am graven there." Cf. Isa. 49:16; John 20:20–27.
88. Heb. 12:2.
89. 1 John 4:16–17.
90. Cf. 1 Cor. 16:9.
91. Matt. 11:12.
92. John 19:30.
93. Cf. Eph. 1:7ff.; Hebr. 9:12ff.
94. Isa. 40:29.
95. I.e., one who professes Christian faith.
96. 1 Sam. 10:11–12.
97. John 15:19.
98. John 15:16.
99. John Wesley, "The Scripture Way of Salvation," *WJW*, VI, p. 53. Cf. *LWJ*, 7, pp. 268, 317.

100. Cf. 1 John 1:7.
101. Matt. 23:19.
102. Cf. Augustine, *On the Trinity, LCC*, VIII; *Confessions, LCC*, VII.
103. Cf. Eph. 4:30.
104. Cf. 2 Cor. 6:17.
105. Cf. Rom. 7:18.
106. 2 Cor. 6:17.
107. Ezek. 36:25.
108. 2 Cor. 6:2.
109. Cf. Matt. 10:1; Mark 3:15; 1 Cor. 9:12; Eph. 1:19, 6:10. The expectation of the reception of power—the power of the Spirit—was a crucial component of the Palmer message.
110. Adam Clarke, *HBC*, on Exod. 29:37. Clarke has only "Lord's property" italicized. The allusion to Matt. 23:19 is made by Clarke.
111. Adam Clarke, *HBC*, NT, vol. 2, on Heb. 13:10, p. 749 (emphases Mrs. Palmer's). It is likely that Mrs. Palmer was substantially influenced by Clarke in her exegetical focus upon the altar as an analogy to Christ.
112. Cf. Luke 2:14.
113. Charles Wesley, "Come, O Thou Traveller Unknown," vv. 7–12. *HUMEC*, 1850, #649–652 (Wrestling Jacob).
114. Johann A. Rothe, translated by John Wesley, "Now I have Found the Ground Wherein," *HMEC*, 1879, #420, v. 3; *CH*, p. 189.
115. Rom. 1:17.
116. Heb. 10:35.
117. Heb. 3:14.
118. Cf. Charlotte Elliott, "Just as I am, Without one Plea," *MHB*, #353.
119. Cf. 1 John 1:7.
120. Cf. *HMEC*, 1879, #243, 314, 726, 841.
121. Cf. Mt. 11:12.
122. Charles Wesley, "Redemption Found," *PWJCW*, I, #280, v. 6; *HMEC*, 1879, #470.
123. Mrs. Palmer offers to her reader the opportunity without delay to enter into this covenant. Its terms must be clear, and should not be entered into naively or without counting the cost.
124. "O Happy Day That Fixed My Choice," *HUMEC*, 1850, #451, v. 1. First line: "Oh, happy bond that seals my vows." *MHB*, 1933, #744.
125. Cf. 1 Cor. 3:16ff., 6:19.
126. Cf. Rev. 22:1–3.
127. Exod. 28:36; Zech. 14:20, 21.
128. Note the radical extent of the dedication: body, soul, mind, spirit, possessions, family, children.
129. Gen. 28:18.
130. Gen. 28:22.
131. Cf. Matt. 6:20.
132. Cf. Matt. 6:19.

133. 2 Tim. 3:16.
134. Cf. Acts 17:11.
135. Dan. 9:4.
136. Cf. Luke 24:49.
137. Cf. Rom. 12:1.
138. Cf. Deut. 30:19, 31:28.
139. Cf. Heb. 12:22–23.
140. Charles Wesley, "He Wills That I Should Holy Be," *HUMEC*, 1850, #482, v. 4. Line 1: "No more I stagger at Thy power."
141. Cf. Phil. 3:20.
142. Cf. Heb. 10:23.
143. Cf. 2 Pet. 1:4.
144. Cf. Matt. 23:19.
145. Exod. 29:37.
146. Cf. Luke 6:19.
147. Cf. Phil. 4:13.
148. Phil. 4:13.
149. Cf. Matt. 7:14.
150. Matt. 16:24.
151. Cf. Jer. 23:33–40.
152. Cf. Matt. 11:30.
153. Matt. 5:47.
154. Cf. Isa. 35:8 and 10.
155. Cf. Luke 12:48.
156. Cf. John 14:23.
157. Cf. Jude 24.

VIII

THE REVIVAL SPREADS
(1844–1859)

I. EPISCOPAL ELECTIONS OF
MRS. PALMER'S FRIENDS (1844)

*Mrs. Palmer's description of the election of her dear friends and com-
patriots, Leonidas Hamline[1] and E.S. Janes,[2] to the Methodist episcopacy
in 1844 sounded a note of triumph. Her diary reveals how earnestly she had
prayed for such an outcome, and quite likely had some influence in it, albeit
indirectly. Her home was something of a hostel[3] nearby the General
Conference[4] for those ministers who were committed to the promotion of
holiness and heart purity. This election was a major victory for the Palmer
circle. Both Hamline and Janes attended when possible the Tuesday Meetings, and remained for many years friends, confidants and regular correspondents of Mrs. Palmer (Memoirs, p. 61–62).*

May, 1844.—This morning witnessed the ordination of Rev. L.L.
Hamline, and E.S. Janes, to the office of Bishop of the M.E. Church. They
are in no ordinary degree, lovers of holiness,[5] and being intimately acquainted with both, I feel like saying that seldom, if ever, has our own, or
any other church been favored with such models of christian excellence at
the head of ecclesiastical affairs.

That two men should be elected to sustain the highest responsibilities
in the church, of such humility of spirit, and purity of life, betokens good
for us as a people. Perhaps two more fully, and experimentally assured that
those who bear the vessels of the Lord should be men of clean hands and
pure hearts,[6] could not have been chosen. Last night, dear Brother Hamline,
(who has been sojourning with us during the sitting of the General Confer-

208

ence),[7] said, with a manner expressive of unutterable solicitude, "Sister Palmer, pray that I may go to the altar on the morrow, with a holy heart. I want to be pure—to 'lift up holy hands'[8]—I feel as if I could never lay my hands upon the heads of others, to set them apart for the sacred office, unless these hands, as also this heart, be pure.'' This morning he again repeated the request. "Pray,'' said he, "that I may be *pure*—that not a *spot* may remain, as I stand before the altar to be set apart for my work.'' He did not mean this as an intimation that he has not a conscious sense of purity.[9] The words were but the outbreathings of his soul and expressive of the important light in which he viewed it as an essential in the office to which he was about to be consecrated.[10]

The scene, as presented to my mind, was one of extraordinary interest, and will ever stand connected in my mind with hallowing associations. Inexpressible interest, and long continued wrestling and intense gratitude shall be brought to remembrance by the recollection of this eventful period.

Mrs. Palmer's long-term relation with Bishop and Mrs. Hamline[11] *was one of utterly self-disclosing intimacy, mutual accountability, long-term covenant commitment, and above all, intercession, as indicated by this striking letter (*Memoirs, *p. 98):*

May 19th, 1844—Brother Hamline asks that I will promise to remember him *daily*, before the Lord. You know it is the disciple's privilege to *tell Jesus all*. I have spread this matter before the Lord, and with *stipulations*, will heartily enter into the engagement. I make it a point to present the individual members of my family, through Christ, the sin-atoning sacrifice, *daily*, before God. A deep and abiding consciousness possesses my soul, that this is not an unmeaning service. . . .

Now, dear Brother H., I suppose you wonder what this has to do with the promise that I will remember you daily. I will hasten to say, that your request shall be regarded in the light of a sacred engagement, and answered in the affirmative, if you will consent to enter into an engagement to make [yourselves] a part of our family.[12] We know that you will soon leave us, but if you will still, when far away, think of us as your own dear brother and sister, we will, in the presence of the High and Holy One, engage to remember you daily as a brother *beloved* in the Lord, and will engage to remember dear Sister Hamline also as a sister beloved in Christ—and for His sake, and in His name, we shall delight to bear you up continually, on the wings of faith and prayer. The endearing friendships we have formed with dear brother and sister Hamline, we ascribed to God, the Giver of every good and perfect gift.[13] May this friendship,—Aye more, *relationship*—be perpetuated through time, in the manner that shall in the highest possible degree glorify God, and through eternity be matter of unending felicity and eternal praise.[14]

William Miller, a Baptist preacher of Low Hampton, New York, early advocate of Adventism,[15] *had predicted that Christ would return to earth in 1843 or 1844 (see Evidence from Scripture and History of the Second Coming of Christ, About the Year 1843, published in 1836). Mrs. Palmer affirmed scriptural teaching of the second coming of the Lord, but taught that "of that day and hour knoweth no man."*[16] *After the anticipated year had passed, Mrs. Palmer wrote to Miller this pointed, yet caring admonition (Memoirs, p. 512):*

New York, October 24th, 1844

To Rev. Wm. Miller:

Dear Sir, * * * By a *sincere,* but, as time has proved, an incorrect movement, you have influenced thousands of minds, and those minds have influenced thousands of circumstances. The many papers devoted to the dissemination of your views state, that East, West, North, and South, have heard the cry, and have been roused by your call. Now, as the trumpet has not given a certain sound,[17] and many have been roused to an action, not suited to the emergency of the time,—should you not call the people back to the duties variously assigned them by the great Head of the Church?[18]

You, brother, were the first to sound the alarm. Your name and your efforts have been greatly helpful in perpetuating it, and now, should you not be among the *first,* and most ready, to advise and urge the people to a return to their various avocations? You know you have urged upon all, in view of the doctrines you believe, to leave all the ordinary duties of life, and yourself and friends were doubtless sincere in regarding the past few months, as a time of demanding this.

And what has been the result? Why, just as should have been foreseen; a confusion of tongues[19] more lamentable, than that from which they have issued, and—I think yourself will acknowledge,—likely to be far more so.

In view of this, I again ask, is it not your *duty* to sound a retreat? Had you not better say, "Every man to his tent, O Israel!"[20]

In the closing days of 1844, Mrs. Palmer reflected upon that year, which began a period in which it appeared to holiness advocates that the Wesleyan teaching could exercise wider influence (Memoirs, p. 133):

Diary, December 29th, 1844.—The past year has been marked with a good degree of outward prosperity[21]—For the greater part of the time I have been more abundant in labors, and the Lord has encouraged my heart by permitting me to see the fruit of my efforts. Holiness in the M.E. Church seems to be gradually on the rise.

Still she felt reticent to speak in public, even with her extensive revival and camp meeting (as well as Tuesday Meeting) experience of the past several years (Memoirs, p. 272):

BORDENTOWN, N.J.
December, 1844.— . . . In the evening, before the hour for service at the church, I attended class-meeting, held at the home of a veteran in Israel, old Father Robbins. I was blest in speaking to a part of the members of the class, and refreshings from God's presence seemed to be realized by all. On going to the church, I was required to exercise in a more public manner than I had anticipated,—Bro. Tuttle mentioning my name to the people, and then calling upon me to make the opening prayer, speak, etc.[22]

How my *nature* still shrinks from this publicity, but I never refuse, and grace *always sustains.* Though nature recoils, yet the divine principle within me always goes out in searching for the mind of the Spirit.

Here is a memorandum from her diary of 1845 reporting a visit to promote holiness at Wesleyan University, which illustrates her intense interest in university religious life (Memoirs, p. 273–274):

Middletown, Conn.[23] Last week, Sister Sarah Lankford and I visited Middletown, Conn., the seat of the Wesleyan University. We have seldom felt more sure of going at the bidding of the Saviour, any where, than to this place. We had several opportunities for "praising the beauty of holiness,"[24] and our gracious God condescended to permit us to see some fruit of our labors. Several became deeply awakened to the importance of holiness, and some who before had only regarded it as a *privilege,* were aroused to the solemn *duty.*

One of the professors of the University frankly acknowledged that he had been faulty in looking at the matter thus,—as though it were optional with himself whether he would perfect holiness in the fear of God,[25] or otherwise, and said he was afraid that too many regarded the matter thus. Alas! how many are unmindful that it is an imperative command, "BE YE HOLY."[26]

An interesting young sister, who is engaged to be married to a young minister about to sail for Africa, felt that she was enabled to enter into the rest of faith, during our visit. Professor Holdich[27] called on us, and wished to be affectionately remembered to you. We met with Mrs. Holdich also, at a class-meeting of the Faculty,[28] held at the University, at which were present three or four ladies of the Professors, with several of the brethren, tutors, and students. We endeavored to present Holiness as the duty of the *present* moment, with faithfulness, and shall hope that God will cause that which was sown in weakness to be raised in power.[29]

2. ILLNESS AND LIMITATION, 1845–1846

Mrs. Palmer fell ill during 1845 and her condition made it almost impossible to travel during much of the following year.[30] She was, nevertheless, able to continue her literary efforts, for it was during this time that she put together the letters of her portfolio published under the title, Faith and Its Effects.[31] *As she sent the manuscript to the printers on March 29, 1846, the following entry was made in her diary, providing several clues concerning the method of her work as a writer, her understanding of her vocation to authorship, and her wretched state of health* (Memoirs, p. 487):

Diary, March 29, 1846.—

If God has called me to the publication of the work, it surely is because He intends to bless it, and I leave the results confidently with the Lord. Every page has been written with much prayer.[32] Now that I, as an instrument in the hand of the Lord, have accomplished the work, I, in the most solemn manner, dedicate it to the Father, Son, and Holy Ghost.

Though I have had the work in contemplation for two or three years past, yet the state of my health has been such, that I have hesitated whether I might presume so far as to prepare the MSS., as close reading, or thinking, still affects my head injuriously.[33]

Her health had deteriorated so far that by 1846 she thought at age thirty-eight she would die. Soberly realizing that she had to cut back drastically on her expenditure of energy, she reflected in her diary upon her ministries of spiritual counsel, teaching, and public witness (Memoirs, p. 90):

Diary, 1846

My health admonishes me that I must ere long, close my earthly labors,[34] unless the progress of disease in my system be arrested. To-day, in contemplating the necessity of giving up a long cherished portion of my work, I wept—not from a desire to retain it, if my Heavenly Father required that I should not, but from a tenderness of feeling which I am sure is warrantable,—long association and its consequences,—*spiritual relationships,* etc., considered. I have written a resignation to the Allen Street S.S.[35] Association, of my Bible class, whose charge was entrusted me about nine years since. Here God has given me spiritual children.[36] Some, who soon after conversion, have been enabled to claim the blessing of full salvation.[37] Here the Holy Spirit has often taken of the things of God, and revealed them unto me;[38] and here many of the lovers of Jesus have received out of the treasures of grace, things new and old.[39] I love this, with other portions of my work, greatly, and see where, if I had, perhaps, been more judicious, and better aware of my danger,[40] I might have been spared longer to do my work.[41] My more public labors have been small, in comparison to my labor, hour after hour, with persons who have called for conversation on religious experience,[42] when laboring under the effect of disease, till now it is spread throughout my system, to a degree which makes my recovery (humanly speaking), extremely dubious. I am well aware, that the Divine government exhibits laws, natural and physical, which must be as truly obeyed,—unless supernaturally reversed,—as those regulating His spiritual kingdom. I fear I have not been as attentive as I might have been, in observing these laws. I have sacrificed myself in communing on religious experience, with an indefinite hope that the goodness of my cause would warrant the innovation,[43] and now, though my Father doth not chide, yet in love he assures me that I might have acted more wisely.

By September she had regained sufficient health to become again fully engaged anew in ever-expanding revival activities. She did not cease writing poetry, however, especially upon anniversary and memorial occasions, as in this recollection on her nineteenth wedding anniversary, when away from her husband, headed for another revival meeting on a North River steamboat (A Mother's Gift, *pp. 100–101). Her years of public witness, even when coupled with poor health, had not robbed her spirit of humor, joy, or romantic sentiment:*

My Wedding Day

On Board Steamboat North River,[44] Sept. 28th, 1846. Beloved One:— For a long time, as you well know, I have been required to lay aside my harp.[45] But will my dear husband forgive my trespass[46] in taking it down on an occasion so special as my wedding day?

Dear pleasant partner of my life,
    How many a happy year
Has passed since I became thy wife,
    And shared with thee life's cheer.

Nineteen most blessed years have past
   Since Heaven pronounced me thine,
Each still more happy than the last,
   Since first I knew thee mine.

Yes, mine! my precious husband thou,
   More than when first thy bride—
Full well I know thou lov'st me now;
   My warmth *thou* wilt not chide.

Stoics have smiled, and poets talked,
   Of love's first fitful boons,
But we in heightening bliss have walked,
   'Neath scores of honey-moons.

While pure Religion's sober ray,
   Diffusing light and love,
Hath gently guided all our way,
   To sweeter bliss above.

Thus far our path through life is trod,
   And now our vows we'll pay,
And highest praise ascribe to God,
   On this our Wedding Day.

By October 1846, she had resumed her Friday class-meeting, and wrote to the Rev. George W. Woodruff[47] of her approach to teaching these young people, focusing upon active, out-going witness rather than inwardly turned subjectivism or self-absorption (Memoirs, pp. 182–83):

October 12th, 1846

   At my class-meeting on Friday evening, a week since, I urged the members to come at once to this point of entire surrender, and to begin to be in verity the *Lord's servants*, assuring them that, ''He that watereth shall be watered. . . . ''[48] Is there not quite too much danger, dear Brother, of Christians absorbing themselves with their *own* experience, to the exclusion of zealous efforts for the salvation of others? I fear that this is a snare of Satan, even with some who would be wholly devoted to God.

   Not that I would divert the minds of believers, from an absorbing interest, relative to receiving the full baptism of the Holy Ghost, but I would direct them to what is *implied* in Holiness, Sanctification, or the baptism of the Holy Ghost.[49] Does it not imply a coming to God *through* Christ, and presenting all our redeemed powers, a *living* sacrifice, or as Dr. Clark[50] terms it, "a *continual* sacrifice."[51] Now, the very moment we lay all upon that altar which sanctifieth the gift,[52] and begin to *act* upon the principle that we are the Lord's—what is this but entering into that state of holiness, without which it is declared no man shall see the Lord,[53] and how *long* should any who profess to believe that they already belong to God, be in coming to this point. O, indeed, it is *unreasonable* not to be holy.

During the decade from 1837 to 1846, she had rigorously sought to remain faithful to her unconditional covenant of 1837. She probed this issue with profound seriousness in her annual spiritual retrospect at the end of 1846 (Memoirs, *pp. 126–27):*

Diary, December 31st, 1846.—This night, in the sanctuary of the Most High, I have been numbered with the witnesses of Jesus. Congregated with his disciples, I have referred to the glory of His grace, to the period ten years since when I entered into solemn covenant, that I would take the soul-inspiring sentiment, "I can do all things through Christ which strengtheneth me,"[54] as my motto for the then ensuing year.[55] What hath God wrought[56] since that eventful hour? Year after year have I rested, with yet stronger confidence on this soul-strengthening assurance. While thus reposing, strength suited to every emergency hath been granted, *just* when needed. . . .

My unworthiness, and the remembrance of my short-coming, would dissuade me, but the knowledge that I have never removed the offering from off the altar, but in the integrity of my heart have ceaseless presented the sacrifice—this knowledge, I would say, blended with an absorbing view of the faithfulness of God, furnishes a scriptural reason for my boldness when I again, with yet increasing confidence, repeat, "who of God is made unto *me,* wisdom, righteousness, sanctification, and redemption."[57]

3. PUBLIC WITNESS, PRIVATE STRUGGLE, (1847–1848)

During the decade of her forties (ca. 1848–58), Phoebe Palmer was dealing often with controversy, further refining her altar theology, extending the revival to Canada and to many new locations in the United States, and intensifying her support of foreign and home mission activity. The following selections are all taken from her diary of this period, published in the Memoirs. *This period ends with the publication of* The Promise of the

Father *(1859), and her decision to go to Britain, a journey which would keep her abroad for "four years in the old world" (1859–63).*

By 1847 Mrs. Palmer was increasingly recognized as a public figure, and hence had to face gross misrepresentations and take on burdens of controversy that had not been required under more private conditions (Memoirs, p. 579–80):

Diary, 1847

I have had some seasons of trial, *deep* trial, of late. The Lord has said to my heart, "Take your brethren, the prophets, as an example of suffering,"[58] etc.; and great has been the courage with which the Lord has inspired me, in view of those who have gone before. I can truly say with Paul, "I know what it is to be abased, and what it is to abound."[59] My views (doctrinal) have been misrepresented by those who do not seem to love holiness, and are not disposed to be at pains to read what I have written.[60]

I am first, now, reminded of this: "Blessed are ye, when men shall revile you, and shall say all manner of evil against you, *falsely,* for my name's sake. Rejoice and be exceedingly glad, for great is your reward in heaven."[61] And again, "What glory is it, if when ye be buffeted for your faults, ye shall take it patiently; but if when ye do *well,* and suffer for it, ye take it patiently; this is acceptable to God."[62]

O, my heart is greatly rejoiced while I write. Joy unutterable and full of glory[63] fills my soul. I see now, in clearer light, that I have in verity been following after Christ.[64] Especially in reading these words, has my courage and confidence been greatly increased. "For even hereunto are ye called; because Christ also *suffered* for us, leaving us an example, that ye should *follow in His steps.*"[65] What an *honor* to be permitted to follow on in the steps of the suffering Saviour.

She had to combat the antinomian view that when one is justified, one is thereby sanctified, and hence there would be no need to make any further commitment beyond that of acceptance of God's act of pardon. She argued for the intrinsic connection between justification and sanctification: Those who are justified are still called by scripture to "perfect holiness in the fear of the Lord." She wrote to a Mrs. Stokes (Memoirs, 580–81):

April 22, 1847.

You speak of a minister who gives it as his opinion, that the soul, when justified, is fully sanctified. If general experience were not at variance with his views, he might with more plausibility, urge this unscriptural and anti-Wesleyan view. Unscriptural, because this doctrine cannot be legitimately drawn from the Word of God. It is true that its partisans affirm it that way.

The general testimony of Scripture is at variance with these sentiments. Paul was writing to his brethren, when he urges upon them the importance of coming out in entire separation from the contaminating influences by which they were surrounded, and then presenting the promises of acceptance and conformity to the divine image, says, "Having these promises, dearly beloved, let us cleanse ourselves from all filthiness of the flesh and spirit, perfecting holiness in the fear of the Lord."[66] Were they already in the enjoyment of a state of holiness, would he have urged them to the attainment of it?

*She struggled frequently against the popular tendency to make private emotions the criterion of witness ("the enthusiastic doctrine, that we are not to do good, unless we feel free to [do] it"). One does not await natural inclination to witness to the full extent of grace, but rather such a profession is a duty emerging directly out of the experience of grace. In September of 1847, while attending a camp meeting near Norwalk, Connecticut, she wrote in her diary (*Memoirs, p. 275):*

I do not wait to witness a manifestation of deep interest on the theme of holiness, before speaking. If but little concern is felt, proportionate zeal should be exhibited in urging the duty. It is not so pleasing to nature, but I act on the principle, that it is a duty to cast aside the enthusiastic doctrine, that we are not to do good, unless we feel free to it.[67] I felt the approval of my Heavenly Father, in pressing the importance of present holiness, this morning.

*She faithfully sustained intimate friendships of profound mutual accountability, such as those with Melinda and Leonidas Hamline (her "dearest brother of the heart"), even at great distances. The joy and warmth of these more-than-friendships in Christ was celebrated in this poem rich in self-disclosure (*Memoirs, p. 486):*

To my much-loved Brother and Sister, Bishop and Mrs. Hamline

That They All May Be One.

When hearts made one in Christ,[68] each other meet,
     And then pour out their blended sympathies,
Upon the universe; how passing sweet!
     Can earth know joys which may compare with these?
Affections flowing out *through* God the Son,

Meeting in the broad channel of His love,
Must here unite, and be divinely *one!*
Is this not bliss like that enjoyed above?

Shall this be called mere *friendship?* Ah, the phrase,
    But tamely answers what my muse would say;
Worldlings thus name a form their ardors raise,
    A thing of earth, which ends with life's short day.

I sing of that which hath immortal birth,
    Of holy ardor, which descends from heaven,
To mould together hearts in love,[69] on earth,
    Which, as the blissful antedate is given,
Of pleasures, such as flow forevermore,
    At God's right hand; when all life's scenes are o'er.

This bliss is ours; *we are in Christ, made one.*
    He is our life,[70] and on His bleeding Heart
We rest: He is our Shield[71]—our Sun.[72]
    In fellowship we walk, no more to part.
The blood of Jesus cleanseth from all sin;[73]
    And now *through Christ,* with blended sympathies,
We'll work out our salvation, whilst He works within;[74]
    When called from earth, we'll meet in paradise.

*   *   *

I love thee, dearest brother of my heart;
    Before my eyes beheld thee face to face,
Our hearts were made acquainted; can we part?
    No! we will still be one through Jesus' grace.
And thou, my sister, dear, most precious one,
    Though we in flesh must part, our hearts shall dwell
In love's embrace, and oft around the throne
    We still will meet; we may not say "Farewell."

                                        Your Sister,
Tuesday, June 22d, 1847   PHOEBE PALMER.

The biblical metaphors of both Martha and Mary shaped her vocational self-understanding, inasmuch as temporal and spiritual matters were viewed as necessarily interrelated (Memoirs, pp. 590–91):

Diary; 1847.—If Christ were present in the flesh, and I were called, with Martha, to minister to the temporal wants of my Saviour and His disciples, it seems to me I should feel as if I were as engaged in His service; and that the affections prompting to this service were as truly pure and spiritual, as though I were with Mary a wholly unencumbered worshiper at His feet. Or, if I were with devoted Mary, and chanced to cast my eye upon the unprepared table, my listenings to His holy teachings would be broken, by a sympathetic, yet invisible cord, leading from the Saviour's heart of pure love, and drawing aside the thoughts and affections of His waiting one, to the performance of the other service.[75] With affections equally ardent, and as sweetly spiritualized, would I hasten to furnish the needful supplies, and as truly would I rejoice that, at the bidding of my Saviour, I had been called with such an "high and holy calling."[76]

While engaged in regular "tract visitation," she went systematically through her district of lower Manhattan tenements, searching from garret to cellar for persons in need, witnessing to Christ not "by proxy" but in person. In this entry in her diary, just after she had visited a neglected sufferer, Mr. S., she reflected upon this method of visiting the poor (Memoirs, pp. 209–10):

May 20, 1848

If it had not been for tract visitation, which admits, or rather invites, and enforces ingress to the highways and hedges, these precious souls might not have been plucked as brands from the burning.[77] They lived in the rear of an alley, and I had several times passed through my district, without even suspecting that there was a dwelling there. But it has been my desire to explore my district thoroughly, and as far as time will allow, to hand the tract, myself, to each family, individually, whether in garret or cellar, believing that to do it by proxy, is not in general, the better way.[78] Mr. S. was an unusually interesting man, who had seen far better days. It is probable that his afflictions brought him to Christ. "He doth not afflict the children of men willingly."[79]

Sensitive to innuendoes of heterodoxy, Mrs. Palmer vigorously defended her teaching as differing in no way from classical Christian orthodoxy (Memoirs, pp. 516–17, in a letter to Mrs. Hamline):

May 22, 1848

The entire Scriptures are the voice of the Holy Spirit. "Holy men of old spake as they were moved by the Holy Ghost."[80] We have been favored with opportunities for knowing the views and experience of Methodists, quite equal to those of ordinary persons; but I never remember to have met with one, who did not believe that "The forgiveness of sin, and the renewing of the heart in righteousness and true holiness, are the work of the Holy Spirit."[81] But there are those who believe that there is vitality in the work of God, and that the "Spirit speaketh *expressly*"[82] through the lively oracles, and many of these have I heard testify, that "he that believeth *hath the witness in himself*."[83]

Love that thinketh no evil, and hopeth all things,[84] constrains to believe that there are but few among us, who regard the word of God as a *dead* letter. If not dead, then there is a living, quickening Spirit in it,[85] and blessed be God, this has been proved by thousands of experimental witnesses, who glory not in themselves, but in the work of the Spirit. None, perhaps, apprehend so fully the deep spiritual meaning of the Saviour's words, "It is the *Spirit* that quickeneth, the flesh profiteth nothing; the *words* that I speak unto [,] you they are *spirit, and they are life*."[86]

. . . Then we will, on the authority of the Bible, say that the promises of God are fulfilled the moment that the waiting one relies fully upon the Promiser, after having complied with the stipulations laid down in His word. I am not conscious of holding any views differing from our orthodox writers.[87]

She viewed duty as privilege, and time as opportunity. After a long summer day, she reviewed her own accountability for that day in specific terms (Memoirs, p. 156):

June 6th, 1848.—Day filled and almost crowded. I often think of the Saviour, who would fain have retired again, and yet again from the multitude;—but they pressed upon him.[88] It is enough that the disciple be as his Master.[89] I trust I am enabled to look upon all my various providential allotments for the filling up of my time as God's *appointments*. I commit my way to Him, and then sweetly rest in the assurance that my ways are ordered of God. This makes duty a privilege. Home mission meeting this morning. A presiding Elder, and his family, from New Jersey, to dine. Meeting, this afternoon. Several friends to tea, and company till quite late this evening. Added to my several meeting engagements, weekly, are the many calls for religious conversation, &c., with the domestic engagements, which of course call for a mother's attention in every family.

Yet, perhaps, I may enumerate as among the most monopolizing demands upon my time, the many letters which I am required to write. These, alone, are numerous enough to make volumes, yearly.[90] I feel, in all these, that I serve the Lord Christ. This is enough.

The resistance felt by holiness advocates was increasing during the late 1840's. The strength of this resistance significantly determined her itinerary at times (Memoirs, p. 79):

New York, August 13, 1848

To our much loved friends, Bishop and Mrs. Hamline;

I returned to my home yesterday, after an absence of three or four days, which was spent at a Camp Meeting, near Philadelphia. Our dear Sister Janes[91] was present. How sweetly does her life exhibit the *beauty* of holiness. I think I never saw an individual more fully possessed of that love that thinketh no evil, than our beloved Sister Janes, yet as she professes the enjoyment of a state of holiness, she has her trials. She feels sadly assured that many ministers of the New Jersey Conference, do not love explicit testimony on this subject. . . .

There are reasons why I shall remember this meeting with thanksgiving to God. I had been strongly urged to attend one which was held at the same time at Eastham near Boston. Here Wesleyan views of holiness are much appreciated, and last year while with them, I witnessed many enter into the enjoyment of holiness. I was perhaps equally urged to attend the meeting in New Jersey; but here I well knew, that the doctrine was depreciated, yet I dared not refuse. When I inquired of the Lord which of the two I should attend, it was suggested that the Saviour would not have left His throne in heaven had His only object been the enjoyment of congenial society, and if I would take Him as my example, my way was clear. I yielded and went to New Jersey. Most abundantly have I been rewarded in my own soul, for this act of self-denial.

She sought to witness anonymously at a Baltimore camp meeting, but her public recognition was so great that it was impossible (Memoirs, p. 280–81):

Late Sept., 1848

Wednesday morning, I attended a general class-meeting, in one of the large tents, at a very early hour. Perhaps from one hundred and fifty to two hundred, were present. In speaking of the dealings of God, I found myself inclined to speak in a manner which might not intimate who I was, but had scarcely commenced speaking, before I perceived that I was recognized. Most sweetly did I feel that the friends of Jesus were my friends, aye, more than friends—brothers and sisters in Christ. The ministers present[92] seemed to drink truly into the same spirit. I was called upon to close the interview with prayer, after which scores gathered around me, who though they had never seen my face in the flesh, expressed themselves acquainted in spirit.[93] Among others who strongly grasped my hand, was Mr. Creamer,[94] the Hymnologist of Baltimore. I was pleased to recognize him, as an ardently devoted Christian. . . .

Thursday. I desire to record to the praise of God the extraordinary liberty felt during the closing exercises at one of the large tents, this morning. It was announced that about twenty had been born into the kingdom of God, during the night. The Lord caused me to realize the awful responsibility of the Church, when new born babes had thus been committed to her keeping. I can indeed say, that it was out of the abundance of my heart that my mouth spoke.[95] Young converts will inevitably backslide, unless they obey the command, and go on unto perfection.[96]

4. FIVE POINTS MISSION AND SERVICE
TO THE URBAN POOR (1848–1852)

Among America's first efforts to establish social services to the urban poor were those initiated by Mrs. Palmer and associates. Vision and original support for the Five Points Mission in New York City came from Mrs. Palmer and a small group of women, working against official church opposition decades before the work of Jane Addams.[97]

The story of her involvement in ministry to the poor dates back to the early 1840's, when she was engaged in a tract ministry to the poor of lower East Side Manhattan, which she called her "Tract District." It involved not only a ministry of conversation and tract distribution, but also a ministry of physical care—feeding, addictive behaviors rehabilitation, orphan rescue, etc.[98]

A wrenching conflict occurred in 1848 that was to create later waves of opposition and misunderstanding directed against Dr. and Mrs. Palmer. They had decided to move their church membership from the more affluent Allen Street Church to a struggling church in a poor neighborhood that desperately needed their support and leadership (Memoirs, p. 189–90):

NEW YORK, October 12th, 1848

BELOVED BROTHER CREAGH:[99]

Seldom have we put pen to paper under what we deem to be more responsible circumstances. It is not without prayerful deliberation that we make known to you, as the pastor of the Allen Street congregation, a *decision* which has been the result of much serious, and *painful* inquiry. This decision is no other than to ask a certificate of dismission, in order that our names may be transferred to the Norfolk Street Church. The request may startle you, and to make it, we can assure you, is indeed, as we have said, *painful*, and the thought that it might also give you pain, and add yet greater weight to your already burdened heart, has caused us to linger in painful suspense, until the way is now made so plain, that we dare no longer resist what we believe to be the order of God.

Our kind pastor may desire to know our reasons for coming to this decision. One important reason is, that our sympathies have been much enlisted for the Norfolk Street Church, on account of its *feebleness*. The pecuniary wants, and the need of laborers in this Church, have already, by its pastor, been made known to Brother Creagh, and we need not to say that we feel ourselves bound to dispense according to the ability given[100] in these respects, and to do this *just in the sphere* where such as God has made us the stewards of, may be most needed, and most effective.[101] In looking at the *wants* of the Norfolk Street Church, Brother Creagh, with ourselves, can have no doubt on the subject.

In relation to the Allen Street Church, we have *long* thought, that in view of what ought to be her resources, both in regard to her pecuniary ability—her long standing as a church, and the amount of piety and talent of her membership, that she has within her pale what ought to have been available, toward the establishment and upbuilding of several churches.

With this view, which has been the sincere conviction of several years past, we feel that it would rather require an apology for remaining so long, rather than for the request for dismission. And if, as inferred, an apology were required, we will say, what may assure you that we do not take this step without some self-denial and serious inconvenience. It is not expedient, doubtless, for us to glory,[102] yet, during the eighteen or twenty years of our membership here,[103] we hope we are not without seals[104] to our labors here, both in regard to the reception of the grace of justification, and sanctification. To these, our hearts are bound in the strong ties of spiritual relationship, and the inquiries which may be awakened in the minds of some such, would be a source of painful solicitude, were it not for the assurance, that the ways of the Lord are perfect, and we are sure that He would not require this duty, without causing the consequences to be such as may glorify His name. Thus we dare to believe it will be. Another motive which may have had some weight toward detaining us here, is the inconvenience to which I shall be subjected, in view of the frequency of my professional calls, even while engaged in sanctuary services.

Yet these matters dwindle, in view of the inquiry, "Can we not, on the whole, bestow our labors on a part of the Lord's vineyard, where they are more needed, than that which we now occupy?" If Brother Creagh will look at the comparative wants of the two churches in question, we think it cannot be otherwise than that he will decide with ourselves, that we have been influenced by the Great Master of the vineyard, to ask a transfer, to go to a portion, which for months past, has been calling loudly for help.

We have chosen this mode of communication, because we could not well bring our minds to the painful duty of communicating verbally. Our minds are *wholly one,* on this subject, and when our classes, which meet, one on Thursday afternoon, and the other on Friday evening, shall be taken in charge by others who may fill our places,[105] we shall ask the benediction of our beloved and honored pastor, and take our leave.

> Yours, as ever, in the bonds of Christian love,
> WALTER C. and PHOEBE PALMER

The move elicited bitterness on the part of the previous pastor, and gave detractors an opening for a wider attack upon the Palmers' theology and churchmanship. Cholera and other epidemics were widespread and deadly in New York City during this period. Several of her friends died, and all were mortally endangered. The cholera epidemic intensified Mrs. Palmer's efforts to improve health and living conditions in the slums, which in time developed into America's first inner city mission to the poor[106] (Memoirs, p. 128–29):

Diary, July 18th, 1849,—The "pestilence that walketh in darkness, and the destruction that wasteth at noonday,"[107] continues its work of destruction.

> "Friend after friend departs,
> Who has not lost a friend."[108]

Bro. Samuel Roberts, one of the trustees of the Allen Street M. E. Church, died last night, of the prevailing epidemic. One might well think of "the pains, the groans, the dying strife," in beholding his agonies for several hours. But in all he endured as seeing the invisible.[109] Though in indescribable distress, he cried out, "All is well, I am going home."

During the past week, nine hundred and ninety-one have departed this life, within the bounds of this city. Over four hundred died of cholera.

"In the way of thy judgments, O, Lord, have we waited for thee. The desire of our soul is to Thy name and to the remembrance of Thee. With my soul have I desired Thee in the night; Yea, with my spirit within me will I seek Thee early; for when thy judgments are in the earth, the inhabitants of the world will learn righteousness."[110]

To her house came a diverse stream of people who shared her vision of a way of holiness. Her ministry of conversation was relentless, yet often softened by evidences of good humor. We get a glimpse of this in the following diary entry, where we learn that at her dining table, games were invented to sharpen biblical awareness (Memoirs, p. 158):

Diary, 1849—A good old brother Sawyer was present, from Canada, whom Dr. Bangs introduced as his spiritual father.[111] Dear mother Stebbins told an affecting portion of her experience, at the supper table. Dr. Bangs, who is ever intent upon bringing out instructive lessons, on such occasions, had been questioning her on the subject of faith. Her answers were most satisfactory, and brought out a recital of experience most interesting and edifying. A number were present, and we truly had a spiritual, as also a temporal repast. We have been in the habit of pursuing a course which we ever realize is favored with a sense of divine approval. It is that of having a portion of the bread of life from each one surrounding the table, in turn. Sometimes the person sitting at the head of the table selects a verse commencing with A, the next repeats one commencing with B, and thus we progress until the alphabet is finished.

Whether audiences were receptive or resistant, she worked with them where they were, as indicated in this letter to her husband from Red Lion camp meeting in Delaware (Memoirs, p. 285):

August 10[112]
The Spirit's process is not quite as rapid, (though always equally sure) under some circumstances, as others. At some places where I go, I find a people prepared for the Lord, and I only seem required to gather the harvest. At others, the fallow ground is to be broken up, and then the seed is to be sown, and the fruit, of course, cannot be so quickly gathered. It is somewhat thus under present circumstances. But I think we shall have a glorious ingathering, before the close of our labors.

Through these years her special interest in young people continued. On the eve of the momentous decade of the 1850's, which was to witness an accelerating holiness revival[113] that would take her repeatedly throughout New England and Canada, she wrote this inspirational poem for declamation by youth. The transition from elegiac meter to a shorter meter in the third verse marks a transition from an eschatological vision to one of penitence and supplication (A Mother's Gift, pp. 163–66):

A Thought for the Year 1950[114]

Friends will have met ere then, yes, those long parted
   By destiny forbid to mingle hearts,
That 'neath the pangs of hope deferred[115] had smarted,
   Have met at last where friendship never parts.

Foes too have met where once high malice stealing
   Upon the strings of life, they both gave way,
The curtain drop of death is now revealing
   Scenes that have filled the soul with sad dismay.

     Taught by Thy word of truth,
       That children came to Thee;[116]
     We come, a company of youth,
       Before Thy majesty.

    Lord, we have ever been
      The children of thy care;
And as a Father we have seen
      That Thou dost with us bear.

Though we have often erred,
      And fear we grieve Thee much,
We learn from Thy most holy Word,
      That Thou dost pity such.[117]

Oh! through the coming year,
      Whilst we instruction gain,
May it by all we do appear,
      That it is not in vain.

    Mrs. Palmer's efforts were early linked with those of transAtlantic[118] *evangelist James Caughey*[119] *whose pattern-setting revival mission was destined to have wide influence in Ireland and England. She had urgently invited Rev. Caughey to visit New York. Within a decade she would be following his British revival circuits in England and Ireland* (Memoirs, p. 191):

Rev. James Caughey, May 29th, 1850
   . . . It is true your answers are discouraging, and with these in view,

our importunities might cease, were it not that we *believe God* has a work for you to do here. We are sure you would not willingly be disobedient to this calling, if you knew just how the matter has stood, and now stands.

Caughey responded affirmatively to this stirring call, and held a series of meetings at Norfolk Street Church.[120]

By 1851 Mrs. Palmer had begun a precedent-setting ministry to prisoners in one of the worst prisons in America: the Tombs in Lower Manhattan, New York City (Memoirs, p. 216):

Diary, February 9th, 1851.—Sister Sarah Lankford, and Sister Keene, accompanied me to the Tombs. Mrs. Upham met us there, and we had an interesting time with the prisoners. We spent the remainder of the afternoon at the Five Points Mission.

She worked with alcoholics at early morning hours, distributed Bibles, reaching out constantly for the welfare of the souls and bodies of the dispossessed and poor.[121] *Here is a sample from her 1851 diary (Memoirs, p. 210):*

March 30th, 1851.—Went out this morning at an early hour, to do something toward reclaiming an inebriate, Mr. B. Begged him, on my knees, to lay his hand on the Bible, and promise the God of the Bible that he would neither "Touch, taste, nor handle"[122] spiritous liquors. This afternoon, on his knees, he solemnly pledged himself. Thank the Lord!.

March 31st.—Long conversation with Mr. B., about the divinity of the word of God. Said he never saw the Scriptures in such a light before. Gave him a pocket Bible, which he says he ever intends to carry *close to his heart.* My sympathies have been greatly enlisted in his behalf. . . .

April 1st.—Mr. B. was reading the Bible as I entered the room, early this morning. Pointing to the fifty-first chapter of Isaiah, "See," said he, "what I accidentally opened upon." "Not *accidentally*," I replied, "*God* gave it to you, for before I came to the room, I thought of directing your mind to it."[123] My soul is filled with joy in his behalf, *the joy of Christ.*

At the Tombs, she regularly pursued her ministry to women prisoners under wretched conditions. There, in stark contrast with her meetings for the promotion of holiness, she was confronted by the despair and squalor that caused desperation on the part of the prisoners, as this diary entry reveals (Memoirs, p. 216):

June 15th, 1851.—Held a meeting with the female prisoners at the City Prison. Witnessed a dreadful sight. One of the male prisoners had tied a handkerchief around his neck and strangled himself. There he lay in his pine coffin, with the kerchief still about his neck, and his face awfully discolored, looking more like a fiend than a human being. How unlike the sight I witnessed yesterday. There lay the sweet, placid form of the now sainted Brewster, angel gentleness and love already stamped on his countenance, though suddenly precipitated into eternity; his life and even his look seemed to say it was sudden glory.

Her view of the purity and unity of the church was poignantly set forth in this detailed letter to Bishop Janes, whose ordination she had so warmly applauded. This delicate communication reveals how vexing had become the thorny controversy with Hiram Mattison[124] *(Memoirs, pp. 551–53):*

NEW YORK, January 25th, 1852.

TO REV. BISHOP JANES:

I am indulging the humble hope of soon walking the streets of the Heavenly Jerusalem, with the dear brother whom I now address. I have been asking the Lord for wisdom to say now, about what I shall wish I had said, after we have entered upon our eternal state. I would not expose myself to the appearance of officiousness, which the mention of matters which I am about to suggest, might indicate, were it not, that I believe you know the integrity of my heart. Over fourteen years since, the Lord brought me to a willingness to be of no reputation for Him, who made himself of no reputation for me.[125] The day of your ordination as Bishop,[126] was one of the most eventful days of my life. For years had I been pleading that God would raise up instrumentalities, whose influence might be felt through the length and breadth of our land, in arousing our people to the relative importance of holiness. That there should not be, perhaps, more than one in fifty among us, professing the attainment of this grace, when the distinguishing doctrine of our creed is a belief in the attainableness of holiness in the present life, to me did not seem answerable to the claims of God upon us. On the day of your, and our Brother Hamline's ordination, as superintendents, I felt that the Lord had indeed looked upon His people for good,[127] and was now about to fulfill my desire. My heart, in almost a bewilderment of grateful feeling, cried out, *"What* shall I render unto the Lord, for all His benefits?"*[128]—His mercy in raising up two *such* men, to such a position, in a time when they were so much needed,—when such an evident want of internal holiness in the church, had plunged her into such difficulties; *What* shall I render?" The answer of the Holy Spirit was, "Present yourself as a whole burnt sacrifice, upon the altar of the service of the church, for the promotion of holiness.'' I did so,—and Abraham, when he saw the fire descend, and consume his sacrifice,[129] could not, I think, have more sensibly realized the acceptance of his offering, than I realized the consuming energies of the Holy Spirit, penetrating, as it were, every fibre of my being.[130] I had before felt that my interests were all identified with the interests of my Redeemer's kingdom, but ever since that eventful day, have I felt such an absorption in everything that stands connected with the internal purification of the church, that I can scarcely speak of interests apart from it. Our unity, as a people,[131] and our well-being in every regard, I believe stands in connection with right realizations of our responsibilities, in relation to this important theme. God has set us as a city upon a hill[132] in regard to this subject, and if our ministers indulge in controverting truths, which by our standard authors are regarded as of vital importance, I believe God will punish us with dissentions.[133] Two or three months before the excitement commenced in Philadelphia, a minister of New Jersey Conference said to me, ''They are having very warm times in discussing the subject of holiness, in Philadelphia, at the preachers' meeting,'' etc. I felt in my heart that God would not have the force of truth weakened in the minds of the people, after this sort, without visiting for it. He raised up an adversary to Solomon and He can raise up an adversary to us. The next thing I heard from Philadelphia was the excitement about a lay delegation, which a careful observer of the movement tells me, will doubtless end in serious disunion. This brother, though he knew nothing of my thoughts, put precisely the same version on it, as I have given. This was Brother Longacre of Philadelphia. But the Philadelphia controversy on the subject, will but slightly compare with the far-reaching harm which is being done by the articles of brother Mattison in the ''Northern Christian Advocate.''[134] Here the subject of holiness has been controverted in almost every conceivable way,[135] and I think I will speak truly before God, when I say, that the professors of it have been divided, until I should think hundreds of them are now covering their heads in shame.

If your time would admit, I would love to spread out before you some of the letters I have received from some of the most useful and accredited presiding elders and ministers in our connection.[136]

As your name has been more freely used in this controversy, than the name of any other bishop,[137] I have been endeavoring to ask the Lord in faith, to direct your attention to it, but I have learned that I am not to expect God to do through spiritual influences, that which ought to be done through a human instrumentality. Faith without *works*, is dead.[138] Let this be the apology for my present work. I hoped that you had been induced, before now, to look at brother Mattison's articles, but on asking Dr. P., last night, he informed me you had not.[139] Since which, my heart has been *very* heavy. Shall the names of our bishops, be sounded through the length and breadth of the land, as men not favoring the *profession of holiness?* Does it signify much, that the attainment of holiness in the present life, is a distinguishing doctrine of our creed, if the profession, when attained, is not encouraged? I think there are but few of other denominations of the present day, but will admit, that it is a present duty to obey the command, "Be ye holy."[140] But when witnesses, that God does empower the soul to obey the command, are raised up among them, from time to time, they are persecuted as fanatical and presumptuous. Shall this state of things be brought in among us, and not be reproved by those in authority?[141]

Your Sister in Jesus.

5. THE EXTENSION OF MISSION TO NEW AREAS
(1853–1856)

Mrs. Palmer earnestly sought to persuade the Missionary Society to initiate a Palestinian mission in 1853.[142] She felt distinctly the call of God to help activate and support a witness to Christ in Arab lands (Memoirs, pp. 233–34):

New York, February 12th, 1853

To Rev. Dr. Durbin, Sec. of the Miss. of the M.E.C.:[143]
    Dear Brother,—I have for some time indulged an earnest desire, that the pure uncompromising principles of Methodism might be planted in Palestine. In view of the apostolic zeal of the founder of Methodism, it seems not only right, but evidently called for, that his sons in the gospel should go forth and in the spirit of the apostles, proclaim the Gospel as the power of God, unto the salvation of men. If Methodism is in fact, as it has been denominated, "*Christianity in earnest*,"[144] then who can doubt that the Head of the Church calls her to undertake a Mission in Palestine.[145]

The effort did not succeed (Memoirs, p. 234):

February 17th, 1853

To Rev. Mr. Hartwell:
    About nine o'clock A.M. Dr. P. took me to the mission rooms to see Dr. Durbin. Dr. D. and ourselves had a long talk about Palestine. Though

all, and more than all, we have said about the need of missionary effort in P. is true, yet Dr. D. thinks the field so unpromising that he dares not encourage the hope of success. Time and again the field has been entered and abandoned as hopeless. The American Board has now withdrawn her mission, and the London Missionary Society alone, I believe, has the field, and it is conjectured that this may be more in view of *political* effect than anything else; besides, ecclesiastical comity forbade interference with the work of other churches in his opinion.[146] I can scarcely say, at the present moment what decision it may be better to come to. In view of what my yearnings over this portion of God's vineyard, once so favoured, are, I cannot regret the efforts I have made to bring it into remembrance.[147]

While away on one of her revival journeys, Mrs. Palmer wrote to her husband of her concern over their growing children, who were now twenty, fourteen, and eleven years old (Memoirs, p. 145):

Jan. 19, 1854

My heart was much drawn out, as it ever is, for our dear children. The Lord only knows how continually they are on my heart,—how much I desire their present usefulness and happiness.[148] The Lord has given them so much light by which to discern that holiness, usefulness, and happiness, are inseparably connected. I well know that they can not really enjoy themselves unless they aim at entire devotion to God. The burden of my heart for them constantly is, that they may be living examples of "the beauty of holiness,"[149] for well do they know as dear Aunt Mary[150] said, "*There is no such thing as a half-hearted Christian.*" I have often wished, if it were the will of God, that my heart were as a window, where my dear children might look in and witness all the spiritual and natural movements of their mother's heart toward them.[151]

Six years after their transfer to the poor neighborhood Norfolk Street Church,[152] Mrs. Palmer wrote to one of its members, "Brother B.," who was considering leaving it. Here she stated why she regarded service to the poor neighborhood of the Norfolk Street Church as analogous to a mission station requiring special support (Memoirs, p. 193–95):

May 30, 1854

I have heard (rather as a secret, and what I hope may remain such,) that you have expectations of taking your transfer from the Norfolk Street charge. I hope this may be a mistake, but if it should not be, let me ask my dear Brother whether he feels quite sure, that this is the step which will be most pleasing to God. I do not ask this because I do not think it possible

with God to raise up another to take your place. We know the Church belongs to *God,* not to *us.* We know it is nothing with God to help, whether
with many or few. The silver and the gold are His, and the cattle on a thousand hills.[153] The best of us are but stewards, whether our possessions be
in money, or in intellectual gifts. And if we are permitted to minister in the
Church of God, whether it be in gift or speech, or in money, we only dispense according to the ability which *God* giveth,[154] for what have we but
what we have received.

. . . Dr. P., and myself, would not have left a strong and popular
Church, directly in our neighborhood, for one weak in its resources, and
less popular, and at a greater distance, if it were not that the Lord had assured our hearts, that we must not live for ourselves. Religion assured us
that the claims of the stronger ought to yield to the weaker.[155] In view of
the necessities of the N——— Street Church, we tore ourselves away from
a field of labor, which, from almost our youthful days, we had been endeavoring more or less to cultivate. What we suffered in doing this, the Lord
only knows.

Now suppose, because we have had some trials about our minister, and
some other things occurring, not quite pleasing, we shall desert the Church
in the hour of her greatest need. Would not the Master of the vineyard chide
us, and refuse to employ us in another portion of his vineyard, if, to please
ourselves, and, unbidden by him, we should leave where he has so evidently
placed us? We find our attendance at N——— Street, attended with serious
and various inconveniences. From year to year, we have been waiting, hoping that, from among the number who are being born there, some one may
be raised up to take our place, but our scattered, and ever scattering congregation seems to betoken that the Lord intends the N——— Street Church,
as a sort of Mission Church, differing from other Mission Stations, in that
it is being sustained by a few.

*In August of 1854 she held a meeting at Millennial Grove, Eastham,
Massachusetts, with Benjamin Adams, the minister of the Five Points Mission. Her travelling experiences were at times harrowing. She wrote to the
Hamlines of a life-threatening steamship accident on Long Island Sound, a
dangerous nighttime fire while returning from the New England camp
meetings*[156] *(Memoirs, pp. 306–07):*

August, 1854
. . . I must record a remarkable preservation of our lives on our return
from the New England camp-meetings. While on board the elegant steamer
"Empire State," between ten and eleven o'clock at night, and the passengers mostly retired, the boiler burst. Truly, we could now, judging from

appearances, say, "There is but a step between me and death." The consternation among the passengers was awful. Among the hundreds on board, we did not observe any among them that gave indication of a preparation for eternity. "Thanks be to God, who giveth us the victory through our Lord Jesus Christ,"[157] such a sweet consciousness had I, of victory over death, that "all was calm and heaven within. . . . "[158]

Sister Sarah united with me, and we sang the words to the beautiful, plaintive tones of the tune, "We're going home to die no more."[159] It really seemed, as we were singing, as though we were aided by a supernatural power, and I do not doubt but the strains fell in almost unearthly tones on the listeners. Immediately the scene began to change from wild consternation, to more unimpassioned thoughts of the future, bringing into striking contrast, the peaceful trust of the christian and the sad insecurity of the worldling, who is trusting in the God of this world, for happiness.

After we had finished these stanzas, we were entreated to repeat them. By this time Dr. P. came in, and we commenced the hymn, "How do Thy mercies close me round,"[160] and with his beautiful bass, the Lord helped us to discourse music which I do not doubt told on hundreds of hearts.

By the time we finished, the boat's company was calm, and the immediate and imminent danger seemed to have subsided.

The deck outside the ladies' cabin, was filled with a dense fog, whether from the bursted boiler, or the boat being on fire, or both.

The officers of the boat seemed unwilling to inform the people of the facts in the case. Which ever was the case, the difficulty was in some way braved, and after several hours detention in the midst of Long Island Sound, we were again slowly on our way, reaching the city of New York the next afternoon, instead of early the next morning, as due.

"There are some Methodists here!" exclaimed a passenger, in the hearing of Dr. Palmer, as the sweet strains of the sanctified singers fell on the ears of the hushed and breathless throng of men, who jammed the door and passage way of the ladies' cabin,—anxious for the safety of female friends. What a powerful testimony to the value of Methodistic doctrine and experience, the involuntary exclamation was, is apparent to all.

Her valuing of each soul infinitely is clearly stated in this letter to a Brother Harper, concerning an invitation to provide leadership for a camp meeting in the Brampton District of Canada (Memoirs, p. 137):

[Undated, probably 1854][161]

I have settled it in my mind that, *one soul out-weighs the universe.* I have asked myself, whether it is not probable that one soul more might be saved, either directly, or indirectly, through our efforts, by going, rather than by staying, and the scale preponderates towards going. *I have a passion for soul-saving.*

Her interest in a mission to the Jews, which had surfaced earlier[162] *in her effort to establish a mission in Palestine, now focused upon Christian witness among Jews in New York. This concern became intensely personalized in the Palmer's decision to adopt an imprisoned Jewish lad, apparently a convert, Leopold Solomon (Memoirs, p. 213):*

NEW YORK, April 28th, 1855

TO BISHOP AND MRS. HAMLINE

Well, we have also, in yet more immediate prospect, another dear child. When you come, we hope to have the privilege of introducing you to Leopold Solomon Palmer, our Jewish boy. You will remember that he was thrown into prison for embracing the Christian faith. We expect to receive his indenture tomorrow.[163] He is bound to us by the city authorities. We take him as our child, in the name of the Methodist public, to train him for the ministry to which he feels himself called.

May 8th, 1855

To the same:

I told you in my last, of our newly adopted son, Leopold Solomon Palmer. He has now been with us several days. He is indeed most lovable and loving. We already take much comfort in him, and expect that he will be a blessing to thousands of the house of Israel. He has been relating his intensely interesting experience as a Christian, to me, this morning. You would be filled with wonder and joy, could you hear him tell of what things he has suffered for Christ's sake. Pray that he may be an instrument eminently fitted for the Master's use, and ever be deeply humble and holy.

Phoebe and Walter Palmer's daughter, Phoebe, married Joseph Knapp, who founded the Metropolitan Life Insurance Company.[164] *Shortly after their marriage, Mrs. Palmer wrote affectionately to them an admonition that their marriage be "in the Lord" (Memoirs, p. 147):*

June 17th, 1855

I want you, my dear Phoebe and Joseph, to be deeply devoted to God,—to resolve, should the Lord spare you to each other, that your lives shall unitedly flow out upon the world in rich blessings.

Do, my dear children, at this early period in your union, resolve not to live for *yourselves*. If you will do this, I think the Lord may spare you long to each other. This is being united in the Lord. But if you do not resolve on this, I feel jealous for the Lord of Hosts. He will have no other Gods before Him.[165] I want you to aim at the highest and most extended usefulness, and then will you live happily and God will be glorified.

Eminent holiness, usefulness and happiness are inseparably connected.[166]

A mother's blessing be on my dear son and daughter.

By August of 1855, Dr. and Mrs. Palmer's modest, unpretentious, personalized mission to immigrant Jews was fully operational. The Palmers had largely funded it, and provided their own home as a residence for its leader (to Mrs. Hamline, Memoirs, p. 229):

August 8th, 1855

Did I tell you that our Jewish Mission is at last fairly commenced? We have as yet no chapel, with steeple and church-going bell, but we meet in the chapel which was solemnly consecrated to the service of the Almighty God under our roof. Here our mission has been commenced, and here the sons of Israel meet. Last night, we had a meeting, and the God of Jacob was present. Three Jewish missionaries who had been converted from Judaism, and another preparing for the ministry, with several other converted Jews, were present. It was a good meeting. Last week we had our first meeting. We were reminded of the company assembled in an upper room in the earliest days of Christianity. We had memorable assurances that He who baptizeth with the Holy Ghost and with fire, was with us. He favored us with tokens of His presence and approval. Our missionary at present resides in the house with us, as our guest.

Her way of dealing non-defensively with opposition—quietly with intercession, trusting in providence—is best expressed in an article in the Christian Advocate *of December 5th, 1855.[167] This irenic view, willing to bear reproach for Christ's sake, was destined to have wide influence upon many in the holiness and pentecostal traditions:*

Coals of Fire

"In so doing, thou shalt bear coals of fire on his head." Rom. 12:20.

I might tell you of one of your friends who is never troubled very seriously for any length of time, with hard feelings about any one. Not that she does not sometimes have trials of this sort, calculated to perplex, but there are some things which Satan cannot endure, and it is well to find out what these things are. Well, here is one. He cannot bear to witness exhibitions of love to our enemies, or to have us bless and pray for them that despitefully use and persecute us.[168]

When the enemy obtrudes with new trials of this sort, she scarcely trusts herself to dwell on the merits or demerits of the case; but shielding herself afresh in Christ, she breathes out in words of love, blessings on her enemies. And the more the enemy magnifies the extent of the wrong, and tempts her to indulge in hard feelings against those who despitefully use her, the more earnestly does she ejaculate, "Lord, bless them! Lord, bless them!" And thus has she continued to repeat blessings, until the enemy has been vanquished.

Having suffered several harsh public attacks during the previous year, her diary contained a probing "last testimony" included in a New Year's self-examination of 1856, in which she reflected profoundly[169] *upon suffering as requisite to the deepening of faith*[170] *(Memoirs, pp. 129–30):*

Diary, January 1st, 1856.—I feel that my union with God is inward, *vital* and *real*. Most consciously do I realize that all my interests are identified with the interests of Christ's kingdom. If this should be my last testimony, I would wish to say before God, angels, and men, that from my own heart experiences, I know that God can, through the power of the Holy Spirit, so subdue the heart, as to bring the whole soul into a *joyous obedience to Christ*. Jesus saves me from my sins. I *feel* the Triune Deity—God the Father, Son, and Spirit, has undertaken the work of my salvation, and through grace, I have been enabled to submit to the saving, sanctifying, and ever-purifying processes through which I am led. God is leading me forth by a right way. The process of late has often been crucifying to the flesh. I have been called to *endure*. But I have victory *through* our Lord Jesus Christ. I have laid myself a whole burnt sacrifice upon the altar of the service of the church, and I am permitted of late, often painfully, to feel that the sacrifice is being *consumed*. The profession of holiness has of late been publicly and seriously assailed by those who ought to have defended it. I have been personally assailed as standing at the head and front of offending. But I feel that Christ is gloriously with me. He is even now saying to my inmost soul, "Great is the holy One in the midst of thee."[171] Though my nature, at times, recoils, yet grace triumphs over nature, and I seem almost lost in view of the glory that will follow. "Christ shall be magnified,"[172]

Truth shall triumph, and I feel that I am indeed enabled to "glory in tribulation."[173] Often have I had occasion to exclaim, "The reproaches of them that reproached Thee are fallen upon me."[174] In view of these things, *nature,* in sympathy with the outward, will more or less *suffer,* but in the midst of all, my spirit will often in joyous song burst forth in the words,

> "And I enjoy the glorious shame
> The scandal of the cross."[175]

As a witness of the power of saving and sustaining grace, let me say, it can empower the soul to be *joyous* in tribulation. Indeed, I feel almost like chiding myself, when I speak of tribulation. It is enough for the disciple that he be as his Master, yet he that is perfect, shall be even as his Master.[176] How few are my *trials,* in view of my many triumphs! Truly, "The servant is above his Lord."[177] The recent persecution[178] against the profession and professors of holiness, seems only to have increased their holy courage. The interest in the precious theme of holiness, as a whole, seems manifestly on the increase.[179] Those who enjoy the blessing, seem disposed with yet greater explicitness and earnestness, to "hold fast the *profession* of their faith, without wavering."[180] Hallelujah! The Lord God omnipotent reigneth! "From henceforth, let no man trouble me, for I bear in my body the marks of the Lord Jesus Christ."[181] Never have I felt more like saying with holy boldness, and a degree of exultation, "I am crucified to the world, and the world to me."[182] O, it is indeed blessed to feel a conscious identification with the interests of a suffering Saviour. It is blessed to have a heart, "His *joys* and *griefs* to feel."[183] It is blessed to feel that He takes our entire being, and lays upon it His own blessed heart of love, and causes all its pulsations to flow out in unison with His own nature and purposes. Though the flesh may dislike the way, yet faith approves it well, and it is indeed most blessed to have the entire being so identified with Christ, as to feel at rest in the will of God, even though the prayer may be answered,

> "My spirit to Calvary bear,
> To suffer and triumph with Thee."[184]

Never have the words seemed so significantly glorious to me as of late, "If we suffer with Him, we shall also be glorified together."[185]

*In a soberly realistic mood, on election day of 1856 she wrote this rare political reflection in her diary (*Memoirs, *1856):*

This is election day. Our Presidential election has called forth an enlistment of interest and feeling, perhaps quite beyond precedent. Many prayers have been presented that the God of nations may overrule. It is not in my heart to censure the servants of the Most High God, for being earnestly active in manifesting their preference in the election of "the powers that be."[186]

We can scarcely hope that the powers that be, will be "ordained of God,"[187] unless God's servants unite in earnest activities, in the use of the means to secure this end.[188] The servants of the God of this world, will be untiring in their efforts to secure the election of such rulers as will serve the purposes of the "Prince of this world."[189] Satan has, for centuries, been vaunting himself in boastful claim on the kingdoms of this world. Perhaps the most strangely audacious record of Satan's assumptions, on the annals of time, is found where he said to the Son of God: "All these things will I give thee, if Thou wilt fall down and worship me."[190] The kingdoms of this world belong to our God and His CHRIST.[191] Christians are *they*, who, after having acknowledged the claims of Christ, as the world's Redeemer, and yielded up their mortal bodies that He may reign—"Whose right it is to reign,"[192]—employ all their powers to bring the world over to Christ.

I would not infer that the most effectual way to do this may be by engaging in political strife. But I do think that Christians ought to PRAY *much*, and also by careful *foresight* and earnest endeavor—seek to have *God-fearing* candidates for office; and then in pious, united, persevering zeal, strive for the election of such candidates. And perhaps thus only, may our prayer for God-fearing rulers be answered.

6. THE CANADA CAMPAIGN (1856–1859)

As early as 1853, Mrs. Palmer had initiated a far-reaching mission to Canada, first in Ontario: Napanee in 1853, Bond Head in 1854, Earnesttown and Barrie in 1855. This effort intensified during the last three years before she left for England (1856–59). In 1856 she visited Coburg and London, Canada. In 1857, often referred to as the annus mirabilis[193] (miracle year), she held meetings with exceptional responses in Quebec (Montreal, St. Andrews) and Ontario (Brighton, Millbrook, Port Hope, Spencer-town, Acton, Hamilton, and London). In 1858 she shifted her focus toward eastern Canada, visiting New Brunswick (Woodstock, Frederickton, St. Johns, Monckton, Sackville), Nova Scotia (Halifax, Truro, River John), and Prince Edward's Island. The lay witness emphasis,[194] and proto-Pentecostal theology[195] and language began to gain clearer expression during this period. Few letters from this period exist, partly due to the intense activity.

One that suggests the excitement of the Canadian campaign was written from Coburg, Ontario just after she had held an extended meeting at Victoria College (Memoirs, p. 313):

September 25th, 1856

TO BISHOP AND MRS. HAMLINE:

With inextinguishable ardor did a number of those young students from the school of the prophets, Victoria College—begin to ask for the baptism of fire.[196] Its results on the future of the meeting were glorious. Scores of seekers, some pleading for pardon, and others for purity, were ready to rush forward at every invitation. Many were saved. O, it seemed as if Pentecostal times had in verity, come upon us.[197] Truly did the Lord pour out His Spirit upon His servants and his handmaidens, upon His sons and His daughters.[198] With each passing day and hour, did the manifestations of divine power in the awakening of sinners, the sanctification of believers, and the quickening of the saints, increase. And thus matters progressed, until Tuesday, the fourth day after my dear mother had entered her heavenly rest. It was evening, and all day, angels had been hovering over us, bearing the news to heaven, of souls newly repenting, newly forgiven, and newly sanctified. To scores of redeemed spirits had the blood of sprinkling been newly applied, and with the redeemed company within the vale, we had again and again joined in the song,

"Glory to the Lamb," etc.[199]

Ah! I did not then know, that that dear mother, who first taught my infant lips to repeat the praises of the Lamb, had been mingling in the chorus with us. Just at twilight, a messenger (a dear minister), came from twenty miles distant, bringing a telegraphic dispatch, by which we were assured, that our dear mother had reached her long sought rest. It was a new trial. God had done it, and hidden it from us. Never, perhaps, did I more deeply feel the need of grace, to enable me to endure, in such a manner, as to glorify Him in my body and spirit. . . .

Word of her mother's death shook her deeply, but she continued her itinerary[200] (Memoirs, pp. 314–15, written Sept. 25, 1856):

And now I felt newly commissioned for my work—more than ever detached from earth—newly winged from heaven. Surely, God takes our treasure to heaven that our hearts may be there also. From this hour, I resolved that the death of my mother should be made the occasion of spiritual life to many. "Instant in season, out of season,"[201] I resolved to pursue my way, making every strait, through which I might be brought, whether afflictive or joyous, subservient to the salvation of souls.

She returned to New York for the winter (of 1856–57), but was back again in Canada the following summer, accompanied by Dr. Palmer who by this time had become an important regular participant in her revival activities. From Millbrook, Ontario, Canada, she wrote to her sister Sarah a carefully crafted, detailed letter describing an ordinary day of a Canadian-style camp meeting.[202] This letter discloses her firm conviction that the Pentecostal Spirit had already fully reappeared amid these meetings, and that the baptism of the Holy Spirit[203] and fire was "in their midst."[204] The summer of 1857, therefore, must be marked as an important date in the history of proto-Pentecostalism, far earlier than it is often dated (Memoirs, pp. 318–20):

July 6th, 1857

TO MRS. S. A. LANKFORD,

Suppose you follow us for one day, and you take it mostly as a specimen of the manner in which many of our other days are spent, during our repeated absences from home. We arose about six o'clock, after having closed a meeting before the preachers' stand, near midnight, the night previous.[205] Dr. P. is always, in this region, given in charge of all the meetings before the stand. We sleep about one-third of a mile from the encampment. Soon after we arose, a conveyance was brought to the door, to take us to the ground. But the kind brother with whom we abide, who is the owner of the ground, was resolved that we should remain and breakfast with the family at the house, and therefore, the vehicle is kept standing until after we have dispatched our breakfast. Scarcely have we finished, and read a portion of the ever blessed Word, and knelt in prayer with the family, and put our things hurriedly on, to go to the ground, before four large, able-bodied men come in, one after another. They have traveled forty miles on horseback, to attend the meeting, and are now come to get their horses, in order to return to their homes. We find, on inquiry, that they all enlisted, about one year since, in the service of the Captain of their salvation. They came to the ground on Saturday evening, and it is now Monday morning. We ask them how it is with their souls, and are informed that they came seeking the blessing of entire sanctification, but have not yet attained the grace. We speak of the open fountain[206]—the readiness of the Sanctifier to do it *now*. He who baptizeth with the Holy Ghost, and with fire,[207] is in our midst. In about one-half hour, all three were filled with wondering amazement. The

Holy Ghost, as a gift of power, light, and life, has lighted upon each one of them, and all are unutterably filled with glory and with God, and return to their homes, filled with new wine,[208] as warriors in Immanuel's army—fully equipped, and mighty, through the Spirit, to do battle for God.[209] And now we go to the encampment. The eight o'clock[210] preaching service is already in progress. The servant of Christ is preaching from the text, "God sent not his Son into the world to condemn the world, but that the world, through Him, might be saved.''[211] The discourse finished, we are called upon to address the congregation.[212] With a feeling of conscious, and absolute dependence on the Holy Spirit, we speak of the Christian's high calling—of the glory of the present dispensation, and its responsibilities on individual professors. We speak of the day of Pentecost, as fully come[213]—no need of waiting, in view of the fact, that He who baptizeth with the Holy Ghost, and with fire, is in the midst.[214] Conscious of the Spirit's impellings, I speak on, and on, till a half hour passes, as though it were but a few moments. Dr. P., now in an earnest exhortation, invited all who will, to draw high, and partake of the gospel feast, assuring them, in the name of the heavenly Provider, that all things are now ready,[215]—Pardon, and Holiness, and Heaven. From sixty to eighty present themselves. God's Spirit is poured out in such copious measure, in the conversion of sinners, and the sanctification of believers, that the measurement of time is forgotten. Preachers, and people unite as one. Victory succeeds victory, till, ere we are aware, it is one o'clock, and we are urged to take something to eat, and find, that the time for the ten o'clock service, has passed by without our having taken note of time. One case after another presses upon us, and we find it difficult to release ourselves, so as to get time to eat. And now we dine. No boarding tents here, or nothing answerable thereunto. All things are common, as in the primitive days of Christianity.[216] Hundreds have been on the ground as visitors, but so hearty and impelling is the hospitality, it really seems as if those who succeed in getting the greatest number to partake of their profusely set tables, are the most happy. No charges for ground, sextonship, or anything of the sort. Everything is done in the spirit of bounteous sacrifice, as though each, in pious noble resolve, had long since learned to say with David, "Shall I sacrifice that which cost me nothing?''[217]

Some Roman Catholic participation in Mrs. Palmer's Canadian camp meetings (rare for that period) was attested in this letter (Memoirs, p. 324):

New York, August 3d, 1857

TO MRS. HAMLINE:
      . . . We reached St. Andrew's about mid-day. This meeting was the first of the sort ever held in this region. It was held in the midst of a Catholic

population, and was looked upon by all, as an EXPERIMENT. Several months since, we were advised with, in regard to a camp-meeting being held in Lower Canada, and were asked if we would come, in case it should be thought expedient to make the effort. Under such circumstances, you may be assured that we felt no small responsibility. The ground chosen for the encampment was within three minutes' walk of the Catholic church, which stood at the entrance of the wood, as we approached the ground, and daily did their vesper bell salute our ears. Many of the Catholics attended the services on the encampment. . . .

The Canadian revivals of 1856–59 were largely lay-led occasions.[218] *They were to some degree distinguished from their U.S. counterparts in encouraging more lay leadership, and in the pervasiveness of the Pentecostal metaphor. Entire devotion to God was frequently concretized and symbolized by "bringing tithes into the Lord's storehouse." The Palmers were constantly attentive to the Spirit's unexpected direction in sudden re-arrangements of her itinerary, as this letter dramatically portrayed* (Memoirs, pp. 328f.):

HAMILTON, October 10th, 1857

TO MRS. S.A. LANKFORD:
    We arrived at Hamilton about dark, and Dr. P. made an effort to check his baggage through for Friday, so as to reach home by the Albany boat, on Saturday morning. But *God* has, in a wonderful manner, detained us at every step. Dr. P. was frustrated in his attempt to leave his baggage, and we went to the house of a friend, to remain over night, intending to leave for home early in the morning. It was the usual evening for prayer-meeting in the three churches here. Two of the ministers received information of our unexpected visit, and before we had finished our tea, were with us. They immediately made arrangements for uniting the prayer-meetings. As we proceeded to the meeting, the Spirit of the Lord urged the text, "Call upon me and I will answer thee, and show thee great and mighty things, things that thou knewest not."[219] And while talking in the meeting, I felt a Divine power pressing me mightily to urge upon the people to set themselves apart at once, to work for God, in promoting a revival. I felt the Holy Spirit working in my own heart powerfully, and assured the people if they would at once "bring all the tithes into the Lord's store house,"[220] and prove Him therewith, that He would open the windows of heaven and pour out such a blessing as would overflow the regions round about, and result in hundreds on hundreds being brought home to God.[221] I asked that as many as would thus bring all the tithes of *time, talent, estate,* etc., into the Lord's treasury,

and begin *at once* to act on the principle that the tithes of *time, reputation, talents,* whether of influence, estate, body of mind, should be devoted to the work of soul saving, would manifest their resolve to do so by raising the right hand. Thirty, perhaps, or more of those present lifted their hand in the solemn presence of God that they would begin to work *immediately.* Thus it was that the battle was at once, in the most unlooked-for manner, pushed to the gate. One of the ministers, speaking of this since, said, "The battle was set in array so suddenly, that Satan himself had not time to contemplate a defence." We *dared* not leave, but promised in case that all would thus go abroad at once, and give the gospel invitation, we would remain with them over the next evening. There were in all, probably about sixty or seventy present at the meeting. During the night, my spirit was awake with God, much of the time, and I received a divine conviction that God was about to bring out the people in multitudes and stamp our ideas of a "laity for the times," with signal success.

The next letter reported this remarkable sequel (Memoirs, pp. 330–31):

HAMILTON. C.W., October 14th, 1857

TO MRS. S.A. LANKFORD:

. . . Such a sabbath as yesterday, we never saw. Meetings were being held from seven o'clock in the morning till ten in the evening, in all of which I believe some were saved. We have had but very little preaching. I mean preaching in the technical sense, according to the ordinary idea of preaching in the present day. And though I would not be understood to speak lightly of the value of well beaten oil for the service of the sanctuary, yet never have I been so confirmed in a belief long since adopted, in regard to the sort of preaching needed at the present day. It is the preaching of apostolic times, when all the church membership were "scattered throughout the regions of Judea and Samaria, *except* the apostles."[222] And these scattered bands, of newly baptised disciples, though so young in faith, and composed of men, women, and children, went everywhere preaching the Word.[223] Surely, dear Sister Sarah, this, in the most emphatic sense, is the sort of preaching which has been made instrumental in this great revival. Though few churches can boast of such ministers for talent and devotedness, and we are earnest in our acknowledgements that as shepherds of this newly gathered flock, their care, and also affectionate teachings and guidance, are *absolutely* needful, yet we will again say, that though favored with the constant aid of their three resident ministers, and other ministers, visitors of high position, district chairmen, etc.—yet this revival took its rise mainly with the laity.[224] It did not commence in laborious pulpit effort, neither has it progressed in this way. We had but one very short sermon, during the whole week. One of the ministers would generally say a few introductory stirring words, and then leave the meeting with ourselves, to follow up the remarks. Dr. P.'s prayer-meeting tact is of course brought into constant requisition, to bring up the rear.[225]

Returning to Canada in October 1858, she wrote to Mrs. Lankford from Charlottetown, Prince Edward's Island, of Pentecost-like happenings (Memoirs, p. 342):

5th of October, 1858

Many had, during the heart searching exercises of the preceding days, come to a point where they had a right to look for the present fulfillment of the promise of the Father.[226] The sacrifice had been brought to the altar, but it is *faith* that brings the power,[227] and claims the *tongue of fire*.[228] And how thankful we ought to be that our faithful Lord does not require us to believe anything, but what he gives a reason from his *Word,* for believing, etc. Oh, what extraordinary demonstrations of the power of faith followed. Surely, the scene we witnessed could not have been greatly unlike that witnessed on the day of Pentecost.[229]

Notes

1. Leonidas Lent Hamline (1797–1865), admitted to Ohio bar, received on trial in the Ohio Conference, 1832, assistant editor of the *Western Christian Advocate,* 1836, editor of *The Ladies' Repository,* 1841, elected bishop, 1844. Resigned episcopal office in 1852 due to ill health, retired to Mount Pleasant, Iowa. See *Works of Rev. Leonidas L. Hamline,* edited by F.G. Hibbard, 2 vols. (Cincinnati: Hitchcock and Walden, 1869–71); and F. G. Hibbard, *Biography of Rev. L.L. Hamline* (Cincinnati: Hitchcock and Walden, 1880).

2. Edmund Storer Janes (1807–1876), born in Sheffield, Mass., studied law, received into Philadelphia Conference in 1830, appointed agent for Dickinson College in 1838, elected financial secretary of the American Bible Society in 1840. Elected bishop in 1844, served for thirty-one years in the episcopal office. Provided leadership for the promotion of holiness teaching, the Missionary Society, Sunday-School Union, Wesleyan and Drew Universities.

3. And probably locus of some strategic planning and discussion.

4. This was the fate-laden General Conference of 1844 in which the church split into the Methodist Episcopal Church and the Methodist Episcopal Church, South. Mrs. Palmer's friends and associates virtually all had northern abolitionist

sympathies. Hamline and Bangs were on the committee that made the decision and provided the oversight for the separation of the two church bodies.

5. The holiness advocates had become a distinct voice in Methodism by 1844, and held considerable influence from 1844 till the end of the century. See *CM*, for biographies; Buckley, *HMUS;* Peters, *CPAM.* James Porter, *A Compendium of Methodism* (Boston: Charles H. Pierce, 1851), reveals the general state of Methodism at mid-century.

6. Ps. 24:4.

7. He had just been elected, and was to be consecrated the following day. A warm supporter of holiness teaching, he was resident at the Palmer-Lankford home throughout the Conference.

8. 1 Tim. 2:8.

9. Hamline did not lack a conscious sense that grace had cleansed him thoroughly; rather he was asking the prayers of his mentor to sustain this unconditional commitment, not just through the service of episcopal ordination, but through an extended enactment of that office. For a fuller account of her admonitions to Hamline prior to his election, see her long memorandum in *Memoirs*, pp. 548–51—a remarkable case study of candor in crisis vocational counseling (slightly revised in *GTH* 7:[1845]127–30).

10. Mrs. Palmer and her friends were convinced that only a sanctified ministry could lead an errant church to the way of holiness. Renewal had to begin with radically recommitted pastoral leadership.

11. Melinda Hamline, born in 1801 in Hillsdale, N.Y., married Prof. Truesdell, of Augusta College, Kentucky (later Transylvania College), 1820–35, and subsequently was married to Leonidas Hamline, editor of *The Ladies' Repository,* for which she occasionally wrote contributions. The couple retired in 1857 to Mount Pleasant, Iowa, where they were visited by Mrs. Palmer, who sustained a steady correspondence with the Hamlines for over two decades. After Bishop Hamline's death in 1865, Mrs. Hamline moved to Evanston, Ill., where she was visited by Mrs. Palmer.

12. The analogy was a striking one: she would pray for the Bishop and his family as if they were her own family members, if they would consider themselves as such.

13. James 1:17.

14. What is being described here was something more than a friendship. It was a divinely accountable "*relationship*" (italicized) to be viewed in the light of eternal claims and hopes, enlivened by daily intercession, supported by regular correspondence, and characterized by utter candor, loving admonition, and continuing process of radical self-disclosure. Many subsequent letters from the Palmers and Hamlines indicate that this sort of relationship was indeed sustained with no apparent interruptions throughout the remainder of their lives.

15. See Arthur W. Spaulding, *Origin and History of the Seventh Day Adventists,* 2 vols. (Washington, D.C.: Review and Herald Publishing Association, 1962).

16. Matt. 24:36.

17. Cf. 1 Cor. 14:7–8.

18. The danger Mrs. Palmer sensed as intrinsic to an embryonic, somewhat chiliastic Adventism was the loss of "usefulness," and quietistic withdrawal from stations of duty and service. Her temperament was decidedly activist, not withdrawalist, from life's ordinary duties, and focused upon scripturally reasoned duty, not on speculative enthusiasm.

19. Cf. Gen. 11:8, 9. This is not a reference to glossolalia, or "speaking in tongues" (1 Cor. 14:26–33). This is an important issue in seeking to understand the relation of Mrs. Palmer to the later history of Pentecostalism, where glossolalia became one of the key evidences of the baptism of the Holy Spirit. Although most of the elements of Pentecostal theology were clearly anticipated by Mrs. Palmer, glossolalia appears to be an exception.

20. Cf. Deut. 5:30.

21. She was referring less to financial prosperity than the prospering of the witness to sanctifying grace.

22. Note that by 1844 she was increasingly being invited to speak in church services. This would prepare the way for the argument that would ensue in 1859 in *The Promise of the Father*, in defense of women witnessing in public church services.

23. Probably written in August 1845, following the August 17, 1845, note.

24. Cf. 2 Chron. 20:21.

25. Cf. 2 Cor. 7:1.

26. Cf. 1 Pet. 1:16; Lev. 11:44.

27. Joseph Holdich, born 1804, Philadelphia Conference, taught moral science at Wesleyan, wrote *The Life of Wilbur Fisk*.

28. Wesleyan University was sufficiently Wesleyan in its orientation at that time that the faculty apparently had regular class-meetings in the Wesleyan style for prayer, scripture study and self-examination. Cf. Julia M. Olin, *Life and Letters of Stephen Olin, Late President of Wesleyan University*, 2 vols (New York: Harper & Bros., 1853).

29. 1 Cor. 15:43.

30. Short articles written during this time included "Christian Communings," *GTH* 7 (1845): 97; "Be Specific in Confession," *GTH* 7 (1845): 127; "Religious Correspondence," *GTH* 7 (1845): 29–32; "Extract of a Letter from a Friend," *GTH* 8 (1846): 93; and "He Led Them Forth by the Right Way," *GTH* 9 (1846): 135–37.

31. Wheatley mistakenly argued in *Memoirs*, p. 274, that it was during this illness of 1846 that she "composed and published, '*The Way of Holiness.*' " This could not be the case, since the first serial edition was published in *CAJ*, 1842, and the first book edition in 1843.

32. Most of this book is composed of letters of spiritual counsel, which, as we learn elsewhere, were often written while literally on her knees in prayer.

33. Her illness greatly hampered her work as a writer, and prevented her accepting invitations to engage widely and energetically in a public ministry during this period.

34. She would live almost twenty-eight more years.

35. Sunday School.

36. Recall the traumas of 1829, 1830, and 1836 when she lost three of her own children. These "spiritual children" had become very important to her.

37. Sic. Sentence incomplete in text.

38. Cf. 1 Cor. 2:10.

39. Matt. 13:52.

40. Neglect of health.

41. This letter has special poignancy because it appears that she was convinced she would die soon.

42. Her ministry during this period of illness was largely limited to a ministry of counsel, conversation, letter writing, and some literary productivity, which continued even when the public ministry had been drastically reduced.

43. The innovation of centering a lay ministry of witness to holiness primarily around conversation.

44. Estuary of the Hudson River between New York and New Jersey.

45. A reference to her poetry.

46. According to one reading, it might seem that Dr. Palmer only put up with her poetry; but it seems more likely that this was merely a self-effacing jest, or as Paul Bassett suggests, that she was circumventing "doctor's orders," perhaps Walter's own orders.

47. Woodruff, educated at Oberlin, became a pastor in the New York Conference beginning in 1845, and was elected secretary of the General Conferences of 1872 and 1876.

48. Prov. 11:25.

49. Here the Baptism of the Holy Ghost is directly identified with sanctification. Cf. John Morgan, "The Gift of the Holy Ghost," *Oberlin Quarterly Review* 1 (1845): 90–116. This point marks a key issue in the discussion of the early history of proto-Pentecostalism; cf. the views of M. Dieter, C. White, F. Brunner, D. Dayton, V. Synan, and T. Smith, op. cit.

50. Adam Clarke.

51. Adam Clarke, *HBC*, vol. VI, p. 75, on Rom. 12.

52. Cf. Matt. 23:19.

53. Heb. 12:14.

54. Phil. 4:13.

55. See diary reference above, Jan. 3, 1837.

56. Num. 23:23.

57. 1 Cor. 1:30.

58. James 5:10; King James Version: "Take, my brethren, the prophets . . ."

59. Phil. 4:12.

60. Mrs. Palmer was temperamentally less prepared defensively to fend off polemical attacks than to lead the offense in revival activism.

61. Matt. 5:11–12; (her emphasis).

62. 1 Pet. 2:20 (her emphasis).

63. Cf. 1 Pet. 1:8.

64. Anyone who reads the lives of Phoebe Palmer and Søren Kierkegaard as parallel stories cannot help but be astonished at some of their remarkable similarities. Just about this time (1840's), as SK was writing his *Upbuilding Discourses in Various Spirits, Works of Love,* and *Christian Discourses,* the theme of the joy of following Christ's suffering was being experientially rediscovered and powerfully set forth. He wrote of the "joy of it—that affliction does not bereave of hope, but recruits hope," (*CD,* pp. 11–119); and that "it is blessed nevertheless—to suffer derision in a good cause" (*CD,* pp. 228–39).

65. 1 Pet. 2:21 (her emphasis).

66. 2 Cor. 7:1.

67. The problem with this "enthusiastic doctrine" was that it focused more upon the subjective, emotive state of the seeker than upon the promise of scripture.

68. Cf. Eph. 2:3–14.

69. Cf. Col. 2:2.

70. Cf. Col. 3:4.

71. Cf. Ps. 84:11.

72. Cf. Mal. 4:2.

73. 1 John 1:9.

74. Cf. Phil. 2:12–13.

75. Cf. Luke 10:38–42.

76. Cf. Phil. 3:14; 2 Tim. 1:9.

77. Cf. Amos 4:11; Zech. 3:2; the same image was used of Wesley when he was rescued from the fire at the Epworth vicarage, *JJW,* 4, p. 90.

78. Note the personalization of tract ministry and holiness revivalism. It does not work by proxy, or exclusively by the written word, but by personal communication.

79. Lam. 3:33.

80. 2 Pet. 1:21.

81. Cf. Titus 3:5.

82. 1 Tim. 4:1 (her emphasis).

83. 1 John 5:10 (her emphasis).

84. Cf. 1 Cor. 13:6–7.

85. Cf. Heb. 4:12.

86. John 6:63 (her emphasis).

87. This is followed by a quote from Wesley, "The Scripture Way of Salvation," *WJW,* VI, p. 53; cf. *WSS,* 2, p. 458.

88. Cf. Matt. 14:13–14, and Luke 5:1.

89. Matt. 10:25.

90. Where are all these letters today? Have they survived or been destroyed? Scholars interested in Phoebe Palmer have a major task ahead to locate and study them. No adequate manuscript bibliography of Mrs. Palmer's letters has yet been compiled. This writer made several unsuccessful attempts to locate further manuscript materials, and still holds the belief that some are likely to have survived, per-

haps through the Palmer, Knapp, Lankford, or Worrall families, or in uncatalogued archives.

91. Wife of Bishop Edmund S. Janes.

92. The preacher was William Taylor, later (1884) elected Bishop. Served as missionary to California, and was a key contributor to Methodist mission in India (1870–74), Latin America (1877–83), and Africa; a leading proponent of the idea of "self-support missions," *HMM,* 3, pp. 229–35, 510ff.

93. This passage is an indication of her public recognition level.

94. David Creamer, "the earliest American student of hymnology, and collector of hymns" (*DH,* p. 268), whose hymnological library of 800 volumes is now in the Archives at Drew University. Author of *Methodist Hymnology* (New York: Creamer, 1848); founding editor of the *Baltimore Monument,* weekly journal of music, science and literature.

95. Cf. Matt. 12:34.

96. Cf. Heb. 6:1. This entry indicates how seriously Mrs. Palmer was beginning to take up the neglected task of follow-up after revival conversions. Her ministry focused significantly upon this problem, heretofore somewhat neglected in the camp meeting tradition.

97. According to *CM,* the Five Points Mission, on the site of the Old Brewery, was organized by the Ladies Home Missionary Society, which was organized in 1844, and whose 1848 Annual Report pledged to establish a center in this area (p. 364). Mrs. Palmer was a Founding Directress of the Society (p. 679). Space was acquired for Sunday School teaching in 1850 on the corner of Cross and Little Water Streets. J. Luckey was pastor. The Old Brewery was purchased on the corner of Park and Cross Streets, demolished in 1852, and the new building built in 1853, providing housing (rent-free for widows and children), "barrells of bread which supply a daily luncheon to the children," day-school, clothing, and a reading room (p. 364). For further discussion, see *Ladies of the Five Points Mission, The Old Brewery and the New Mission House at Five Points* (New York: Stringer and Townsend, 1854); "The Five Points House of Industry," *American Church Monthly* 3 (1858): 209–22; E. R. Wells, "Five Points Mission," *CAJ* 35 (1860): 173; W. P. Strickland, "The Five Points," *CAJ* 38 (1863): 330; Lewis E. Jackson, *Gospel Work in New York City: A Memorial of Fifty Years in City Missions* (New York: NYC Mission, 1878); Timothy L. Smith, *RSR,* pp. 169ff.; Norris Magnuson, "Salvation in the Slums: Evangelical Social Work, 1865–1920 (Metuchen, NJ: Scarecrow Press, 1977); Carroll Smith Rosenberg, "Protestants and Five Pointers: The Five Points House of Industry," *New York Historical Society Quarterly* 48/4 (1964): 327–47.

98. Cf. J.T. Peck, et al., *Systematic Beneficence* (New York: Carlton & Phillips, 1856).

99. Bartholomew Creagh (1804–52) emigrated from Ireland, served ten years in New York and Brooklyn; elected delegate to General Conference in 1848 and 1852.

100. Cf. Acts 11:29, and 1 Pet. 4:11.

101. The principle involved: Christians are called to exercise stewardship ac-

cording to the greatest needs and according to their abilities given. This is sometimes thought to be an exclusively Marxist dictum, but was well-known in the tradition of Christian preaching on Acts.

102. 2 Cor. 12:1.

103. This suggests that they joined Allen Street Church shortly after their marriage.

104. I.e., validating signs.

105. Both Walter and Phoebe Palmer were Class Leaders. Both were strong supporters of the Missionary Society, and leading exponents of sanctificationist theology. Doubtless the Allen Street Church expected to feel their loss intensely.

106. Timothy L. Smith, op. cit., p. 169n.

107. Ps. 91:6.

108. James Montgomery, "Friend after friend departs," *HUMEC*, 1850, #1077, v. 1.

109. Cf. Heb. 11:27.

110. Isa. 26:8–9.

111. Bangs by this time had become one of the leading American Methodist theologians and historians, and a key interpreter of Methodism, soon to publish *The Present State, Prospects, and Responsibilities of the Methodist Episcopal Church* (New York: Lane and Scott, 1850). During the period to follow, Bangs wrote several articles in *CAJ* where he discussed issues bearing upon Mrs. Palmer's views: "Is it Right to Profess the Experience of Perfect Love?", *CAJ* (1851): 185; "More Witnesses in Favor of Perfect Love," *CAJ* (1851): 189; and a series of five articles "On the Profession of Holiness," *CAJ* (1852): 1, 5, 9, 13, 17, largely defending Mrs. Palmer, but with some salient criticisms.

112. Could be 1849 or 1850.

113. Among books appearing during this period that would show evidence of a wider audience of seekers after Christian perfection were those by Episcopal minister Stephen Higgison Tyng (1800–85), Rector of Holy Trinity, New York, *Christ is All* (New York: Robert Carter, 1849) (Mrs. Palmer would later dedicate one of her books to Stephen Tyng); and Merritt Caldwell, (1806–48), professor at Dickinson College, *Philosophy of Christian Perfection* (Philadelphia: Sorin & Ball, 1848).

114. It could be that, as Charles E. White argues, 1950 is not a misprint— that Mrs. Palmer was seeking to prepare young people to live in 1850 in a way that would bear fruit in 1950. Another hypothesis is that 1950 is a misprint in the text of the *Memoirs*, and that 1850 was intended. Since the poem refers to "the coming year," the latter hypothesis seems probable.

115. Prov. 13:12: "Hope deferred maketh the heart sick"; cf. Samuel Becket, *Waiting For Godot*.

116. Cf. Matt. 19:13–14.

117. Ps. 103:13.

118. Cf. John Kent, *HF*, pp. 77ff., and Richard Carwardine, *TAR*, pp. 107ff., 126ff.

119. James Caughey, born in Ireland, admitted to the Troy, New York, An-

nual Conference of the Methodist Episcopal Church in 1834; author of *Methodism in Earnest: Being a History of a Great Revival in Great Britain* (Boston: C.H. Pierce, 1850). As an active and uniquely energetic evangelist, he became famous on both sides of the Atlantic. William and Catherine Booth, founders of the Salvation Army, were influenced by the preaching of both Caughey and the Palmers. Cf. Kent, *HF,* pp. 325ff.

120. *Memoirs,* p. 192.

121. For similar work in Boston, see William E. Boardman, *Faith Work under Dr. Cullis in Boston* (Boston: Willard Tract Repository, 1874).

122. Cf. Col. 2:21, ironically exegeted by the Temperance Movement to mean precisely what it did not mean for the author of Colossians, wherein injunctions like "Do not taste!", as applied to religious festivals, were thought to be a "shadow of things that were to come," (v. 17), and are "human commands," "destined to perish with use" (*NIV,* v. 22).

123. One of many instances reported in which she understood herself to be communicating telepathically. Although she did not speculate on how such extrasensory perceptions might have occurred, she experienced and reported them frequently. Some three decades later in London the study of parapsychology would become a distinct object of serious scientific investigation and empirical inquiry.

124. Prof. Mattison, author of *Thoughts on Entire Sanctification* (New York: Land & Scott, 1852), taught at Falley Seminary (1850), served New York City churches, elected to General Conferences of 1848, 1852, and 1856; withdrew from the Methodist Episcopal Church in 1861 on abolitionist grounds, returned in 1865; wrote stinging polemics against Mrs. Palmer. Virtually a professional polemicist, his attacks on her began in 1851: "Professing Holiness," *CAJ* (1851): 201, and *CAJ* (1852): 17; cf. *CAJ* (1855): 121, 181, 189, 195, 201–202. The controversy would extend till 1856, when Mattison wrote *An Answer to Dr. Perry's Reply to the Calm Review* (New York: Miller and Holman, 1856); and J.H. Perry wrote *Reply to Prof. Mattison's 'Answer' "* (New York: John A. Gray, 1856). Cf. Editorials in *CAJ,* "On Mattison's Misrepresentation," 16 (1842): 83, "Condemnation of H. Mattison," 34 (1859): 63. Mrs. Palmer's first reply is found in "False Statement Corrected," *CAJ* (1852): 27. White has an excellent summary of the controversy, *BH,* pp. 53–58, 245ff. See also Bangs' intervention, in Abel Stevens, *The Life & Times of Nathan Bangs,* N.Y.: Carlton and Porter, 1863, pp. 350–353, 396–402.

125. Cf. Phil. 2:7.

126. See May 1844 entries.

127. Cf. Ex. 2:25.

128. Ps. 116:12.

129. Cf. Gen. 15:10–17.

130. She envisioned her own sacrificial offering as her whole being—body, soul, and spirit—on the altar being ever anew consumed by the flame of the Spirit penetrating every fibre. This is her distinctive, personal, and existential sense of being on fire with the Spirit. It is the commitment to understand herself in this way that she would repeatedly say she had never defaulted, never "taken off the altar," since July 26, 1837.

131. I.e., Methodist people.

132. Cf. Matt. 5:14.

133. She viewed contentiousness among Methodists as evidence that God was rejecting their tendency to neglect their distinctive contribution: experiential holiness.

134. *CAJ;* cf. N. Vansant, *Work Here, Rest Hereafter, The Life and Character of Rev. Hiram Mattison* (New York: N. Tibbals, 1970).

135. See J.T. Peck, "Holiness," *Methodist Quarterly Review* 33 (1851): 505–29.

136. She is hoping to demonstrate to Bishop Janes that she has considerable support, despite these detractors.

137. Bishop Janes had a long and established association with the movement to promote holiness, but he had also had to deal with unsympathetic clergy in New Jersey.

138. Cf. James 2:26.

139. It was deeply disappointing to Mrs. Palmer that Bishop Janes had not kept abreast of the issue, and was seeking to keep somewhat aloof from the debate. She is urging his deliberate engagement in the discussion.

140. 1 Pet. 1:16.

141. She thought Janes owed it as a duty to the church to reprove actively the detractors of holiness teaching. She did not think that he himself was resisting holiness teaching, but found him at this stage relatively uncommitted and unwilling to come actively to their defense. The frank, admonitory tone of this letter to a Bishop and longtime friend indicates the relation of spiritual candor that must have pervaded their relationship. Much later Janes would write further on the issues of the Mattison-Palmer debate, see E.S. Janes, H. Mattison, D. Curry, J.M. Buckley, S.D. Brown, *Perfect Love, Speeches on Sanctification* (New York: N. Tibbals, 1868).

142. Her views on this subject are elaborated in a Tract: Israel's Speedy Restoration and Conversion Contemplated, or Signs of the Times, *in Familiar Letters* (New York: John A. Gray, 1854).

143. Missionary Society of the Methodist Episcopal Church. John Price Durbin, 1800–76, was elected editor of the *Christian Advocate and Journal* (following Nathan Bangs, who continued to edit the *Quarterly Review*) and of Sunday School Books in 1832, with Timothy Merritt (one of Mrs. Palmer's early mentors) as his assistant. Durbin became President of Dickinson College 1832–44, served Philadelphia pastorates, 1844–50, and followed Dr. Pitman as missionary secretary in 1850. The *Cyclopedia of Methodism* states that "all the foreign missions grew up under his personal supervision" (*CM*, p. 319).

144. Cf. James Caughey, *Earnest Christianity* (New York: W.C. Palmer, Jr., 1868).

145. The Palmers concretely supported this proposal by pledging a thousand dollars, a substantial sum for that time (*Memoirs*, p. 234).

146. Even at this relatively early stage of missionary activity, it appears that territorial assumptions somewhat analogous to colonial paradigms were presup-

posed in making such assessments. With such reasoning Mrs. Palmer doubtless was impatient, but finally acceded.

147. They would continue, see Israel's Speedy Restoration, op. cit. Her efforts in 1853 to establish a mission to Palestine would late be transmuted (see entries of April 28ff., 1855) into a home mission for Jewish immigrants in Lower Manhattan, which also failed.

148. It appears that Dr. Palmer took on a considerable weight of responsibility in nurturing and guiding the children during extended periods of Mrs. Palmer's absence. The pattern they apparently worked out seems to be a rare example of a nineteenth century couple anticipating what we today regard as patterns of joint responsibility in parenting.

149. Cf. Ps. 96:9.

150. Possibly Mary Jane Worrall Kellogg, Phoebe Palmer's younger sister.

151. The will to full disclosure between parent and child is beautifully expressed in this metaphor.

152. Norfolk Street is on the Lower East Side of Manhattan, east of Essex Street (Avenue A), between Delancey Street (Williamsburg Bridge) and East Houston Street. It remains a very depressed area.

153. Cf. Ps. 50:10.

154. Cf. 1 Pet. 4:11.

155. At this point their reasoning becomes clear concerning the claims of the poor upon those who have resources, especially in connection with their wrenching decision to move their church membership (despite opposition) to Norfolk Street— it was a weaker and more vulnerable church in a poorer neighborhood, facing a more difficult situation.

156. Wheatley infers that the letter was written from Hartford (perhaps some time after the incident) while visiting with the wife of the mayor of Hartford, Mrs. Hammersley.

157. 1 Cor. 15:57.

158. Cf. Joseph Stennett, "I Return, My Soul, Enjoy Thy Rest," *HMEC,* 1879, #82, which speaks of "This heavenly calm within the breast."

159. William Hunter, "My Heavenly Home is Bright and Far," *Methodist Hymnal* (Nashville: Smith and Turner, 1906), #628, v. 1: "I'm going home to die no more."

160. Charles Wesley, *HMEC,* 1879, #170, v. 1; *MHB,* 1908, #912, v. 1; in *Hymns and Sacred Poems,* 3, 1740; *DH,* p. 1261.

161. The date is inferred from Wheatley's sequence (pp. 136ff.). This is among the earliest evidences of her growing involvement with Canadian ecumenical revivalism.

162. See Feb. 12 and 17 of 1853.

163. He was considered a member of the Palmer family. The grant of indenture was apparently required to gain release from prison. That he was not treated as an indentured servant is evident from the next entry.

164. Ironically, this would bring Phoebe Palmer Knapp (the daughter of Phoebe Palmer, the tract distributor in the Bowery area) into the highest social cir-

cles, where she would entertain in her home several Presidents (Grant, Cleveland, and Harrison, *BH*, p. 58). She continued to support the *Guide to Holiness*, and wrote hymn tunes, notably, "Blessed Assurance," to which Fanny Crosby added the lyrics.

165. Exod. 20:3.

166. *WJW*, III, pp. 271ff.; VI, pp. 431ff.

167. This would be her last public statement on the Mattison controversy.

168. Cf. Matt. 5:44.

169. Again reminiscent of Kierkegaard reflecting upon the *Corsair* attacks only a few years before this (see *Journals and Papers of Søren Kierkegaard*). Kierkegaard's views of culture-Protestantism ("Christendom in Denmark") are analogous to Mrs. Palmer's views of an unserious Christian profession that pretends conversion without the fruits of faith.

170. Cf. Kierkegaard, *Christian Discourses;* Albert T. Bledsoe, *A Theodicy* (New York: Carlton & Phillips, 1853).

171. Cf. Exod. 33:3ff.; Ps. 46:5.

172. Phil. 1:20.

173. Cf. Rom. 12:12.

174. Ps. 69:9.

175. Cf. Acts 5:41; *HMEC*, 1879, #736, 850.

176. Luke 6:40: "A student is not above his teacher, but everyone who is fully trained, will be like his teacher" (NIV).

177. The reference is again to Luke 6:40 (cf. Matt. 10:24): "The disciple is not above his master." This could either be a misprint in the text, omitting "not," or an ironic reference (having fewer trials, she felt more kindly treated than Jesus).

178. Probably a reference to the attacks made upon her views by Hiram Mattison.

179. For contemporary discussions that continue to develop and enlarge this theme, see Delbert Rose, *Vital Holiness* (Minneapolis: Bethany Fellowship, 1975); J.B. Atkinson, *The Beauty of Holiness* (New York: Philosophical Library, 1963); Leslie D. Wilcox, *Be Ye Holy: A Study of the Teaching of the Scripture Relative to Entire Sanctification with a Sketch of the History and Literature of the Holiness Movement* (Cincinnati: Revivalist Press, 1965). For discussions of the theme of holiness from within the Lutheran and Calvinist tradition, see A. Koberle, *The Quest for Holiness* (Minneapolis, Augsburg, 1938); and A. Kuyper, *The Work of the Holy Spirit* (Grand Rapids: Eerdmans, 1956).

180. Heb. 10:23.

181. Gal. 6:17.

182. Cf. Gal. 6:14.

183. Cf. Philip Doddridge, "How Swift the Torrent Rolls," *The Methodist Hymnal* (Nashville: Lamar & Smith, 1906), #580, v. 2.

184. *MHB*, 1970, #423, v. 2.

185. Rom. 8:17.

186. Rom. 13:1. James Buchanan (D.–Penn.) defeated John C. Fremont (R.–Cal.), 1856.

187. Rom. 13:1.

188. Hence it is not expected in Christian thinking about political responsibility that the political order could be simplistically turned over to God as if without any use of human reason, imagination, or effort.

189. John 14:30, 16:11.

190. Matt. 4:9.

191. Cf. Rev. 11:15.

192. Cf. Rom. 6:12ff., 8:21; 1 Cor. 15:25.

193. *Memoirs*, pp. 315ff.; cf. T. Smith, *CUH*.

194. One of her most important essays, "A Laity for the Times," was published in 1857, *CAJ*, calling for greater participatory initiative on the part of the laity in the renewal of the church; cf. "A Voice from the Laity," *CAJ*, 1855.

195. Cf. Karl Roebling, *Pentecostal Origins and Trends, Early and Modern* (New York: Paragon, 1983); D. Gee, *The Pentecostal Movement* (Luton: Assemblies of God Publishing House, 1949); J.T. Nichol, *Pentecostalism* (New York: Harper & Row, 1966).

196. Matt. 3:11; Luke 3:16; cf. 1 Cor. 3:13; a metaphor for Christian purity, entire consecration, and the reception of sanctifying grace.

197. The Pentecost metaphor henceforth would be repeatedly and increasingly employed.

198. Note both genders. It was the increasing influence of the Book of Acts on her preaching that eventually led to the writing of *The Promise of the Father* (condensed to "Tongue of Fire," see above, chapter 1).

199. The Lamb, an atonement metaphor, was a frequent theme of camp meeting hymnody, *HMEC,* 1879, #12, 26, 51, 991. For further discussion of the hymnody which was actively produced by the camp meeting revival movement, see Julian, *DH:* R. G. McCutchan, *Our Hymnody* (New York: Abingdon, 1937); Sandra S. Sizer, *Gospel Hymns and Social Religion: The Rhetoric of Nineteenth-Century Revivalism* (Philadelphia: Temple University Press, 1978). Cf. H. Lillenas, *Modern Gospel Song Stories* (Kansas City: Lillenas Publishing Co., 1952).

200. The Greenwood Cemetery tombstone of Doretha Worrall, Phoebe's mother, reads: "Born Feb. 13, 1786, died September 13 [could be 16 or 19—very worn], 1856."

201. 2 Tim. 4:2.

202. Compare this with a similar account of an American camp meeting, Amos P. Mead, *Manna in the Wilderness: Of the Grove and Its Altar, Containing a History of the Origin and Rise of Camp Meetings and a Defense of This Remarkable Means of Grace: also an account of the Wyoming Camp Meeting* (Philadelphia: Perkinpine and Higgins, 1860). Mrs. Palmer defended the camp meeting format in "The Inquiry Answered: Do Camp-Meetings Do More Harm Than Good?", *Beauty of Holiness,* 1857.

203. For further discussion, see Phoebe Palmer, "The Doctrine of the Sealing of the Spirit," *GTH* 32 (1857): 50; F.G. Hibbard, "Thoughts on the Baptism of the Holy Ghost," *GTH* 51 (1867): 77–79; cf. Donald W. Dayton, "The Doctrine of the Baptism of the Holy Spirit: Its Emergence and Significance," *WTJ* 13 (1978): 114–

26; and Harold Hunter, *Spirit Baptism* (New York: University Press of America, 1983).

204. From this period, see Smith N. Platt, *The Gift of Power* (New York: Carlton & Porter, 1856); J.T. Peck, *The Central Idea of Christianity* (Boston: H.V. Degen, 1856); cf. George Allen Turner, "The Baptism of the Holy Spirit in the Wesleyan Tradition," *WTJ* 14/1 (1979): 60–76.

205. Allowing travel time, they could hardly have had more than about five hours sleep.

206. Cf. William Cowper, "There is a Fountain Filled with Blood," *MHB*, 1933, #201, v. 1.

207. Matt. 3:11.

208. Cf. Acts 2:13; Mark 2:22.

209. Cf. Eph. 4–6; Rev. 19.

210. A.M.

211. John 3:17.

212. This was frequently the format of the services in which Mrs. Palmer spoke—after a discourse or sermon had been heard, she was called upon to bear testimony in an informal way. Hence she did not call her participation "preaching, technically so called," *PF*, p. 1.

213. This was a characteristic awareness of the revival of 1856–58. See Howard F. Shipps, "The Revival of 1858 in Mid-America," *Methodist History* 16 (1977): 128–51; Carl Spicer, "The Great Awakening of 1857 and 1859," Ohio State Univ. dissertation, 1935; Francis E. Russell, "Pentecost: 1858. A Study in Religious Revivalism," Ph.D. dissertation, Univ. of Penna., 1948; James W. Alexander, *The New York Pulpit in the Revival of 1858* (New York: Sheldon, Blakeman, 1858).

214. The present occurrence of Pentecostal gifts is one of the keys to the ethos of Pentecostalism. In the Canadian holiness revivals of 1856–58, this was repeatedly attested.

215. Luke 14:17.

216. Acts 2:44.

217. 2 Sam. 24:24.

218. Cf. Phoebe Palmer, "The Cost of Faith's Superstructure," *GTH* 31 (1857): 67.

219. Cf. Jer. 33:3.

220. Cf. Mal. 3:10.

221. She was subsequently led on numerous occasions to propose this as an act of good faith symbolizing seriousness about giving up one's idolatries. The notion that if one brings tithes, direct blessings will follow, would later be turned into a ploy plagued by distortions and fraudulent motives completely foreign to Mrs. Palmer's spirit.

222. Acts 8:1.

223. Lay preaching done also by women and young people, as in the apostolic tradition, according to the pattern of Acts, was commended.

224. That Proto-Pentecostal preaching was largely lay preaching is evident

here. The Canada mission was a turning point on this issue, learned through experience. Heretofore, she had been relatively more accommodative to clergy-led revivalism.

225. Dr. Palmer was an energetic and significant member of this team, often beginning and/or following the addresses of Mrs. Palmer. This pattern would continue in their British mission.

226. Acts 1:4; i.e., a present appearance of the power of the Spirit that first appeared at Pentecost. At this time Mrs. Palmer was deeply engaged in preparation of the argument of *The Promise of the Father;* see "A Forthcoming Volume," *GTH* 34 (1858): 63, 96.

227. I.e., the power of faith awakened by the Spirit, (not faith considered autonomously). The experiential dynamics of this power were her central concern.

228. Acts 2:3.

229. Many themes of this paragraph are reflected in William Edwin Boardman, *The Higher Christian Life* (Boston: Henry Hoyt, 1858).

IX

FOUR YEARS IN THE
OLD WORLD (1859–1863)

A European journey had been seriously contemplated as early as 1845, and again in 1856. The Palmers had already become well-known among British evangelicals. Her books had been widely read. Her work in England and Ireland had been preceded by the preaching missions of James Caughey[1] (whose British mission had proceeded from 1841 to 1847) and Charles Finney (who had preached and lectured in England in 1849 and 1851),[2] and by certain Anglican writers on holiness.[3] Finally, having considered for several years a mission to the Old World, on June 4, 1859, in response to repeated invitations,[4] the Palmers set out on board the steamship "City of Baltimore" for Liverpool.

Most of the selections that follow are from Four Years in the Old World, *(hereafter, FYOW [New York: Foster and Palmer, 1864], compiled from her letters and diary upon their return), from her Memoirs, and a few selections are from* Some Account of the Recent Revival in the North of England and Glasgow *([Manchester: W. Bremner, 1860], hereafter SARR, most of which appears almost identically in FYOW).*

Her first letter was written aboard the ship on their fourth day out. She was keenly aware of her distance from her circle of friends, and of her affectionate feelings toward England, her father's homeland (FYOW, pp. 15–16):

Here I am in the midst of the ocean, endeavoring to steady my position amid heaving billows, hoping that I may be able to write a few intelligible lines to my dear S.[5]

On Saturday[6] we parted with you at twelve o'clock. It is now Tuesday. I am sitting in the large dining-saloon, and the time-piece before me says ten minutes past three o'clock. And here I sit surrounded by over a score of fellow-passengers. Oh, how unlike the companionship of the hour to that last Tuesday between three and four o'clock![7]

My spirit flies to the precious disciples of Jesus, who at various points assemble this afternoon. Not only in New York and Philadelphia, but in England, and several other places, do we hear of the formation of Tuesday-afternoon meetings. . . .

Your dear papa just now informs me that we are eight hundred miles on our journey (lat.44° 39') toward England, our fatherland. You smile and say, Nay, don't begin to claim relationship with Old England so soon.

But do you not remember that England is indeed my fatherland. It is only a little over fifty years ago that my father of most precious memory left good Old England to establish himself in Young America.[8] That honored father, though he greatly loved his adopted country, could not, of course, but venerate his fatherland; and that his daughter should affectionately acknowledge her relationship to England, and confess, under God, the debt of gratitude she owes that country for the gift of such a father, is only seemly, and what she loves to do.

After arrival at Liverpool, being unexpectedly met and welcomed by a Wesleyan minister[9] who had read a notice of their ship boarding in the Guide to Holiness, *they proceeded to London. Staying at Brixton Hill, London, at the residence of J. K——, Esq., they visited the services of the very young Rev. Charles Spurgeon,[10] Wesley's City Road Chapel and residence, and various London sites. They led services in Bowden, near Manchester, where the following letter was penned to Mrs. Gov. Wright.[11] It reveals one of her major purposes in the trip: to follow Wesley's footsteps and recollect Methodist hagiography. She saw all England with distinctly Wesleyan eyes* (Memoirs, *pp. 349–50):*

Bowden, July 9, 1859

The next day[12] we took the cars[13] for London. From childhood, I loved to treasure up recordings of the pioneers of Methodism, in England.[14] I have been accustomed to follow the footsteps of the sainted Wesley, and his coadjutors.[15] And as we rapidly coursed our way by the steam-cars, from place to place, interesting memories would crowd rapidly, one upon another. Surely, memory is imperishable! As we passed through Oxford,[16] we looked upon the University, where the Wesleys and Whitfield spent their early days. What has God wrought, since that little band met in those halls, and resolved to conform to such *Methods* of self-sacrifice and devotedness to God, as might lead to eminent usefulness. How has the little leaven leavened the lump,[17] so that there is scarcely a city or town in Europe or America, but has been blest with the leavening influences of Methodism.

I. EARLY CAMPAIGNS IN IRELAND
AND THE NEWCASTLE AREA (1859)

By July 19, 1859, the Palmers were in Belfast, Ireland, participating in open-air revival meetings at Donegal Square led, to their surprise, by Presbyterians (FYOW, pp. 45–46):

The revival is not confined to any particular denomination. If one has shared more largely than another, it has been the Presbyterian. But in these regions, this denomination, prior to this wondrous visitation of the Holy Spirit, has not been characterized, as in some other parts of the world, for enlightened views of Christian privilege. For an individual to speak of a divine conviction of sins forgiven, would, by many, be thought fanatical, if not presumptuous. But what a change! Now, you may go into a Presbyterian church but a few minutes' walk from where I write, and you will hear young men and maidens, old men and children, speaking, with tongues touched with living fire,[18] of the wonderful works of God. Hitherto where only the slow measured psalm was sung is now heard the soul-inspiring revival melodies as among our most earnest Methodist friends.

From the Mayor of Belfast to mill workers gathering in the rain to hold an open-air prayer meeting before work, the revival was having a powerful effect upon the entire community of Belfast. Note also the reported effect of these meetings upon Catholics. It was Mrs. Palmer's first experience of "revival fever" Irish style (FYOW, pp. 58–62):

Belfast, July 26, 1859

I am impressed with the conviction that the Lord has much for the Methodists to do as a people in this revival, if we would be answerable to the *speciality* of our calling. Thank God for the Calebs and Joshuas, who, within the past week, have been raised up to testify from their own experimental realizations, "We are well able to go up and possess the good land."[19]

The Mayor of Belfast called at the residence of our host, his brother-in-law, today; and says, in passing his mills this morning, he saw between two and three hundred of his operatives gathered in the open air, holding a prayer-meeting, despite the falling rain. This was between eight and nine o'clock, the breakfast hour. Thus these newly received disciples, in their longings for a spiritual repast with the Master, were devoting one-half of the time allotted for breakfast to feast with Jesus; and who can doubt but he, who after his resurrection, met his disciples at a table already provided by a divine hand with broiled fish and honeycomb,[20] met these his humble disciples, and feasted them richly with divine dainties? . . .

These sudden and remarkable awakenings are not confined to any particular people, church, or place. I have been credibly informed that seven were stricken in a Romish church, and were carried in their state of helplessness to the adjacent nunnery. Strong men, as well as females, have been suddenly struck down in the street, the public road, and their own houses. In general, a deep sympathy is felt, even among the most sceptical, for those who are called, in common phrase, "the *sufferers;*"[21] and everything is done for their relief with earnest and affectionate promptness.

From Belfast they proceeded to ecumenical[22] services at Coleraine, in the northernmost part of Ireland, where revival fever almost stopped the publication of a newspaper, and brought estranged denominations of Christians together (FYOW, pp. 70–73):

Coleraine, July 31, 1859

The revival is the all-absorbing topic. Young and old, and people of all classes, are subjects of the wonder-working influences. What would you think of a united prayer-meeting at which from four to five thousand attend *daily?* Such has been held in these regions. The stricken cases occur at all places and under the most extraordinary circumstances.

The editor of a weekly paper, the "Coleraine Chronicle," giving as a reason for the non-delivery of his paper in due time, states that sixteen cases of prostration occurred in one house; "and of these, three are of our newspaper staff, and we have had difficulty in getting out the 'Chronicle.' " This good editor adds, "Rich and poor are now partaking of the special anointing of the Holy Ghost. . . . "

In almost every house, a stricken soul was lying; and the sound of praise and the voice of prayer were heard at every step, mingling with the moans and supplications of the stricken ones. . . .

The ministers of the Presbyterian Church, the Wesleyan ministers, with the rector of the parish, held an open-air service, which was attended by thousands. The rector opened the meeting, and requested him[23] to address the audience, which he did. Everything went on quietly for a short time; but the Spirit of God was at work, for on all sides the people began to fall. It was a wonderful scene, and all attempts to preserve order were unavailing. The field was strewn over with men and women, and the moans and cries were such as to remind him forcibly of descriptions he had read of a field of battle.[24]

She considered, but decided against, a mission to France (to Mrs. Hamline, Memoirs, p. 354):

Bowden, England, August 15, 1859

We have just received an encouraging letter from the minister who has translated our works into the French language. He says about 2,000 of the "Way of Holiness"[25] have been sold, and "Faith and Effects"[26] is ready to be issued. If we were able to speak the French language with sufficient fluency to make ourselves intelligible, we should rejoice to go there, but in view of our inability to do so, I think we shall not go.

By August of 1859, the Palmers were back in Bowden, from which they launched campaigns in September to Walsingham, Weardale, and Newcastle (FYOW, p. 93, in a letter to Brother Boyer, Sept. 16, 1859; also in SARR, p. 3):

The God of the armies of Israel[27] has commenced to display his all-conquering power here in the north of England. A work is progressing, which, my heart seems to assure me, is destined to spread over England, provided human limitations do not obstruct, and the ministry and laity, as workers together with God,[28] unite in spreading the flame.

We have been engaged in many revivals in America, and more recently in Ireland, and have seen thousands saved, but never remember to have witnessed a more glorious work than has been going on here within the last few days.[29]

The work in the Newcastle area had inaugurated a spectacular series of meetings that would shake English Christianity to its foundations. The lives of William[30] and Catherine Booth (founders of the Salvation Army) would be deeply affected by her ministry in the Newcastle Area.[31] Catherine Booth defended her view of women bearing religious testimony against attacks seeking to discredit her.[32] Mrs. Palmer wrote to a "Dear Brother in Jesus" of those who through total commitment were coming to an "experimental realization" of the way of holiness (SARR, pp. 16–19):

Newcastle-on-Tyne, Oct. 12, 1859

. . . World-loving and worldly-conformed professors are apprehending as never before, that the God of the scriptures means just what He says, when He enjoins separation from the world. "Come out from among them and be ye separate, saith the Lord, and touch not the unclean thing,"[33] has become an obvious and experimental realization. A minister once said to us, "Mrs. Palmer, how do you get people to believe so easily?" Our answer was, "Because we never attempt to persuade anyone to appropriate a promise, until we have reason to know they are on *promised ground*."[34] The promise, "I will receive you,"[35] is only applicable to whose who, through the enabling grace of God, separate themselves from the spirit of the world. . . .[36]

One gentleman came all the way from Scotland, groaning after the witness of inward purity. Whilst he was kneeling at the altar of prayer, and we were pointing the living way by which the Holy Spirit led us into the holiest, through the blood of the everlasting covenant, he was enabled to cast anchor within the vail,[37] and returned home to be mighty through the Spirit in pulling down the strongholds of Satan.[38] O this blessed doctrine of the full baptism of the Spirit[39] is our might, and to just the degree we are answerable to the specialty of our calling, and are a witnessing people, to just that degree God will be mindful of us, and exalt us before the people of all lands,[40] and we shall be called "The repairer of the breach, the restorer of the paths to dwell in."[41] What but the revival of our ancient doctrine, "Holiness to the Lord,"[42] making it a present and experimental realization, has caused the wonderful out-burst of power, by which hundreds have, within the past thirty-five days, been brought under the influence of saving grace?

From Newcastle they proceeded to receptive audiences at Sunderland in one of their most memorable seasons, where over two thousand registered themselves as seekers, and two hundred attested reception of the "witness of purity," i.e., sanctifying grace (FYOW, pp. 122–123):

Sunderland, Nov. 14, 1859

We seem to have been kept in the heat of this glorious battle to such a degree as to preclude attention to any thing else. Such has been the pressure of other calls, that we came here quite settled in purpose that we must not remain over two weeks. But we have already numbered twenty-nine days, and still it seems impossible that we should leave. During the past week, about one hundred have been saved daily. Oh, how glorious have been the manifestations of awakening, converting, and sanctifying power!

It is not now difficult for faith to apprehend how a nation may be born in a day.[43]

Since the commencement of this work, the secretaries of the meeting have recorded the names of two thousand and eleven who have presented themselves as seekers.[44] Of these, we trust about two hundred from near and remote regions have received the witness of purity. "Create in me a clean heart O God! and renew a right spirit within me. Then will I teach transgressors thy ways, and sinners shall be converted unto thee."[45] So says the Psalmist; and the development of power which has resulted in the sudden ingathering of such a multitude of the unsaved still gives demonstration of the fact, that purity is power;[46] or, in other words, that the creation of a clean heart,[47] and the reception of increased ability to teach transgressors truths[48] which may lead to their conversion, is still the divine order.

The whole town seems to be permeated with the power of restraining, transforming truth. To a remarkable degree is the Lord of the armies of Israel[49] owning and guarding this work, and the instrumentalities engaged in its promotion.

Everywhere she went, she tirelessly tracked down the Wesleyan connections, reminiscences and historical sites. In this letter to the Hamlines, she showed evidence that she had been a careful reader of Wesley's irenic and editorial works (to the Hamlines, Memoirs, pp. 358–59, Dec. 17, 1859; cf. FYOW, pp. 148ff.):

North Shields, Mr. Wesley's Study, Dec. 17, 1859

This letter is dated as you observe, from "Mr. Wesley's study." Mr. Wesley's study at North Shields?—you ask. Yes, here is the veritable place where the indefatigable Wesley penned many of the precious things which have been blessed to thousands in Europe and America, and will continue to be prized yet more and more till the end of time.

"Here," says a writer in Christian Miscellany, "much of Mr. Wesley's precious time was spent"; here also, as various intimations in his journal show, he loved to be. "Thursday, August 8th, 1765," while at this place, he writes, "I scarcely ever saw the people here so much alive to God, particularly those who believe they are saved from sin. I was ready to say it is good for me to be here!—But I must not build tabernacles,[50] I am to be a wanderer on earth, and desire no rest till my spirit returns to God."[51] Could the timbers of this hallowed spot be rendered vocal, to how many scenes of interest, and numberless pleadings with God, and visitations from on high etc., might they bear testimony. Here, in part at least, was written Mr. Wesley's correspondence with Dr. Thomas Seeker,[52] then Bishop of

Oxford, afterward Archbishop of Canterbury, who under the assumed name of John Smith, controverted Mr. Wesley's views on some important points in doctrine.[53] Here, Mr. Wesley in 1748, formed the purpose of publishing in three-score or four-score volumes, all that is most valuable in English literature, in order to form a complete library[54] for all who fear God. This structure was erected on the roof of the orphan house built by Mr. Wesley, in Newcastle-on-Tyne. It is a wooden structure about eleven feet square, with a tiled covering. The orphan house has recently been rebuilt, and the "Study," preserved as a precious relic, has been removed to the beautiful grounds of Mr. Solomon Mease, Esq., a worthy and influential magistrate of North Shields, with whom we are guests during the period of our labors in this place. He is one of the magistrates to whom I referred in a former part of my letter, as having received such a blessed baptism of the Spirit, at one of our afternoon services. Here also, we see many other precious relics. Dr. Palmer has been presented by the estimable lady of Mr. Mease, with a manuscript sermon of Mr. Fletcher's,[55] in his *own handwriting*. I have also been presented with Mrs. Fletcher's Testament. This bears on the cover the name of "John Fletcher, Madeley" as written by himself.[56] It was doubtless Fletcher's closet companion *before* his marriage with Mrs. Fletcher.[57] Afterward, it was unquestionably the closet companion of Mrs. Fletcher, during the years of her widowhood. Here is hardly a page but whose margin bears the impress of Mrs. Fletcher's pen, and on some, many *verses* are marked, as our dear Sister Hamline has her Bible marked through and through.

On New Year's Day of 1860, the Palmers were visiting in Jarrow, where the venerable Bede had written his history, and where their friend, Samuel Mease, had a country residence. She soberly reviewed the astonishing events of the year 1859 (FYOW, p. 164):

East Jarrow, Jan. 2, 1860

. . . What hath God wrought during the past twelve months! We look back with amazement. What multitudes have we witnessed in the valley of decision![58] The year began with seeing souls turning from darkness to light in our own dear America. The last evening of the expiring year was spent here in the Old World. Three thousand miles intervening between this and our former scenes of labor find us yet nearer to our blissful home in heaven, and engaged in similar endeavors in winning souls to Christ.

We came to this place feeling that a short respite was needful from more arduous labors, and believing that the Lord of the vineyard[59] might have us gather some fruit. The cause of vital godliness here has been low.

The Wesleyan society has numbered but twelve; but there were elements of power which God would have brought into action; or, in other words, there were seeds which had been vitalized by the prayer of faith, and watered with tears[60] which have now come up in remembrance before God.

2. CAMPAIGNS OF 1860–1862

The middle period of the Palmers' stay in Britain involved an extensive series of itineraries. In 1860 they travelled north to Scotland and far south to Wight (and nearby Poole, Cowes, and Swanage), as well as London, Banbury and Oxford. In 1861 they would hold services in Maidenhead and Windsor, then proceed to the central area of England (Rochedale, Macclesfield), east to Boston and Epworth, north to Darlington and Barnard Castle, and then back to Liverpool. In 1862 after a sentimental journey to Madeley, they would conduct an extensive campaign in Wales (Cardiff, Merthyr Tydvil, Abergavenney), then visit the Isle of Man, thence to Ireland (Portadown), and return to Leeds. The full account is detailed in Four Years in the Old World, *from which only a few selections are here included.*

Their first visit to Scotland elicited some of Mrs. Palmer's most incisive reflections on the relation of Christianity and culture[61] (FYOW, pp. 170–72; cf. Memoirs, *p. 361):*

Glasgow, Diary, Feb. 3, 1860

. . . The established religion, as you will remember, is the church of Scotland. The opinion is quite general among both ministers and people, that it is possible for persons to be converted without knowing it, unmindful of the fact, that all true believers, "receive of that Spirit whereby they *know* the things freely given to them of God."[62]

It is unpopular not to be a church-member. Almost any or every one maintaining any sort of position, belongs to either the Established Church of Scotland, or some other church, and partakes of the sacrament once a quarter.

I have just been conversing with an intelligent lady, who speaks of the exceeding injuriousness of this, inasmuch as it is a quietus,[63] and conscience sleeps under the opiate of a religious profession; but as the ministers are not willing to baptize the children of those who are not church-members, and it is regarded as heathenish not to have children baptized, it becomes a sort of necessity to unite with the church.[64] Hence, it is common for church-members to know nothing experimentally about a change of heart. . . .

We had been somewhat dissuaded from going to Scotland; but, having been most pressingly and affectionately invited by the superintendent minister and official board to come, we consented. We were told that the people were cold, and slow to move, and so settled in doctrinal dogmas calculated to repel such efforts as we might put forth, that there were not the same probabilities of success as awaited us elsewhere; but we at once found open, loving hearts, and most willing hands.

The Church came up to the help of the Lord. Persons of all denominations attended largely. The Scotch, as a people, are *theologians;* and are remarkable for religious technicalities, and the strength of their prejudices. They are, as a nation, greater adepts in hair-splitting and making a man an offender for a word,[65] than any people I ever saw. For this they are famed.

She loved the English, but resisted their inveterate class consciousness. She displayed good humor in comparing English upper class consciousness with more egalitarian American assumptions. In the incident that follows, she offered polite but firm resistance to the conspicuous consumption of the aristocratic class (from Penrith, in FYOW, pp. 223, 225):

April 24, 1860

England is in many things quite unlike America. The ground is highly cultivated. There are many beautiful gardens. The hawthorn fence is common all over England. Think of farms in every direction divided by a beautiful green fence!

You would have smiled if you had seen us riding along here yesterday. Our postilion was dressed in bright-blue broadcloth bordered with yellow, bright-blue buttons, white pantaloons, and light-topped boots. He rode one of the horses. English habits differ from American in many respects, but in nothing perhaps that would be more observable to an American than the difference there is between the common people and the higher classes.

We have just visited the castle of the Earl of Lonsdale, called Lowther Castle. This is a magnificent structure. It stands in a park of six hundred acres, studded with large umbrageous trees, many of whom have outlived the oldest inhabitants of these regions.

. . . At the porter's lodge a book is kept for the purpose of receiving visitor's names. We wrote our names as from America. I could not forbear appending to mine, "Godliness with contentment is great gain; for we brought nothing into this world, and it is certain we can carry nothing out; having food and raiment let us be therewith content".[65]

By July she was back in London, recollecting her first full year in England, and wondering how to assess whether it would have lasting effect (FYOW, pp. 276–77):

London, July 1, 1860

One year ago, as we were approaching London, fresh from the New World, we asked for a promise upon which we might stay our soul. The answer was given, "I will show thee great and mighty things."[66] Has the promise been fulfilled? Let the hundreds of newly baptized disciples answer; ay, let the thousands of redeemed ones, newly brought up out of Egyptian bondage, join in hosannas of praise to our faithful promise-keeping Jehovah.[67]

But has the work been abiding?[68] Some, disposed to be sceptical in regard to the expediency of revival efforts, might assume the contrary. We leave such to answer for their reportings to the third person in the holy Trinity, whose work alone it is to convince of sin; and to Christ the Saviour of the world, but for whose sacred presence not one convicted sinner had been saved, and but for whose ever-speaking blood not one believer had been washed in the purifying fountain; and to God the Father, the Lord and Judge of all, who in fulfilment of his faithful word has made bare his arm,[69] and permitted us to witness "great and mighty things"[70] in the presence of his people.

The Palmers spent August 1 to September 22, 1860, on the Isle of Wight, where the Queen was in residence. During these nine weeks of revival services, it was estimated that the church membership on the island doubled.[71] *Mrs. Palmer politely sought to communicate with the Queen, presented her, through her private secretary, a copy of* The Promise of the Father; *received a note from Sir Charles Phipps of "Her majesty's gracious acceptance,"*[72] *and dutifully reported her efforts to the Hamlines (*Memoirs, *pp. 368–69):*

COWES, August 20, 1860

TO BISHOP AND MRS. HAMLINE:
Last week I wrote to Queen Victoria. The subject had been resting on my mind with most solemn bearing, for several weeks. The duty was made very plain. There are some things which you know, may be made very plain, between God and our own soul. And so I sat down, as in the more immediate presence of the King of kings, and wrote a letter whose results I expect to meet, when, with an assembled universe, I shall stand before the great white throne.[73]

As a Queen, she doubtless merits their admiration. But as an experimental Christian, she cannot be regarded, so long as she patronizes the theatre, and the horse race, etc. I have sometimes thought what her ideas may have been, on witnessing in many places, as she has been riding through the Island, the large placards announcing "Revival services," with our names, as visitors, appended. Of course she must have her curiosity excited occasionally, as other people, and how often have I wished it might lead her to hear such things as stand in connection with the eternal interests of her soul.

Last week I sought unto the Lord with great carefulness, and became settled in my convictions in regard to the duty of unburdening my heart in a letter to Her Majesty. And in regard to few duties, have I felt more divinely assured, or more conscious of being aided by a power beyond myself. I have reserved a copy of the letter, and perhaps at some future day you may see it.[74]

After the Isle of Wight, services were held in Poole, Stroud, Lynn, Leamington, and Banbury. Her enthusiasm over Wesleyan memorabilia was taken to excess at Oxford—one can picture her peeking into the window of Wesley's room at Lincoln College under the awkward circumstances of the death of its recent occupant (FYOW, p. 389):

Oxford, Dec. 29, 1860

We were not able to gain access to the rooms occupied by John Wesley when Fellow of this college; the professor occupying the suite of rooms having died within the past day or two, and his body now awaiting burial from the same spot. But as we gazed into the windows of that room, which is still designated as Wesley's room, we thought of the mighty blaze now spreading over the earth through the power of that form of Christianity here first developed, and in derision called Methodism, and exclaimed, "What hath God wrought!"[75]

During early 1861 the Palmers held services in Maidenhead, Windsor, Rochdale, Great Grimsby, and Loughborough. At Macclesfield she met the Rev. Mr. Ryle.[76] En route to Epworth she visited the Old Bradford Church, where her father had worshipped and had heard Wesley preach, and her father's birthplace at Ughill near Sheffield, reported in a letter to her daughter, Sarah (Mrs. Elon Foster, Memoirs, pp. 374–75):

Ughill, May, 1861

Ughill is a scattered village, situated on a range of hills, and soon after entering it, I began to figure to myself the venerated spot I had so long wished to see. On looking at a large antiquated farm-house, situated on an eminence, with commodious outbuildings a little back from the road, I exclaimed, "There, that place just suits my ideas of the place where my precious father was born." It looked as if it might have stood the ravages of five hundred years, and might stand till the end of time. Our inquiries on the premises, did not seem to be in favor of my anticipations, and we were directed to a person bearing the name of Worrall, a few minutes' walk beyond. And here we found, Henry Worrall, youngest son of father's youngest brother, Benjamin.

We found him a very pleasant, communicative, good-looking young man, with an interesting young wife and baby. I imagine he must have looked very much as our honored father did, when of his age. An unusually fair complexion, cheeks a little ruddy, and a clear blue eye.

You will not wonder when I say that his frankness and independence took my fancy. Though a young farmer, I could see an independent bearing about him that reminded me strongly of father, and would suggest that his equanimity would not have been disturbed, though her majesty had made him a call, instead of our humble selves. His mother, the widow of our deceased uncle Benjamin, lives in the next farm-house. He took us to see her. Here we saw the old family Bible, containing the family records. I regretted we could not remain long enough to take a copy. On inquiring in which of the houses our beloved father was born, we were directed back again, to the house first mentioned, and the one I had singled out as the place, soon after entering the village.

In late 1861[77] the Palmers held services in Epworth (the home of John Wesley), Crowle, Boston, Darlington, Barnard Castle, and Berwick-on-Tweed, before they returned to Liverpool for recuperation amid the reports of Civil War that had already started in America. The "Trent Affair," wherein a U.S. vessel, acting without orders, intercepted and boarded a British ship, taking two Confederate diplomats into custody, caused intense British hostility against the Union. The Palmers, who usually supported President Lincoln, in this case wished that he had apologized sooner. Mrs. Palmer was placed in the position of defending the Union cause against prevailing British sympathies at that time with the South. Although she was not prone to use her public platform as an arena of political debate, this letter reveals that she had political intuitions that were richly informed by biblical faith. Afraid that war between Britain and America might be imminent, she pensively wrote of the tragedy of war and slavery (FYOW, pp. 498–502; cf. Memoirs, p. 378):

Liverpool, October, 1861

To say that England is in a state of breathless suspense, would be incorrect. At the moment I write, she is awaiting, in bewildering, angry excitement, the arrival of the steamer, which may furnish an occasion for the commencement of war with America. "The British flag has been outraged," is the one exciting idea of the outer world; and that the offence should be speedily punished, seems to be the prevailing sentiment of the populace. Newsboys, by way of insuring a more ready sale for their papers, cry, "War with America! war with America!" The question may arise, "And how do Americans resident in England feel, amid such surroundings?"

We can only speak for ourselves, and say that we feel perhaps more security on this point, than those around us may apprehend. We cannot believe that our country would be willing to plunge herself into a war, at present, and would prefer to make the *amende honorable,* rather than to gratify the war spirit of England, or to give the advantage to the Southern States, which would ensue, in case England should join them in hostilities.

Warlike preparations on a gigantic scale are going on. The Cunard steamships "Persia" and "Australasian" have been taken up by the government for conveying troops and stores to Canada, and are to sail this week. . . .

If it might be confidently affirmed that the results of this war would in fact be the ultimate and absolute extirpation of slavery, then the manifest want of English sympathy were more inexcusable; but what are we doing, or have we hitherto done, which may be regarded as a guaranty to England, or any other nation, that the end of the war will be the wiping-away of the foul blot of slavery from the American nation? . . .

God grant that the war-ship may quickly find her moorings by the adoption of right principles, and no longer be compelled to drift through a sea of the life-blood of some of America's bravest sons, and the briney tears of new made widows and fatherless children, and broken-hearted mothers, sisters, brothers, and friends; and to this every true Christian and loyal-hearted American will haste to respond "Amen, AMEN!"

Pardon me for writing so long on this subject; but of course, my heart is so occupied with the tremendous blow contemplated against our beloved country, that my only relief is in looking to the God of nations, and pleading that he will not forsake us in our hour of trial, but give our senators wisdom, and in case of war with England, turn the counsel of our adversaries to foolishness.[78] It is nothing for God to save, whether with many or few. Surely our help cometh from God alone.[79]

At the close of 1861, it was Dr. Palmer who fell seriously ill in Liverpool. They would have returned to America at that stage, but he was too ill to travel.[80] *By early 1862, however, they were again actively engaged in fruitful new campaigns at Madeley (John Fletcher's parish), and in Wales at Bridgend, Cowbridge, and Cardiff.*[81] *From Merthyr Tydvil she mused upon historic divisions among Methodists due to Calvinism (FYOW, p. 556, 558):*

Merthyr Tydvil, April 15, 1862

Having spent about ten weeks in Wales, and witnessed the salvation of over one thousand souls, and the quickening of hundreds of believers into new spiritual life, we are now about taking our departure for Abergavenny, a town situated a little beyond the line separating Wales from England. . . .

The Calvinistic Methodists form far the most numerous body in Wales. They still have in full operation their School of the Prophets, at Trevecca, which was founded in the days of Lady Huntingdon, and of which the devoted Fletcher was one of the first instructors. When we read, in our childhood days, the interesting details of the formation of the Trevecca College, and the trials of the excellent Fletcher in connection with the Calvinistic question which resulted in the disunion of the parties, how little did we conceive whereunto this would grow!

In South Wales they met audiences that were both intensely responsive (at Abergavenny), and in some cases quite unresponsive (as at Blaina, FYOW, p. 569):

Blaina, Wales, May 12, 1862

Our first service was not encouraging. The people, having heard of the remarkable outpouring of the Spirit in other places we had visited, acted as though they thought that we poor helpless mortals must, of course, bring salvation with us, irrespective of their being *workers* together with God, and us his unworthy servants.[82] We were burdened in spirit, and told them, as ever, that the divine order is *absolute,* and we could only work where it is obeyed. "Judgment *must* begin at the house of God."[83] We urged the necessity of a personal, immediate, and unconditional recognition of God's order on the part of every professed Christian, irrespective of name or sect. From that hour, the Spirit began to move mightily among the people. With amazement have we listened to the joyous recitals of some who have received the tongue of fire.[84]

Her descriptive powers were elaborately applied to a Welsh funeral (FYOW, p. 571):

Aberdare, S. Wales, May 20, 1862

The Welsh people have customs of their own, contradistinquished from the English. A funeral has just passed my window. My attention was attracted to the solemn procession by the melody of voices attuned to a mournful dirge. The persons accompanying the corpse do not follow in orderly procession; but men and women, forming a large concourse, are blending in an indiscriminate walking mass, and the bier is carried along in the midst, not on men's shoulders, but placed on poles, and borne by four. The singing, though very pathetic, is sonorous, and forms a volume of solemn sound sufficiently strong to be heard quite in the distance by the surrounding community, proclaiming that Death has been gathering a new victim.

Three funerals have passed within one hour. How rapidly is Death doing his work! His sickle is ever sharp, and ready for use; and where is the place exempt from his reapings?

At Douglas on the Isle of Man, she described the stunning effect that her spontaneous call for total commitment had upon hearers (FYOW, pp. 579–80):

Douglas, Isle of Man, June 20, 1862

From the first of the evening's service, the presence of the High and Holy One was a felt reality. About an hour after the commencement of the service, such a remarkable effusion of the Spirit occurred, that not an individual present can ever forget the gracious event. In the midst of a solemn appeal to entire devotedness of heart and life, I seemed constrained to pause suddenly, and said, "I feel divinely impressed with the conviction, that if all who have named the name of Christ will at once bring their tithes into the Lord's storehouse, and prove God herewith, we shall have the windows of heaven opened upon us, and such an outpouring of the Spirit[85] as has never before been witnessed in this place, which will result in such a revival as has not been seen on the Isle of Man."[86]

There was a most solemn pause; and all seemingly, in that large assembly, that could free themselves from their crowded position, fell on their knees before God. For about three minutes, all was silence, with the exception of stifled sobs on the part of the contrite, and suppressed exclamations of praise, when the tide of divine power and holy joy rose to an irrepressible point. "Glory, glory, hallelujah!" burst from every part of the house. The tithes had been brought in, and the overflowing blessing had been poured out; and, judging from the effect, many hearts were saying,—

"It comes in floods we can't contain."[87]

Many, before the close of the service, were sanctified wholly. Scores of heaven-illuminated countenances seemed to bespeak unmistakably the reception of an indwelling power, which, we trust, will be diffusing on others its hallowing influences during all the future of their lives.

During their second brief campaign in Ireland, Mrs. Palmer suffered a "very serious and critical illness," "one of the most formidable and protracted illnesses of my life," in late summer of 1862, which brought her once again very near death. Dr. Palmer struggled to return her to Liverpool for medical care, thinking seriously of an immediate return to America, but then proceeded to London for slow recuperation. From her grave description, one might have imagined that their work in Britain would be quite finished (FYOW, pp. 600–601):

Liverpool, Everton Brow, Sept. 29, [1862][88]

After closing our work at Portadown, we stood announced for a public breakfast-meeting, in connection with the new chapel enterprise, at Enniskillen Town Hall, in anticipation of leaving the next day for Londonderry. For several days, I had seemed quite too ill to labor; but, having stood for some time announced, we resolved, if possible, that our yea should be yea.[89] I was unable to accompany Dr. P— to Enniskillen. We met, by arrangements, on the road to Londonderry the next day.

Special meetings commenced on the succeeding day, which were largely attended; but I was only able to attend the evening meeting, after which I was for several days prostrated with a very serious and critical illness. Our home was at the parsonage, with the minister's family, the beloved and devoted Mr. and Mrs. Dwyer, who did every thing that Christian courtesy and affection could devise for my restoration and comfort. As I grew rapidly worse, and medical council suited to Dr P—'s wishes could not be obtained in Londonderry, we concluded to risk the seemingly hazardous attempt, and return to England. Through great mercy I was sustained, and, though seriously ill when I started, found myself no worse on reaching our English home at Everton Brow than when we started. And here I have been suffering from a severe attack of congestive fever over three weeks, but am now, through much mercy, gaining in health, though still almost too ill to use my pen. Several days I was flickering between the two worlds. I seemed so near the haven of rest, that I had little expectation of returning; and yet I had no intimation of what the Lord was about to do with me. Such was the rapid force of disease, day after day, that I knew not which wave would bear me to the eternal shore.

In the midst of all, I felt that the everlasting arms were underneath and around me;[90] and for worlds I would not have taken my destiny into my own hands, whether to live or to die. Still, when I looked abroad over the world, and saw the great work to be done, and the laborers so few,[91] and thought of the little I had done in comparison to what I might have done, my heart was almost ready to break in agony for souls.

3. CAMPAIGNS OF 1863[92]

It became a point of critical deliberation whether the Palmers would return home or continue. While in Ireland, the Wesleyan Annual Conference had voted to prohibit its societies from bringing in traveling evangelists who were not members of their Connection, thus providing resistance not only to the Palmers but also to William Booth and James Caughey. Others begged them to continue their ministry. She reviewed their dilemma and the whole year of 1862 in a letter to the Hamlines (Memoirs, 391–93):

Leeds, England, Jan. 7, 1863

. . . I do not wonder that you express yourselves as you do in regard to our coming home, and though we have thousands of friends here who would fain have us linger, yet our dear ones at home, and yearning for the work there, would incline us to respond *heartily,* "WE COME." But we dare not come, until we are sure it is by the command of the Lord of the vineyard. Twice, though we could not feel quite sure it was at the Master's bidding, we made the attempt.

On the first occasion, the Lord laid his hand upon Dr. P. He was taken so severely ill that had we made the attempt to cross the ocean, his spirit, I presume, would have taken its departure for the eternal world, ere we reached our native shore. We had come to take passage from Liverpool. On account of his health, we were *compelled* to give it up. As soon as possibly able, he joined me, and over one thousand were saved in a few weeks. We then went to Madeley, memorialized as the scene where the immortal Mr. and Mrs. Fletcher exercised their ministry. Here the Lord began to pour out His Spirit, as we had scarcely before witnessed, in this, or any other land. As the result the revival, over one thousand souls were saved on the Madeley and Wellington circuits. Nine hundred were added on trial on the Madeley circuit, and four hundred on the Wellington circuit, beside many others who came forward and sought and obtained mercy, who were in the habit of going to the Established and other churches.

We then went to Wales, and the names of about one thousand five hundred were recorded by the secretaries of the meetings, who professed to have been translated out of the kingdom of darkness into the kingdom of God's dear Son.[93] Then we came back to Liverpool again, intending, as before, to set sail for America, having sent word to our loved ones at home, that they might expect to see us in the spring, or early summer.

But our earnest Irish friends, who had advertised us as expected at their camp-meeting, the summer previous, maintained that they had a *claim* upon us now, and were unyielding. . . .

We left Enniskillen for Portadown. Here the large altar was nightly surrounded with seekers and penitents, and many were saved. I presume one hundred would be a very low computation, but as there was no secretary appointed, as is usual where we labor, I cannot write definitely. From Portadown, we went to Londonderry (the birthplace of Dr. Eliot,[94] I believe). Here my health utterly failed. The time had again arrived, when we would have set our face homeward. But the idea of doing so was utterly impossible.

It was with difficulty that I was brought back to England, where I passed through one of the most formidable and protracted illnesses of my life. This wholly precluded our return in the autumn.

I have thus given you a glance of a year's labor. Can we doubt but it was the hand of infinite love that was laid upon Dr. P., preventing his return.

But you will say, "What now?" I can only say we are waiting the Lord's bidding. Wide doors of usefulness are in every direction, inviting us to enter. We are importunately urged to Manchester, Bristol, and several other important towns which we have not yet been able to visit. Still we feel that our health seems to demand a respite. We have serious thoughts of going to Palestine.[95] If we go to the Holy Land, we will go shortly, in view of returning to America, early in the summer.

Mrs. Palmer made good use of this period of recuperation by inquiring further into Wesley's biography and thought. She sought to explain to American readers of the Guide *the enigmatic divisions and varieties of "Methodism in England," (GTH 43, 1863: 145–47; written Feb. 4, 1863; see FYOW, pp. 630ff.; cf. Memoirs, p. 394):*

"Methodism in England"

WESLEY'S RECEPTION AT WALSALL

Walsall has been noted in my own mind since childhood as the place where the good Mr. Wesley came so near losing his life by the ruffianly mob in 1743.[96] Truth seems stranger than fiction as one reviews those scenes. The river in which he came so near being drowned is within a minute's walk of the place where I write.

The founder of Methodism could little have imagined, when he with his few devoted friends at Oxford University were endeavoring to live methodically good, that is, by the "same rule" of holy living, that their endeavors were destined to give rise to a cognomen[97] by which several distinct denominations should be distinguished all over the land. There are but few towns of any considerable size in England where may not be found the Wesleyan Methodists, the New Connexion Methodists, the Primitive Methodists, and the Free Church Methodists.

When Wesley was being so roughly handled by the rioters in Walsall that the blood issued from his mouth, and part of his coat was torn from him, and he dragged from one magistrate to another as a disturber of the peace, and for no other crime than that of talking to the people about their souls and psalm singing, could he have conjectured that here would be three or four distinct bodies all ambitious to bear his name, and acknowledge him as their founder under God? Yet so it is.

BRANCHES OF METHODISM[98]

Walsall has now four or five Methodist Churches, divided in a way little known in America, but as is usual here. Our efforts to do good in a general way often places us in contact with these various branches of Methodism, and we have reason to know that each is blessed with not a few good men, and we will trust each, as so many separate families are performing a mission which either one singly might not so well perform. While the circumstances which originated the dividing lines were to be regretted, He who alone can call forth things that are not as though they were,[99] knows how to make things which, if taken singly, seem disastrous, when taken together work for good.[100]

A letter just received from an excellent superintendent Wesleyan minister in whose circuit we have labored says: " . . . I do believe as the case stands they are mutual checks and incentives to good works, and that in all probability there are more spiritual results from their aggregate labors than could have been otherwise, had all the Methodists of the United Kingdom been under one banner. Political objects might have been accomplished which may not be attempted in our divided condition. . . . O for the baptism of the Holy Ghost to be bestowed on all the churches throughout Christendom!''

HARMONIZING EFFECTS OF A REVIVAL.

We are now witnessing scenes in this ancient town, in connexion with the various branches of Methodism, over which angels and the spirits of the just made perfect[101] must rejoice. Within the past twenty-six days over three hundred have been born into the kingdom of grace at the Whittimore-Street Methodist chapel. Here we are daily beholding what we have long been wishing to see—people hailing under five or six church banners, all laboring as one in bringing the unsaved to Jesus. . . .

SPIRIT BAPTISED CONVERTS.

We have long been settled in our convictions that it is the privilege of young converts to be holy. Mr. Wesley gives many instances of persons who were sanctified wholly, some within a few hours after conversion. Many will remember the case of Grace Paddy, of whom Mr. Wesley says, ''Such an instance I never knew before; of such an instance I never read; a person convicted of sin, converted to God, and renewed in love within twelve hours! Yet it is by no means incredible, seeing one day is with God as a thousand years.''[102] I do not know that we can record prodigies of grace quite equal to this here, but we have seen many who within a few days after their conversion have sought and obtained the full baptism of the Spirit, and the effect of the blessing has made them mighty in pulling down the strongholds of Satan.[103] I have no sympathy for mysticism[104] in religion. Any attainment of grace, however lofty, that does not energise the soul and bring it into sympathy with Jesus in the great work of soul-saving, leading to holy activities, does not to my conceptions, reach the Bible standard of Christian holiness.

While deeply engaged in revival efforts, Mrs. Palmer was not oblivious to the tragic events happening in the United States in 1863.[105] Long before the Civil War, Mrs. Palmer had expected divine judgment to descend upon America for the crimes of slavery. Her deep sympathy for Lincoln became increasingly transparent (FYOW, pp. 647, 648):

Wolverhampton, Feb. 12, 1863

What have been our feelings while observing the state of our country politically we will not attempt to describe. Though three thousand miles distant, we have closely watched the rising and retiring clouds of political strife. Long before the portentous clouds darkened our heavens, we were anticipating days of sadness, when the righteous Judge would chastise us as a nation for the wrongs permitted. For many years it has not seemed possible that judgment could much longer linger over the cruel wrongs of the slave, and the martyr-blood of such men as the righteous Buley and others. . . .

The name of Lincoln, so much abused through Southern perfidy, and mistaken conservative politicians of the United States, is now being embalmed in the minds of thousands in England as one of the great benefactors of the age. The proposition and attempt to establish a nation on the basis of slavery is now looked upon by tens of thousands as infamous beyond parallel.

At Nottingham,[106] *she defended vigorously the role of women testifying in public worship, although she was not inclined to think of that testimony as being "preaching in a technical sense" (FYOW, p. 677):*

Nottingham, June 21, 1863

It is our aim, in addressing the people previous to the prayer-meeting services, to simplify the way of faith to seekers of pardon; and we also try to tell the seekers of purity just the way to the cleansing fountain, as we and others have found it; and often do we hear of those, who, while a present acceptance of present grace is thus being urged upon them, receive the purchased gift. Preach we do not; that is, not in a *technical* sense. We would do it, if called; but we have never felt it our duty to sermonize in any way by dividing and subdividing with metaphysical hair-splittings in theology.[107] We have nothing to do more than Mary, when, by the command of the Head of the Church, she proclaimed a risen Jesus to her brethren.[108]

The experimental character of Irish revivalism would later have significant effects upon the American scene. The summer camp meeting would become an increasingly refined means of American holiness revivalism. In her third campaign in Enniskillen, Ireland, she observed (FYOW, pp. 686–87):

Enniskillen, Ireland, Aug. 3, 1863

This is the third summer since the Wesleyans in Ireland have been testing the advantages of camp-meetings with good success. One is now going
on within a mile of this town. The encampment is on a rise of ground about
two minutes' walk from the beautiful Lough Erne, a lake many miles in
length, with three hundred and sixty-five islands. The encampment is situated midway, within an enclosure whose entrance is guarded by a porter's
lodge over a quarter of a mile distant on either side. The road leading to it
is finely shaded by a choice variety of majestic trees. Each person entering
pays a half-penny, which, though a trifle, helps towards defraying incidental expenses, and may not be unimportant in guarding the sacredness of the
place from mere idlers. The grounds are handsomely cultivated, having
been recently occupied by a wealthy gentleman, who, though a Churchman,
gives it free of charge.

A large tent has been purchased, costing over a thousand dollars, capable of holding about three thousand persons. This, with a few smaller
tents, furnishes ample accommodations. Having been officially invited,[109]
and feeling a great desire that the hosts of Israel might be encouraged with
conquests here, as at these highly favored means of grace in our native land,
we concluded to defer our homeward course a little longer, and give our
humble aid.

*As their stay in England drew to a close, they felt the outpouring ap-
preciation of many, and the need for extended rest. Their efforts in England,
Scotland, Wales, and Ireland would soon be followed by the development
of the Brighton Convention[110] and the Keswick Movement (1875ff.) which
would extend and amend to some degree her holiness theology[111] (Memoirs, p. 39):*

Louth, Lincolnshire, September, 1863

. . . Dr. P. seems to bear up lately, much better than myself. My head
has grown weary, very weary, and absolutely requires *rest*. It is on this
account we have almost hesitated in informing you of the precise time when
you may expect us, as we shall require *quiet* a few weeks after our return.

We closed our services at Louth, night before last. Our farewell meeting was one of exceeding interest. I would love to tell you all about it, but
must forbear. Not less than two hundred were at the railroad station, waving
their last tearful adieus, as the train bore us rapidly away.

*Her last entry while in the Old World was filled with grateful recol-
lections of the outpouring of divine grace (FYOW, pp. 694–96):*

Manchester, Harpurhey, Oct. 2, 1863

Having already secured our passage in the steamer "City of New York," destined to sail from the shores of England Oct. 7, I have concluded to date my last letter from the Old World for dear ones at home. As we are about to launch away from these distant shores, our hearts are filled with adoring gratitude in reviewing the way by which the Lord hath led us since we left our native land.

. . . We are not unmindful of the strife of opinion now waging between the two countries; and, in relation to this, the deeply pious in both countries seem only to be drawn in closer fellowship with the right. While the wicked politicians and semi-Christians would, like Herod and Pilate, meet in friendliness when the object is to crucify truth, single-minded Christians in both lands not only deprecate the idea of war between the two countries, but every thing leading to it.. . . .

We have indeed witnessed the mighty things of our Almighty Lord wherever we have been called to labor. When the longings for loved ones at home would have prompted us to an earlier return, and we would have made arrangements to leave before our work was finished, the richness of God's goodness, as manifested in yet greater effusions of his Spirit, has prevented. On two occasions, when, from causes we cannot now state, we had fixed our time to leave, Infinite Love stayed us by severe and critical illness, rendering it utterly impossible for us to be answerable to our appointment; yet in all the results proving that our seeming disappointments had in a most marked manner been the appointments of Infinite Wisdom and Love.

The Palmers were warmly greeted back to America by friends,[112] *and immediately back in harness, as she promptly reported to Bishop and Mrs. Hamline (Memoirs, p. 403):*

We had not been at home two hours,[113] before we were waited upon by a number of brethren, composing the Quarterly Conference of the Allen Street M. E. Church, with the Presiding Elder and Pastor,[114] requesting that we would, if able, enter upon labors at once. We consented to spend our first Sabbath at Allen Street, though much worn, and needing rest.[115]

Notes

1. Caughey, *Helps to a Life of Holiness and Usefulness, or Revival Miscellanies* (Boston: James P. Magee, 1856). Later the Palmers would publish several of

Caughey's books: *Arrows from My Quiver*, (1867); *Earnest Christianity Illustrated* (1868); *Glimpses of Life in Soul-Saving: Selections from the Journal* (1868).

2. Mrs. Palmer knew and affirmed the work of both Caughey and Finney. For a fuller account of Trans-Atlantic evangelism, see Kent, *HF*, and Richard Carwardine, *Trans-Atlantic Revivalism: Popular Evangelicalism in Britain and America, 1790–1865* (Westport, Conn.: Greenwood Press, 1978); cf. James E. Orr, *The Second Evangelical Awakening in Britain* (London: Marshall, Morgan and Scott, 1949).

3. Frederick William Faber (1814–63), *Growth in Holiness* (London: T. Richardson, 1854); and exponents of Anglo-Catholic Revivalism, cf. Kent, *HF*, pp. 236ff.; J. Embry, *The Catholic Movement and the Society of the Holy Cross* London: The Faith Press 1931; L.D. Eliott-Binns, *Religion in the Victorian Era* (London: Lutterworth, 1936); A.T. Pierson, *Forward Movements of the Last Half Century* (New York: Funk & Wagnalls, 1905); Handley C.G. Moule, *The Cross and the Spirit* (London, Pickering & English, n.d.).

4. The reason for the Palmers' trip to Britain has been grossly misunderstood by John Kent, who wrote that "the Palmer's reaction to the threat of the American Civil War had been to leave America and sit out the conflict in England, clinging to what Donald Dayton has called a 'parlour' version of holiness," *HF*, p. 355; cf. Dayton, "The Holiness Heritage between Calvinism and Wesleyanism," paper at the Oxford Institute of Methodist Theology, July 1977. Almost every clause of Kent's sentence is incorrect: There is no evidence that the Palmer's motive for the British campaign was in any way connected with avoidance of civil strife. They actively resisted the early British tendencies to identify with the South in the Civil War. They did not "sit out" anything in England, as their itinerary shows—an extremely active four years. Very little in their intense activities can accurately be described as a "clinging" or a parlor withdrawal from their active vocation of proclamation and teaching.

5. Probably Phoebe's daughter, Sarah Palmer Foster.

6. June 4, 1859.

7. The Tuesday Meeting for the Promotion of Holiness; see entries for December 1839, January 1840.

8. Hence it appears that Henry Worrall probably immigrated to America a little after the turn of the century.

9. Rev. Thornelow of Prescot.

10. Charles Spurgeon, 1834–92, Baptist preacher, by age twenty-two became one of London's leading preachers, holding services after 1861 at the Metropolitan Tabernacle. At this time Spurgeon was about 25 years old.

11. The wife of Joseph A. Wright, a Methodist, elected governor of Indiana in 1849 and served for two terms of four years each, *CM*, p. 966. At the time this letter was written, Mrs. Wright may have been with him in Berlin where he served the U.S. government as minister, 1857–61, following his governorship. Mrs. Wright (formerly Mrs. C.R. Duel) had served with Phoebe Palmer in the founding of the Five Points Mission, as Second Founding Directress (Mrs. Palmer was Third Directress), cf. *CM*, p. 679.

12. About July 9, 1859.

13. By steam railway.

14. It is worth noting that she does not say as a young girl, but "since childhood." If true, this reinforces the view that her Methodist education began very young. This would suggest that she is not the author of "The Experience of Mrs. P.P.," GTH 19 (1851):135.

15. Mrs. Palmer appears to be extraordinarily well-informed on early Wesleyan preachers and leaders, both men and women; cf. *PF*, pp. 96ff.; *FYOW*, passim. By this time there was considerable interest in Wesleyana, cf. A. Clarke, *Memoirs of the Wesley Family* (New York: Lane and Tippett, 1848); John Nelson, *Extract from the Journal of John Nelson* (New York: Carlton & Porter, 1856).

16. She would later return to Oxford, see entry of Dec. 29, 1860.

17. 1 Cor. 5:6, 7; Gal. 5:9; Luke 13:21.

18. Those looking for glossolalia in the Palmers' revivals might imagine in such a passage some preliminary evidence for it; but rather than glossolalia, it apparently is referring simply to inspired utterance.

19. Num. 13:30.

20. Cf. Luke 24:33–43.

21. Viz., suffering the pains of earnest penitence and confession.

22. Cf. John Wesley White, "The Influence of North American Evangelism in Great Britain Between 1830 and 1914 on the Origin and Development of the Ecumenical Movement," Ph.D. thesis, Mansfield College, Oxford, 1963. "Ecumenical" is used here in the sense of Protestant evangelical proto-ecumenism, anteceding to developments that later would emerge as the ecumenical movement. Cf. Ruth Rouse and S.C. Neill, eds., *A History of the Ecumenical Movement, 1517–1948* (London: 1954).

23. The Presbyterian minister.

24. The military metaphors abound in Mrs. Palmer's descriptions of the campaigns of 1859.

25. Le Chemin de la sainteté, translated by John Wesley Lelievre (Paris: Grassart, 1859).

26. La foi et ses effets, translated by John Wesley Lelievre (Paris: Grassart, 1859).

27. Cf. 1 Sam. 17:45.

28. Cf. 2 Cor. 6:1.

29. Cf. Robert Young, The Importance of Prayer Meetings in the Revival of Religion (New York: Carlton & Porter, n.d.).

30. William Booth (1829–1912), founder of the Salvation Army, born into Church of England, ordained Methodist preacher in 1858 (New Connection), followed Wesley's teaching on sanctification. Married Catherine Mumford in 1855; heard Mrs. Palmer in her 1859 Newcastle campaign in England; withdrew from Methodists in 1861, and by 1865 had begun his mission to the poor of East London, which was to result in the formation of the Salvation Army.

31. Catherine Booth, *Godliness* (Boston: McDonald, Gill, 1893). Kent writes: "'Mrs. Booth's letters . . . make it quite clear that she and her husband had

completely accepted Phoebe Palmer's doctrine of holiness'', *HF*, p. 326. Cf. F. de L. Booth-Tucker, *Life of Catherine Booth*, 2 vols. (New York: Fleming H. Revell, 1892), I, pp. 343ff.

32. P.J. Jarbo published "A Letter to Mrs. Palmer," in *Reference to Women Speaking in Public* (North Shields, England: 1859). Arthur Augustus Rees published a pamphlet against women preaching, to which Catherine Booth wrote a response, *Female Ministry: Woman's Right to Preach the Gospel* (London: Morgan and Chase, 1859); 2nd ed., *Female Teaching: Or the Rev. A.A. Rees versus Mrs. Palmer, being a reply to the pamphlet by the above gentleman on the Sunderland Revival* (London: 1861). Catherine Booth's defense of Mrs. Palmer constituted a major turning point in her personal history, especially concerning the duty of women to speak, cf. White, *BH*, pp. 71f.

33. 2 Cor. 6:17; this separationist theme was later to take a turn against Methodism itself, in the form of the "come-outers" who would leave the Methodist Episcopal Church to form new churches and societies for the promotion of holiness.

34. Cf. Rom. 4:21.

35. 2 Cor. 6:17.

36. Cf. 1 Cor. 2:12.

37. Cf. Heb. 10:19–20, with Heb. 6:19.

38. Cf. 2 Cor. 10:4.

39. "Full baptism of the Spirit" is her way of speaking of entire sanctification, the reception of sanctifying grace. Cf. Mark 1:8, Matt. 3:11, Acts 1:5.

40. Cf. Ps. 37:34.

41. Isa. 58:12.

42. Zech. 14:20; by "ancient doctrine" she probably is referring to the biblical teaching of holiness, but also could be referring to those patristic teachers of the way of holiness, upon whom Wesley's teaching of sanctification depended ("Macarius the Egyptian," Ephraim Syrus, Gregory of Nyssa, Augustine; cf. Albert C. Outler, *WJWB*, Sermons, volume 1, introduction; ed. John Wesley, *LPT*, intro.; R. Newton Flew, *The Idea of Perfection in Christian Theology* [New York: Humanities Press, 1968]).

43. Cf. Isa. 66:8.

44. The system of secretarial recording of names of persons making commitments, and turning them over to local church pastors for follow-up, was a significant development of the Caughey-Palmer revivals, both for the purposes of nurture, and for keeping accurate records. The salient distinction in record-keeping was that between seekers of salvation (conversion) and recipients of heart purity (sanctification).

45. Ps. 51:10–13, v. 11 omitted.

46. This is one of the key links between Wesleyanism and Pentecostalism; cf. Keswick Convention, 1875, emphasizing the baptism of the Holy Spirit, making a relative shift from the themes of purity and cleansing to the power of the Spirit (cf. T. Smith, *Called Unto Holiness*, ch. 1).

47. Cf. Ps. 51:10.

48. Cf. Ps. 51:13.

49. Cf. 1 Sam. 17:45.

50. Cf. Matt. 17:4.

51. *WJW*, III, p. 232; quote slightly amended (cf. *Journal*, ed. N. Curnock, V, p. 140).

52. Secker.

53. Frank Baker has expressed doubt that it was Archbishop Thomas Secker (1693–1768) who wrote under the pseudonym, "John Smith," *WJWB*, Letters, II, p. 138n.

54. Wesley's Christian Library included works by patristic and Protestant writers, many on themes of holy living.

55. John Fletcher (1729–85), vicar of Madeley, early Methodist theologian, opponent of antinomianism, and exponent of Christian perfection. Born in Switzerland de la Flechere, educated in Geneva, came in touch with the Methodists as a tutor in England. Ordained Church of England priest in 1757. Became superintendent of seminary at Trevecca, Wales, in 1768, resigned after three years due to doctrinal dispute. His *Checks to Antinomianism* defended Arminian-Wesleyan doctrines against orthodox Calvinist objections. See Joseph Benson, *The Life of the Rev. John W. de la Flechere* (New York: Wade and Mason, 1833). Fletcher's work was to have significant effect upon the holiness movement in general, and Mrs. Palmer in particular, cf. John A. Knight, "John Fletcher's Influence on the Development of Wesleyan Theology in America," *WTJ* 13 (1978): 13–33; Timothy Smith, "How John Fletcher Became the Theologian of Wesleyan Perfectionism, 1770–1776," *WTJ* 15/1 (1980): 68–87; E. Dale Dunlap, *Methodist Theology in Great Britain in the Nineteenth Century* (Ann Arbor: University Microfilms, 1968).

56. Probably the copy now in the United Methodist Archives at Drew University.

57. Mary Bosanquet Fletcher (1739–1805), was a principal model for Phoebe Palmer's ministries of witness and service. She opened her own house at Laytonstone as an asylum for the poor. After four years of marriage to John Fletcher, following his death, she continued to serve at Madely. Cf. Taft, *HW;* Coles, *Heroines of Methodism*, op. cit.; and Henry Moore, *The Life of Mrs. Mary Fletcher, from Her Journal* (Birmingham: J. Peart, 1817); (New York: Emory and Waugh, 1830).

58. Joel 3:14.

59. Luke 2:9ff.

60. Cf. Isa. 16:9; Jer. 9:1.

61. Although she had never read Kierkegaard or Marx (available then only in Danish or German), her observations on the state of religion in Scotland are ancitipatory of phrases that have affinities with both (similar in some ways to SK's *Attack Upon "Christendom,"* and to Marx's image of religion as an opiate: "conscience sleeps under the opiate of a religious profession"). It is arguable that her influence through world-wide revival movements (Methodist, holiness, charismatic, and Pentecostal) has indirectly had effect upon human history of similarly vast proportions, though far less recognized.

62. Cf. 1 Cor. 2:12.

63. Discharge from duty.

64. Cf. Kierkegaard, *Attack Upon "Christendom,"* and *Judge for Yourselves!*

65. Isa. 29:21.

65. 1 Tim. 6:6–8; this was Mrs. Palmer's way of protesting conspicuous consumption.

66. Jer. 33:3.

67. Cf. Matt. 21:9ff.; Mark 11:9ff.

68. Compared with other traveling revivalists, Mrs. Palmer showed extraordinary interest in what today is called "followup," or nurturing the Christian life in Christian community following the experience of divine grace in a revivalist or para-church setting. Compared with Wesley, however, Mrs. Palmer did less justice to this concern. Wesley showed more sustained commitment and interest in developing communities of mutual care, confession, accountability, and nurture (*WJW*, VIII, pp. 252ff.). This pattern was indeed largely followed in Mrs. Palmer's Tuesday Meetings. Wesley was not inclined to assume that class-members had received sanctifying grace until they gave evidence of this by good works over a period of time, so as to be rigorously tested through a sustained experience of an intensive group in dialogue, study, admonition, and mutual care (cf. Oden, *The Intensive Group Experience* [Philadelphia: Westminster, 1973], ch. 2).

69. Cf. Isa. 52:10.

70. Jer. 33:3; cf. Ps. 106:21; Luke 1:49.

71. *Memoirs*, p. 318; cf. newspaper accounts of the period.

72. *Memoirs*, p. 368.

73. Rev. 20:11.

74. There is no indication that she visited the Queen.

75. Num. 23:23.

76. Quite likely a reference to J.C. Ryle (1816–1900), who would later become Bishop of Liverpool, and major spiritual mentor of modern evangelical Anglicanism. Ryle would later write of one of the most important treatises of the nineteenth century entitled *Holiness* (Cambridge: Jas. Clarke, 1956), focusing upon the premise of radical sin. This followed a pre-Wesleyan Evangelical Anglican position on sanctification (as defined by Anglican and Reformed writers like Thomas Watson, Robert Trail, Thomas Brooks, John Jewell, Richard Baxter, John Owen, Philip Doddridge, etc., guardedly stated in a way that Wesley could have hardly found objectionable), and was critical of the Keswick Movement (1875ff.) that would follow Mrs. Palmer's revival activities in Britain.

77. For continuing reports to her American readers on the progress of the British revival, see *GTH* 39 (1861): 15, 85, 99, 149; 40 (1861): 13f., 85, 122, 153f.

78. Cf. Prov. 19:3.

79. Ps. 121:2.

80. *Memoirs*, p. 392.

81. For periodic reports to her American readers during this period, see *GTH* 41 (1862): 39–42, 57, 185; 42 (1862): 23, 26, 62, 92, 122, 151–55, 183f.

82. Cf. 2 Cor. 6:1; Luke 17:10.

83. Cf. 1 Pet. 4:17.

84. Possibly a proto-glossolalic reference, but more likely a metaphor for sanctification.

85. Cf. Mal. 3:10.

86. The form of this invitation had been previously offered in the Canadian Revival.

87. The poetic allusion is to Mal. 3:10; cf. 2 Chron. 6:18; Ps. 93:3. Cf. similar allusions in Nicholas von Zinzendorf, "O Thou, to Whom All-Searching Sight," *The Methodist Hymnal* (Nashville: Smith & Lamar, 1908), #359, v. 3; hymn source uncertain, cf. *HMEC,* 1879, #290, 341, 431.

88. *FYOW* indicates 1863, but probably it is a typographical error and actually refers to 1862, otherwise the sequence organized by Mrs. Palmer herself would be out of order.

89. Cf. James 5:12.

90. Cf. Deut. 33:27.

91. Cf. Luke 10:2.

92. For periodic reports of these events to her American readers, see *GTH* 43 (1863): 14, 62, 82, 145; 44 (1863): 46, 49, 73, 97, 121, 161, 178, 186; and *CAJ* 38 (1863): 4 (editorial), 153, 233, 281.

93. Cf. Col. 1:13.

94. Probably Charles Eliot (1792–1869), whose actual birthplace was Green-conwayu, County Donegal, Ireland; a Wesleyan minister who came to the United States in 1815, he joined the Ohio Conference, taught at Madison College, Union-town, Pa., and for thirteen years was editor of the *Western Christian Advocate;* became President of Iowa Wesleyan College (*EWM,* I, p. 766).

95. They did not go.

96. *WJW,* I, pp. 453ff.

97. Nickname.

98. Cf. John Kent, *The Clash Between Radicalism and Conservatism in Methodism, 1815–1848* (Cambridge: Cambridge University, 1950), (available on microfilm); *The Age of Disunity* (London: Epworth, 1966).

99. Cf. Rom. 4:17.

100. Cf. Rom. 8:28.

101. Cf. Heb. 12:22–23.

102. *WJW,* III, p. 235; cf. 2 Pet. 3:8.

103. Cf. 2 Cor. 10:4.

104. Mrs. Palmer's chief association with the term "mysticism" was quietism. Following Luther and Wesley, she disliked the term and its implied passivity.

105. Contra Kent, *HF,* p. 355; cf. editorial, "When Will the War End," *GTH* 44 (1863):58.

106. She had been preceded at Nottingham by James Caughey; cf. *The Triumph of Truth, and Continental Letters and Sketches, from the Journal, Letters and Sermons of the Rev. James, Caughey, as Illustrated in the Two Great Revivals in Nottingham and Lincoln* (Philadelphia: Higgins and Perkinpine, 1857).

107. This is her standard caricature of "theology."

108. She was alert to the fact that Mary was the first person to bear testimony

to Jesus' resurrection (John 20:11–18). Mrs. Palmer is one of the few exegetes in the historic Christian tradition to point out this simple fact: It was women who first bore testimony to the resurrection of Jesus (*Promise of the Father*, chs. 2–4, pp. 14–51).

109. Apparently some of the earlier resistance of Irish Wesleyan officials to itinerant revivalism had been overcome.

110. *Record of the Convention for the Promotion of Scriptural Holiness, Brighton, 29 May to 7 June 1875* (Brighton and London: 1875).

111. Charles F. Harford, ed., *The Keswick Convention: Its Message, Its Method, and Its Men* (London: Marshall, 1907).

112. Nathan Bangs had died while she was abroad, May 3, 1862; see Edmund S. Janes, *Sermons on the Death of Nathan Bangs* (New York: Carlton & Porter, 1862).

113. Arrival date: Oct. 19, 1863.

114. The pastor was J. A. Roche.

115. See editorial, "Palmers Return to New York," *GTH* 44 (1863): 37.

X

THE LAST DECADE (1864–1874)

I. GUIDE TO HOLINESS: ENGENDERING A NEW
GENERATION OF LEADERSHIP (1864–1866)

Upon their return from Europe, Dr. and Mrs. Palmer purchased the major journal of the holiness revival movement, Guide to Holiness *(the journal started by Timothy Merritt with Mrs. Palmer's encouragement as* Guide to Christian Perfection, *1839 to 1846, entitled* Guide to Holiness *from 1846 to 1864),*[1] *and Mrs. Palmer increasingly took on its editorial responsibilities.*[2] *The Palmers were soon back on the road to numerous points west not previously visited.*

During the deadly year 1864, one of the fiercest of the Civil War, Mrs. Palmer continued her revival activity non-stop, almost as if to signal that she too was at war. During that year she held meetings in New York (Troy, Poughkeepsie, Brewster, Mt. Kisco), Massachusetts (Lawrence, Boston), Illinois (Rock Island City), Michigan (Detroit), then to Iowa (Mt. Pleasant) to visit Bishop and Mrs. Hamline, and finally to Canada (Peterborough, Yarmouth, Nova Scotia, Percy and Pictou). She renewed many friendships among those whom she had not seen during the several years she was abroad. In a spring article on "Camp-Meetings" (GTH 46 (1864) pp. 42–43), she anticipated the summer season of camp meetings by briefly recounting their history and the solemn expectations that each participant rightly brings to such an event:

We would suggest to all who are on the eve of going, that as far as their physical condition will allow, they set apart a day for special prayer and fasting, or abstinence, for the reception of a deeper baptism of the Spirit on their own souls, and in pleadings that an extraordinary effusion of the Spirit may be realized at all the services on the encampment.

Let all the professed servants of Christ lay themselves on the divine altar as a *whole burnt sacrifice,* in view of engaging in the work of the Lord. . . .

The more you exemplify by your daily doings and words the loving compassions, lowliness, and burning zeal of your Saviour, the more truly will your professions of *perfect love* exert a vitalizing, persuasive influence, and in most winning assurances, will demonstrate that those who profess perfect love do in fact do more than others. Live in the spirit of sacrifice. Let it be seen that you are willing to sacrifice that which costs you something in ease, reputation, and according as God hath prospered you[3] in money, for the establishment of Christ's kingdom on earth. Thus shall it be known by the testimony of your life and lips, that holiness is the power, or, in other words, the great lever by which a fallen redeemed world is to be raised from earth to heaven.[4]

While the Civil War was yet raging, in June of 1864, on the way to Chicago and Iowa,[5] Mrs. Palmer was in a railway accident but came through unscathed. Her report to her readers ("Notes by the Way," GTH 46 [1864]: 67–69) described the event and her subsequent meeting with Bishop Hamline in Iowa. Written during the summer of 1864, it contains a poignant interpretation (by Bishop Hamline, which she affirmed) of the Civil War as divine judgment upon national sin:

We left New York City on Tuesday morning, June 7th, by the Erie Railroad, and passing through a picturesque region of 332 miles, arrived at Hornellsville[6] in time to take tea. . . . Just before reaching Cleveland on the Atlantic and Great Western Railroad we had an accident which seriously perilled life and limb. We were rounding a curve in the road at a furious, and certainly unwarrantable, speed, when we were dashed against a freight-train throwing it off the track and breaking several cars to pieces. Our own baggage-car was also much injured and thrown off the track. The engine broke loose and dashed a distance beyond, or we might have entered the blissful mansions prepared for us above before reaching the mansion of our beloved Bishop Hamline. . . . [7]

Friday morning, nine o'clock, we were again on our way, After journeying all day, passing through some populous towns,—Aurora, Mendota, Galesburgh, etc.,—we arrived about twilight on the banks of the beautiful Mississippi. Seldom, perhaps never, did we witness a more enchanting scene than that which presented itself as we crossed the Mississippi to the town of Burlington. The sun was lying on a bed of golden clouds, diffusing a roseate hue over the meandering waters, rich landscapes, and evening sky.

The day's journey had been exceedingly tiresome and the heat of the sun excessive; but now fresh breezes fanned our brow and invited to repose. After a comfortable night's rest at Burlington, we took the train for Mount Pleasant, Iowa. Before eleven o'clock, on the morning of June 11th, we were again permitted to greet our long-loved, cherished friends, Bishop and Mrs. Hamline, after a separation of seven years.[8] What a change do we observe in the appearance of our excellent Bishop H. One might judge that a score of years had intervened since we last gazed upon him instead of seven. His flowing white beard and snowy hair give him a most venerable appearance, reminding us of what we imagine the ancient Bishop Polycarp[9] might have been. . . .

The bishop has never, I presume, been what is termed *conservative* on the subject of slavery. We have known him intimately over twenty years, and he has ever been outspoken in his abhorrence of the system, in all its developments from first to last. He is now more than ready to give of his means as largely as possible toward the sustainment of the government in its present fearful crisis. He believes the terrible things we have witnessed are the righteous retribution of the High and Holy One. Said he, ''I can never ask that the sword may cease to devour and peace be restored, without first pleading for the poor slave, and the entire abolition of slavery, believing that God is now punishing us for our complicity with this sin.''[10]

By June 29, 1864, she was in Detroit. She wrote to Sarah of her surprise at finding the Tuesday Meeting pattern being diligently practiced on the frontier. She described a woman in Rock Island City[11] whom she identified only as "Aunt Harris" (Memoirs, pp. 247–48):

Detroit, June 29, 1864

. . . She has kept up a meeting at her own house on the subject of holiness, the past four or five years, and is exerting a most gracious leavening influence in the Church community. I asked her *when* and *where* she received the blessing. She looked surprised, and said, ''Why, do you not know? It was at the *Tuesday* meeting in New York, during my visit there several years ago.'' So she came home, resolved that she would establish a Tuesday meeting, in Rock Island City, which has been going on ever since. Surely, our Tuesday meeting has spread into bands. Who can tell how diffusive its influence,—and where it may end? Surely, its effects will be seen long as eternity endures.

During the last decade of her life, Mrs. Palmer was alert to encourage leadership in the holiness revival that was destined to grow exponentially. This is exemplified by the talented couple, Rev. and Mrs. John S. Inskip.[12] The reception of sanctifying grace by Mrs. Inskip was to prove a momentous occurrence that would presage significant developments following after Mrs. Palmer's ministry in the last half of the nineteenth century. For Mrs. Inskip was to lead her minister husband—already an outstanding leader of New York Methodism—into the experiential reception of sanctifying grace, and he was later to take major leadership in the National Camp Meeting Association that was to give strength and growing unity to the holiness movement and proto-Pentecostal theology.[13] This letter, presumably to Bishop and Mrs. Hamline, dated Sept. 25, 1864, describes the experience of Rev. and Mrs. Inskip (Memoirs, pp. 66–67):

NEW YORK, September 25, 1864

You will remember Brother Inskip, and I am inclined to think you have some knowledge of Sister Inskip as a Christian Sister of more than ordinary energy of character. Neither our Brother nor Sister Inskip are disposed to be slow or uninfluential, and I have longed that their power to sway might all be turned wholly in a sanctified channel. The desire of my heart has been gloriously fulfilled.

At the Sing Sing Camp Meeting, through the influence of our beloved Sister Sarah Lankford, mainly, Sister Inskip was enabled to claim Jesus as a Saviour able to save to the uttermost. Sister Sarah is a host. She has meetings in her tent, where many ministers and people received the full baptism.[14] While Sister Inskip was attending these meetings from time to time, the enemy tempted her that she was devoting too much time to herself personally, and ought to be at work in other tents where she might be leading sinners to the Saviour. On mentioning this temptation to Sister Sarah, she said, "Dear darling, get the blessing of holiness, and it will be a gift of power by which you will be enabled to do much more in helping sinners to Jesus." I mention this, because the result proved it to be so gloriously true. Sister Inskip received, and testified before many hundreds, that she had obtained the witness before leaving the encampment. It was only as might have been anticipated, that her husband should be affected, and drawn to a consideration of the subject, through her testimony. Two weeks passed, his mind gradually preparing, and his heart becoming yet more deeply impressed in regard to his need of personal holiness, till on Sabbath morning, while preaching from Heb. 12, 1st, he experienced the blessing in great power. It was while earnestly exhorting his people to lay aside *every* weight,[15] and to do it *now*, that he received power to say "I am doing it

NOW! I *have* DONE IT NOW*!* Glory! Glory! Glory!'' The power of the Lord came down upon the people in a very remarkable manner, and many wept and others praised the Lord, and the whole congregation was moved in a very extraordinary manner. The evening of that day proved to [be] a demonstration, that HOLINESS IS POWER.[16]

Sister I. told me that she never heard her husband preach with the unction he did that night. Sinners were awakened all over the house.[17]

By the end of the year[18] she was, once more, exhausted from travel. She had just passed through another period of grave illness "not knowing but at any hour I might pass the portals of time," thereby eliciting this sober thought upon her finitude and physical vulnerability (Memoirs, p. 73):[19]

. . . My illness was induced by taxing myself too severely, in labors abundant. So pressing have been the claims on our time, constraining us to unremitting labors, that I look back with astonishment that we have endured so long. If spared, we shall be more careful in future, and not suffer ourselves to be *overpersuaded.* I have not yet recovered,—still feel a pressure on my head, which admonishes me to carefulness.

It was in this context of her own intense awareness of her own finitude that Mrs. Palmer reflected on her grief concerning the assassination of President Lincoln on April 14, 1865, having visited his funeral bier in New York (Memoirs, p. 60):

The whole of the past week in regard to business, has been as a Sabbath. So signally set apart to mournful devisings and doings. On Monday, the remains of the President were brought by the way of Philadelphia, to this city. Tens of thousands looked upon his lifeless remains, as they lay in state at the City Hall. We chose the midnight hour, thinking we might be able to gain access, which thousands, by the pressure of the crowd, were denied.

It was just as the city clock was pointing the solemn midnight hour, that we gazed upon all that was mortal of the beloved man that we had loved and revered as the second Washington of our nation. Would that I could depict the *solemnity* of that countenance. There was something so *speaking* about it, that its strangely solemn features have ever since been telling on both heart and mind.

I would love to tell you, beloved one, all I feel on this subject. Surely, the Judge of all the earth, would, by the solemnities and atrocities of this astounding event, teach us as a people, lessons which we must not fail to learn, if we would not have something yet more terrific befal [sic] us. Yesterday afternoon, the funeral procession passed from City Hall, through Broadway and Fifth avenue, to 34th st., occupying several hours. Such an assemblage, I presume, was never before witnessed in this, or any other city in America.

2. POST-WAR JOURNEYS WEST AND SOUTH
(MICHIGAN, ILLINOIS, OHIO, MISSOURI, KANSAS, WEST VIRGINIA, MARYLAND, MISSISSIPI, AND LOUISIANA, 1866–1869)

During the period immediately following the war, she was not spared controversy. She was challenged by the Unitarians and Universalists, and by anti-sanctificationists in the Methodist fold.[20] *Her view of the way of holiness, sometimes misinterpreted as being wildly utopian or optimistic, was grounded upon a soberly realistic estimate of the persistence and subtlety of sin, as is revealed in this letter to Mrs. Lankford from Upper Newton Falls, Massachusetts, dated May 12, 1866 (Memoirs, pp. 417–18):*

With Unitarianism and Universalism, and general obtuseness on the subject of everything that constitutes an orthodox Christianity, we are being called to contend. Even members of the M. E. Church think that revival services are too *exciting,* and that we are making quite too much ado in getting people forward to the altar, the thing being new to them. Some of them also quarrel with the subject of holiness.

A noted Universalist minister of these parts, said in comparing the two—Unitarianism and Universalism, ''The difference is this: ''Universalists believe God is too good to damn the people. Unitarians believe that they are too good to be damned.'' The large church edifice in which we worship has been recently purchased from the Unitarians, one of the leading Methodist men having recently bought it. Wishing to have the seats all rented, so as to ensure a return for his money, he has advised the minister to be reserved in regard to preaching on the doctrine of future punishment.[21] Yet, in the midst of all, the Lord is working. The altar is nightly surrounded and souls are born into the kingdom, at both afternoon and evening services.

Mrs. Palmer's avid interest in leadership in higher education is revealed in her account written to her sister Sarah from Jackson, Michigan, concerning her cordial visits to Asa Mahan, President of Adrian University in Michigan, and Erastus Haven, president of the University of Michigan[22]—*both longtime associates of the Palmers. It was during her tes-*

timony at the Chicago camp meeting that Frances Willard, later to become founder of the Women's Christian Temperance Union, experienced the fullness of salvation.[23] *Following Chicago, in the same letter in which she reported her call upon the wife of the governor of Illinois, she reflected gravely upon the cost of the war to a single family (Memoirs, pp. 426–31):*

Palmyra, Mich., Aug. 15, 1866

Here we were delighted to meet our long-valued Christian brother, Dr. Mahan;[24] for several years past President of the Adrian University. His name has long been as ointment poured forth,[25] to the lovers of heart-purity, in both hemispheres. Some of our readers are familiar with his work on "Christian Perfection". He tells us that he intends shortly to give to the Christian world a work on the baptism of the Holy Spirit, which we doubt not will be hailed with delight, by thousands. . . . [26]

After leaving the camp-meeting, we returned to the town of Ann-Arbor, in time for the evening meeting at the Methodist Episcopal Church, where we stood pledged for a service. We had a gracious season. Spent the night with Dr. Haven, President of the Michigan University, with whom and his excellent lady, we have long been favorably acquainted.[27] The doctor's position is one of great responsibility. About twelve hundred students are in attendance. The University is not sectarian or nominally religious; but the doctor preaches on the Sabbath, in the University Chapel, and is thus furnished with an opportunity to diffuse a religious influence. . . . [28]

We took tea with Mrs. Gov. E———,[29] and other pleasant friends, and left the encampment a little after seven o'clock in the evening, feeling that our stay, though short, had not been in vain.

We remained in Chicago over night, and very early the next morning, were on our way to the Goshen-district camp-meeting.[30] We were met, toward evening of the same day, at Sturgis, Ind., by Rev. R. Newton, of Lima, and introduced to Mr. D. Sharp with whom we enjoyed a pleasant home, during our stay at the campmeeting. Many have made sacrifices for the war, but few have paid so dearly as this dear, kind family. Four beloved sons, under the age of twenty-three, were laid on the altar of the service of their country, and fill soldiers' graves. How sad the bereavement!

During 1867 Dr. and Mrs. Palmer's revival activity pressed further west (St. Louis, Missouri, and Leavenworth, Kansas), and further south than ever before (to New Orleans). After visiting Leavenworth and Kansas City, they led an extended meeting at Lebanon, Illinois, where Mrs. Palmer wrote Mrs. Hamline (Memoirs, p. 438, Feb. 25, 1867):

. . . We have been here about two weeks. He who alone doeth wonders,[31] has wrought in power. Many have, we trust, obtained the blessing of holiness, and between one and two hundred have been added to the Lord. The exact number I have not yet learned, but the excellent minister, Rev. Mr. Earp,[32] told me, last week, that he had taken more than one hundred names of the converts. Over fifty, I think, are students of McKendree College. Far the largest proportion of the converts are men, mainly, the most wealthy and influential of the town. You will with us, unite in giving glory to God in the highest.[33]

The work here still goes on gloriously. An unusual feature of the revival is, that most of the converts are men. One hundred and forty have joined the M. E. C. since we came, and about one hundred and seventy professed conversion. Our afternoon meetings, we devoted mainly to the subject of holiness. President Allyn[34] came out clearly in the profession of the blessing, yesterday, and his son also (one of the students), came forward as a seeker of holiness, and professed to find. He has been converted since we came. Several other students, converted within the past few days, were among the seekers of the great salvation, some of whom professed to find the gift of power. About sixty were forward, seeking holiness.

Only two years after the Civil War, Mrs. Palmer set out on a poignant, tentative, exploratory journey into the deep South.[35] This was her only trip to the Mississippi side of the deep South.[36] Only one letter has survived from that trip. She felt keenly the demoralization of the southern church and society in the wake of the war. In this letter she offered a condensed version of her startling theory of the beginning of the Civil War (later to be more seriously developed and elaborated by respected American historians):[37] that the division of the two Methodisms constituted the opening wedge that later led to the division of the United States into north and south, and ultimately to war. She had personally witnessed that division of Methodism in the General Conference of 1844 at New York. She was earnestly convinced that it was Methodism's lack of holiness that in part elicited the war, and if Methodism had only fulfilled its historic task, the war could have been avoided (Memoirs, pp. 438–40, in a letter to Mrs. Hamline, dated March 30th, 1867, while traveling on the Mississippi River):

We had a prosperous passage, pausing on our way at Cairo, Vicksburg, Natchez, and a few other places memorialized by sanguinary strife, in the history of the late war. At the places mentioned, we called on the ministers, or as the beloved John might say, on the angels of the churches.[38]

Nothing can be more sure than that the churches South generally are in a very low condition, spiritually, and also financially. The ministers mourn over the desolations of Zion.[39] They say that the people of their charges are demoralized. . . . Everywhere, we found the Southern ministers acquainted with us, by reputation, and disposed to be affectionately appreciative. At Vicksburg, as we called at the parsonage, the minister, Dr. Camp,[40] though personally unacquainted, was so affected at sight of us, that he turned aside and wept. He afterward apologized for it, saying, that for years he had been interested with our writings on the precious theme of holiness, and had longed to see us,—thought of coming to New York,—but now, behold the Lord had sent us to see him. . . .

We have had very serious thoughts whether the Lord might not have something for us to do with these Southern people.[41] The want of perfect love caused their disasters. So we think. I have always thought that the separation of the M. E. C., North and South, was the entering wedge, and in part through political intrigue, preparatory to a bolder step—the separation of the States. What a pity that the ministers of the church South do not see their error. But though they mourn their desolations, I fear that they are not yet sufficiently humble to learn the lessons that infinite wisdom would teach.

After returning to New York, the Palmers set out in late June of 1867 on the steamer "Daniel Drew" on a long journey down the Erie Canal that eventually took them to Oberlin for a visit with President Charles G. Finney, leading Congregationalist in the sanctificationist revivals. This visit was followed by a wide swing of revival meetings through Illinois, Indiana, Michigan, Canada, and Vermont, to Philadelphia, and Trenton, New Jersey. The year's work would culminate in a campaign in Washington, D.C., at Wesley Chapel, where the wife and daughter of General Grant attended their services, to which she alluded in a letter to Mrs. Hamline, Nov. 20, 1867. This letter shows evidence of a long precedent of communication between American revival leaders and American political figures—a form of "civil religion" that Mrs. Palmer did not find uncomfortable (Memoirs, p. 444):

Do pray for us *daily,* while at Washington. We go to the Wesleyan chapel. When we were laboring at Cincinnati, last spring, Gen. Grant's mother and sister came from Covington, to the services. We were at that time urged to go to Washington, as we had been, repeatedly before, to hold services at the *Hamline* church. We mentioned this to Mrs. Grant and daughter, when we visited them. An earnest desire was expressed that we might be able to go, and they said that they were *sure* Gen. Grant would attend the services. Now, I want you to unite with me in praying daily for a few days to come, that not only General Grant and family may be induced to come and get salvation, but that there may be a great moving among the dry bones in Washington.[42] How *greatly* is it needed! All things are possible with God,[43] and all things are possible to him that *believeth*,[44] and for mighty faith that *cannot* ask in vain.[45]

The theme of spiritual vigilance, or watchfulness in the face of demonic temptation, was developed in this diary entry of the following February (Memoirs, p. 131):

Dairy, February 20th, 1868.—My mind is deeply impressed with the conviction, that if I would make my life, in all its *particulars,* a power for God, and really make it a practical demonstration of "the beauty of holiness,"[46] I must be ever on the watch-tower. "Watch and pray, lest ye enter into temptation,"[47] is the Divine command. In the Divine order, *watching* precedes *praying*. If, as with the prophet Elisha, our interior eye might be ever open on both worlds, we would see, not only the host of God, for our defence, but the army of aliens.[48] Some of these are robed as angels of light.[49] How much spiritual discernment, watchfulness and meekness of wisdom is necessary, in order to ensure perfect victory. Surely, a watchful eye and a constant looking to Jesus[50] will insure perfect victory. God the Father, God the Son, God the Holy Ghost is for us: good angels are for us; all the ministers of the redeemed and saved hosts in heaven and on earth are for us, and why should not the entire[51] of life, in all its *particulars,* be one continual triumph?

The heart of Mrs. Palmer's views of church and ministry were expressed in this dedicatory hymn written for a church in Utica in the spring of 1869 (Memoirs, pp. 449–50):

O, God most high! in wondrous grace,
    Behold the house we've reared for thee,
Regard it as Thy resting place,
    And fill it with Thy majesty.[52]

With outstretched hands, on Thee we call;
    Before Thy throne, O Lord, we bow,
Let hallowing fire upon us fall,[53]
    Accept us, and our offering now.

Thus by Thy presence sanctify,
    This earthly sanctuary, Lord,[54]

To this, Thy house, be ever nigh
And here Thy hallowed name record.

When from this altar shall arise,
Joint supplication to Thy name,
Accept, O, Lord, our sacrifice,
Thyself our answering God proclaim.

When here Thy ministers shall stand,
O, give them hearts and tongues of flame,
Hold them as stars in Thy right hand,[55]
And seal the truth in Thine own name.

Now, therefore, O our God arise,
In this, Thine ark of strength appear,[56]
And let Thy people's longing eyes,
Behold Thee fix Thy dwelling here.

This was the period of the beginnings and rapid upbuilding of theological schools in American Methodism, and it is clear that Mrs. Palmer prayed earnestly for the effective fulfillment of their mission. On the occasion of her visit to the newly founded Garrett Biblical Institute in May of 1869, she declared her distinctive hope and expectation for theological education (as quoted by Wheatley in the Memoirs, *p. 451):*

May this school of the prophets ever be a praise on the earth, not only for literary advantages and soundness of creed, but for richness of divine unction; or in other words, for the reception of the full baptism of the Holy Ghost,[57] on the part of all who, in coming time, shall be trained within these walls for the holy ministry. Surely, a holy work demands, first of all, a holy heart.

*At other centers of learning such as Bloomington, Illinois, the home of Illinois Wesleyan University, she encountered considerable resistance (*Memoirs, *p. 452, in a letter to Mrs. Hamline, May 27, 1869, from Bloomington):*

We have never, to my recollection, labored in a region of country, where what Wesley calls "the Methodist testimony" has been so slightly regarded. One of the more prominent ministers said to a friend of ours, that, ninety-nine ministers out of one hundred of the Conference, including these regions, were resolved to keep down everything in the Conference favoring holiness as a *specialty,* and said that they didn't believe in it, etc. Our friend asked, in view of his being a Methodist minister, "But what do you do in view of the fact of its being a *Wesleyan* doctrine?" His reply was, "We hold to *progress,*—Mr. Wesley lived a hundred years ago, etc."[58] When we first came to these parts, we felt that it would be a luxury if divinely permitted to fly home. But in despite of these retarding influences, the Lord is working mightily. Would that I had time to tell you of some of the victories, but time will not allow, at present.

The hearing was more hospitable at Fort Wayne College in Indiana (Memoirs, p. 456, in a letter to Mrs. Hamline, from Fort Wayne, Ind., Nov. 28, 1869):

This is the seat of Fort Wayne College.[59] The Lord has been showing the people great and mighty things.[60] All the students, both male and female, have been converted, with the exception of perhaps one or two. The President of the College[61] told us, as we were rejoicing over a young man just born into the kingdom, a few hours since, "This was the only unconverted student remaining." One of the female students has since told us that one or two, she thinks, are not yet saved.

3. JOURNEY TO CALIFORNIA (1870)

The Palmers' 1870 itinerary would take them on a wide ranging journey from Corning, New York, to Montreal, from Minnesota to Kansas. In the summer of 1870, at age sixty-two and hardly in excellent health, Mrs. Palmer set out for California by rail, river steamer, and coach, accompanied by Dr. Palmer. They were responding to urgent calls from California churches to visit that emergent state. In deciding to take on the promise and hazard of frontier California, she was adhering to a long settled principle of itinerary selection, stated forthrightly in a letter to Mrs. Hamline from Leavittsburg, Ohio, March 18th, 1870 (Memoirs, p. 458):

We have endeavored more strictly than ever, to adhere to Mr. Wesley's advice to his helpers, that is, to go, not where most *wanted,* but where most *needed.* In doing this, we have turned aside from some large places, and visited smaller places, where Satan had entrenched himself strongly, and the great want of revival influence had been long felt.[62]

All along the line of her lengthy itinerary, she held meetings wherever possible (Memoirs, p. 461, in a letter written while on the Upper Mississippi River, after meetings in Minnesota, to Mrs. Hamline):

Minneapolis, July, 1870

In passing from one district to another, special meetings were appointed at Hastings and Northfield,[63] so that every day has been filled up. Since Cannon's Falls camp-meeting, we have had two meetings daily, in two of the largest towns and churches. Sabbath before last, we commenced our labors at St. Paul. Scores crowded the altar, seeking sanctifying power.

The pattern of a traveling revivalist utilizing the latest technology—in this case, transcontinental rail and steam transport,—was well established by the Palmers and others in the mid-nineteenth century.[64] Their circuitous itinerary apparently followed invitations that they had received. It took them from Minneapolis through Quincy, Illinois, Leavenworth, Kansas, and Evanstown, Utah, on the way to Sacramento and San Francisco. This suggests that they were on the first transcontinental railway link, the Union Pacific, all the way to California only seven months after it had been completed, May 10, 1869[65] (Memoirs, p. 461, in a letter to Mrs. Hamline, August 11, 1870, from Evanstown, Utah):

We have since spent a Sabbath in labors for Jesus, at Quincy, Ill., after which we attended a camp-meeting, a long, long distance away, in Southern Kansas, only ten miles from the Indian Territory.[66] Though seemingly at the ends of the earth,[67] Jesus was gloriously present in sanctifying, soul-saving power.

Last week we attended another meeting, to which we had long since been engaged, near Leavenworth, Kansas.

The largest camp meetings ever held in California to that date were held by the Palmers (Memoirs, p. 462, in a letter from Woodland, California, August 19, 1870, to Mrs. Lankford):

The Lord of hosts is with us, the God of Jacob is our refuge.[68]

Never have we had stronger assurance of a call from God, than in having accepted the call of the churches here.

We arrived last Saturday, Aug. 13th. We are now in attendance on a camp-meeting which is being owned of God in an extraordinary manner. Such a camp-meeting of power and largeness of attendance has never before been held in California. We always take one or two public services at the stand, daily, beside prayer-meeting services, children's meetings, etc.

So, you see, we do not write home letters, because we have not[69] other demands on our time.

The calls here, from every part of the coast, are numerous and imperative.

From Sacramento, California, Sept. 3, 1870, she wrote to Sarah Lankford (Memoirs, p. 462):

The camp-meeting to which we were invited, held fourteen days. All unite in saying that such a meeting was never before known in California. We are now holding afternoon and evening meetings in this city, which are largely attended, and the altar is nightly surrounded with penitents and seekers of the great salvation. Last night, the minister of the Presbyterian church asked if we would not hold meetings in his church. The minister of the church South, also sat on the platform, and opened the meeting. But Oh, what a work there is to do in this far off *beautiful* land! So much fallow ground.

The Palmers remained in California from August to November of 1870. Her description of the meeting held in Rev. Mr. Heacock's[70] church in September indicates that the San Francisco of 1870 was an international city,[71] and that Mrs. Palmer had firmly established an international reputation that was to follow her wherever she went (Memoirs, p. 463):

Multitudes crowded around the altar, as candidates for the Spirit's baptism.[72] At the close of the service, persons that we had lost sight of, five, ten, twenty, and thirty years, came crowding around us; some by way of refreshing our memories saying, "I saw you in Philadelphia"; another, "I met you in Liverpool, England"; another, "Do you not remember seeing me on Prince Edward's Island"; another, "I met you at Enniskillen, Ireland"; others, long since from New York, Canada, etc. It was indeed a *jubilant time.*

At Santa Clara they were in attendance at the laying of the cornerstone of the Pacific University at Santa Clara. In a note dated only "the closing days of 1870," but probably written en route from California in November, she summarized her impressions of her ministry in California (Memoirs, p. 464):

. . . From San Jose we went to Stockton. . . . Stupendous have been the manifestations of converting and sanctifying power! At the call of the churches, we have, during the past eleven months,[73] traveled between twelve and thirteen thousand miles. Besides going to many other places, at the bidding of the Master, we have traveled across the continent, from sea to sea. "Now, thanks be unto God, which always causeth us to triumph in Christ, and maketh manifest the savor of His knowledge by us, in every place."[74] And here, during the closing days of 1870, let me renewedly raise an *Ebenezer* of exalted *Praise!*[75]

4. RECOGNIZED MATRIARCH OF THE HOLINESS MOVEMENT (1870–1873)

Immediately upon returning to New York in November of 1870, the Palmers dedicated their new house, and the extended ministry it afforded, with the following hymn written for the occasion by Mrs. Palmer. It was in this house that she would spend her final days, widely celebrated as the leading figure of the holiness revival. Her house would continue to be her major locus of ministry, even with her waning health, through the Tuesday Meetings (A Mother's Gift, pp. 131–33; Memoirs, pp. 151–52):

Dedication Hymn

[Sung at the Tuesday afternoon meeting, Nov. 29th, 1870,[76] on the occasion of the Dedication of the House 316 East 15th Street.[77]]

O Thou Most High! in heaven adored,
    While angels bow with veiled face,
And cry, O Holy! Holy! Holy! Lord,
    Behold! we worship from this place.

Though Zion's gates Thou lovest best,
    In wondrous grace Thou dost ordain
That Jacob's dwelling shall be blest,
    And in them Thou dost live and reign.

And now, O Lord, behold and see!
    Thy people in Thy name have met,
To dedicate this house to Thee,
    Here let Thy holy seal be set.

And in this house wilt thou abide;
    We consecrate it to Thy name,
In every room and heart reside,
    And here Thy hallowing grace proclaim.

Head of the Church! O wilt thou still
    Thy Church in this our house behold,
With greater grace thy people fill,
    Give power beyond the days of old?

Here let the Holy Ghost abide,
    And Pentecostal gifts be given,[78]
And Christ—the living Christ—reside
    In human hearts made meet for heaven.

*Her own family was growing, and she enjoyed the grandmotherly role,
as indicated in this hymn for her grandchildren* (A Mother's Gift, *pp. 132–
33):*

Hymn of Consecration.

[Affectionately inscribed to our children, Walter and Mary, on the occasion of the baptism of their babes, and the dedication of their new home.]

Thou Great Eternal One in Three!
    With grateful hearts we come
To dedicate our all to Thee,
    OURSELVES, our BABES, our HOME.

Ourselves!—redeemed by Jesus' grace,
    We would to Thee resign
The offspring of a godly race,
    Now make and seal us thine.

Our BABES! sweet pledges of our love,
    We take as *lent,* not *given,*
To rear them for a home above
    With *Thee;* with *us,* in heaven.

And now in the baptismal rite
    The covenant blessing give,
Oh, seal them Thine! and in thy sight
    May they forever live.

Thou, once a homeless wanderer here,
    To us a HOME hast given,

We consecrate it to thy fear;
Make it a type of heaven.

And here may Love and Friendship meet,
And grateful songs arise,
And morn and evening incense sweet,
Ascend the upper skies.

Although her health would continue to deteriorate after the California trip, she did respond to invitations in 1871 to hold meetings in Hamilton, Toronto, Cookstown, and Owen Sound, Canada, as well as Ohio, West Virginia, Chautauqua, New York, and Ocean Grove, New Jersey. The following letter to Mrs. Hamline, written April 15, 1871 from Toronto, shows how profoundly the holiness revival anticipated and encouraged the early forms of the ecumenical movement[79] (Memoirs, p. 57):

Have you observed how greatly the Lord is blessing the ministers and people of other denominations in connection with the "Conventions on Holiness" held in churches of various denominations? We attended one of the Conventions held in an old established Episcopal Church, a few weeks ago. It was a season of Holy Ghost power. Male and female disciples participating with unreserved freedom. Congregational, Episcopal, Baptist, Presbyterian and Methodist ministers, as one, witnessing of the great salvation.

The Tuesday meeting seems to be the general rallying point with these dear brethren of various denominations. The Lord is blessing and diffusing the savor of the meeting in a remarkable manner.

Looking back on her ministry of three and a half decades since her covenantal transformation in 1837, she summarized her view of the way of holiness in 1871 (Memoirs, pp. 525–26; cf. Guide to Holiness, 59 [1871]: 131):

There is but one way, from earth to heaven, and the Lord has given that one way a name. It is our purpose to make every step of ascent to that way so plain, that even by the most unsophisticated, there may be no misapprehension.

The Bible teaches progression. Men are first justified, and then sanctified wholly. We believe also in the direct witness of the Spirit.[80]

If justified in the sight of God, it is the privilege of the believer to have the witnessing Spirit, assuring him of the fact that he stands justified before God.

We believe, and also teach from the Scriptures, that if sanctified wholly, the Holy Spirit beareth witness with the spirit of the believer,[81] that the work is wrought. "We have received of that Spirit whereby we *know* the things freely given to us of God."[82]

We have also long believed and taught, that all the disciples of our Lord, under the present dispensation of power, may, and *must* receive the *baptism of fire*.[83] We have, over thirty years past, been earnestly pressing upon all believers, as an immediate necessity,—an endowment of power available to all, by an *act of faith*, and a gift of hallowing power, that must be obtained by all who would be true to the duties of their heavenly calling.[84]

Between thirty and forty years, we have, with consuming earnestness, been urging upon the religious world, these great cardinal doctrines of our divine Christianity. It seems due to the grace of God that we should say, in all humility, that a divine constraint has been laid upon us, to declare our experimental conviction of these momentous, fundamental truths.

She provided this moving description of the peace she experienced in her last years (Memoirs, p. 75):

May 16th, 1871.—To-day Jesus reigns in my soul as the Prince of Peace. How wonderful that the Lord should rejoice over his people with singing; yet so it stands written, "He will rejoice over thee with joy. He will rest on His love, He will joy over thee with *singing*."[85] In responsive strains, my soul echoes back, "Glory to God in the highest, peace on earth, and good will toward men!"[86] When my soul entered into rest over thirty years ago, the Lord showed me that the special heritage of the sanctified believer was *peace*. "*My* peace I give unto you, *My* peace I leave with you."[87] Holiness is a *state*, not particularly of great rapture, but where all controversies between God and the soul are forever settled, and conscience has the advantage of every question.[88] The atmosphere of my soul is *peace*. "Being justified by faith, I have peace with God through our Lord Jesus Christ."[89]

In her diary of June, 1871, she used an image from John Bunyan to describe her awareness of approaching death (Memoirs, pp. 620):

Christiana, of Bunyan's "Pilgrim," received a shining *token* in the form of a lance, which gently penetrated her heart, by which she was assured that she would in ten days be called to see the King in His beauty.[90] I presume I shall not be called quite so soon; but unless the disease with which I am now afflicted is arrested, the shining token is sure. Never have these words been so much on my mind, and invested with so much sweetness, as of late: "For we know that if the earthly house of our tabernacle were dissolved, we have a building of God, a house not made with hands, eternal in the heavens."[91] O, the blessed hope of immortality and eternal life.

Again in a letter to Mrs. Hamline, June 1871, she employed the same metaphor to describe her encroaching illness[92] *(Memoirs, pp. 620–21):*

I have been thinking quite a good deal about finishing life's short journey, ere long. I had indeed imagined that the token as received by Christiana, after she entered the Beulah land,[93] had been received. It came in the form of painful disease, which for a long time has lingered in my system, but has developed itself in acuteness, affecting my entire system seriously, during the past few months. But my soul rests in the bosom of infinite *LOVE*. "He doeth all things well."[94] You know that I sometimes breathe forth the sentiments of my heart, in verse. I will enclose a few lines, written for daughter Phoebe, who had asked that I would write her some lines that she might set to music. I will get dear Dr. P. to copy them for you. Phoebe wept when her Pa read them to her, and exclaimed, "I can't write music for those words." And when asked, "Why not?" She replied, "If Ma was *well*, I could, but as she is not well, I cannot." I feared, while I was writing the verses, that she might feel so, and tried to write something else. But having knelt down with my blank sheet, as I generally do, before writing, and asked that the Lord would give *matter* and *manner*,[95] I seemed constrained to write either the lines as here given, or nothing.[96]

In a letter to "My much loved Sister H.,"[97] *whom she could not think of "as other than strong in spirit," she recounted her vigorous pace through Canada, Ohio, Virginia, West Virginia, and New York. She wrote from near Chautauqua Lake, N. Y., Sept. 21, 1871, after a five hundred mile trip in one day. Never before had evangelists had the advantage of such rapid transportation (Memoirs, p. 468):*

We have just returned from a journey, having traveled about five hundred miles, during the last twenty-four hours.[98] I hoped that we might have found a letter informing us of your improved health.

Never do I remember to have crowded so much work into spring, summer, and autumn. You may recall our three weeks' labors with the churches in Hamilton, Canada West. After a hurried stay home, to prepare the "Guide,"[99] we spent another three weeks in Canada, at Toronto. Then returning home to prepare the next month's magazine, we attended two camp-meetings, beside a week's meetings, two sessions daily, at Owen Sound, and also several other meetings at three or four other towns. In the midst of the summer, we had the privilege of visiting you at your pleasant home.

The next day after leaving you, we arrived at the Ohio State camp-meeting. It was a season of great spiritual power. Next week, after the close of the Ohio State meeting, we attended the Virginia State camp-meeting,[100] which was marked with the hallowing presence of the High and Holy One. On the day that the Virginia State camp-meeting closed, we hastened to the one already commenced on the Allegheny Mountains.[101] Of all the meetings we have attended this summer, none was more signally crowned with the mighty out-pourings of the Spirit, than this.

We have just returned from the Chatauqua[102] Lake camp-meeting. Beautiful for situation, and attended with much of the presence of the Sanctifier, I could give many particulars that would interest you, but time fails. Mainly, my health is not worse than when I saw you. If you knew the particulars, you would say with me, that it is amazing grace—wondrous mercy—almighty power alone, that sustains, amid such incessant labor.

After forty-four years of marriage, her wit and romantic zest had not grown dull (A Mother's Gift, *p. 101, Sept., 1871*).

Bride of Forty and Four Years.
(To Her Husband)

JOY! to our happy wedding-day,
    Full forty years and four,
'Mid brightening skies have passed away,
    Each happier than before.

Matches are made in Heaven 'tis said,
    With us I'm sure 'tis true,
As years on joyous wing have sped,
    In higher bliss with you.

A pensive entry in her journal of May 9, 1872, recounts a visit to the Palmer plot of the Greenwood Cemetery in Brooklyn, where her father and children were buried. The pain of the loss of her children which so significantly spurred her religious development was recollected, and the faith transcending that pain (Memoirs, *pp. 621–22):*

Husband and myself visited that beautiful city of the dead,—Greenwood. What a multitude of dear ones, with whom we have taken sweet counsel,[103] lie sleeping here. And there, within a beautiful enclosure, in a peaceful, quiet spot, stands a monument, bearing on its base, "Palmer." It is awaiting the time when this now active frame, shall cease its pulsations, and the spirit ascend to the God that gave it. On one part of the monument, that awaits the inscription of our own departure, is that of our precious little darlings, who have been long mingling with the cherub band in Paradise. The inscription reads thus:

OUR LOVED ONES.

Alexander H.,	Born September 28 [1828][104]
	Died, July 2d, 1829.
Samuel M.,	Born, April 29th [1830]
	Died, June 19th, 1830.
Eliza,	Born, August 28th, 1835.
	Died, July 29th, 1836.[105]

To which the following lines, written by their mother, are subjoined:

What though this urn their ashes keep;
    Their spirits took an upward flight.
On Jesus' breast, they fell asleep,
    He bore them to the realms of light.
And when the reign of death is o'er
    And Christ descends to claim His own,
Our loved ones, then, we'll greet once more;
    And ever mingle round the throne.

At the General Conference of 1872, of eight new bishops elected, four were close associates of Mrs. Palmer and "decided friends of the holiness movement":[106] Jesse T. Peck, Randolph Sinks Foster, Stephen M. Merrill, and Gilbert Haven.[107] Three and a half decades after the beginning of the Tuesday Meetings on Feb. 9, 1836, she reflected upon their remarkable influence (Memoirs, p. 256):

Diary, May, 1872.—The Tuesday afternoon meetings have been wonderfully crowned with the Divine benediction, during several weeks. Members of General Conference and visitors from abroad, from almost every region, California, Oregon, North, South, East and West, have met on the grand platform of perfect love. Glorious, beyond description, have been the manifestations of the approval and presence of the Head of the church. Who am I, or what was my Father's house, that the ark of the Lord should so long abide at our house?[108] It is now about thirty-five years since these precious meetings commenced under our roof.

Her diary entry of June 6, 1872, is especially intriguing in its indication that she had received visitors from "the Orthodox order." She is probably referring to the Yearly Meeting of Orthodox Friends, which she attended periodically (cf. Memoirs, pp. 577–78). Her influence on Friends' thought was significant, especially through Hannah Whitall Smith and David B. Updegraff[109] (Memoirs, p. 256):

We had, I presume, over a score of brethren and sister friends of the Orthodox order. Many of them spoke with sweetness and power,—doubtless as the *Spirit* gave utterance.[110]

It is the time for their yearly meeting, and we hope to be at one of their meetings to-morrow, as we have been strongly invited.

Her journal entry of June 13, 1872, probed her "actuating principle," the source of her energetic activism (Memoirs, p. 50):

O, yes! this body is the temple of the Holy Ghost.[111] Whence this absence of all desire to live for self? Whence these ceaseless inworkings, to work, live, think, and speak for God? Whence this absorbing, controlling love for God and his cause? Conscious, deeply conscious, that I have received the sentence of death in myself.[112] Whence this realization of reliance, momentary reliance, on Him that raiseth the dead?[113] Is it not because the Holy Spirit, as a living, actuating principle, has taken full possession of, and is now working in me to will and do of His good pleasure?[114]

Even late in life she did not cease her habit of an annual recollection of her wedding anniversary as a spiritual landmark (Memoirs, p. 144):

Diary, September 28th, 1872.—My wedding-day. This evening, forty-five years ago, I was united in holy wedlock, to my beloved W. C. P. Six dear children have been given us. Three are waiting to welcome us on the shores of immortality, and three are with us amid the scene of probation. May all make their calling and election sure,[115] and at last appear an unbroken family in heaven. Husband and I feel that we have been wedded forever. We are most blessedly one in the Lord, and in each other.

"Our aims, our joys, our hopes, are one,
Our comforts, and our cares."[116]

Like Søren Kierkegaard, whose life resembles hers in so many ways, Mrs. Palmer had expected to die early, and continued throughout her life to be keenly aware of her own finitude (Memoirs, p. 482, from her diary, Jan. 1, 1873):

Among the things I have cause to praise the Lord for, without ceasing, is that He so continuously permits sweet encouragements to flow in upon me, in connection with my humble writings. When the "Way of Holiness" was written, I was in a very low state of health, from which I had but little expectation of ever recovering. Much of it was written, while in almost an agony of pain. After the manuscript was finished, I knelt down with it in my hand, and in the most solemn manner dedicated it in the name of the Triune Deity, conscious that it was by divine aid, spiritually, mentally, and physically, that the work had been completed. I then expected that my spirit would be mingling with the redeemed, blood-washed company around the throne, and my body in the tomb, before the publication of the work. But God has permitted me to live thirty years since, and declare His goodness by pen, life, and lip. What hath God wrought,[117] since that time. Hundreds have, by the steps marked out in the *"Way of Holiness,"* defining the manner by which Jesus led me, as His lowly disciple, been brought into the King's highway, and thousands, as years have rapidly passed on, have been brought through the Spirit's leadings, by us, out of spiritual Egypt, and their feet set in the way to heaven. When the faint dottings of each day shall be brought out into the light of eternity, things which have seemed so trivial, as scarcely to have left a trace on memory, will perhaps appear among the more important of our lives.

5. THE LAST YEAR (1874)

By the summer of 1873, large, regional camp meetings like Ocean Grove, N.J., had become an established aspect of American revivalism, to which Mrs. Palmer's gifts were extraordinarily well suited (Memoirs, p. 474):

Diary.—OCEAN GROVE, N. J., August 24th [1873].—A congregation of, I presume, not less than four or five thousand, listened to the Word, this morning. Dr. P., and myself spoke of the readiness and ability of Jesus to save to the uttermost.[118] We had a most gracious, memorable season.

Life under grace must be continually renewed by grace (Memoirs, pp. 88–89, from a diary entry of Oct. 5, 1873):

. . . As it is in our being sustained in natural existence, we get so accustomed to the momentary act of inhaling the vital air, that it becomes natural, and we seldom dwell on the thought that we are sustained by the power of God. Yet so it is. Past grace will not meet present necessities. The longer I live, the more deeply does my soul cry out,

"Every moment, Lord, I need
The merits of Thy death."[119]

In a diary entry of Dec. 10, 1873, Mrs. Palmer spoke of her own distinct sense of calling (Memoirs, p. 83):

Of these wonderful solemnities and responsibilities, I have not a slight experimental apprehension. That God has called me to stand before the people, and proclaim His truth, has long been beyond question. So fully has God made my commission known to my own soul, and so truly has He set His seal upon it, before the upper and lower world, in the conversion of thousands of precious souls, and the sanctification of a multitude of believers, that even Satan does not seem to question that my call is divine. It has been many years since I remember to have had a temptation to doubt. Well do I, as a daughter of the Lord Almighty, remember the baptism of fire that fell upon me, over thirty years since. Not more assuringly, perhaps, did the tongues of fire fall in energizing, hallowing influences on the sons and daughters of the Almighty, when they ALL spake as the Spirit gave utterance, on the day of Pentecost,[120] than I felt its consuming, hallowing, energizing influences fall on me, empowering me for holy activities and burning utterances.[121]

Ever since that sacred, eventful hour, I have had an ever-abiding conviction that I have received the sentence of death in myself, that I should not trust in myself, but in Him that raiseth the dead.[122] The idea that I can do anything myself, seems so extinct, that the enemy is not apt to tempt me in that direction.

In a letter to Mrs. Hamline, Feb. 18, 1874, she described her halting yet joyful participation in a Tuesday Meeting of her last year (Memoirs, pp. 622–23):

. . . While at the Tuesday meeting, last week, not able to hear much that was said, and suffering with the gathering in my ear, it was suggested, "Can you now say,

"Thankful, I take the cup from Thee,
Prepared and mingled by Thy skill."[123]

All praise to the Great Physician of souls, who has so long had my case in hand, that I was enabled to answer, "Yes, *thankful,* I take the cup. Infinite love has prepared it. Surely I shall not be permitted to suffer one pang too much."

Taking up the precious Word, a short time later, I opened on the passage, "Now, this I say, brethren, that flesh and blood cannot inherit the kingdom of God, neither doth corruption inherit incorruption."[124] "For this corruptible *must* put on incorruption, and this mortal *must* put on immortality,"[125] . . . "then shall be brought to pass the saying, 'Death is swallowed up of victory.' "[126] When I thought of the many prayers, and the continuous efforts of the past two or three years, to detain me, amid the manifest dissolution of nature, I saw a striking appropriateness and beauty in the passage above quoted, never before apprehended.

I do not wish you to think that I am in anticipation of immediate dissolution, but I do feel that this earthly house of my tabernacle is being dissolved,[127] and unless I improve soon there remains but little hope of doing much more. But whatever the result may be, I know all will be right. The Lord will not call me till my work is done.

Mrs. Palmer died on November 2, 1874. Even in the last year of her life amid waning health, however, she did not refuse invitations to speak at camp meetings and revival services in Canada, New York, Connecticut, Ohio, and Illinois. Her last meeting was at the Ohio State camp meeting at Mansfield, beginning on August 13, 1874, which she dutifully reported (Memoirs, p. 478):

. . . On Monday, we had our closing service, and took the parting hand, with many dear ones, whom we shall probably see no more, till we meet in our Father's kingdom.[128]

Notes

1. The Palmers merged *GTH* with another journal purchased about the same time, *Beauty of Holiness and Sabbath Miscellany,* and from 1864 to 1867 the journal was entitled *Guide to, and Beauty of Holiness and Revival Miscellany,* revised to *Guide to Holiness and Revival Miscellany* from 1867 to 1896, and *Guide to Holiness and Pentecostal Life* from 1896 until its last numbers in 1901. However through all these name changes, the numerical sequence remained intact, indicating that the

essential continuity of the journal had remained; hence we use the single abbreviation for all these titles: *GTH.*

2. For a more detailed account of the Palmers' long involvement with religious publishing, see George Hughes, *Fifty Years of Holiness Publishing Work, 1830–1869* (New York: Palmer and Hughes, 1889). Cf. Walter C. Palmer, Jr., *Catalogue of Works on the Higher Christian Life* (New York: Walter C. Palmer, Jr., 1870) *General Devotional Works and Books for Sunday School Libraries* (New York: Walter C. Palmer, Jr., 1870).

3. Cf. 1 Cor. 16:2.

4. It was clear to her, however, that the lever does not work by merit or works-righteousness, but only by grace evoking free human responsiveness.

5. The Chicago trip was apparently not included in Wheatley's sequence (*Memoirs,* pp. 405–11). Although *BH,* p. 96, assumes that their primary purpose for visiting Iowa was to hold a "series of meetings," the more definite purpose was probably to visit with Bishop and Mrs. Hamline after their long period of separation.

6. Or Hornell, Steuben County, New York, on the Erie Railroad.

7. At this point her account digresses with a quaint description of Chicago in the year 1864: "situated on the shore of Lake Michigan and is adorned with several costly churches and fine dwellings. A wide, beautiful street runs along the margin of the lake." She had accepted the invitation of Mr. O. Lunt "to take tea with his family and accompany him in his phaeton to take a drive through the city and its environs," *GTH* 46 (1864–65):67.

8. During this period, 1857–64, Mrs. Palmer had maintained a steady correspondence with the Hamlines.

9. It is illuminating that Mrs. Palmer associated the holiness of Hamline's life not with a Reformation or early modern figure, but with the Apostolic Father, Polycarp (ca. 70–155/160 A.D.), bishop of Smyrna and martyr. This reinforces the premise that Mrs. Palmer's teaching of holiness was understood by her as a reappropriation of the same ancient Christianity that immediately succeeded the New Testament.

10. For similar reflections, see Luther Lee, *Five Sermons and a Tract* (Chicago: Holrad House, 1975).

11. Illinois.

12. Lawrence E. Breeze, "The Inskips: Union in Holiness," *Methodist History* 13 (1975): 25–45.

13. English born John Swannell Inskip (1816–84), served in the Philadelphia and New York East Conferences, was editor of the *Christian Standard,* and principal organizer of National Camp Meeting Association; authored *Methodism: Explained and Defended* (Cincinnati, H. and J. Applegate, 1851). Inskip is credited with being the first to have encouraged his (Springfield, Ohio) congregation to sit together in church as families—heretofore the practice had been to seat women and men on opposite sides of the church. See *CM,* and *EWM,* "Inskip"; William McDonald and J.E. Searles, *The Life of Rev. John S. Inskip, President of the National Association for the Promotion of Holiness* (Chicago: Christian Witness, 1885).

14. The dedication of all one's redeemed powers to God, i.e., the reception of sanctifying grace.

15. Heb. 12:1.

16. All talk of power, and every realization of power, is admittedly subject to abuse. It is unclear the extent to which Mrs. Palmer grasped or anticipated the potential distortions of this equation that could follow. It is clear that she viewed the holy life and the profession of holiness as a powerfully experienceable reality capable of moving persons to remarkable transformations of character, energetic activities, and social betterment.

17. The letter continues to describe John Inskip's attendance and testimony at the Tuesday Meeting and subsequent testimony in New York Churches.

18. 1864.

19. This letter appears to have been written to Mrs. Hamline on Dec. 5, 1864.

20. Samuel Franklin (Illinois Conference), *A Critical Review of Wesleyan Perfection* (New York: Methodist Book Concern, 1866), argues that entire sanctification is objectionable, and that only regeneration, which accompanies justification, is taught in the Bible, pp. 1ff., 166ff.

21. It is well not to miss the humor in Mrs. Palmer's description. Pew rental was such a volatile controversial subject that it caused a major split in Methodism (Free Methodist Church). The delicacy of this issue was combined with that of the softening of preaching (as on the theme of judgment).

22. Not Gilbert Haven, *BH*, p. 97. Both Gilbert and Erastus would in due time become Methodist bishops.

23. It was at the Chicago District Campground (*Memoirs*, p. 429), that Frances Willard, later to provide major leadership in the temperance movement and early women's rights causes, devoted herself entirely to God after Mrs. Palmer had spoken. Later Frances Willard would write that she had come no longer to feel "that heaven in the soul, of which I came to know in Mrs. Palmer's meeting" (see S. Olin Garrison, ed., *Forty Witnesses, Covering the Whole Range of Christian Experience* [New York: Eaton and Mains, 1888], pp. 94–98). See F. Willard, *Glimpses of Fifty Years: The Autobiography of an American Woman* (New York: Hacker Art Books, 1970, reprint of the 1889 edition).

24. Asa T. Mahan, a longtime friend of the Palmers, was the first president of Adrian College (1859–64; 1867–71), formerly president of Oberlin College; a sanctificationist who promoted antislavery and social reforms; an early advocate of coeducation.

25. Song of Solomon 1:3.

26. The Palmers later published Mahan's book, *Baptism of the Holy Ghost* (New York: Walter C. Palmer, Jr., 1870), often considered a groundbreaking book in holiness theology.

27. Erastus Otis Haven (1820–81) had served the 24th Street Church and the Mulberry St. Church in New York City, where he became acquainted with the Palmers. He was appointed Professor of Latin at Michigan University in 1853, was elected its president in 1863, and subsequently became president of Northwestern

University in 1869, and of Syracuse University in 1877. He was subsequently a bishop of the Methodist Episcopal Church.

28. After leaving Ann Arbor, she visited Mrs. Hamline, now (after Bishop Hamline's death on Feb. 22, 1865) resident in Evanston, Ill., and friends in Chicago.

29. Mrs. Gov. E——— could have been the wife of the former Governor of Illinois, Wm. L.D. Ewing (1834). Many Illinois Regiments had been fighting in the south only recently.

30. Indiana.

31. Cf. Ps. 136:4.

32. Probably Joseph Earp (1820–94; cf. *Southern Illinois Conference Minutes,* 1894, p. 33).

33. Cf. Luke 2:14.

34. Robert Allyn, who had served in the Rhode Island Legislature in 1852 and 1854, was elected president of McKendree College in 1863.

35. There were many readers of *GTH* in the South, and leading advocates in southern Methodism of views similar to Mrs. Palmer's, cf. Thomas O. Summers, *Holiness: A Treatise on Sanctification* (Richmond, J. Early, 1850); Samuel D. Akin, *Christian Perfection as Taught in the Bible* (Nashville: So. Meth. Publ. House, 1860).

36. Later she would visit Florida (Jacksonville, 1874).

37. Richard Cameron, *Methodism and Society in Historical Perspective,* NY: Abingdon, 1961, I, pp. 173ff.; Donald G. Jones, *The Sectional Crisis and Northern Methodism* (Metuchen, N.J.: Scarecrow, 1979), 29ff.; cf. S.D. Hillman, "The United States and Methodism," *MOR* 49 (Jan. 1867): 31, 40ff., 49; Barbara M. Swartz, *The Methodist Episcopal Church and the Civil War* (Cincinnati: Meth. Book Concern, 1912); Frederick Norwood, Sourcebook of American Methodism, Nashville: Abingdon, 1982: William Warren Sweet, Methodism and American History, NY: Methodist Book Concern, 1933.

38. I.e., pastors, cf. Rev. 1:20.

39. Cf. Isa. 64:10; Daniel 9:2.

40. Possibly W. F. Camp, M.E. Church, South, *Minutes,* 1879 (see *Southwest Missouri Conference,* 1879, p. 92).

41. The Palmers seriously considered a more extensively campaign in the South, among both blacks and whites. In New Orleans they spoke to a large black congregation of some fifteen hundred, and to the white congregation of M.E.C. missionaries, the Newmans; cf. *GTH* 51 (1867): 149–54. Although cordially received in Natchez, Baton Rouge and New Orleans, they decided that the time was not ripe for an extended mission.

42. Modern observers of the American public's cynicism toward Washington will be amused to see it appear in such an undisguised form in 1866. General Grant did not attend.

43. Cf. Matt. 19:26.

44. Mark 9:23.

45. Cf. Matt. 7:7ff.; Luke 11:9ff.; John 16:23ff.

46. Ps. 29:2.
47. Cf. Mark 14:38.
48. Cf. 2 Kings 6:17.
49. Cf. 2 Cor. 11:14.
50. Cf. Heb. 12:2.
51. Entirety.
52. Cf. Ps. 29:4.
53. Acts 2:3; Heb. 12:29.
54. Cf. Exod. 29:44; 40:10ff.; Isa. 29:23.
55. Rev. 1:16; 2:1ff.
56. Cf. Ps. 132:8.
57. Clearly her hope for Methodist theological education was that it might elicit through study the life of holiness.
58. This conversation concisely recapitulated the history of Methodist theology of the nineteenth century, moving from Wesley to modernity. Cf. Langford, *PD,* ch. 1ff., and Oden, *Agenda for Theology* (San Francisco: Harper & Row, 1979), ch. 1ff.
59. Ft. Wayne Female College was founded in 1846 by the North Indiana Conference. Around the turn of the century it was moved to Upland, Indiana to become Taylor University.
60. Cf. Gen. 18:18; Deut. 3:24; 11:2; Jer. 32:18.
61. J.B. Robinson, president of Fort Wayne College in 1869, 1870.
62. The Palmers' principle in selection of revival locations is questioned by John Kent, *HF,* and R. Carwardine, *TAR,* on the grounds that urban locations were relatively neglected. This rule shows why she made these selections. They were not based upon a prudential assessment of results, but upon their understanding of the divine address through need.
63. Minnesota.
64. Holiness tradition electronic evangelists continue this tradition of utilizing advanced technology for the "promotion of holiness."
65. The Union Pacific Railroad map shows Evanstown or Evanston in Wyoming, very near the Utah border (*The Railroaders* [New York: Time-Life Books, 1973], p. 140). In 1870 one could travel first class from Omaha to Sacramento for $100. The itinerary went through North Platte, Cheyenne, Ogden, Elko, and Reno.
66. This camp meeting could have been held at or near Dodge City or Abilene if she was traveling on the Sante Fe Railway, which she could have taken from Kansas City. If so, she would have gone through these cattle-rail connection towns at the heyday of their wild west fame. If so, she underestimated the distance to Indian Territory. If she was literally correct about being only ten miles from Indian Territory, the location is more likely Arkansas City (on the Acheson, Topeka, and Santa Fe) than Winfield (Acheson, Topeka, and Santa Fe), Parsons (Missouri, Kansas and Texas), Independence (St. Louis & San Francisco), or Liberal (Chicago, Rock Island, and Pacific).
67. It should be recalled that in 1870 the Plains Indians still controlled much

of the territory through which the Palmers were travelling. That it was a hazardous journey did not seem to deter her, but rather intensified her awareness of grace.

68. Ps. 46:7.

69. The double negative (perhaps a misprint in the original text) confuses her meaning, which apparently is that she has not been able to write because of so many demands upon her time.

70. Probably Henry Ball Heacock (1838–1915), ordained an elder by Bishop Simpson in 1865, appointed to San Francisco in 1870.

71. Cf. William Taylor, *Seven Years' Street Preaching in San Francisco* (California, New York: Phillips & Hunt, 1856).

72. Asa Mahan's book, *The Baptism of the Holy Ghost,* was published by the Palmers in 1870.

73. This suggests either that it was written in November of the period of January through November, or in December of the period of February through December. The former is more likely.

74. 2 Cor. 2:14.

75. Robert Robinson, "Come Thou Fount of Every Blessing," *MHB,* 1933, #417, v. 2.

76. There is some uncertainty about whether Dr. and Mrs. Palmer were actually at this dedication, since her letter en route from California suggests that it was written "during the closing days of 1870" (see above), yet in that same letter she reviewed "the past eleven months," which suggests that that letter was written in November. Hence it is more probable that they did make it home to New York by the Nov. 29, 1870 dedication.

77. This home on 316 East 15th St. was later donated to the Salvation Army and became a home for unwed mothers. Later, in conjunction with adjacent properties, it became a general hospital. Eventually the hospital was removed to become the Booth Memorial Medical Center, Flushing, New York.

78. The Pentecost metaphor continued ever stronger in her last years.

79. Cf. John Wesley White, "The Influence of North American Evangelism in Great Britain Between 1830 and 1914 on the Origin and Development of the Ecumenical Movement," Ph.D. dissertation, Oxford University, 1963.

80. *WJW,* V, pp. 112ff.; XI, 420ff.

81. Cf. Rom. 8:16, with 1 John 5:10.

82. Cf. 1 Cor. 2:12.

83. Matt. 3:11; Luke 3:16.

84. Her emphasis upon the *power* received through sanctifying grace seems to have appeared early and increased steadily over the years. The shift of emphasis from cleansing of sin to power seems already to have taken place years before the Brighton and Keswick Conventions in which this same shift took place more visibly; cf. Timothy Smith, *Called Unto Holiness* p. 25; C.F. Harford, ed., *The Keswick Convention* (London: Marshall, 1907).

85. Cf. Zeph. 3:17.

86. Luke 2:14.

87. Cf. John 14:27.

88. On "good conscience" see 1 Tim. 1:5, 19; Heb. 13:8; 1 Pet. 3:16–21; *WJW*, V, pp. 135ff.

89. Cf. Rom. 5:1.

90. John Bunyan, *Pilgrim's Progress* (Grand Rapids: Zondervan, 1973).

91. 2 Cor. 5:1.

92. Nephritis, or Bright's disease.

93. The metaphor of Beulah Land would later become a standard fixture of holiness preaching, and would enter especially powerfully into the tradition of black preaching.

94. Cf. Mark 7:37.

95. Her specific manner of receiving divine instruction for her ministry of correspondence is here vividly described: She literally wrote on her knees.

96. The poem has not survived.

97. Hamline.

98. They had apparently come from the West Virginia State camp meeting.

99. By this time she, with help from her family, had edited the *Guide* for about seven years—a demanding task, demonstrating extraordinary executive ability. She is better known as a revivalist than editor. The study of her work as an editor has been neglected, and deserves a separate monograph.

100. Probably a reference to the West Virginia State camp meeting.

101. The precise dates of the busy itinerary are uncertain, but it is clear that she spent three weeks in Hamilton, Canada in March, three weeks in Toronto in April, and visited Cookstown, Canada, in June. During the period between July 10 and Sept. 21 of 1871 she attended camp meetings in Owen Sound, Ontario, Ohio, West Virginia, and Chautauqua, New York.

102. Current spelling is Chautauqua. It would subsequently become a household word for an educational assembly with a combination of lectures, entertainment, self-examination, and outdoor life, modeled after the Chautauqua, New York, assembly grounds (in the Finger Lakes District) that were inaugurated by these advocates of the promotion of holiness.

103. Cf. Ps. 55:14.

104. *Memoirs,* p. 26, indicates that Alexander was born September 27, 1828.

105. The Palmer-Worrall-Foster plot of Greenwood Cemetery in Brooklyn (purchased in 1846) is in sections 68 and 57 (Lots 1574–76). In addition to the grave marker reported in the text, birth and death dates on the gravestones (some stones are drastically worn, hence some dates uncertain) are as follows: Phoebe Palmer, bn. Dec. 18, 1807, d. Nov. 2, 1874. Walter C. Palmer, bn. Feb. 9, 1804, d. July 10, 1883. Henry Worrall (Phoebe's father), bn. Nov. 15, 1771 in Bradfield, near Sheffield, England, d. April 29, 1849. Dorothea (or as the gravestone says: Doretha) Worrall (Phoebe's mother), bn. Feb. 13, 1786, d. Sept. 13, 1856. John Wesley Worrall (relation uncertain, probably Phoebe's nephew or brother), died Nov. 11, 1836 after eleven years and eight months (hence born about March, 1825). William W. Worrall was buried July 19, 1867, and Wesley Worrall was buried May 31, 1866. Sarah Lankford Palmer (Phoebe's sister, and after Phoebe's death, married to Walter C. Palmer), bn. in New York, April 23, 1806, d. April 28, 1896. Thomas

A. Lankford (Phoebe's brother-in-law, first marriage of Sarah), bn. May 22, 1800, d. Mar. 6, 1873. Joseph W. Kellogg (Phoebe's brother-in-law, married to her sister, Mary Jane), bn. Jan. 6, 1809, d. Dec. 3, 1862. William L. Kellogg (son of Joseph and Mary Kellogg, Phoebe's nephew), bn. 1842, d. April 10, 1862. Sarah Palmer Foster (Phoebe's daughter), bn. April 16, 1834, d. Nov. 25, 1919. Rev. Elon Foster (Phoebe's son in law, married to Sarah, who shared responsibilities with the Palmers in the publishing business), bn. June 22, 1833, Moretown, Vt., d. Nov. 10, 1898, Brooklyn. Phoebe Palmer Foster (Phoebe's granddaughter, daughter of Elon and Sarah Foster), bn. June 18, 1858, d. Nov. 27, 1922. Elon Foster (relation uncertain, probably Phoebe's great-grandchild), bn. Brooklyn, Sept. 14, 1892, d. July 17, 1957, Riverside, Conn. Mary Witherbee Foster (wife of Elon Foster, immediately above), born in Brooklyn, June 16, 1896, d. in Gwynedd or Gowynedd, Penna., April 22, 1978. Miles Wesley Palmer (1822–1914), married to Hannah Worrall (1828–93), had a son, Arthur Worrall Palmer, M.D. (1861–1915), who married Luella Angelina Palmer (1867–1934), and they had a son, Arthur Worrall Palmer, Jr., (1898–1959).

106. *HAM*, p. 614.

107. Their writings bear the signature of Phoebe Palmer's language: Randolph Sinks Foster, *The Nature and Blessedness of Christian Purity* (New York: Lane and Scott, 1851); Jesse T. Peck, *The Central Idea of Christianity* (Boston, H. V. Degen, 1856). Foster's and Peck's work are included in *Christian Perfection: A Compilation of Six Holiness Classics,* vol. 1 (Salem, Ohio: Schmul, 1974). See also Stephen M. Merrill, *Sanctification: Right Views and Other Views* (Cincinnati: Jennings and Pye, 1901); Gilbert Haven, *Sermons, Speeches and Letters on Slavery and War* (Boston: Lee and Shepherd, 1869); and M. Simpson, ed., *CM*.

108. Cf. 2 Sam. 7:18.

109. Garrison, *FW*, pp. 25ff., 144ff.

110. Cf. Acts 2:4.

111. Cf. 1 Cor. 6:19.

112. Cf. 2 Cor. 1:9.

113. Cf. 2 Cor. 1:9.

114. Cf. Phil. 2:13.

115. Cf. 2 Pet. 1:10.

116. John Fawcett (1740–1817), "Bless't Be the Tie that Binds," *Methodist Hymnal* (Nashville: Methodist Episcopal Church, South, 1906), #556, v. 2., slightly misquoted: "Our fears, our hopes, our aims are one. . . . "

117. Cf. Num. 23:23.

118. Cf. Heb. 7:25.

119. *MHB,* 1907, #468, v. 4.

120. Cf. Acts 2:1–4.

121. The themes of empowerment and holy utterance would be leading themes of the Keswick movement and early Pentecostal theology. Cf. J.B. Figgis, *Keswick From Within* (London: Marshall, 1914); Vinson Synan, *HPM;* A.M. Hills, *Scriptural Holiness and Keswick Teaching Compared* (Manchester: Star Hall, 1900).

122. Cf. 2 Cor. 1:9.

123. Charles Wesley, "Eternal Beam of Light Divine," *HUMEC*, 1850, #757, v. 3.

124. 1 Cor. 15:50.

125. 1 Cor. 15:53, her emphasis.

126. Cf. 1 Cor. 15:54.

127. Cf. 2 Cor. 5:1.

128. Her biographer, Wheatley, regarded this as "Mrs. Palmer's last record of public labors" (*Memoirs*, p. 478).

CONCLUSION

REFINING PROCESSES (1874)

Just before her death, Mrs. Palmer wrote an explicit description of the experience that grounded her call to public ministry, which had occurred in 1840, some thirty-four years earlier. Although she had written often about her own experiences, she had withheld this from view until she was very near death. It was made available shortly after her death in her own firm handwriting in a primitive facsimile form (New York: W.C. Palmer, Jr., 1875).[1] This powerful account of her calling is now for the first time being made available in print in its original unedited form.

REFINING PROCESSES

"I have chosen thee."[2] "Great Trials," Great Triumphs

Have you not noticed that in all the homeward way of the believer, new and unthought of phases of experience present themselves: I do not mean that these are experiences of which a wherefore may not be found infered from the Scriptures. These are in fact the divine chart which alone describes the way by which the redeemed of the Lord return to Zion.[3]

But I have had during the past summer months[4] some new experiences which I am sure I could have known little about, if my course had not been onward and upward. There is untold significance in the passage, "Then shall ye know if ye follow on to know."[5] And let me assure you that my soul has of late been following hard after God.[6] O with what indiscribable longings have I been pressing after greater conformity to the image of the heavenly.[7] That these breathings after God and soul communings with Him have been transforming, I do not doubt.

322

The peculiar experience of which I am about to speak occurred August 1840, was preceeded by humiliations of soul that I can scarcely attempt to describe. I am sure I know what David meant when he exclaimed "I am a worm and no man."[8] I knew, and *felt* that I was shielded by the atonement, and therefore there was no condemnation, but the *Word of the Lord* was intensified, in a manner that human language cannot portray. For days, and nights in succession it penetrated my soul, as if it would part it asunder "sharper than any two-edged sword, piercing even to the dividing of soul, and spirit, and of the joints and marrow, and as a discerner of the thoughts and intents of the heart."[9] My naked soul seemed to be tending as in the more immediate presence of the All-seeing, to whom all things are naked and open. Such piercing views of my utter nothingness, and the intense spirituality of the *Word of God,* seemingly would have crushed me, but I pleaded that my spirit might not fail before Him.[10] In a sense beyond any former experiences I could say "I have heard of thee by the hearing of the ear; but now mine eye seeth thee, wherefore I abhor myself in dust and ashes."[11]

Previous to this deep realization of the sharpness of the two-edged sword, my experience had generally been joyous. Though I had not been without oft repeated conflicts, conquest had so quickly succeeded each conflict, that the joy of victory was ever in my heart, and on my lips. For many days in succession all sensible, joyous experiences were withheld, and I was shut up to the exercise of "naked faith in a naked promise."[12] The cruel tempter said, that the Lord whom I loved supremely, had forsaken me, that I had surely in some unknown way offended. But I kept hold of the promise, "If in any thing ye be otherwise minded, God will reveal even this to you."[13] And as God in answer to special and importunate prayer did not reveal anything, I still held strongly the shield of faith,[14] saying sooner will I die than doubt. Often amid this great trial of my faith, did the providences of God seem to contradict the promises. Yet knowing that the ways of God are all perfect,[15] I knew that in the end He would bring order out of apparent confusion.

Day and night the fight of *faith* went on. With the veteran warrier[16] David I could say, night after night "He holdeth my eyes waking."[17] And during all this season of conflict, it did not seem expedient that I should open my mind to any earthly friend. Believing then, as I do now, that God had hidden purposes, in these trainings of grace, intended for my instruction as an individual, and therefore not to be understood by another.[18]

One morning, after a night of wakefulness spent as in the more immediate presence of Him who searcheth the heart and trieth the reins,[19] I took the Word of the Lord in my hand. Before opening it I said, "O thou who in an ancient time did'st speak through the urim and thummin,[20] wilt

Thou not now speak to me through the *Word,* cause me now to learn the lesson that Thou wouldst teach me by these extraordinary exercises. I would not ask signs but only desire to apprehend the design of these peculiarly trying, penetrating, soul-searching influences.

It is the Holy Spirit alone that incited the Word, that can reveal to the soul its hidden meaning. On opening the precious Word as it lay before me my eye rested on the words, "In that day, saith the Lord of hosts, will I take thee O Zerubbabel my servant saith the Lord, and will make thee as a signet; for I have chosen thee saith the Lord of hosts."[21] If I could disclose to you the revelations of that hour, the peculiarity of some tests through which I have passed would not seem mysterious, but only as might have been anticipated from the forshowings[22] of that memorable hour.

The curtain of the future seemed uplifted. Yes! The Spirit took of things to come and revealed them to me. Perceptions of the great blessedness of the work to which the Lord might call me in identification with the great fundamental truth of Christianity *"Holiness to the Lord,"*[23] were granted, but with these glorious perceptions, a view was also given of the trials I should be called to endure, in connection with my open identification with Truth. Yea, said the Spirit, "A sword shall pierce through thine own soul also; that the thoughts of many hearts may be revealed."[24]

Since that hour I have experimentally apprehended the solemn significance of my holy calling as never before. Perhaps you have wondered that when an onset against the doctrine or profession of holiness has been attempted, by partisans, it is oftener than with any one else that the name of your friend has been victimized. But in all, how wonderously has truth triumphed! And this leads me to what I have been wishing to record to the praise of infinite grace,—. Thus far my trials have been triumphs. Every new conflict has furnished an occasion for a new victory.

And now in praise of the faithfulness of God I wish to say, that just the lesson that the Lord taught me in that eventful hour thirty four years ago[25] when He said, *"I have chosen thee as a signet,"*[26] has been most graciously fulfilled.

While He revealed to me that I should have great trials, He also assured me that I should have great triumphs. So great and continuous have been the triumphs of truth in connection with the precious theme of Holiness, that my life has been one great Psalm of *"Glory to God in the highest."*[27]

Notes

1. The official title as published was *Mrs. Phoebe Palmer's Testimony to the Faithfulness of the Covenant-Keeping God.* This was somewhat confused by adding

the superfluous title: "Crowning Testimonies" on the cover. Since "Refining Processes" was her own title, it is preferred here.

2. Hag. 2:23; cf. John 15:16.

3. Zech. 8:3.

4. Probably 1874.

5. Cf. Hosea 6:3.

6. Cf. Ps. 63:8.

7. Cf. 1 Cor. 15:49.

8. Ps. 22:6.

9. Cf. Heb. 4:12.

10. Cf. Isa. 57:16.

11. Cf. Job 42:6.

12. The predominating metaphor—nakedness, vulnerability, lacking covering or pretenses before God—has been sustained throughout her adult lifetime; cf. entries from July 1837; John Wesley, *WJW*, VII, p. 322; J. Benson, *Life of the Rev. John W. de la Flechere*, p. 85; White, *BH*, p. 261.

13. Phil. 3:15.

14. Eph. 6:16.

15. Cf. Ps. 18:30.

16. Warrior misspelled in text.

17. Cf. Ps. 77:4.

18. Cf. the secrecy theme in Kierkegaard, *Fear and Trembling* and *Repetition.*

19. Cf. Jer. 17:10.

20. Cf. Deut. 33:8.

21. Cf. Hag. 2:23.

22. Foreshowings.

23. Exod. 28:36.

24. Luke 2:35.

25. Hence she is writing in her last year, 1874, since as she stated earlier, the experience of which she speaks occurred about 1840.

26. Hag. 2:23. *NIV:* "I will make you like my signet ring."

27. Luke 2:14.

ABBREVIATIONS

ANF *The Ante-Nicene Fathers,* edited by A. Roberts and J. Donaldson. 10 vols., 1885–96, reprint edition. Grand Rapids: Eerdmans, 1979.

BCMH *Baketel Concordance to the Methodist Hymnal.* Oliver Sherman Baketel. New York: Eaton and Mains, 1907 (in reference to the 1905 Hymnal).

BCP *Book of Common Prayer,* Philadelphia: Church Pension Fund, 1945.

BH *The Beauty of Holiness: Phoebe Palmer as Theologian, Revivalist, Feminist, and Humanitarian.* Charles Edward White. Grand Rapids: Francis Asbury Press, Zondervan, 1986.

CAJ New York Christian Advocate and Journal. New York: 1826–1956.

CBTEL *Cyclopedia of Biblical, Theological, and Ecclesiastical Literature.* Edited by J. M'Clintock and J. Strong. 12 vols. New York: Harper & Bro., 1867–87. Reprinted, New York: Arno Press, 1968.

CD *Christian Discourses* (1849). Søren Kierkegaard. London: Oxford University Press, 1940.

CE *Catholic Encyclopedia.* 17 vols. New York: Encyclopedia Press, 1907–22. ed Charles G. Herbermann, Edward A. Pace, Condé B. Pallen, Thomas J. Shahan, John J. Wynne.

CH *A Collection of Hymns.* London: Wesleyan Conference Office 1877.

CM *Cyclopedia of Methodism.* Edited by Matthew Simpson. Philadelphia: Everts and Stewart, 1876.

CMC Camp-Meeting Chorister. Philadelphia: W.A. Leary, 1844.

Codville William Codville, *A Concordance to the Hymnal.* New York: Phillips and Hunt, 1880.

CPAM *Christian Perfection in American Methodism.* John L. Peters. Nashville: Abingdon, 1956.

CUH *Called Unto Holiness: The Story of the Nazarenes, the Formative Years.* Timothy L. Smith. Kansas City, Mo.: Nazarene Publishing Co.

CUP *Concluding Unscientific Postscript.* Søren Kierkegaard. Princeton: Princeton University Press, 1941.

DH   *A Dictionary of Hymnology.* Edited by J. Julian. London: J. Murray, 1915.

EMPP   *"The Experience of Mrs. P.P.,"* Guide to Holiness, 19: (1851) 133ff., (authorship uncertain).

ERE   *Encyclopedia of Religion and Ethics.* Edited by James Hastings. 13 vols. Edinburgh: T&T Clark, 1908–26.

EWM   *Encyclopedia of World Methodism.* Edited by Nolan B. Harmon. 2 vols. Nashville: United Methodist Publishing House, 1974.

FC   *The Fathers of the Church: A New Translation.* Edited by R. J. Deferrari. 77 vols. to date. Washington: Catholic University of America Press, 1948ff.

F&E   *Faith and Its Effects.* Phoebe Palmer. NY: Walter C. Palmer, 1867 NY: Garland Pub, 1985.

FW   *Forty Witnesses.* Edited by Stephen Olin Garrison. New York: Eaton and Mains, 1888.

FYOW   *Four Years in the Old World.* Phoebe Palmer. New York: Foster & Palmer, 1867.

GTH   *Guide to Holiness* Boston, New York, 1839–1901.

HBC   *The Holy Bible with a Commentary and Critical Notes.* Adam Clarke. 6 vols. New York: J. Emory and B. Waugh, 1829.

HBN   *The Holy Bible With Notes.* Joseph Benson. 5 vols. New York: Harper, 1823.

HF   *Holding the Fort.* John Kent, London: Epworth, 1978.

HM   *Heroines of Methodism.* George Coles. New York: Carlton and Porter, 1857.

HMEC   *Hymnal of the Methodist Episcopal Church.* New York: Nelson and Phillips, 1879.

HMM   *History of Methodist Missions.* Edited by Wade Crawford Barclay 4 vols. New York: Board of Mission, 1949.

HMUS   *History of the Methodist Episcopal Church in the U.S.* Abel Stevens. 4 vols. New York: Carlton & Lanahan, 1864.

HPM   *The Holiness-Pentecostal Movement in the United States.* Vinson Synan. Grand Rapids: Eerdmans, 1971.

HRNC   *The Holiness Revival in the Nineteenth Century.* Melvin E. Dieter. Metuchen, NJ: Scarecrow Press.

HUMEC   *Hymns for the Use of the Methodist Episcopal Church.* New York: Lane and Scott, 1850.

HW   Holy Women, or Biographical Sketches of the Lives and Public Ministry of Various Holy Women, in Which Are Included Several Letters from the Rev. John Wesley Never Before Published. Zechariah Taft. 2 vols. London: Kershaw, 1825; Leeds: Cullingworth, 1828.

IPCT   The Idea of Perfection in Christian Theology. R. Newton Flew. New York: Humanities Press, 1968.

JJW   Journal of John Wesley. Edited by Nehemiah Curnock. 8 vols. London: Epworth, 1938.

KJV   King James Version

LCC   Library of Christian Classics. Edited by J. Baillie, J. T. McNiell, and H. P. Van Dusen. Philadelphia: Westminster, 1953–61.

LHS   A Lineal Index to The Wesleyan Hymn Book. Edited by Richard Herlan. London: Wesleyan Conference Office, 1878.

LJW   The Letters of the Rev. John Wesley. Edited by John Telford. 8 vols. London: Epworth, 1931.

LLA   Library of Liberal Arts. NY: Bobbs Merrill Series.

LR   Ladies Repository, Cincinnati, Ohio and New York, 1841–76.

LSLP   The Life of Sarah A. Lankford Palmer. J. A. Roche. New York: Geo. Hughes, 1898.

LST   Lectures on Systematic Theology. Charles G. Finney. Oberlin: James M. Fitch. Boston: Crocker & Brewster, 1846.

LTNB   Life and Times of Nathan Bangs, Abel Stevens, NY: Carlton and Porter, 1863.

Memoirs   The Life and Letters of Mrs. Phoebe Palmer. Richard Wheatley. NY: Palmer & Hughes 1884 NY: Garland Pub., 1984.

MG   A Mother's Gift. Palmer, Phoebe, New York: Palmer, 1875; London: F.F. Longley, 1875.

MHB   The Methodist Hymn-Book. London: Wesleyan Conference, 1907.

MYC   Mary, Or the Young Christian. Phoebe Palmer published anonymously. New York: Carlton & Porter, Sunday School Union, 1841.

NIV   New International Version.

NPNF   A Select Library of the Nicene and Post-Nicene Fathers of the Christian Church. 1st Series, 14 vols.; 2nd series, 14 vols. Edited by H. Wace and P. Schaff. New York: Christian, 1887–92. Reprint edition, Grand Rapids: Eerdman, 1952–57, 1979–83.

OCDD   Oxford Dictionary of the Christian Church. Edited by F.L. Cross

(1957). Revised by F.L. Cross and E.A. Livingstone. Oxford: Oxford University Press, 1974.

PBL   Paul Bassett, Letter to Thomas C. Oden, June 2, 1986, Drew University Library Archives, Madison, N.J.

PD   Practical Divinity: Theology in the Wesleyan Tradition. Thomas Langford. Nashville: Abingdon, 1983.

PE   Pioneer Experiences. Edited by Phoebe Palmer. New York: W.C. Palmer, Jr., 1868.

PF   The Promise of the Father. Phoebe Palmer. NY: Palmer 1859. Salem, OH: Schmul Pub. 1981.

PM   The Pentecostal Movement. Nils Bloch-Hoell. London: Allen and Unwin, 1964.

PPHAM   Perfectionist Persuasion: The Holiness Movement and American Methodism, 1867–1936. Charles Edwin Jones. Metuchen, N.J.: Scarecrow, 1979.

PWJCW   The Poetical Works of John and Charles Wesley, 13 vols. London: Wesleyan Methodist Conference, 1868–1872.

RGG   Die Religion in Geschichte und Gegenwart: Handwoerterbuch fuer Theologie und Religionswissenschaft. Edited by K. Galling et al., 3rd ed. 7 vols. Tuebingen: J.C.B. Mohr, 1957–65.

RSR   Revivalism and Social Reform. Timothy L. Smith. Nashville: Abingdon, 1957.

RSV   Revised Standard Version.

SA   The Structure of Awareness, Thomas C. Oden. Abingdon, 1968.

SARR   Some Account of Recent Revivals in the North of England. Phoebe Palmer. Manchester: Bremner, 1859.

SCDHL   A Serious Call to the Devout and Holy Life. William Law. Grand Rapids: Baker, 1977.

SEAA   The Second Evangelical Awakening in America. J.E. Orr. London: Marshall, Morgan and Scott, 1953.

SEAB   The Second Evangelical Awakening in Britain. J.E. Orr. London: Marshall, Morgan, and Scott, 1949.

SINE   Social Idea of the Northern Evangelists. Charles E. Coles, Jr. New York: Octagon, 1866.

ST   Summa Theologica. St. Thomas Aquinas. 3 vols. New York: Benziger, 1947.

TAR   Trans-Atlantic Revivalism: Popular Evangelicalism in Britain and

America, 1790–1865, Richard Carwardine, Westport, Conn.: Greenwood Press, 1978.

TES Thoughts on Entire Sanctification. Hiram Mattison. New York: Lane & Scott, 1852.

TFDL Tongue of Fire on the Daughters of the Lord. Phoebe W. Palmer.New York: Palmer, 1869. (A shortened version of *PF*).

THS A Theology of the Holy Spirit: The Pentecostal Experience and the New Testament Witness. Frederick Dale Bruner. Grand Rapids: Eerdmans, 1970.

TM Fragrant Memories of the Tuesday Meeting. George Hughes. New York: Palmer and Hughes (*TM1*); *TM2*, University Microfilms edition. 1981.

TRP Theological Roots of Pentecostalism, Donald W. Dayton, Grand Rapids: Francis Asbury Press, 1987.

TTAM Theological Transition in American Methodism: 1790–1935. Robert E. Chiles. New York: Abingdon, 1965.

TWS Theology in the Wesleyan Spirit. Albert C. Outler. Nashville: Tidings, 1975.

WAPR Women in American Protestant Religion, 1800–1930. 36 vols. Edited by Carolyn De Swarte Gifford. New York: Garland Publishing Co., 1985ff.

WJF The Works of the Rev. John Fletcher. 4 vols. New York: Carlton & Porter, n.d.

WJW Works of John Wesley. Jackson edition. 14 vols. Grand Rapids: Baker, 1958–1959.

WJWB Works of John Wesley, Bicentennial edition. Edited by Frank Baker. (1975–83, New York: Oxford U.P.) (1984-Nashville: Abingdon).

WOH The Way of Holiness: With Notes By the Way. Phoebe Palmer. New York: G. Lane and C. B. Tippett, 1845.

WM The Women of Methodism. Abel Stevens. New York: Carlton & Porter, 1866.

WSS Wesley's Standard Sermons. Edited by Edward H. Sugden. 2 vols. London: Epworth, 1921.

WTJ Wesleyan Theological Journal.

BIBLIOGRAPHY

UNPUBLISHED MANUSCRIPTS

Palmer, Walter and Phoebe. Nineteen "Letters" to Walter and Phoebe Palmer. Palmer Folder. Drew University Archives Manuscript Collection, Madison, New Jersey.

————"Letters." Catalog Nos. 460, 461. New York Methodist Historical Society Collection.

————Methodist Episcopal Church Records Collection. Allen Street Methodist Episcopal Church. Records. Catalog nos. 138a–152, 156, 161, 168–72. "Letters." Inventory No. 430. New York Public Library Manuscript Collection.

————"Letter to Gersham F. Cox, 29 January 1844." New England Methodist Historical Society Collection, Boston.

PRIMARY SOURCES: PHOEBE WORRALL PALMER

Boynton, Jeremy. *Sanctification Practical: A Book for The Times, With Introduction and Appendix by Mrs. Palmer*. New York: Foster & Palmer, 1867.

Palmer, Phoebe. *A Mother's Gift; or, A Wreath for my Darlings*. Introduction by E.S. Janes. New York: Walter C. Palmer, Jr., 1875 (*MG*).

————*Faith and its Effects: Or Fragments from My Portfolio*. New York: Author, 1854 (F&E). Reprint edition, *The Devotional Writings of Phoebe Palmer*, "Higher Christian Life" Series. New York: Garland, 1986.

————*Four Years in the Old World: Comprising the Travels, Incidents and*

331

Evangelistic Labors of Dr. and Mrs. Palmer in England, Ireland, Scotland, and Wales. New York: Foster & Palmer, 1867 (*FYOW*).

_____*Full Salvation: Its Doctrines and Duties.* (English edition, selections from *Incidental Illustrations*); reprint ed., Salem, Ohio: Schmul Publishers, 1979.

_____"I Resolved To Be a Bible Christian." *Tracts on Holiness,* No. 20. New York: Walter C. Palmer, n.d.

_____*Incidental Illustrations of the Economy of Salvation, Its Doctrines and Duties.* Boston: Henry V. Degen, 1855. Selections republished by Schmul Publishing Co., Salem, Ohio, as Full Salvation.

_____*Israel's Speedy Restoration and Conversion Contemplated, or Signs of the Times.* In familiar letters. New York: John A. Gray, 1854.

_____(published anonymously). *Mary, Or the Young Christian.* New York: Carlton and Porter, Sunday School Union, 1841.

_____*The Parting Gift to Fellow Laborers and Young Converts.* New York: Walter C. Palmer, 1869.

_____(ed.). *Pioneer Experiences: Or the Gift of Power Received by Faith and Confirmed by the Testimony of Eighty Living Ministers of Various Denominations.* New York: W. C. Palmer, Jr., Office for Works on the Higher Christian Life, 1868 (*PE*).

_____*A Present for My Friend on Entire Devotion to God.* New York: Author, 1853. Republished by Schmul Publishing House, Salem, Ohio, as *Entire Devotion to God* (*EDG*).

_____*The Promise of the Father: Or a Neglected Speciality of the Last Days.* Boston: H.V. Degen, 1859; New York: Foster and Palmer, 1866 (*PF*). Reprint editions: Salem, Ohio: Schmul, 1981, and New York: Garland, 1986.

_____*Recollections and Gathered Fragments of Mrs. Lydia N. Cox.* New York: Piersy and Reed, 1845.

_____*Refining Processes: Crowning Testimony. Testimony to the Faithfulness of Covenant-keeping God.* New York: Walter C. Palmer, Jr., 1875 (original fascimile of a handwritten document).

_____*Some Account of the Recent Revivals in the North of England and Glasgow.* Manchester: W. Bremner, 1859 (*SARR*).

_____*Sweet Mary.* London: Simpkin Marshall & Co., 1862.

_____*Tongue of Fire On Daughters of the Lord.* New York: Walter C. Palmer, Jr., 1869.

_____*Tracts on Holiness.* New York: W.C. Palmer, Jr., n.d.

_____*The Useful Disciple; or, A Narrative of Mrs. Mary Gardner.* Cincinnati: Swormstedt & Poe, 1853.

_____*The Way of Holiness, with Notes by the Way: Being a Narrative of Religious Experience, Resulting from a Determination to Be a Bible*

Christian. New York, Piercy and Reed, 1843; New York: G. Lane and C. B. Tippett, 1845, 2nd ed.; New York: Lane and Scott, 1850; New York: Palmer and Hughes, 1867. Reprint edition, *The Devotional Writings of Phoebe Palmer.* "Higher Christian Life" Series. New York: Garland, 1986.

Palmer, Walter Clark. *Life and Letters of Leonidas L. Hamline, D.D.* New York: Carlton and Porter, 1866.

Wheatley, Richard. *The Life and Letters of Mrs. Phoebe Palmer.* New York: W.C. Palmer, Jr. 1876. Reprint edition, New York: Garland, 1886.

PERIODICALS

Advocate of Christian Holiness. Boston. 1870–82.

American Wesleyan. Syracuse, N.Y. 1860–83.

Beauty of Holiness and Sabbath Miscellany. Columbus, Ohio. 1853–64.

Christian Advocate and Journal (New York). 1826–1956 *(CAJ).*

Guide to Christian Perfection, and Guide to Holiness. Boston, New York, and Philadelphia. 1839–1901 *(GTH).*

Ladies Repository. Cincinnati. 1841–75 *(LR).*

Methodist Quarterly Review. New York. 1835–90.

Zion's Herald and Wesleyan Journal. Boston. 1835–75.

ARTICLES BY PHOEBE PALMER IN PERIODICALS:

In the *New York Christian Advocate and Journal (CAJ)*:

1841 Holiness; What Is Gospel Holiness or Sanctification? How May We Enter into the Enjoyment of Sanctification? What Will Be the Advantages of Living in the Enjoyment of the Witness of Holiness to Ourselves and Others?

1842 Is There Not a Shorter Way?

1843 The Blind.

1852 False Statement Corrected.

1855 A Voice from the Laity. Preaching at Camp Meeting. Believe That Ye Have It and Ye Have It. Coals of Fire.

1857 Laity For the Times (written by Mrs. Palmer, attributed to "A Distinguished Layman." *Memoirs,* p. 502).

1860 Isle of Wight Letter. Letter to the Editor.

1861 English Correspondence, #1, #2, #3. Letter from England.

1862 London and Its Environs. Letter from Wales. Revival In Wales. Letter From England, #1, #2, #3.

1863 Letter from the Old World. Letter from England, #1, #2, #3.
In the *Beauty of Holiness* (*BOH*):
1856 The Infidel. The Infidel Induced to Pray. The Infidel at the Altar. Scraps from my Writing Desk. Our Ascended Elijah. Music the Dialect of Heaven. Semi-Centennial Marriage.
1857 Our Dear Kitty, #1, #2. Reachings of Faith. The Inquiry Answered: Do Camp-Meetings Do More Harm Than Good?
1859 Reply to the Address to Dr. and Mrs. Palmer. Believe That Ye Have It, and Ye Have It. Extract of a Letter from Mrs. Palmer.
In the *Guide to Christian Perfection* (Boston, 1839–45, *GTH*):
1839 Letter from a Lady to Her Friend, 1.
1840 Letter from a Lady to Her Friend, 2.
1841 Letter from a Lady to Her Friend, 3. Closet Reflections on the Subject of Gospel Holiness.
1842 Holiness, Parts 1–4.
1843 The Way of Holiness. 1, 2.
Note: Before July, 1844, each volume covered a full year, July to June. Hence volume 1 ran from July 1839 to June 1840, vol. 2, July 1840–June 1841; vol 3, July 1841–June 1842; vol. 4, July 1842–June 1843; vol. 5, July 1843–June, 1844. After July, 1844, each volume contained six monthly issues, July to January, or January to July.
1844 Notes by the Way, 1–4. Triumphs of Holiness. Holiness, Not Numbers, the Glory of the Church.
1845 Christian Communings (7:97). Be Specific in Confession (7:127). Religious Correspondence (7:29–32).
In the *Guide to Holiness* (Boston and New York: 1846–64, *GTH*):
1846 Extract of a Letter From a Friend (8:93). He Led Them Forth by the Right Way. (9:135–137).
1849 Religious Correspondence, No. 1 (15:12), 2, (15:39), 3, (15:65).
1853 Not Ignorant of Satan's Devices (21:49); The Doctrine of Entire Sanctification Simplified (23:52); Our Last Family Gathering (23:175); Gatherings by the Way (24:79).
1854 Profession of Perfect Love (25:19); Do I Walk Worthy of My Father? (25:128); Will You Know the Secret? (25:171); The Methodist Ministry (26:1); Is the Relation of Christian Experience a Duty? (26:9); A Singular Vow (26:55); Publish It. Tell It. (26:137); I Don't Believe in Holiness (26:78); Letter to a Minister (26:97).
1855 The Shorter Way (27:14); Polluted Sacrifices (27:50); Rules for a Bible Christian (27:73); A Dream—Why They Do Not Slip (27:75) To the Memory of a Beloved Sister (27:105); The Man Who Didn't Know Where He Was (27:176); An Act of Faith (28:136); Illustrations of Christian Experience (28:79); Religious Counsels (28:163).

1856 A Speedy Way of Overcoming (29:18); A Letter to the Editors (29:154–5); Scraps from My Writing Desk (29:167); Gentle Words (29:170); Prayers Not Always Answered (30:8); Two Steps to the Blessing (30:33); A Noble Band of Helpers (30:112).

1857 The Fulness of Love (31:82); Scraps from My Writing Desk (31:74, 32:152); Cost of Faith's Superstructure (31:167); A Mother's Portrait, or the Model Mother (31:33, 65, 97, 129, 161); Sketches and Incidents (32:74); Doctrine of the Sealing of the Spirit (32:50); Reachings of Faith (32:24); Mrs. Palmer's Works in England (32:62).

1858 Gracious Reviewings (33:10, 38); To Our Absent Loved Ones (33:52); Christian Vigilance Bands (33:65); A Witness of Perfect Love (33:120); Antidote to Backsliding (34:6); A Forthcoming Volume (34:63; 34:96, notice of Promise of the Father); Letter from St. John, New Brunswick (34:83, from Dr. Palmer); Mrs. Palmer Still Absent (34:124, a letter from her); Letter to the Editor, from Prince Edward Island, Canada (34:174, 175).

1859 Promise of the Father (35:30, 61, 95, notices); Letter from Mrs. Palmer (35:70, from on board Steamer in the Bay of Fundy); Mrs. Palmer in England and Ireland (36:97).

1860 Letters from Dr. and Mrs. Palmer (37:18–22, 58–61, 84, 138, 169, 38:1, 129, 176); Dr. and Mrs. Palmer (report from Edward Boyer, 37:17, news report, 37:186); Revival Letters and Incidents (37:43–53); Dr. and Mrs. P. in Glasgow (letters from others, 37:103); Farewell to Dr. and Mrs. P.—Penrith, England, (38:5).

1861 Dr. and Mrs. Palmer in England (news reports, 39:99, 39:85, 40:14); Letter from Mrs. Palmer (39:15); New York Correspondence (extract from Mrs. Palmer's Last Letter, 39:149); Extact from Mrs. Palmer's Letter (40:122); Letter from Mrs. Palmer (from Grimsby, 40:13); Letters from Mrs. Palmer (40:153, 154); Notes by the Way (40:85, from Oxford).

1862 Letters from Mrs. Palmer (41:57, 42:23, 122, 151–155, 183); News From England (letter from Mrs. P., 41:118); Revival Incidents (Letters from Mrs. Palmer, 41:39–42); Revival in Wales (41–185); The Meeting in Rivington Street—continuing while the Palmers are Abroad (42:26, 92, 184); Dr. and Mrs. Palmer's Revival Services (news report, 42:62).

1863 The Beatific Vision (43:14); Dr. and Mrs. Palmer (43:62, 44:46, 161, 186, news of the Palmers' return home); Revival in Leeds, England (43:82); Letter From Mrs. Palmer (44:39); Revival in England (#1, 44:49; #2 44:97); Letter to the Wesleyan Times, June 15th (44:73); Revival in Ireland (44:121); Methodism in England (43:145); Letter From Dr. Palmer (44:178).

In 1864, upon their return from Britain, Dr. and Mrs. Palmer bought the *Guide to Holiness* and merged it with *Beauty of Holiness and Sabbath Miscellany*. The volume numbers continued, but with a new title: *Guide to, and Beauty of Holiness and Revival Miscellany* (New York, 1864–67), which later was changed to *Guide to Holiness and Revival Miscellany* (New York, 1867–98). For convenience, we are following Charles E. White's practice of designating all of these titles as *GTH*, for despite the name changes the journal's continuity remained. A separate monograph is needed to specify accurately the Palmer materials in *GTH*, especially after 1864.

NINETEENTH CENTURY SOURCES
RELATING TO PHOEBE PALMER

Adams, Charles. *Evangelism in the Middle of the Nineteenth Century; or an Exhibit, Descriptive and Statistical of the Present Condition of Evangelical Religion in All Countries of the World.* Boston: Charles H. Pierce, 1851.

"Address to Dr. and Mrs. Palmer." *Beauty of Holiness* 10 (1859):9.

Akin, Samuel D. *Christian Perfection as Taught in the Bible.* Nashville: Southern Methodist Publishing House, 1860.

Alexander, James Waddell. *The New York Pulpit in the Revival of 1858.* New York: Sheldon, Blakeman and Co. 1858.

Allen, R. W., and Wise, Daniel. *Methodism in Earnest.* Boston: Charles H. Pierce, 1850.

Arthur, William. *The Tongue of Fire: or the True Power of Christianity.* New York: Harper and Brothers, 1880; first edition, 1856.

Atwood, Anthony. *Causes of the Marvelous Success of Methodism in This Country within the Past Century.* Philadelphia: National Publishing Association for the Promotion of Holiness, 1884.

Bangs, Heman. *The Autobiography and Journal of Rev. Heman Bangs.* New York, N. Tibbals & Sons 1872.

Bangs, Nathan. *The Errors of Hopkinsianism Detected and Exposed.* New York: John C. Totten, 1815.

_____*A History of the Methodist Episcopal Church.* 4 vols. New York: Mason and Lane, 1838–41.

_____*The Necessity, Nature and Fruits of Entire Sanctification.* New York: Phillips and Hunt, 1888.

_____*The Present State, Prospects, and Responsibilities of the Methodist Episcopal Church.* New York: Lane and Scott, 1850.

————"The Recent Revival." *Christian Advocate and Journal* 33 (1858): 9, 117.

Benson, Joseph. *An Apology for the People Called Methodists.* London: G. Story, 1801.

————*Holy Bible with Notes.* 5 vols. New York: Harper, 1823.

————*The Life of the Rev. John W. de la Flechere.* New York: B. Wade and T. Mason, 1833.

Black, Warren C. *Christian Womanhood.* Nashville: Publishing House of M.E.C., South, 1888.

Bledsoe, Albert T. *A Theodicy.* New York: Carlton & Phillips, 1853.

Boardman, William Edwin. *The Higher Christian Life.* Boston: Henry Hoyt, 1858.

————*Faith Work under Dr. Cullis in Boston.* Boston: Willard Tract Repository, 1874.

Boland, J.M. *The Problem of Methodism: Being a Review of the Residue Theory of Regeneration and the Second Change Theory of Sanctification and the Philosophy of Christian Perfection.* Nashville: Publishing House, MEC, South, 1888.

Booth, Catherine. *Godliness.* Boston: McDonald, Gill and Co., 1893.

————*Female Ministry: Woman's Right to Preach the Gospel.* London: Morgan & Chase, 1859; cf. *Female Teaching: Or the Rev. A.A. Rees versus Mrs. Palmer, being a reply to the pamphlet by the above gentleman on the Sunderland Revival.* 2nd ed. London: 1861; reprint, New York: Salvation Army, 1975.

Booth-Tucker, F. de L. *The Life of Catherine Booth, the Mother of the Salvation Army.* 2 vols. New York: Fleming H. Revell, 1892.

Bourne, Hugh. *Remarks on the Ministry of Women.* Bemersley, Eng.: Office of the Primitive Methodist Connection, 1808.

Brooks, John R. *Scriptural Sanctification: An Attempted Solution of the Holiness Problem.* Nashville: M.E.C., South, 1899.

Bucke, Emory Stevens, ed.. *History of American Methodism.* 3 vols. Nashville: Abingdon, 1964.

Buckley, James Monroe. *A History of Methodism in the United States.* 2 vols. New York: Harper & Bros., 1989.

Bunyan, John. *Pilgrim's Progress.* London: Collins, 1979 (reprint).

Caldwell, Merritt. *The Philosophy of Christian Perfection.* Philadelphia: Sorin and Ball, 1848.

Carvosso, William. *The Great Efficacy of Simple Faith in the Atonement of Christ.* Edited by Benjamin Carvosso. New York: Lane and Tippet, 1847.

Cartwright, Peter. *Autobiography.* Nashville: Abingdon, 1956.

Caughey, James. *Arrows from My Quiver.* New York: W.C. Palmer, Jr. 1867.

_____*Earnest Christianity Illustrated: Or, Selections from the Journal of the Rev. James Caughey.* Boston: J.P. Magee, 1854; New York: W.C. Palmer, Jr., 1868.

_____*Helps to a Life of Holiness and Usefulness, or Revival Miscellanies.* Boston: James P. Magee, 1856.

_____*Glimpses of Life in Soul-Saving: Or, Selections from the Journal and Writings of the Rev. James Caughey.* New York: W.C. Palmer, Jr., 1868.

_____*Methodism in Earnest: Being the History of a Great Revival in Great Britain.* Letters edited by Dan Wise. Boston: C.H. Pierce, 1850.

_____*Revival Miscellanies, Containing Twelve Revival Sermons, and Thoughts on Entire Sanctification.* NY: W.C. Palmer, Jr., 1868.

_____*The Triumph of Truth, and Continental Letters and Sketches, from the Journal, Letters and Sermons of the Rev. James Caughey, as Illustrated in Two Great Revivals in Nottingham and Lincoln, England.* Philadelphia: Higgins and Perkinpine, 1857.

Clarke, Adam. *Christian Theology.* New York: Lane and Scott, 1851; reprint edition, Salem, Ohio: Schmul Publishing Co., n.d.

_____*Discourses.* 2 vols. New York: Waugh and Mason, 1832.

_____*The Holy Bible, Containing the Old and New Testaments, with a Commentary and Critical Notes.* 6 vols. New York: B. Waugh and T. Mason, 1833; 2nd ed., T. Mason and G. Lane, 1837.

_____*Memoirs of the Wesley Family.* New York: Lane and Tippett, 1848; reprint edition, South Bend, Ind.: World Harvest Press, n.d.

Coles, George. *Heroines of Methodism: Or, Pen and Ink Sketches of the Mothers and Daughters of the Church.* New York: Carlton & Porter, 1857.

Conant, William C. *Narratives of Remarkable Conversions and Revival Incidents; including . . . an account of the rise and progress of the Great Awakening of 1857–58.* New York: Derby & Jackson 1858.

Crosby, Sarah. "The Grace of God Manifested in the Account of Mrs. Crosby of Leeds." Edited by Elizabeth Richie Mortimer. *Arminian Magazine* (London) 29/9 (Sept. 1806): 418–73, 516–21, 563–68, 610–71.

Crooks, George R. *The Life of Matthew Simpson.* New York: Harper & Bros., 1890.

Cullis, Charles. *History of the Consumptive Homes.* Boston: A Williams and Co., 1869.

Curry, Daniel. *Fragments: Religious and Theological.* New York: Phillips and Hunt, 1880.

Daniels, Morris, S. *The Story of Ocean Grove: Related in the Year of Its Golden Jubilee, 1869–1919.* New York: Methodist Book Concern, 1919.

Disosway, Gabriel P. *Our Excellent Women of the Methodist Church in England and America.* New York: James Miller, 1873.

Dow, Lorenzo. *History of Cosmopolite. . . . Journal From Childhood to 1815. Also His Polemical Writings.* 2nd ed. Philadelphia: Joseph Rakestraw, 1815.

Dunn, Lewis Romaine. *Relations of the Holy Spirit to the Work of Entire Sanctification.* New York: W. C. Palmer, 1883.

Editorials in *Christian Advocate and Journal,* "On Mattison's Misrepresentation" 16 (1842): 83; "Condemnation of H. Mattison" 34 (1859): 63; "Status of Palmer's European Tour" 38 (1863):4.

Editorials in *Guide to Holiness:* "Dr. and Mrs. Palmer in Birmingham" 44 (1863):46; "Grace Destroys the Dominion of Sin" 43 (1863): 185–87; "Mrs. Palmer—Our Engraving" 31 (1857): 1–2; "Mrs. Palmer—Views Entertained of Her by Other Sects" 30 (1856):64; "Palmer's Return to New York" 44 (1863): 37; "When Will the War End" 44 (1863):58.

Faber, Frederick William. *Growth in Holiness.* London: T. Richardson, 1854.

Finney, Charles Grandison. *Lectures on Revivals of Religion* (1835). Reprint title: *Revival Lectures.* Old Tappan, N.J.: Revell, n.d.;

———*Lectures on Systematic Theology.* Oberlin: E.J. Goodrich, 1878.

———*Views on Sanctification.* Oberlin, Ohio: James Steele, 1840.

"The Five Points House of Industry." *American Church Monthly* 3 (1858): 209–22.

Fletcher, John. *Christian Perfection, an extract/selections from "Last Check to Antinomianism," with letter by Thomas Rutherford.* New York: Tho. Mason and Geo. Lane, 1837.

———*The Works of the Reverend John Fletcher.* 4 vols. New York: Carlton & Porter, 1849; reprint edition, Salem, Ohio: Schmul, 1974.

Fletcher, Mary Bosanquet. *Jesus Altogether Lovely: Or, A Letter to Some of the Single Women in the Methodist Society.* Bristol: N.P. 1766.

———*Thoughts on Community with Happy Spirits.* Birmingham, Engl.: King, n.d.

Forsyth, P.T. *Christian Perfection.* London: Hodder and Stoughton, 1899.

Foster, Randolph Sinks. *Nature and Blessedness of Christian Purity.* Introduction by Bishop Edmund Janes. New York: Lane & Scott, 1851.

Franklin, Samuel. *A Critical Review of Wesleyan Perfection.* New York: Methodist Book Concern, 1866.

Garrison, Stephen Olin, ed. *Forty Witnesses.* Introduction by C.D. Foss. New York: Eaton and Mains, 1888.

Gorham, B.W. *Camp Meeting Manual.* Boston: H.V. Degen, 1854.

Gregory, Benjamin. *Sidelights on the Conflicts of Methodism, 1827–1852.* London: Cassell 1898.

Hamline, Leonidas L. *Works of Rev. Leonidas L. Hamline.* Edited by P.G. Hibbard. 2 vols. Cincinnati: Hitchcock and Walden, 1869–71.

Harford, Charles F., ed. *The Keswick Convention: Its Message, Its Method, and Its Men.* London: Marshall, 1907.

Haven, Gilbert. *Sermons, Speeches and Letters on Slavery and Its War.* Boston: Lee and Shepherd, 1869.

Headley, Phineas Camp. *Evangelists in the Church.* Boston: H. Hoyt, 1875.

Hibbard, F. G. *Biography of Rev. Leonidas L. Hamline.* Cincinnati: Hitchcock and Walden, 1880.

————. "Thoughts on the Baptism of the Holy Ghost." *GTH* 51 (1867): 77–79.

Hills, Aaron Merritt. *Scriptural Holiness and Keswick Teaching Compared.* Manchester: Star Hall, 1900.

Hobbs, James. *Methodist Standard Holiness Gems.* New York: Palmer and Hughes, 1888.

Holdich, Joseph. *The Life of Wilbur Fisk.* New York: Harper & Bro., 1842.

Holiness Miscellany: Essays of Adam Clarke, Richard Watson, Bishop Foster, George Peck, Alfred Cookman, J. A. Wood, Edgar Levy, and Daniel Steele. Philadelphia: National Publication Association for the Promotion of Holiness, 1882.

Horner, R. C. *Notes on Boland: Or Mr. Wesley and the Second Work of Grace.* Boston: McDonald, Gill, 1893.

Hughes, George. *The Beloved Physician, Walter C. Palmer, M.D.* New York: Palmer and Hughes, ca. 1884.

————. *Days of Power in the Forest Temple: A Review of the Wonderful Work of God at Fourteen National Camp-meetings from 1867 to 1872.* Introduction by Bishop Haven. Boston: John Bent and Co., 1873.

————. *The Double Cure; or Echoes from National Camp-Meetings.* Boston: Christian Witness, 1894.

————. *Fifty Years of Holiness Publishing Work, 1839–1889.* New York: Palmer and Hughes, 1889.

————. *Fragrant Memories of the Tuesday Meeting and the Guide to Holiness and Their Fifty Years' Work for Jesus.* New York: Palmer & Hughes, 1886; microfiche, ATLA, 1981.

————. "Letters From England," *Christian Advocate and Journal* 38 (1863): 153, 233, 281.

_____. "Memorium, Death of Walter C. Palmer." *GTH* 52 (1883): 65–100.

_____. *Ministerial Life Pictures*. Introduction by Alfred Cookman. Philadelphia: Methodist Home Journal, 1869.

_____. "Testimony. Influence of the Palmers." *Guide to Holiness* 47 (1865):97–99.

Hunt, John. *Entire Sanctification: Its Nature, The Way of Its Attainment, Motives for Its Pursuit*. London: John Mason, 1860.

Inskip, John S. *Methodism Explained and Defended*. Cincinnati: H.J. and J. Applegate, 1851.

_____. ed. *Songs of Triumph Adapted to Prayer Meetings, Camp Meetings and All Other Seasons of Religious Worship*. Philadelphia: National Publishing Association for the Promotion of Holiness, 1882.

Jackson, Lewis E. *Gospel Work in New York City: a Memorial of Fifty Years in City Missions*. New York: New York City Mission, 1878.

_____. *Walks About New York: Facts and Figures Gathered from Various Sources*. New York: New York City Mission and Tract Society, 1865.

Janes, Edmund S. *Sermons on the Death of Nathan Bangs*. New York: Carlton and Porter, 1862.

Janes, E. S., Mattison, H., Curry, D., Buckley, J. M., and Brown, S. D. *Perfect Love, Speeches on Sanctification*. New York: N. Tibbals and Co., 1868.

Jarbo, P. J. *A Letter to Mrs. Palmer, in reference to Women Speaking in Public*. North Shields, England: N.P. 1859.

Journals of the General Conference of the Methodist Episcopal Church. New York: Carlton and Porter, 1848–64.

Ladies of the Five Points Mission. The Old Brewery and the New Mission House at the Five Points. New York: Stringer and Townsend, 1854.

Lancaster, John. *The Life of Darcy, Lady Maxwell, of Pollock; Late of Edinburgh*. New York: T. Mason and G. Lane, 1837.

Law, William. *Serious Call to the Devout and Holy Life*. Grand Rapids: Baker, 1977.

_____. *Christian Perfection*. Carol Stream: Creation House, 1975.

Lee, Luther. *Five Sermons*. Edited by Donald W. Dayton. Chicago: Bethany Fellowship, 1981.

_____. *Wesleyan Manual: A Defense of the Organization of the Wesleyan Methodist Connection*. Syracuse, N.Y.: Samuel Lee, 1862.

Lummus, Aaron. *Essays on Holiness*. Boston: Timothy Ashley, 1826.

McClintock, John. "Distinctive Features of Methodism." *Guide to Holiness* 52 (1867): 72.

McClintock, John, and Strong, James. *Cyclopedia of Biblical, Theological, and Ecclesiastical Literature.* 12 vols. New York: Harper & Bros. 1880.

McDonald, William, et al., eds. *Songs of Joy and Gladness.* Boston: McDonald, Gill, 1885.

McDonald, William and Hartsough, L. *Beulah Songs: A Choice Collection of Popular Hymns and Music.* Philadelphia: National Publishing Association for the Promotion of Holiness, 1881.

McDonald, William, and Searles, John E. *The Life of Rev. John S. Inskip, President of the National Association for the Promotion of Holiness.* Chicago: The Christian Witness Co., 1885.

McLean, A. and Eaton, J. W., eds. *Penuel: Or Face to Face with God.* New York: W. C. Palmer, Jr. 1869.

Mahan, Asa. *The Baptism of the Holy Ghost.* New York: W. C. Palmer, Jr., 1870.

_____. "Oberlin Perfectionism." *Christian Advocate and Journal* 19 (1885): 169–70.

_____. *Scripture Doctrine of Christian Perfection.* Boston: D. S. King, 1839.

Matlack, Lucius C. *The History of American Slavery and Methodism, from 1780 to 1849; and History of the Wesleyan Methodist Connection of America.* New York: Wesleyan Methodist Book Room, 1849.

Mattison, Hiram. *A Calm Review of Dr. Perry's Late Article.* New York: John A. Gray, 1856.

_____. *An Answer to Dr. Perry's Reply to the Calm Review.* New York: Miller and Holman, 1856.

_____. *Thoughts on Entire Sanctification.* New York: Lane and Scott, 1852.

Mead, Amos P. *Manna in the Wilderness: Or the Grove and Its Altar, Containing a History of the Origin and Rise of Camp Meetings and a Defense of This Remarkable Means of Grace; also an Account of the Wyoming Camp Meeting, Together with Sketches of Sermons and Preachers.* Introduction by J. B. Wakely of New York. Philadelphia: Perkinpine and Higgins, 1860.

Merrill, Stephen M. *Sanctification: Right Views and Other Views.* Cincinnati: Jennings and Pye, 1901.

Merritt, Timothy. *The Christian's Manual.* New York: N. Bangs and J. Emory, 1827.

Miley, John. *Treatise on Class Meetings.* Cincinnati: Poe and Hitchcock, 1866.

Moore, Henry. *The Life of Mrs. Mary Fletcher, Consort and Relict of the Rev. John Fletcher. Compiled from Her Journal.* Birmingham, Engl.: J. Peart, 1817; New York: J. Emory and B. Waugh, 1830.

Morgan, John. "The Gift of the Holy Ghost." *The Oberlin Quarterly Review* 1 (1845): 90–116.

Moule, Handley Carr Glyn. *The Cross and the Spirit.* London: Pickering and Inglis, n.d.

Mudge, James. *Growth In Holiness Toward Perfection: Or Progressive Sanctification.* New York: Hunt and Eaton, 1895.

Nelson, John. *Extract from the Journal of John Nelson.* New York: Carlton & Porter, 1856.

Olin, Julia M., ed. *Life and Letters of Stephen Olin, Late President of Wesleyan University.* 2 vols. New York: Harper & Brothers, 1853.

Palmer, Walter C. "In Memoriam. Mrs. Phoebe Palmer." *GTH* (1874): 161–86.

Palmer, Walter C., Jr. *Catalogue of Works on the Higher Christian Life, also General Devotional Works and Books for Sunday School Libraries.* New York: Walter C. Palmer, Jr., 1870.

Peck, George. *The Scripture Doctrine of Christian Perfection Stated and Defended: With a Critical and Historical Examination of the Controversy, both Ancient and Modern.* New York: Lane and Sandford, 1842.

———. *The Life and Times of Rev. George Peck.* New York: Nelson & Phillips, 1874.

Peck, Jesse T. *The Central Idea of Christianity.* Boston: H. V. Degen, 1856.

———. "Holiness." *Methodist Quarterly Review* 33 (1851): 505–29.

———. et al. *Systematic Beneficence.* New York: Carlton & Phillips, 1856.

———. *True Woman; or, Life and Happiness at Home and Abroad.* New York: Carlton and Porter, 1857.

Perry, J. H. *Reply to Prof. Mattison's "Answer," Etc.; Being the Summing up of the Case of Professor Mattison Against Mrs. Palmer.* New York: John A. Gray, 1856.

Philip, Robert. *Devotional Guides.* Introduction by Albert Barnes. 2 vols. New York: Appleton, 1837.

Platt, Smith N. *The Gift of Power: Or the Special Influence of the Holy Spirit: The Need of the Church.* New York: Carlton & Porter, 1856.

Pomery, B. *Visions From Modern Mounts: Namely, Vineland, Manheim, Round Lake, Hamilton, Oakington, Canton, with Other Selections.* Albany: Van Benthuysen, 1871.

Pope, William Burt. *A Compendium of Christian Theology.* 3 vols. New York: Phillips and Hunt, 1881.

Record of the Convention for the Promotion of Scriptural Holiness Held at Brighton, May 29 to June 7, 1875. Brighton and London: W. J. Smith, 1875.

"Revival in Camp," Editorial, *GTH* 45 (1864): 21.

Ridgaway, Henry B. *The Life of the Rev. Alfred Cookman.* Introduction by Randolph Sinks Foster. New York: Harper & Bros. 1873.

Roberts, Benjamin Titus. *Holiness Teachings Compiled from the Editorial Writings of the Late Rev. Benjamin Titus Roberts.* Edited by B. H. Roberts. North Chili, N.Y.: The Earnest Christian Publishing House, 1893; reprint ed. Salem, Ohio: Schmul Publishing Co., 1983.

_____. *Why Another Sect: Containing a Review by Bishop Simpson and Others on the Free Methodist Church.* Rochester: The Earnest Christian Publishing House, 1879.

Roche, John A. *The Life of Mrs. Sarah A. Lankford Palmer, Who for Sixty Years Was the Able Teacher of Entire Holiness.* Introduction by John P. Newman. New York: Geo. Hughes, 1898.

_____. "Mrs. Phoebe Palmer." *Ladies Repository* (Feb. 1866). 65–70.

Rogers, Hester Ann. *An Account of the Experience of Hester Ann Rogers. Also, A Sermon, Preached on the Occasion of Her Death, Oct. 26, 1794,* by the Rev. Thomas Coke. New York: N. Bangs and J. Emory, 1828.

Ryle, John C. *Holiness.* London: Hunt, 1883.

Searles, J. E. *A Sermon Preached by the Request of the National Camp Meeting at Pitman Grove, NJ, Aug. 5, 1887 on the History of the Present Holiness Revival.* Boston: McDonald, Gill & Co. 1887.

See, Isaac M. *The Rest of Faith.* New York: W. C. Palmer, 1871.

Sigston, James. *Memoir of the Life and Ministry of Mr. William Bramwell.* 3rd American edition. New York: J. Emory and B. Waugh, 1830.

Simpson, A. B. *The Four-fold Gospel.* New York: Christian Alliance, 1890.

Simpson, Matthew, ed. *Cyclopedia of Methodism.* Philadelphia: Everts and Stewart, 1878.

Smith, Amanda. *An Autobiography: The Story of the Lord's Dealings with Mrs. Amanda Smith, Containing the Account of Her Life Work of Faith, and Her Travel in America, England, Ireland, Scotland, India, and Africa as an Independent Missionary.* Chicago: Meyer and Bros. 1893.

Smith, Hannah Whitall. *Philadelphia Quaker: The Letters of Hannah Whitall Smith.* Edited by Logan Pearsall Smith. New York: Harcourt and Brace, 1950.

Smith, Robert Pearsall. *Holiness Through Faith: Light on the Way of Holiness.* Boston: Willard St. Tract Repository, 1870.

Spener, Philip Jacob. "The Spiritual Priesthood" (1677). In Henry E. Jacobs, ed., *A Summary of Christian Faith,* Philadelphia: General Council Board of Publications, 1905, pp. 581–95.

Spicer, Tobias. *Autobiography of Rev. Tobias Spicer: Containing incidents and observations; also some account of his visit to England.* Boston: C. H. Pierce & Co., 1851.

"Status of the Temperance Movement." *CAJ* 16 (1842): 124.

Steele, Daniel. *A Defense of Christian Perfection.* New York: Hunt and Eaton, 1896.

_____. *Love Enthroned: Essays on Evangelical Perfection.* New York: Hunt & Eaton, 1875.

Stevens, Abel. *Life and Times of Nathan Bangs.* New York: Carlton and Porter, 1863.

_____. *History of the Methodist Episcopal Church in the United States.* 4 vols. New York: Carlton and Lanahan, 1864.

_____. *The Women of Methodism.* New York: Carlton and Porter, 1866.

Stokes, Ellwood H., ed. *Ocean Grove, Its Origin and Progress.* Philadelphia: Haddock, 1874.

Strickland, W. P. "The Five Points." *CAJ* 38 (1863):330.

Summers, Thomas G. *Holiness, A Treatise on Sanctification.* Richmond: J. Early, 1850.

_____. *Systematic Theology: Lectures on the Twenty-Five Articles of Religion.* Edited by John J. Tigert. 2 vols. Nashville: Publishing House of the MEC, South, 1888.

Taft, Mary Barritt. *Memoirs of the Life of Mrs. Mary Taft.* Ripon: John Stevens, 1827.

Taft, Zachariah. *Biographical Sketches of the Lives and Public Ministry of Various Holy Women, in which are included Several Letters from the Rev. John Wesley Never Before Published.* 2 vols. London: Kershaw, 1825; Leeds: Cullingworth, 1828.

_____. *Thought on Female Preaching, with extracts from the Writings of Locke, Henry, Martin, etc.* Dover: G. Ledger, 1803.

Taylor, William. *Seven Years' Street Preaching in San Francisco, California.* New York: Phillips & Hunt, 1856.

Tyng, Stephen H. *Christ is All.* New York: Robert Carter and Bros., 1849.

Upham, Thomas C. *Treatise on Divine Union.* New York: Walter C. Palmer, Jr., 1870.

_____. *Life and Religious Opinions and Experience of Madame de La Mothe Guyon.* New York: Harper & Bro., 1846.

_____. *The Life of Faith, Embracing Some of the Scriptural Principles or Doctrines of Faith, The Power or Effects of Faith in the Regulation of Man's Inward Nature, and the Relation of Faith to the Divine Guidance.* Boston: Waite, Pierce, and Co., 1845.

_____. *The Principles of the Interior or Hidden Life, Designed Particu-*

larly for the Consideration of Those Who are Seeking Assurance of Faith and Perfect Love. Boston: D. S. King, 1843.

Van Cott, Maggie Newton. *The Harvest and the Reaper.* Introduction by Gilbert Haven. New York: N. Tibbals & Sons, 1876.

Vansant, M. *Entire Holiness, Is It a Gradual or an Instantaneous Work?* New York: W. C. Palmer, 1881.

————. *Work Here, Rest Hereafter: or The Life and Character of Rev. Hiram Mattison.* New York: N. Tibbals & Sons, 1870.

Vincent, H. *History of the Camp-meeting and Grounds at Wesley Grove Martha's Vineyard, for the Years Ending with the Meeting of 1869, with Glances at the Earlier Years.* Boston: Lee and Shepard, 1870.

Warner, Daniel Sidney. *Bible Proofs of the Second Work of Grace; or Entire Sanctification as a Distinct Experience Subsequent to Justification.* Goshen, Ind.: E.U. Mennonite Publ. Soc., 1880.

Watson, Richard. *Theological Institutes.* 3 vols. New York: Emory and Waugh, 1828. 26th edition by John McClintock. 2 vols. New York: Carlton & Lanaham, 1850.

Wells, E. R. "Five Points Mission." *Christian Advocate and Journal* 35 (1860): 173.

Wesley, John. *The Journal of the Rev. John Wesley.* Edited by Nehemiah Curnock. 8 vols. London: Epworth, 1838.

————. *The Letters of the Rev. John Wesley.* Edited by John Telford. 8 vols. London: Epworth, 1931.

————. *The Works of John Wesley.* Edited by Thomas Jackson. 3rd edition. 14 vols. London: Wesleyan Methodist Book Room, 1872; reprint edition, Grand Rapids: Baker, 1979.

————. *The Works of John Wesley.* Bicentennial Edition. Edited by Frank Baker. New York: Oxford University Press, Nashville: Abingdon, 1975ff.

Whedon, Daniel. *Entire Sanctification: John Wesley's View.* New York: Hunt and Eaton, n.d.

————. *Essays, Reviews, and Discourses.* Edited by J. S. Whedon. New York: Phillips and Hunt, 1887.

————. *The Freedom of the Will.* New York: Carlton & Porter, 1864.

Willard, Frances. *Glimpses of Fifty Years: The Autobiography of an American Woman.* New York: Hacker Art Books, 1970. Reprint of the 1889 edition.

————. *Women in the Pulpit.* Chicago: Woman's Temperance Pub. Association, 1889.

Winebrenner, John. *Doctrinal and Practical Sermons.* Lebanon, Pa.: Church of God, 1868.

Young, Robert. *The Importance of Prayer Meetings in Promoting the Revival of Religion.* New York: Carlton & Porter, n.d.

TWENTIETH CENTURY BOOKS AND ARTICLES
RELATING TO PHOEBE PALMER AND HER TIMES

Unpublished Dissertations

Behnke, Donna Alberta. "Created in God's Image: Religious Issues in the Women's Rights Movement of the 19th Century." Ph.D. dissertation, Northwestern University, 1975.

Carwardine, Richard. "American Religious Revivalism in Great Britain, c. 1826–c. 1863." D.Phil. thesis, Oxford University, 1974.

Fankhauser, Craig. "The Heritage of Faith: Historical Evaluation of the Holiness Movement in America." M.A. thesis, Pittsburgh State University, 1983.

Francis, Russell E. "Pentecost: 1858. A study in Religious Revivalism." Ph.D. dissertation, University of Pennsylvania, 1948.

Gaddis, Merrill Elmer. "Christian Perfectionism in America." Ph.D. dissertation, University of Chicago, 1929.

Greer, George Dixon. "A Psychological Study of Sanctification as a Second Work of Divine Grace." Ph.D. dissertation, Drew University, 1936.

Hardesty, Nancy A. "Your Daughters Shall Prophesy: Revivalism and Feminism in the Age of Finney." Ph.D. dissertation, University of Chicago, 1976.

Knapp, John Franklin. "The Doctrine of Holiness in the Light of Early Theological and Philosophical Conceptions." M.A. thesis, University of Cincinnati, 1924.

Salter, Darius. "Thomas Upham and Nineteenth Century Holiness Theology." Ph.D. dissertation, Drew University, 1983.

Scott, Leland H. "Methodist Theology in America in the 19th Century." Ph.D. dissertation, Yale University, 1960.

Spicer, Carl. "The Great Awakening of 1857 and 1858." Ph.D. dissertation, Ohio State University, 1935.

Thompson, Claude H. "The Witness of American Methodism to the Historical Doctrine of Christian Perfection." Ph.D. dissertation, Drew University, 1949.

White, John Wesley. "The Influence of North American Evangelism in

Great Britain Between 1830 and 1914 on the Origin and Development of the Ecumenical Movement.'' Ph.D. thesis, Mansfield College, Oxford, 1963.

Zikmund, Barbara Brown. "Asa Mahan and Oberlin Perfectionism." Ph.D. dissertation, Duke University, 1969.

SECONDARY SOURCES

Anderson, Robert M. *Vision of the Disinherited: Making of American Pentecostalism.* New York: Oxford University Press, 1979.

Appleton's Cyclopedia of American Biography. Article on Phoebe Palmer.

Arnett, William M. "The Role of the Holy Spirit in Entire Sanctification in the Writings of John Wesley." *WTJ* 14/2 (Fall 1979): 15–30.

Atkinson, J. Baines. *The Beauty of Holiness.* New York: Philosophical Library, 1963.

Ayars, John E. *Holiness Revival of the Past Century.* Phila: Author, n.d.

Baker, Frank. *From Wesley to Asbury: Studies in Early American Methodism.* Durham, N.C.: Duke University Press, 1976.

Barclay, Wade Crawford. *History of Methodist Missions.* 4 vols. New York: Board of Missions, 1949.

Bassett, Paul. M. "A Study in the Theology of the Early Holiness Movement." *Methodist History* 13 (April 1975): 61–84.

Beardsley, F. G. *A History of American Revivals.* New York: American Tract Society, 1912.

Berg, Barbara J. *The Remembered Gate: Origins of American Feminism, The Woman and the City, 1800–1860.* New York: Oxford Univ. Press, 1973.

Bible, Ken. "The Wesleys' Hymns on Full Redemption and Pentecost: A Brief Comparison." *WTJ* 17/2 (Fall 1982): 79–87.

Bloch-Hoell, Nils. *The Pentecostal Movement.* London: Allen and Unwin, 1964.

Boylian, Anne M. "Women in Groups: An Analysis of Women's Benevolent Organizations in New York and Boston, 1797–1840." *Journal of American History* 71/3 (December 1984): 497–523.

Breeze, Lawrence E. "The Inskips: Union in Holiness." *Methodist History* 13 (July 1975): 25–45.

Brown, Earl Kent. *Women of Mr. Wesley's Methodism. Studies in Women and Religion,* vol. 11. New York: New York University Press, 1956.

Bruner, Frederick Dale. *A Theology of the Holy Spirit: The Pentecostal Experience and the New Testament Witness.* Grand Rapids: William B. Eerdmans, 1970.

Carwardine, Richard. *Trans-Atlantic Revivalism: Popular Evangelicalism in Britain and America, 1790–1865.* Westport, CT: Greenwood Press, 1978.

Chapman, James Blaine. *The Terminology of Holiness.* Kansas City, Mo.: Beacon Hill Press, 1947.

Chiles, Robert E. *Theological Transition in American Methodism: 1790–1935.* New York: Abingdon Press, 1965.

Coles, Charles C., Jr. *The Social Ideas of the Northern Evangelists, 1826–1860.* New York: Octagon Books, 1966.

Cohard, S. L. C. *Entire Sanctification from 1739 to 1900.* Louisville, Ky.: Pentecostal Herald Press, 1900.

Cook, Alice Isabel. *Women of the Warm Heart.* London: Epworth Press, 1952.

Coppedge, Allan. "Entire Sanctification in Early American Methodism." *WTJ* 13 (Spring 1978): 34–50.

Cross, Whitney R. *The Burned-over District: The Social and Intellectual History of Enthusiastic Religion in Western New York, 1800–1850.* New York: Harper Torchbooks, 1950.

Cubie, David L. "Perfection in Wesley and Fletcher: Inaugural or Teleological?" *WTJ* 11 (Spring 1976): 22–27.

Dallimore, Arnold. *Forerunners of the Charismatic Movement.* Chicago: Moody, 1983.

Davison, Leslie. *Pathway to Power: The Charismatic Movement in Historical Perspective.* Watchung, N.J.: Logos Books, 1972.

Dayton, Donald W. *The American Holiness Movement: A Bibliographic Introduction.* Wilmore, KY: B. L. Fisher Library, Asbury Theol. Seminary, 1971.

——. "Asa Mahan and the Development of American Holiness Theology." *WTJ* 9 (Spring 1974): 60–69.

——. *Discovering an Evangelical Heritage.* New York: Harper & Row, 1986.

——. *Theological Roots of Pentecostalism,* Grand Rapids: Francis Asbury Press, 1987. TRP.

——. "The Doctrine of the Baptism of the Holy Spirit: Its Emergence and Significance." *WTJ* 13 (Spring 1978): 114–26.

Dayton, Lucille Sider and Donald W. "Your Daughters Shall Prophecy: Feminism in the Holiness Movement." *Methodist History* 14 (1976):67–92.

——. "Women as Preachers: Evangelical Precedents." *Christianity Today,* 23 May 1975, 4–7

Dictionary of American Biography. 22 vols. NY: Scribner's, 1927–57. See Inskip, Palmer, Hamline, Foster, et al. Ed. by Allen Johnson.

Dictionary of American Religious Biography. Henry W. Bowden, Columbia, SC: Greenwood Press, 1976. See Palmer.

Dieter, Melvin Easterday. "From Vineland and Manheim to Brighton and Berlin: The Holiness Revival in Nineteenth-Century Europe." *WTJ* 9 (1974): 15–27.

————. *The Holiness Revival of the Nineteenth Century.* Studies in Evangelicalism, no. 1. Metuchen, N.J.: Scarecrow Press, 1980.

Douglas, Ann. *The Feminization of American Culture.* New York: Avon Books, 1977.

Drummond, Lewis A. *Charles Grandison Finney and the Birth of Modern Evangelism.* London: Hodder and Stoughton, 1983.

Dunlop, E. Dale. *Methodist Theology in Great Britain in the Nineteenth Century.* Ann Arbor, Mich.: University Microfilms, 1968.

————. "Tuesday Meetings, Camp Meetings, and Cabinet Meetings: A Perspective on the Holiness Movement in the Methodist Church in the Nineteenth Century." *Methodist History* 13 (April 1975): 85–106.

Durbin, Linda M. "The Nature of Ordination in Wesley's View of the Ministry." *Methodist History* 9 (1971): 3–20.

Elliott-Binns, L. D. *Religion in the Victorian Era.* London: Lutterworth, 1936.

Encyclopedia of World Methodism. Edited by Nolan Harmon 2 vols. Nashville: Abingdon, 1974.

Ferguson, Charles W. *Organizing to Beat the Devil: Methodism and the Making of America.* Garden City, New York: Doubleday, 1972.

Figgis, J. B. *Keswick from Within.* London: Marshall, 1914.

Fletcher, Robert. *History of Oberlin College.* 2 vols. Oberlin: 1943.

Flew, Newton. *The Idea of Perfection in Christian Theology: Historical Study of the Christian Ideal for the Present Life.* London: Oxford, 1934.

Flew, Newton, and Davies, R. E., eds. *The Catholicity of Protestantism.* London: Lutterworth, 1953.

Foss, Martin. *The Idea of Perfection in the Western World.* Princeton, N.J.: Princeton Univ. Press, 1946.

Gaustad, Edwin S. *A Religious History of America.* New York: Harper & Row, 1966.

Gee, Donald. *The Pentecostal Movement.* London: Elim, 1949.

Hardesty, Nancy. *Great Women of Faith.* Nashville: Abingdon, 1982.

————. *Women Called to Witness: Evangelical Feminism in the Nineteenth Century.* Nashville: Abingdon, 1984.

Hardesty, Nancy, and Dayton, Lucille Sider and Donald W. "Women in the Holiness Movement: Feminism in the Evangelical Tradition."

Women of Spirit. Edited by Rosemary Ruether and Eleanor Mc-Loughlin, New York: Simon and Schuster, 1979.

Harrison, Brian. *Drink and the Victorians: The Temperance Question in England, 1815–1872*. London: Faber and Faber, 1971.

Hollenweger, W. J. *The Pentecostals*. Minneapolis, Augsburg, 1972.

Hovet, Theodore. "Phoebe Palmer's 'Altar Phraseology' and the Spiritual Dimensions of Woman's Sphere." *Journal of Religion* 63 (July 1983): 264–80.

Howard, Ivan. "Wesley vs. Phoebe Palmer: An Extended Controversy." *Wesleyan Theological Journal* 6 (Spring 1971), 31–40.

Hunter, Harold. *Spirit Baptism*. New York: University Press of America, 1983.

Hurst, John F. *The History of Methodism*. 7 vols. New York: Eaton & Mains, 1902.

Jessop, Harry E. *We the Holiness People*. Chicago: Chicago Evangelistic Institute, 1948.

Jones, Charles Edwin. *A Guide to the Study of the Holiness Movement*. Metuchen: Scarecrow Press, Inc., ATLA, 1974.

————. *Perfectionist Persuasion: The Holiness Movement and American Methodism, 1867–1936*. ATLA Monograph Series, no. 5. Metuchen, NJ: Scarecrow Press, 1974.

Jones, Donald G. *The Sectional Crisis and Northern Methodism: A Study in Piety, Political Ethics and Civil Religion*. Metuchen: Scarecrow Press, 1979.

Joy, James R., ed. *The Teachers of Drew, 1867–1942*. Madison, N.J.: Drew University, 1942.

Julian, J., ed. *A Dictionary of Hymnology*. 2nd edition London: J. Murray, 1915; reprint edition, Gordon Press, 1977.

Keller, Rosemary, and Hilah Thomas, eds. *Women in New Worlds*. 2 vols. Nashville: Abingdon, 1981, 1982.

Kendall, H. B. *The Origin and History of the Primitive Methodist Church*. 2 vols. London: Robert Bryant, 1905.

Kent, John. *The Age of Disunity*. London: Epworth Press, 1966.

————. *Holding the Fort: Studies in Victorian Revivalism*. London: Epworth, 1978.

————. *The Clash Between Radicalism and Conservatism in Methodism, 1815–1848*. Cambridge: University of Cambridge Press, 1950 (available on microfilm).

Koberle, A. *The Quest for Holiness*. Minneapolis: Augsburg, 1938.

Kuyper, A. *The Work of the Holy Spirit*. Grand Rapids: W. B. Eerdmans, 1956.

Knight, John A. "John Fletcher's Influence on the Development of Wesleyan Theology in America." *Wesleyan Theological Journal* 13 (Spring 1978): 13–33.

Knox, Ronald. *Enthusiasm: A Chapter in the History of Religion with Reference to the XVII and XVIII Centuries.* New York: Oxford University Press, 1961.

Langford, Thomas A. *Practical Divinity: Theology in the Wesleyan Tradition.* Nashville, Abingdon Press, 1983.

Lee, Jesse. *A Short History of American Methodism.* Rutland, Vt.: Academy Books, 1974. Reprint of first published history, 1810.

Lillenas, Haldor. *Modern Gospel Song Stories.* Kansas City, Mo.: Lillenas Publish Co., 1952.

Loveland, Anne C. "Domesticity and Religion in the Antebellum Period: The Career of Phoebe Palmer." *The Historian* 39, 3 (May 1977): 455–71.

Lovelace, Richard F. *Dynamics of Spiritual Life: An Evangelical Theology of Renewal.* Downers Grove, Ill.: Inter-Varsity Press, 1979.

McCutchan, Robert Guy. *Our Hymnody: A Manual of the Methodist Hymnal.* 2nd edition. NY: Abingdon, 1937.

McCutcheon, W. J. "Phoebe Palmer." In Notable American Women, vol. 3. Cambridge: Harvard Univ. Press, 1971.

McLoughlin, William C., Jr. *Modern Revivalism. Charles Grandison Finney to Billy Graham.* New York: Ronald Press, 1959.

Magnuson, Norris. *Salvation in the Slums: Evangelical Social Work, 1865–1920.* ATLA Monograph Series, no. 10. Metuchen, N.J.: Scarecrow Press, 1977.

Mallalieu, W. F. *The Fullness of the Blessing of the Gospel of Christ.* Cincinnati: Jennings and Pye, 1903.

Melder, Keith E. *Beginnings of Sisterhood: The American Women's Rights Movement in the United States, 1800–1840.* Studies in the Life of Women. New York: Schocken, 1977.

Mitchell, Norma Taylor. "From Social To Radical Feminism: A Survey of Emerging Diversity in Methodist Women's Organizations, 1869–1974." *Methodist History* 13/3 (April 1975): 21–44.

Morrow, Thomas M. *Early Methodist Women.* London: Epworth, 1967.

National Cyclopaedia of American Biography, 63 vols., NY: James T. White, 1892—see Joseph Fairchild Knapp, Walter C. Palmer, et al.

Nichol, John Thomas. *Pentecostalism.* New York: Harper & Row, 1966.

Niebuhr, H. Richard. *The Social Sources of Denominationalism.* New York: Henry Holt, n.d.

Norwood, Frederick A. "Methodist Historical Studies, 1930–1959." *Church History* 28 (1959): 391–417 and 29 (1960): 74–88.

_____. *The Story of American Methodism.* Nashville: Abingdon, 1974.

Notable American Women. 3 vols. Ed. by E. T. James and Janet W. James, Cambridge: Harvard Univ. Press, 1971. S.v. "Palmer, Phoebe Worrall," by W. J. McCutchen.

Oblinger, Carl. *Religious Mimesis: Social Bases for the Holiness Schism in Late Nineteenth-Century Methodism: The Illinois Case, 1869–1885.* Evanston: Inst. for the Study of Amer. Religion, 1973.

Olmstead, Clifton E. *History of Religion in the United States.* Englewood Cliffs: Prentice-Hall, 1960.

Orr, James Edwin. *The Fervent Prayer. The Worldwide Impact of the Great Awakening of 1858.* Chicago: Moody Press, 1974.

_____. *The Second Evangelical Awakening in America.* London: Marshall, Morgan and Scott, 1953.

_____. *The Second Evangelical Awakening in Britain.* London: Marshall, Morgan and Scott, 1949.

Outler, Albert C. ed. *John Wesley.* New York: Oxford University Press, 1964.

_____. *Theology in the Wesleyan Spirit.* Nashville: Tidings, 1974.

Peters, John L. *Christian Perfection and American Methodism.* NY: Abingdon, 1956.

Pierson, A. T. *Forward Movements of the Last Half Century.* New York: Funk & Wagnalls, 1905.

Piette, M. *John Wesley in the Evolution of Protestantism.* London: Sheed and Ward, 1938.

Porter, James. *A Compendium of Methodism.* Boston: Charles H. Pierce, 1851.

Porterfield, Amanda. *Feminine Spirituality in America.* Philadelphia: Temple University Press, 1980.

Quebedeaux, Richard. *The New Charismatics.* San Francisco: Harper & Row, 1983.

Raser, Harold E. "Phoebe Palmer: Ambassador of Holiness." *The Preachers' Magazine,* Sept.–Nov. 1983, 20–33.

_____. *Phoebe Palmer: Her Life and Thought.* Lewiston: Edwin Mellen Press, 1987.

Roebling, Karl. *Pentecostal Origins and Trends: Early and Modern.* Paragon, 1983.

Rose, Delbert. *Vital Holiness: A Theology of Christian Experience.* 3rd edition. Minneapolis: Bethany Fellowship, 1975.

Rosenberg, Carroll Smith. *Religion and the Rise of the American City, The New York Mission Movement, 1812–1870.* Ithaca: Cornell University Press, 1971.

_____. "Protestants and Five Pointers: The Five Points House of Industry." *New York Historical Society Quarterly* XLVIII, no. 4 (Oct. 1964): 327–47.

Rowe, Kenneth E. *Methodist Union Catalog, Pre-1976 Imprints.* 5 vols. Metuchen, N.J.: Scarecrow Press, 1975– (A–H, to date).

_____. *Methodist Women: A Guide to the Literature.* United Methodist Bibliography Series, no. 2. Lake Junaluska, N.C.: General Commission on Archives and History, UMC, 1980.

Ruether, Rosemary Radford and Keller, Rosemary Skinner, eds. *Women and Religion in America: The Nineteenth Century.* San Francisco: Harper & Row, 1981.

Ruether, Rosemary, and Eleanor McLaughlin, eds. *Women of Spirit.* New York: Simon and Schuster, 1979.

Ryan, Mary P. *Womanhood in America: From Colonial Times to the Present.* New York: New Viewpoints, 1978.

Sandall, Robert. *The History of the Salvation Army.* 2 vols. London: Salvation Army, 1947.

Semmel, Bernard. *The Methodist Revolution.* New York: Basic Books, 1973.

Shipley, David Clark. "The Development of Theology in American Methodism in the Nineteenth Century." *The London Quarterly and Holborn Review* 184 (July 1959): 249–264.

Shipps, Howard F. "The Revival of 1858 in Mid-America." *Methodist History* 16 (1977): 128–51.

Sizer, Sanda S. *Gospel Hymns and Social Religion: The Rhetoric of Nineteenth-Century Revivalism.* Philadelphia: Temple University Press, 1978.

Smith, Timothy. *Called Unto Holiness: The Story of the Nazarenes, The Formative Years.* Kansas City, Mo.: Nazarene Publishing Co.

_____. "The Holiness Crusade." In E. S. Bucke, ed., *The History of American Methodism.* 3 vols. Nashville: Abingdon, 1964, 2: 608–27.

_____. "How John Fletcher Became the Theologian of Wesleyan Perfectionism, 1770–1776." *WTJ* 15/1 (Spring 1980): 68–87.

_____. *Revivalism and Social Reform in the Mid-Nineteenth Century America.* New York: Abingdon, 1957.

_____. "The Transfer of Wesleyan Religious Culture from England to America." *Historical Bulletin of the World Methodist Historical Society* 14 (First Quarter 1985): 2–16.

Spaulding, Arthur Whitefield. *Origin and History of the Seventh Day Adventists.* 2 vols. Washington, D.C.: Review and Herald Publishing Association, 1962.

Sweet, Leonard. *The Minister's Wife.* Philadelphia: Temple University Press, 1983.

Sweet, William Warren. *Revivalism in America: Its Origin, Growth and Decline*. New York: Scribners, 1944.

Synan, Vinson. *Aspects of Pentecostal-Charismatic Origins*. Plainfield, N.J.: Bridge Publishing Co., 1975.

_____. *The Holiness-Pentecostal Movement in the United States*. Grand Rapids, Mich: Eerdmans, 1971.

Turner, George Allen. "The Baptism of the Holy Spirit in the Wesleyan Tradition." *WTJ* 14/1 (Spring 1979): 60–76.

Wall, Ernest. "I Commend Unto You Phoebe." *Religion in Life* 26 (Summer 1957): 396–408.

Wallace, Mary. *Pioneer Pentecostal Women*. Word Aflame, 1981.

Walters, Orville S. "The Concept of Attainment in John Wesley's Christian Perfection." *Methodist History* 10 (April 1972): 12–29.

Warfield, Benjamin. *Perfectionism*. 2 vols. New York: Oxford Univ. Press, 1931–32.

Weisberger, Bernard W. *They Gathered at the River: The Story of the Great Revivalists and Their Impact upon Religion in America*. Boston: Little, Brown and Co., 1958.

Welter, Barbara. "The Cult of True Womanhood: 1820–1860." *American Quarterly* Vol 18, 2nd issue (Summer 1966): 151–74.

White, Charles Edward. *The Beauty of Holiness: Phoebe Palmer as Theologian, Revivalist, Feminist, and Humanitarian*. Grand Rapids: Francis Asbury Press, Zondervan, 1986.

Wilcox, Leslie D. *Be Ye Holy: A Study of the Teaching of the Scripture Relative to Entire Sanctification with a Sketch of the History and Literature of the Holiness Movement*. Cincinnati: Revivalist Press, 1965.

Williamson, Douglas J. "Wilbur Fisk and African Colonization: A 'Painful Portion' of American Methodist History." *Methodist History* 23/2 (January 1985): 79–98.

INDEX TO INTRODUCTION

INDEX TO TEXTS

Other Volumes in This Series